Mars Hill Grad
mhgs.edu/library WITHDRAWN

**THE MAJORITY
IN THE MINORITY**

DATE DUE

DEMCO, INC. 38-2931

TE DUE

Mars Hill Graduate School
10018018

Mars Hill Graduate School Library
mhgs.edu/library

THE MAJORITY IN THE MINORITY

Expanding the Representation of Latina/o Faculty, Administrators and Students in Higher Education

Edited by *Jeanett Castellanos and Lee Jones*

FOREWORD BY
Laura I. Rendón

STERLING, VIRGINIA

Stylus Publishing, LLC
22883 Quicksilver Drive
Sterling, Virginia 20166

Copyright © 2003 by Stylus Publishing, LLC

All rights reserved. No part of this book may be reprinted or reproduced in any form or by any electronic, mechanical or other means, now known or hereafter invented, including photocopying, recording and information storage and retrieval, without permission in writing from the publishers.

Library of Congress Cataloging-in-Publication Data

The majority in the minority: expanding the representation of Latina/o faculty, administrators and students in higher education/edited by Jeanett Castellanos and Lee Jones; foreword by Laura I. Rendón—1st ed.

    p. cm.

Includes bibliographical references.

  ISBN 1-57922-072-X (hardcover: alk. paper)—ISBN 1-57922-073-8
  (pbk.: alk. paper)

1. Hispanic Americans—Education (Higher) 2. Educational equalization—United States.
I. Castellanos, Jeanett, 1972– II. Jones, Lee, 1965–
  LC2670.6.M35 2003
  378'.008968—dc21   2002155870

First edition, 2003

Printed in the United States of America

All first editions printed on acid free paper

CONTENTS

PART FOUR: LATINA/O FACULTY EXPERIENCES AND RETENTION

Laura I. Rendón

Laura I. Rendón holds the Veffie Milstead Jones Endowed Chair at California State University, Long Beach. From 1999 to 2000, Dr. Rendón was a Fetzer Institute Fellow, participating in a three-year program to develop and sustain the capacity of individuals to inform their work through the "inner life" of mind and spirit and the outer life of action and service. Previously, Dr. Rendón was a professor at Arizona State University and at North Carolina State University. Dr. Rendón has also served as Director of Assessment in the Ford Foundation's Urban Partnership Program, a K–16 initiative that involved sixteen urban cities in an effort to improve the participa-

tion, retention, and graduation of at-risk students. Dr. Rendón has also been a Senior Research Associate with the National Center for Postsecondary Teaching, Learning, and Assessment.

Dr. Rendón earned her Ph.D. in higher education administration from the University of Michigan, Ann Arbor (1982), an M.A. in counseling and guidance and psychology from Texas A&I University, Kingsville (1975), and a B.A. in English and journalism from the University of Houston.

Dr. Rendón serves on several advisory boards including The National Council of Community and Educational Partnerships, Pathways to College Network Research Panel, National Initiative on Women in Higher Education, Research Policy Analysis Expert Group, Alliance for Equity in Higher Education, and the National Center for the Freshman Year Experience. Dr. Rendón is past President of the Association for the Study of Higher Education (ASHE).

Dr. Rendón has co-edited two books, *Educating a New Majority: Transforming America's Educational System for Diversity* (1996) and the *ASHE Ethnic/Racial Diversity Reader* (1996). Dr. Rendón has authored or co-authored more than sixty book chapters and journal and magazine articles. Her research publications focus on the topics of access, student retention, diversity, K–16 collaborative teaching, and holistic teaching and learning. In addition, Dr. Rendón has delivered over sixty keynote addresses, made over sixty research presentations, and conducted numerous workshops for faculty, education leaders policy analysts, and student affairs administrators.

Dr. Rendón is associate editor of *The Journal of Minorities in Science and Engineering* and *Voices: Journal of Chicana/Latina Studies*. She is also on the editorial boards of *About Campus* and the *Journal of Latino Education*.

FOREWORD

Laura I. Rendón

The future of American higher education, indeed of the nation, is multiracial and multicultural, and Latinos are evolving into the largest ethnic/racial group in the United States. An ironic trend that was beginning to take shape in the last twenty years is now glaringly apparent. Ethnic/racial groups previously categorized as "minorities" are now majorities or the approaching majority in California, Texas, Arizona, New Mexico, Florida, Hawaii, and New York. Presently, New Mexico, Hawaii, and California are the only three states in which Anglos presently comprise less than 50% of the population. Ethnic/racial "minorities" are now finding themselves, as Jeanett Castellanos and Lee Jones futuristically declare, "the majority in the minority."

As a volume destined to be employed by researchers, practitioners, and policy makers, *The Majority in the Minority* appears at the right time in our nation's demographic history. The 2000 census shows that there is nearly a one in two chance that two people selected at random are racially or ethnically different. Moreover, between 1990 and 2000, the nation's White population diminished from 75% to 69%. But as the White population declines, Latinos represent the fastest growing minority in the nation. Constituting 12.5% of the American population, Latinos have now surpassed the Black population (12.1%), once considered the largest minority in the nation. Latino students are expected to outnumber African American college students for the first time around the year 2006 (Carnevale, 1999). Their numbers will rise from 1.4 million in 1995 to 2.5 million in 2015. This is a remarkable 73% increase that makes Hispanics the nation's largest college-going minority, one of every six undergraduates by 2015. While the numbers of White students will also rise, as a percentage of undergraduates Whites are expected to decline from 70.6% in 1995 to 62.8% in 2015 (Carnevale & Fry, 2000). Consequently, Latinos are a social, economic, and political force to be reckoned with as this group is expected to grow both within their subgroups—Mexican Americans or Chicanos, Puerto Ricans, Cubans, Dominicans, Spaniards, Central Americans and South Americans—and within the category of biracial/multiracial cohorts due to soaring intermarriage rates.

Despite these important demographic and social trends, American higher education has not adequately addressed the increasingly diverse and multicultural student body. As Latinos evolve from minority to majority, our nation's educational system must respond to this cohort in a way that acknowledges not only demographic trends, but long-standing issues that remain unresolved: access, retention, graduation, campus climate, and faculty/staff diversity. In terms of access, Sylvia Hurtado and Mark Kamimura (Chapter 8) remind us that there are over 1.3 million Latino students enrolled in college, but only 40% of these appear in four-year institutions. This fact makes Latinos one of the least represented ethnic/racial cohort in four-year colleges and universities. It is projected that by 2015 Hispanic students in the eighteen- to twenty-four-year-old undergraduate population will be underrepresented by more than 500,000 students (Carnevale & Fry, 2000). These trends appear at a critical time when getting into college is becoming more difficult, as the demand for higher education is at an all-time high. For example, in California, the state with the most Latino students, there is a surge of students applying to college. The state's Master Plan, which provides access to college in three tiers (the highly selective University of California, the moderately selective California State University, and least selective community colleges) is being tested for efficiency. As demand for college rises, the admissions bar is being raised even higher to make even moderately selective institutions more selective. Students who attend schools that do not prepare them well for college will remain disadvantaged, and it is well known that Latinos and other low-income racial/ethnic groups are more likely to attend schools with few resources (Rendón & Hope, 1995). Being academically prepared for college has never been more important. Today, being minimally qualified for college is no longer enough to be admitted to many colleges and universities, and Latino students must receive the high-quality academic preparation that will enable them to be competitive as potential college entrants.

Enrolling larger numbers of Latinos into college is only one piece of what needs to be addressed to ensure that this cohort has a high standard of living and is able to participate in leadership positions and in social and political spheres that shape our nation's future. Access must be matched with retention to degree completion. Here, too, *The Majority in the Majority* becomes a useful tool as scholars such as Amaury Nora, Alberta M. Gloria, Jeanett Castellanos, Guadalupe Anaya, and Darnell G. Cole provide research and policy perspectives to address the alarming attrition rate of Latinos in two- and four-year institutions.

Very few scholars address the issues related to recruiting and retaining Latino faculty and administrators. In 1999, Latino faculty constituted less than 3% of all full-time professors and roughly 3% of all full-time administrators in higher education (Harvey, 2002). Given that Latino faculty and administrators remain greatly underrepresented, what can be done to nurture the next generation of Latino faculty and administrators? What barriers persist and need to be overcome? Fortunately, *The Majority in the Minority* benefits from capturing the experiences and perspectives of seasoned Latino faculty and administrators such as Raymond V. Padilla, Richard R. Verdugo, Roberto A. Ibarra, Edward A. Delgado-Romero, Lisa Y. Flores, Alberta M. Gloria, Patricia Arredondo, Jeanett Castellanos, Kathleen Harris Canul, Roberto Haro, and Juan Francisco Lara.

Many books often fail to include the voices of students in their analysis of educational trends and issues. This is not the case with *The Majority in the Minority*. The wonderfully inspiring voices of undergraduate students such as Veronica Orozco and graduate student Raymond "Ramón" Herrera put what we do as educators into perspective. As one reads these narratives, we discover the poignant issues these students deal with on a day-to-day basis: identity development, isolation, language difficulties, separation from family, lack of financial resources, cultural stereotyping, tracking, discrimination, and sex role conflicts. Yet, students also speak eloquently of the experiences that took them over the top—support from family, caring mentors, spirituality, student support networks, and student support programs. Above all, we find that these students are resilient. Like their Aztec, Maya, Ciboney, and Taino ancestors before them, these students' spirits also rise above adversity. In doing so, students overcome oppressive environments, racial conflict, discrimination, and stereotyping.

When I was a doctoral student at the University of Michigan in the early 1980s, I often wondered why there were so few studies that captured the Hispanic student, faculty, and administrator experience. Twenty years ago, we had precious few Latinos and Latinas who had doctorates and who were writing about these issues. Fortunately, my generation of Latino scholars such as Aida Hurtado, Mildred García, Michael Olivas, Amaury Nora, Raymond V. Padilla, Alberto Cabrera, Sylvia Hurtado, among others, had a strong ethnic/racial consciousness. We not only identified as Latino, we were acutely aware of discriminatory practices against *nuestra gente*. We could identify inequities, and we knew that our work had to be more than an academic exercise. Our work had to make a difference for *la raza*. We shattered the silences and filled the research gaps even when we were admonished for writing about *nuestra gente*.

In those days, Latino issues were not always considered valid research areas. When we broke through the barriers to occupy faculty and administrative spaces in academia, we took care to mentor the next generation of Latino scholars and administrators. We, and others who followed, created an extensive body of research that captured and validated the experiences of Latinas and Latinos in higher education. But clearly, this is not enough. Our struggle for the civil right to gain access to college and to faculty and administrative posts remains as important as it was twenty years ago. Collectively, we must continue our quest for equity and democracy in our educational institutions.

When Tomás Rivera, the late former Chancellor of the University of California–Riverside, wrote his poem *The Searchers,* he spoke of the spiritual nobility of Latinos who persistently search for social justice and validation of their existence. Our salvation, Rivera argued, is based on discovering our connectedness with the collective experience of our people. *The Majority in the Minority* reconnects us to the triumphs and tragedies of our Latino collective pasts and leads us to a more hopeful scenario of the future. I applaud and honor the spiritual nobility of the contributing authors of *The Majority in the Minority,* and say *gracias!* for keeping the struggle alive, and for taking us one step closer to a more equitable future for American higher education.

References

Carnevale, A. P. (1999). *Education = success.* Princeton, NJ: Educational Testing Service, Communications Services.

Carnevale, A. P., Fry, R. A. (2000). *Crossing the great divide.* Princeton, NJ: Educational Testing Service, Communications Services.

Harvey, W. B. (2002). *Minorities in higher education 2001–2002.* Nineteenth Annual Status Report. Washington, DC: American Council on Education.

Hurtado, S., & Kamimura, M. (2003). Latina/o Retention in four-year institutions. In Castellanos, J. & Jones, L. (Eds.), *The majority in the minority: Expanding the representation of Latina/o faculty, Administrators, and students in higher education.* Sterling, VA: Stylus Publications.

Rendón, L. I., & Hope, R. (1995). *Educating a new majority.* San Francisco: Jossey-Bass.

Lee Jones and Jeanett Castellanos

Latinos are the fastest growing minority group in the United States. The 2000 census identified 12.5% of the total population of the United States as being of Latino descent. Examining a ten-year span between 1990 and 2000, the U.S. Census reported that that Latinos have attained the highest rate of population growth in American history. More specifically, the population increased by 58%, from 22.4 million in 1990 to 35 million in 2000. Furthermore, it is projected that the Latino population will reach approximately 38 million by the year 2005, an increase of over 10 million from 1995. With the steady growth trend, Latinos will become the largest minority group in the United States by 2010, making up 13.8% of the entire U.S. population (de los Santos & Rigual, 1994; Hernandez, 2000; Rodríguez, Guido-DiBrito, Torres, & Talbot, 2000). Despite these findings, Latinos remain highly underrepresented in higher education. Of all the racial and ethnic minorities, Latinos are the least likely to complete a college degree (Hernandez, 2000). This review concentrates on various trends of Latina/o college students, including historical factors, statistics, and research findings regarding Latina/o participation in higher education, as well as recommendations provided by various researchers to improve Latina/o student retention.

The History of Latina/os in Education

The segregation of Latina/o students in elementary and secondary schools has been considered a major component of the failure rate of many Latina/o students (Donato, Menchaca, & Valencia, 1991). Prior to the 1950s, the treatment of Latina/os was similar to that of African Americans. Latina/o children were denied access to formal schooling as early as 1892 (Donato et al., 1991). The few Latina/o students who managed to receive an education attended segregated schools, usually referred to as Mexican schools, since Mexican Americans were the largest Latino group in the country. These schools were nowhere near equal to schools that educated the White population. The excuse used to justify this separation was based on the idea of a language barrier, that English-speaking and Spanish-speaking children could not attend the same schools. All students with Spanish surnames, whether Spanish-speaking or not, were excluded from the higher quality, English-speaking schools (Contreras & Valverde, 1994).

Mexican Americans were the first of the Latino population to challenge the notion of segregated schools. The first victory for Mexican Americans was achieved in California in 1946 in the case of *Mendez v. Westminster School District,* where the trial court found that segregated schools did not satisfy the provision of equal protection provided by the United States Constitution. Regardless of this decision, school segregation continued throughout California (Contreras & Valverde, 1994).

Discrimination and segregation were more intense in Texas than in other states with large Latino populations. In 1948, the case of *Delgado v. Bastrop Independent School District* found that school segregation violated the Fourteenth Amendment of the Constitution. The court insisted that separate classes for non-English-speaking students were to be held on the same campus as classes for English-speaking students, no longer allowing authorities to rationalize school separation on the basis of language barriers (Contreras & Valverde, 1994).

Statistics for Latina/o College Students

Latina/os have a history of underrepresentation in American higher education. Part of the reason for the history of low enrollment in college is that Latina/os, particularly Mexican Americans, tended to have high attrition rates at both the elementary and high school levels. Surveys collected between 1974 and 1978 produced a nationwide rate of 51% of Mexican Americans completing high school, and a 23% rate of college entry. The rates for Whites were 83% completing high school and 38% entering college (Attinasi, 1989). The percentage of Latina/os graduating from high school in 1992 was 57.3, whereas the percentage of Whites was 83.3. In 1991, 49,000 bachelor's degrees were awarded to Latinos, representing only 4.5% of all bachelor's degrees awarded that year (de los Santos & Rigual, 1994). In 1998, only 53.1% of all Latinos over the age of twenty-five had graduated from high school and completed some college, compared with 86% of the non-Latino White population (Rodríguez et al., 2000).

Latina/os are not evenly distributed across the United States (U.S. Census, 2000). The majority (44%) of Latinos live in the West or South (33%). Most Latinos live in urban areas and account for about 20% of the total population of the nation's nine largest cities. More specifically, a total of 77% of the Latino population is concentrated among seven states of the United States

(California, Texas, New York, Florida, Illinois, Arizona, and New Jersey). California (11 million) and Texas (6.7 million) are the two states that have the largest Latino populations in the country. Latinos in the state of New Mexico represent 42%, the highest proportion of any state.

Latinos are a very diverse group, with the three largest Latino ethnic population groups consisting of Mexican Americans (59%), Puerto Ricans (10%), and Cuban Americans (3.5%), respectively (U.S. Census, 2000). Central Americans represented 4.8%, while South Americans were a total of 3.8% of the Latino population.

The age of the Latino population directly relates to the enrollment patterns of Latina/os in higher education. Increases in Latino college enrollment are projected to continue well into the twenty-first century because the Latino population is relatively young. The median age of the Latino population in 1994 was 26 years, while the median age of the non-Latino population was 36 years. It is estimated that the population of 18 to 24 year olds—the age group that most colleges and universities recruit as the majority of their students—will be approximately 20% Latino by 2020 (de los Santos & Rigual, 1994).

Enrollment for 18 to 24 year olds in college has remained at approximately 25 million during the 1990s. The number of Latinos enrolled in colleges and universities has more than doubled during the past 20 years. In 1997, the Current Populations Reports of the U.S. Department of Commerce revealed that while 27.8% of all adults aged 25 to 29 earned a bachelor's degree or higher, only 11% of Latinos fell into this category. From 1988 to 1997, the number of Latinos enrolled in postsecondary institutions increased 79.2%, the largest increase among the major ethnic groups. The graduation rate of Latinos in 1998 was approximately 45% (DeSousa, 2001).

Retention Efforts for Latina/o College Students

Factors Contributing to Student Attrition

Financial assistance plays a major role regarding the number of Latina/os attending college (Nora, 1990). Annual incomes of Latino households averaged less than $10,500 in 1978 (Olivas, 1986), $23,900 in 1991 (de los Santos & Rigual, 1994), and $23,670 in 1998, in contrast to $41,110 for non-Latino White families in that same year. More specifically, Latino males who were employed in full-time, year-round positions earned approximately 70% of the average income of their White male counterparts. Similarly, Latinas who worked year-round earned a total of $16,760, over $4000 less than their non-Latina White female counterparts. When compacting salary and Latino families' income, the U.S. Census (2000) also showed the unemployment rate in 1994 for Latinos to be 11% compared to 6% for their non-Latino White counterparts. In 1993, approximately 27% of all Latino families were poor, as compared to 11% of non-Latino White households (U.S. Census, 2000). Among the Latino households, poverty ranges from 17% in Cuban families to 35% in Puerto Rican families. In 1999, the percent of Latino households living beneath the poverty level rose to 28% (Jones, 2001).

Lack of financial resources has been identified as one of the most common reasons for student attrition in higher education (Jones, 2001). While the rate of tuition for a college education has increased, the federal government has failed to keep up with this trend. Federal financial aid actually declined between 1982 and 1992 from 80% to 74% (de los Santos & Rigual, 1994). Another area where a change in federal financial aid has significantly impacted student access and retention was in its shift from grant assistance to loan assistance, where students were responsible for paying back their loans shortly after graduation (Jones, 2001; Nora, 1990).

Perhaps the most important contributing factor of student withdrawal, aside from finances, is the lack of integration into the college environment, usually due to the failure of the student to secure sufficient contact with significant members of the campus community, particularly at four-year, residential institutions. Kraemer (1997) offers the idea that minority students tend to withdraw from college because they are unable to conform to the campus environment, which has already been shaped by the dominant culture. Kraemer identified several aspects of successful social integration for college students, including relationships with faculty and administrators, involvement in student organizations, serving on a university or department committee, and participating in intercollegiate sports.

Academic integration was also found to be a factor in Latina/o student retention, especially with students attending two-year institutions and commuter students at four-year institutions. Kraemer (1997) measured academic integration in how students perceive their academic experiences, based on interactions with faculty, counselors, and administrators, and how students perceived the level of career preparation received at the institution.

Factors Contributing to Latina/o Student Retention

Hernandez (2000) suggested that focusing on failure rates of students does not provide a full understanding of student retention, that the focus should also be on students who have overcome obstacles and succeeded in college. Several positive influences were found to affect retention in Latina/o students, many of which directly relate to Kraemer's notion of academic and social integration. Hernandez found that "validating students' desire to succeed and encouraging their optimistic outlook is a central theme for student retention" (p. 581). Hernandez suggests further that faculty and staff need to be aware of the importance of this factor, especially for students who feel that they are unprepared for college and for first-generation college students.

Families of Latina/o students can prove to be effective tools in retention if parents are familiar with the college environment and they are provided the opportunity to develop relationships with faculty and administrators. Latina/o students who developed positive relationships with faculty were more likely to adjust to college life. Programs that cater to developing student-faculty relationships should be encouraged. Co-curricular activities, especially Latina/o student organizations, allowed Latino students to make new friends and develop a caring and supportive community (Hernandez, 2000).

Similar to other ethnic and racial groups, a larger number of Latina women attend college than do men, though their numbers are low in comparison to other ethnic and racial groups. In 1993, only 6.9% of Latinas had successfully completed college, compared to 17.6% of non-Latino White women and 10.2% of African American women (Rodríguez et al., 2000). Latinas face some different challenges when attempting to complete college successfully. Two main factors separate Latinas from Latino men in higher education. One of these factors affects the decision of whether or not to attend college. Gender-role stereotyping of Latinas suggests that they should be submissive and docile, and that their main purpose is to produce children. Some Latinas face conflict with their families, who believe they are not supposed to go to college because a college education is meant for men or the wealthy. A common view among traditional Latino families is that the women are supposed to get married and, therefore, do not need an education. Latinas of newer generations are also forced to deal with parents who expect them to stay close to home, causing them to commute to four-year institutions or attend community colleges; this attitude is particularly common among first-generation college students (Rodríguez et al., 2000).

The Important Role of Latina/o Faculty and Administrators

The employment of Latina/o faculty and administrators in colleges and universities is viewed as an important device in the retention of Latina/o college students. Latina/o faculty and administrators serve as role models, showing young Latina/o students that there are positions of power and influence available to Latina/os and consequently motivating these students to remain in school and be academically successful. Latina/o faculty and administrators serve a secondary purpose for students, acting as outlets for Latina/o students seeking advice (Verdugo, 1995).

Latina/o faculty and administrators are also underrepresented in higher education. The number of full-time Latina/o faculty members increased by

81% from 1975 to 1991, but only accounted for 2.2% of all faculty members. Latina faculty made up only 36% of all Latino faculty in 1991, though more Latinas attended college than Latino men. Latino faculty have lower rates of tenure than do non-Latino faculty, and less often reach the rank of full professor (de los Santos & Rigual, 1994).

The number of Latina/os in full-time administration positions increased 187% between 1975 and 1991, raising the count from 1,203 to 3,453. Despite this increase, only 2.5% of all full-time college administrators were Latina/os and most were employed in positions classified as being of moderate to low prestige. Only 2.6% of the 3,611 colleges and universities in the United States had presidents who were Latina/o in 1993 (de los Santos & Rigual, 1994).

Verdugo (1995) cites the negative effects of racial stratification as the main reason for the underrepresentation of Latina/o professionals in higher education. Racial stratification, as defined by Verdugo, is characterized in two facets, an ideological mechanism and a structural mechanism. Ideologies of racial stratification include the norms, mores, folkways, values, and theories of a given culture. Structural mechanisms are the factors that lead to the segregation of ethnic and racial groups and foster discrimination.

Latina/o faculty and administrators are negatively affected by racial stratification in several ways. There is a common belief in higher education that Latina/o professionals do not possess the appropriate skills needed to be successful in academe. The further notion is that Latina/o faculty lack objectivity in their research and that their topics are irrelevant to higher education as a whole. Consequently, Latina/o faculty tend to be employed with less prestigious institutions in a limited number of academic disciplines and serve on committees that deal only with minority issues (Verdugo, 1995).

The successful retention of Latino students in higher education is similar to that of other minority groups. It is important that Latinos feel a sense of academic security, beginning at the elementary level and continuing on through the college years. It is also essential that qualified Latina/o students have access to the financial resources necessary to successfully obtain a college degree.

The assimilation of the Latina/o college student into the campus environment is partially the responsibility of the student, but the student needs to be provided with opportunities to meet other students of similar backgrounds and develop relationships with faculty and administrators. Student organizations, specifically Latina/o Student Unions and Latina/o fraternities and sororities serve this purpose well. Successful social integration has shown to have a direct affect on student retention to the completion of the bachelor's degree.

The presence of Latina/o faculty and administrators has been found to have a positive effect on Latina/o student retention. Latina/o professionals serve as role models to students and help to keep them academically motivated. It would increase the retention of Latina/o college students if more Latina/o professionals were employed in higher education, in at least equal proportion to the number of Latina/o students enrolled in colleges and universities.

It is very apparent that Latina/os are underrepresented in all areas of higher education. If college faculty and administrators are willing to learn about and adapt to the various needs of minority students, then Latina/os, as well as other minority groups, could be positively represented in all aspects of higher learning.

Defined Terms

Culture   The ideations, symbols, behaviors, values, customs and beliefs that are shared by a human group. Culture is transmitted through language, material objects, rituals and institutions, and is passed from one generation to the next.

Diversity   Recognition and acknowledgment of differences that are unique to each group that is part of the multicultural community.

Multicultural students   The four underrepresented racial/ethnic groups: African American, Asian/Pacific American, Chicano/Latino, and Native American.

Race   A socially and historically defined human grouping hereditarily assigned but not biologically defined. Refers to very large human groups containing diverse populations and ethnic groups.

Recruitment   The process of identifying and informing African American, Asian/Pacific American, Chicano/Latino, and Native American populations in order to provide them with support systems that will facilitate improved and enhanced access to the university with the expectation of increasing enrollment of multicultural students.

Retention   The continuous process of creating, maintaining, and supporting ongoing strategies for meeting the personal, academic, social, and financial needs of multicultural students to ensure academic success and graduation.

Definition of Terms

An unavoidable dilemma when dealing with multicultural issues is that of the terminology used to conceptualize them. It is evident that there is no consensus in the use of terms, particularly in the area of labels for specific groups.

Terms for Specific Groups

Hispanic   This term was introduced into the official government lexicon by the Office of Budget and Management in 1978, creating an ethnic category that included persons of Mexican, Puerto Rican, Cuban, Central America, South American, or some other Spanish origin (Trevinõ, 1987). This label refers to various populations that are bound by a common ancestral language and cultural characteristics but that vastly differ in immigrant history and settlement in the United States.

Latino   Hayes-Bautista and Chapa (1987) introduced the term Latinos, restricting the name to persons residing in the United States whose ancestries are form Latin American countries in the Western Hemisphere. This term is more inclusive than Hispanic. It includes people from Latin America (e.g., Peru, Argentina, Nicaragua, and Guatemala) who do not necessarily speak Spanish (e.g., Brazilian).

Hispanic versus Latino   Both terms are used interchangeably. Many groups reject the term Hispanic because it is too broad and was given to the Latino group without consent. In fact, many have argued in history that the term Hispanic does not acknowledge the heterogeneity in the Latino group. On the other hand, in certain regions, you will find Latinos who prefer the term Hispanic. However, there is a group of Latino college students who prefer the term Latino over Hispanic indicating that Latino is even more sensitive to people with *mestizo* background and not Spanish heritage. The term most used term by government agencies and the media is Hispanic.

Chicano   A term for Mexican Americans meant to reflect Mexican Americans' dual heritages and mixed culture. The term emphasizes the importance of equal American rights, and some Mexican Americans used the word to relate their cultural and political struggles. From a historical perspective, this term also recognizes the struggle of the Mexican Aztecs' quest to survive during the Spanish conquest. Some Mexican Americans do not relate to the term, seeing it as a name that reflects militant activism while others prefer it (Santana & Gonzalez, 2001).

Mestizo This term is the synthesis of Native and European people, cultures, and lifestyles (Ramirez, 1998).

African Americans The terms Afro-American and African American reflect the identity of Blacks based on their origins in Africa and their presence in America. Today, different labels are used to refer to people of African descent residing in the United States. In the southern and eastern parts of the United States, people of African descent more often referred to themselves as Black than African American. In the western part of the United States, they usually referred to themselves as African American more so than Black. Mainly people outside of the group use African American label. For many people of African descent, the reference does not make much of a difference. The contexts in which the terms are being used determine their response to it.

Asian/Pacific Americans Many diverse groups make up Asian Pacific Americans. These include, but are not limited to, Cambodian, Chinese, East Indian, Filipino, Guamanian, Hawaiian, Hmong, Indonesian, Japanese, Korean, Laotian, Samoan, and Vietnamese cultures (Takaki, 1987). The 1980 U.S. Census Bureau also includes smaller groups: Bangladesh, Butanese, Bornean, Burmese, Celbesian, Cernan, Indochinese, Iwo-Jiman, Javanese, Malayan, Maldivian, Nepali, Okinawan, Sikkimese, Singaporean, and Sri Lankan.

American Indian/Native American The term American Indian refers to all indigenous peoples of North America, including Indians in the United States and Canada, Alaska Natives, Aleuts, Eskimos, Metis, or mixed bloods, Mexican Indians, Central Americans Indians, and Brazilian Indians (Herring, 1999; LaFromboise, 1998). Although the term American Indian is preferred among Native people, there remains the objection that this label was given to a tribe indigenous to the islands of the southeastern coast of the United States, which was mistaken for India (Trimble, Fleming, Beauvais, & Jumper-Thurman, 1996). The term Native American refers to indigenous people living in the lower 48 United States. Therefore, when referring to Native people this study will use the term Native American and American Indian.

Throughout this book we want to acknowledge that as editors we respect the right of each contributor to use exchangeable terminology which refers to Latina, Latino, Chicana/o, Hispanic, etc. We recognize that there will be some inconsistencies in the way some people utilize terminology. To assist the readers and users of this writing, some terms have been defined for the purpose of this book (see box on p. xix). Other definitions are also included in an attempt to make the reader aware of the diversity that exists within specific racial/ethnic groups (see box on pp. xx–xxi).

The Content

Throughout this book you will be provided with concrete and substantive chapters that thoroughly examine a myriad of issues that impede the success of Latina/o students, faculty, and administrators within higher education. In many ways, the chapters that follow not only represent an overview of issues but also offer carefully constructed solutions and recommendations. These recommendations are intended to lead to meaningful discussion and action by institutions that are serious about recruiting and retaining Latina/o students, faculty, and administrators in the academy. The book opens with a Foreword by Laura I. Rendón, whose scholarship is perhaps the most heavily cited in literature of Latina/o participation in higher education. Her insightful Foreword summarizes issues affecting Latina/o participation in higher education.

The goal of the Preface is to provide a broad overview of some of the major issues affecting Latina/o students, faculty, and administrators on college campuses. In Chapter 1, the authors attempt to highlight some important data, allowing the readers a glimpse at the gaps in enrollment, retention, and graduation of Latina/o students. The chapter identifies six key areas that tend to affect the success of Latina/o students in higher education. We hope by reviewing these areas policy makers in higher education will develop strategies to address these issues.

Chapter 2 is a well-developed historical perspective of Latina/o access to higher education. MacDonald and García provide a much needed history lesson dating back to 1848. Part One presents three scholarly chapters that address the various factors that impact the retention of Latina/o students in higher education.

Chapter 3 provides a solid review of the graduation and retention rates of Latina/o students. Amaury Nora's chapter speaks to the relevant data on Latina/os in higher education. Alberta M. Gloria and Jeanett Castellanos begin Chapter 4, with a discussion on the experiences of Latina/os and African Americans on predominantly White college campuses. The authors guide us through the research trends and patterns of Latina/o and African American students—and make them come alive by having students speak to us. Finally, a psychosocial cultural framework is offered to assist universities with campus congruity. Guadalupe Anaya and Darnell G. Cole focus Chapter 5 on the role faculty play in maximizing Latina/o students' efforts to reach their educational goals.

Part Two brings in the voices of Latina/o students who are at varying stages of their education. Raymond "Ramón" Herrera (Chapter 6) presents a well-developed, thoroughly articulated case study, which speaks to his journey as a Latino male at a mid-size predominantly White University in the Pacific Northwest. He highlights the developmental stages he endured as a graduate student while he challenges dominant paradigms as a graduate student and student leader on campus. Veronica Orozco (Chapter 7) speaks to her experiences as Latina undergraduate student who struggles with the academy, its environment, and climate. Orozco speaks to cultural incongruity, gender expectations, and means used to navigate through her education to attain success and create a competitive portfolio for graduate education. Part Two ends with Sylvia Hurtado and Mark Kamimura (Chapter 8), who speak specifically to the retention of Latina/o students in higher education. They recommend principles that address the challenges of retaining Latina/o students. The recommendations aim to assist administrators and faculty who are serious about retaining Latina/o students.

Part Three features Latina/o administrators in higher education. Chapter 9, written by Roberto Haro and Juan Francisco Lara, discusses the experiences of Latino administrators in higher education. More specifically, a thorough review of the literature is provided, followed by educational statistics, and the representation of Latinos in high-powered positions in higher education such as presidencies, chancellor appointments, and other significant roles that are key for policy and decision making. In Chapter 10, Kathleen Harris Canul outlines Latino cultural values while navigating through administrative roles. Harris Canul takes us on her own personal journey of self-reflection and personal challenges faced as a Latina administrator. The chapter highlights a series of cultural values espoused by many in the Latina/o community.

The final section of this book focuses on Latina/o faculty. Part Four starts with Chapter 11 by Raymond V. Padilla on the barriers to becoming a faculty member. Padilla represents one of the most vocal advocates on issues relating to Latina/o faculty in higher education. The author begins his discussion with an overview of the background influences of the educational pipeline. He continues this important chapter by reviewing the hiring and tenure and promotion process of Latina/o faculty in higher education. Finally, he provides a general framework which will be useful for understanding Latina/o faculty experiences and ways in which Latina/o faculty can be more successful in academia. Roberto A. Ibarra's Chapter 12 on Latina/o faculty and the tenure process is well-constructed and provides a comprehensive study of the major issues affecting Latina/o faculty retention in higher education. While tenure issues are the primary focus of this chapter, the authors highlight the top ten issues affecting Latina/o faculty and administrators in the academy. Patricia Arredondo's candid interview on Latinas and the professoriate forms the major part of Chapter 13. The role of gender and culture are evaluated within this interview. More specifically, this chapter highlights Latina faculty experiences and their representation in higher education. In Chapter 14, Richard R. Verdugo examines the various factors that impact the criteria for the promotion and retention of Hispanic faculty in higher education. Verdugo collects data for this chapter from the national survey of Hispanic faculty conducted by the National Education Association. In Chapter 15, Delgado-Romero, Flores, Gloria, Arredondo, and Castellanos note the importance of examining the different professional rankings in the professoriate and the developmental processes that are inherent in each rank. The authors refer to subordinate values such as *personalismo, respeto, familismo, simpatía* and other cultural values that shape the experiences of Latina/o faculty in the academy. In addition, they provide an overview of the status of Latina/o faculty in higher education and highlight their experiences through previous literature and personal narratives. In conclusion, a blueprint is provided for Latina/o career development, and recommendations for retention are suggested. Finally, Chapter 16 addresses the need to provide a better infrastructure to accommodate Latina/os in higher education. The authors provide university-wide recommendations to address the retention of students, faculty, and administrators in higher education.

References

Attinasi, L. C., Jr. (1989). Getting in: Mexican Americans' perceptions of university attendance and the implications for freshman year persistence [Electronic version]. *Journal of Higher Education, 60*(3), 247–277.

Contreras, A. R., & Valverde, L. A. (1994). The impact of Brown on the education of Latinos [Electronic version]. *Journal of Negro Education, 63*(3), 470–481.

de los Santos, A., Jr., & Rigual, A. (1994). Progress of Hispanics in American higher education. In M. J. Justiz & R. Wilson (Eds.) *Minorities in higher education* (pp. 173–194). Phoenix, AZ: Oryx Press.

DeSousa, J. (2001). Reexamining the educational pipeline for African-American students. In L. Jones (Ed.), *Retaining African-Americans in higher education* (pp. 21–44). Sterling, VA: Stylus Publishing.

Donato, R., Menchaca, M., & Valencia, R. R., (1991). Segregation, desegregation, and integration of Chicano students: Problems and prospects. In R. R. Valencia (Ed.), *Chicano school failure and success: Research and policy agendas for the 1990s* (pp. 27–63). London: The Falmer Press.

Hayes-Bautista, D. E., & Chapa J., Latino terminology: Conceptual bases for standardized terminology. *American Journal of Public Health,* 77, 61–68.

Hernandez, J. C. (2000). Understanding the retention of Latino college students. *Journal of College Student Development,* 41(6), 575–588.

Herring, R. (1999). *Counseling with Native American Indians and Alaska Natives.* Thousand Oaks, CA: Sage.

Jones, L. (2001). Creating an affirming culture to retain African-American students during the post affirmative action era in higher education. In L. Jones (Ed.), *Retaining African-Americans in higher education* (pp. 3–20). Sterling, VA: Stylus Publishing.

Kraemer, B. A. (1997). The academic and social integration of Hispanic students into college. *The Review of Higher Education,* 20(2), 163–179.

LaFromboise, T. (1998). American Indian health policy. In D. Atkinson, G. Morten, & D. W. Sue (Eds.), *Counseling American minorities* (pp. 137–158). Boston McGraw-Hill.

Nora, A. (1990). Campus-based aid programs as determinants of retention among Hispanic community college students. *Journal of Higher Education,* 61 (3): 312–332.

Olivas, M. (1986). *Latino college students.* New York: Teachers College Press.

Ramirez, M. (1998). *Multicultural/multiracial Psychology: Mestizo perspectives in personality and mental health.* Northvale, NJ: Jason Aronson.

Rodriguez, A. L., Guido-DiBrito, F., Torres, V., Talbot, D. (2000). Latina college students: Issues and challenges for the 21st century. *NASA Journal,* 37(3), 511–527.

Santana, R. M., & Gonzalez, C. (2001). *Latinos in the United States: Words and facts to know.* Presented by The National Association of Hispanic Journalists, http://www.nahj.org/resourceguide/chapter_1.html

Takaki, R. (Ed.) (1987). *From different shores: Perspectives on race and ethnicity in America.* New York: Oxford University Press.

Treviño, F. (1986). Standardized terminology for Hispanic populations. *American Journal of Public Health,* 77, 69–71.

Trimble, J. E., Fleming, C. M., Beauvais, F., and Jumper-Thurman, P. (1996). Essential cultural and social strategies for counseling Native American Indians. In *Counseling across cultures* (4th ed.) (pp. 177–209). Thousand Oaks, CA: Sage Publications.

U.S. Census Bureau, U.S. Department of Commerce (2000). *Overview of race and hispanic origin.* Washington, DC: U.S. Government Publications.

Verdugo, R. R. (1995). Racial stratification and the use of Hispanic faculty as role models: Theory, policy, and practice. *Journal of Higher Education,* 66(6) 669–85.

ACKNOWLEDGMENTS

Words cannot begin to thank the hundreds of people who lent their voices and time to make this book come to fruition. Neither time nor space will allow us to thank all the individuals who helped make this book a reality. First Jeanett and I give full honor and praises to God, for we both know that all things are possible for those who believe. We give full acknowledgment to the spirit of our ancestors. We come from rich heritages that taught us to fight a good fight and never give up on those things that are right, true, and just. What can we say about our parents who through their wisdom have helped keep us focused on our goals? The late Levi and Carrie Jones and Miriam Chavez, Agustin Castellanos, and Adolfo Chavez continue to play an important role in our lives. Moreover, we would not be as strong without our extended family members: our grandparents (Pedro Hernandez, Amanda Jones, Albertina López, María and Miguel Vidarte, Adela and Ricardo Luis Viera); some aunts, uncles, and godparents (Esther and Henry Cardonez, Carmen and Anderson Castro, Marisol Colon, Rosa and Frank Padron); brothers (Agustin Castellano, Eric and David Chavez, and Lazaro and Ozzie Lastre); our cousins (Ivette Faya, Andy and Rosemary Castro, Eileen Esquivel, Leslie and Brian Fattorini, Jacqui and Lisett Garcia, and Anabel Jaramillo); our godchildren, nieces, and nephews who inspire us to fight the struggle (Andrew Christopher Castro, Garbriella Faya and Jr., Steven Michael García, Joseph and Giovanni González, Joshua Lastre, Aimee López, Alex López, Anaís and Annilette Rodríguez, Melanie and Michelle Saco, Alyssa Schonborn, and Stefanie and Jessica Vidarte); and other special family friends (Claudia Antelo, Teresa Carril, Mercedes and Eugenio Esquivel, Mercedes and Allen Fattorini, Miriam and Henry Garcia, Susana Jaramillo, Olivia and Tani Magaña, Ivonne and Jose Mantilla, Mayra and Maritza Manzanares, Aimee Martinez, Dr. Duvan and Betty Mejia, Fernando and Tere Ridoutt, Lucy and Elias Rodriguez, Graciela and Angel Vasquez, and Juan and Debbie Vidarte).

A quality project is not developed and conceptualized over the course of a conversation or some thoughts at breakfast. Instead, a quality project is a result of lively interactions with mentors, community members/leaders, visionaries, and top scholars. It is important to recognize significant figures in the editors' lives who helped make this book a reality through their quest for justice, equality, and representation. Specifically, we give tribute to Cesar Chavez and Dolores Huerta for their efforts to fight injustice and inequality. In addition, we recognize organizations that have dedicated time, money, and energy to educational advancement and the improvement of the quality of life for Latinos in the United States. These include The Congressional Hispanic Caucus Institute, Hispanic Scholarship Fund, Hispanic Association of Colleges and Universities (HACU), United States Hispanic Leadership Institute, Council of La Raza, MEChA, Office of Minorities in Higher Education (OMHE) with American on Council Education, Society for the Psychological Study of Ethnic Minority Issues, Division 45 with the American Psychological Association, the National Latina/o Psychological Association, and The Latino Coalition.

Excellent mentors and role models include Dr. Fran Hale Jr., Dr. Na'im Akbar, Dr. Brendon Jarmon, Dr. Joseph White, Dr. Alberta M. Gloria, Dr. Thomas Parham, Dr. Michael Pavel, Dr. Kathleen Harris Canul, Dr. Caesar Sereseres, Sally Peterson, Dr. Bernard Oliver, Dr. Juan Lara, Dr. Steve Burkett, Dr. Doug Robinson, Dr. Manuel Gomez, Dr. Guadalupe Anaya, and John Curd, who always believed in the dream, who assisted in the process of attaining the dream, and who continuously offered support even when doors were closed and windows locked shut. These individuals helped us in myriad ways, reminding us of our history and culture, and the struggles to improve our current circumstances. In addition, we thank some special colleagues (Sylvia P. Gomez, Brett Waterfield, Brian McNeill, Milton Lang, Roberto J. Velasquez, Darnell Cole, Steve Tajiri, Gerardo Canul, Keith Harrison, Jeff Hird, Leon Caldwell, Kevin Cokley, and Nita Tewari); other friends who have left imprints of knowledge and wisdom in our lives (Lazara Diaz, Rosalinda Rendon, Arlette Ridoutt, and Eddie Schonborn); and the specific educational institutions that helped shape our experiences, gain access, and opportunities in our paths as professionals [St. Matthias High School, St. Gertrude's Elementary School, TELACU, INROADS, UC Irvine, Washington State University, and Indiana University–Bloomington (particularly the Minority Fellowship Program)].

In addition, we thank our students who helped us to better understand their needs and our community's current issues. Among the many students were 2000–2002 SAEP cohorts: Sandra Avila, Doriane Besson, Arlene Carrasco, Patty Cerda, Noel Donovan, Roberto Escobar, Vern Farber, Andrew

Gonzales, Humberto (Beto) Hernandez, Derek Iwamoto, Alexandria James, Mark Kamimura, Daniel Kim, Szu-Hui Lee, Monique Lewis, Ambrocia Lopez, Jose Lopez, Karen Lucero, Vanessa Martinez, Jaime Mayo, Melissa Mayorga, Monique Mendoza, Lilia Miramontes, Patti Moya, Kevin Nadal, Ezemanari Obasi, Veronica Orozco, Cintia Otero, Yong Park, Nima Patel, Evelyn Perez, Shannon Robertson, Rocio Rosales, Christina Salas, Sharon Santana, Jeanette Torres, Francisco Villegas, and Nola Wanta.

This book would not have been possible without the scholarship and diligence of our contributors: Guadalupe Anaya, Patricia Arredondo, Kathleen Harris Canul, Darnell G. Cole, Edward A. Delgado-Romero, Lisa Y. Flores, Teresa García, Alberta M. Gloria, Roberto Haro, Raymond "Ramón" Herrera, Sylvia Hurtado, Roberto A. Ibarra, Mark Kamimura, Juan F. Lara, Victoria-María MacDonald, Amaury Nora, Veronica Orozco, Raymond V. Padilla, Laura I. Rendón, and Richard R. Verdugo.

We thank our staffs and colleagues at Florida State University and the University of California–Irvine. Marsha Strickland, who collected and organized thou-sands of pages, played a significant role with the administrative mechanics of this book. She will never know how much Jeanett and I appreciate her. Thank you Dr. Caesar D. Sereseres, the School of Social Sciences, Gillian Kumm, the Social Science Academic Resource Center, especially the 2002–2003 student staff (Monica Franco, Alina Hartounian, Alexandria James, Maya Kinatukara, Rosalilia Mendoza, Seena Moongananiyil, and Andrea Reyna), the Social Science Counseling Office staff, Dr. Michael Scavio, the UC Irvine Cross Cultural Center, and the Department of Chicano/Latino Studies (Dr. Leo Chavez and Stella Ginez) at UC Irvine for your continuous support in your efforts to retain Latinos and other ethnic racial minorities in the academy. We thank Wendy Wang, Ph.D. candidate in Higher Education at Florida State University, Lilia Miramontes, Nola Wanta, Anna Burdin, Arlene Carrasco, and Vern Farber who collected much research for this manuscript.

We truly owe a special word of gratitude to Laura I. Rendón, who took time from her busy schedule to write the Foreword. Her reputation, as a scholar and master professor, like so many in this book, is impeccable! Finally, we thank John and Robin von Knorring for once again providing yet another book to voice one of the most untold stories in higher education. We hope that you will reflect, review, and take proactive action as you read *The Majority in the Minority*.

Jeanett Castellanos

Jeanett Castellanos currently serves as the director for the Social Science Academic Resource Center in the School of Social Sciences at the University of California, Irvine. Dr. Castellanos is responsible for coordinating many functions within the Center, including the Social Science Internship Program, Letter of Recommendation Services, Post Baccalaureate Opportunities Program, and Graduate School Preparation services. In addition to her administrative duties, Dr. Castellanos serves as a lecturer for the department of social sciences and the Chicano/Latino studies program. In this capacity, she has taught classes such as racial ethnic minorities in higher education, Chicano/Latino families, multicultural counseling, field studies through ethnography, and research methods. In addition, she has served as a consultant for various higher education institutions in the area of cultural competency.

Dr. Castellanos holds her baccalaureate from the University of California, Irvine. Her M.A. is in the field of counseling psychology and she earned a Ph.D. in education from Washington State University. She also completed a summer postdoctoral fellowship at Indiana University–Bloomington and has taught, as visiting faculty, at the University of Wisconsin, Madison.

Her research focuses on the college experience of ethnic/racial students and the psychosociocultural factors that affect their retention. Other research interests include cultural competency in university settings, the underutilization of psychotherapy among ethnic minority college students, and coping strategies leading to resilience among Cuban refugees.

Lee Jones

Lee Jones currently serves as the associate dean for academic affairs and instruction in the College of Education and associate professor of educational leadership and policy studies at Florida State University. He is a member of the Dean's Administrative Team. Dr. Jones is responsible for coordinating many functions within the College of Education, including the Offices of Clinical Partnerships, Academic Services, Learning Resource Center, Curriculum Resource Center, Living Learning Center, and Student Access, Recruitment, and Retention.

Dr. Jones holds a B.A. from Delaware State University, in drama, speech, communication, and theater. While at DSU he was elected president of the student body. He has an M.A. in higher education administration and one in business and administration, as well as a Ph.D. in organizational development from The Ohio State University.

He is the editor of three books, *Brothers of the Academy: Up and Coming Black Scholars Earning Our Way in Higher Education* (2000), *Retaining African Americans in Higher Education: Challenging Paradigms for Retaining Students, Faculty and Administrators* (2001), *Making It on Broken Promises: African American Male Scholars Confront the Culture of Higher Education* (2002), and *Black in America: When a Ph.D. Is Still Not Enough* (2003).

I

LATINA/O UNDERGRADUATE EXPERIENCES IN AMERICAN HIGHER EDUCATION

Jeanett Castellanos and Lee Jones

The United States is undergoing a radical change in its demographics. It is estimated that by the year 2020, today's ethnic minorities will be the U.S. population majority. The increase in immigration rates has made the United States an "American mosaic," with a diverse population consisting of a multitude of cultures. With the strong desire for social mobility, many immigrant children pursue education for social and economic mobility. Many of these first-generation students are attempting to gain access to a quality education and many are struggling to enter higher education and complete a college degree.

The lack of educational attainment among Latina/os affects their political and socioeconomic status in the United States. Education, however, is the primary means of upward mobility, particularly for those who are socially and economically disadvantaged (*The Condition of Education,* 1995). Unfortunately, the low levels of academic achievement of Latina/os means they are woefully unprepared to access employment and to meaningfully contribute to social change (Gloria, 1998). Most Latina/os are unable to change their low socioeconomic status, because they do not have the preparation to acquire a high paying job. It is undoubtedly true that high paying jobs lead to prestige and a higher status in society. Latina/os' lack of educational attainment also affects their political power to make the changes necessary to improve their communities.

This chapter will examine the retention issue of Latina/os in postsecondary settings. Specifically, the chapter will highlight educational statistics and some of the challenges encountered in higher education by Latina/os. The first section will overview their educational status, followed by a summary of the current retention literature for Latina/os.

Overview of Latina/o Students in Higher Education

Latina/os are the fastest growing ethnic population in the United States, constituting 12.5% of the population, (35.5 million people; Census, 2000). It is projected that Latina/os will be the largest racial and ethnic minority group by the year 2010 (de los Santos & Rigual, 1994; Hernandez, 2000; Rodriguez, Guido-DiBrito, Torres, & Talbot, 2000). Although Latina/os are growing proportionally in the population, their substantial increase is not reflective in their representation in the U.S. education system. Gonzalez and Ortiz (2000) report that Latina/o students "enter school later, leave school earlier, and receive proportionately fewer high school diplomas" (p. 67). As Latina/os progress through the educational pipeline, they are less likely to complete a college degree (Hernandez, 2000).

Educational Status

A comprehensive review of Latina/o student representation in higher education demonstrates slow progress throughout the years (Brown, 1992; Olivas, 1986; Rendón & Hope, 1996). The number of Latina/o students enrolled in U.S. postsecondary institutions rose from 384,000 (fall 1976) to 624,000 (fall 1986), a 62% increase (Levine, 1989). However, of every 100 young Latina/o adults in 1985, only 59% were high school graduates, and of this group only 29% were enrolled in college. During the 1990s, Latina/os experienced educational gains, but their 1995 participation rate of 35% was nearly identical to the 36% recorded 20 years previous (Carter & Wilson, 1996).

Postsecondary enrollment   Although Latina/os have gained representation in postsecondary institutions, they constitute only 4% of all college undergraduates. Latina/os continue to be underrepresented compared to their total share of the population, 29 million (11%) (National Center for Education Statistics [NCES], 1995; Quintana, Vogel, & Ybarra, 1991; U.S. Census Bureau, 1997; U.S. Department of Education, 1995). Despite the total college participation rate having increased 5%, the increase was from 3% to 8% over the course of 1976 to 1995. The total number of Latina/o students enrolled in U.S. postsecondary institutions in 1995 was approximately 1,093,900, a total of 480,200 men and 613,700 women. Of those attending higher education, a large proportion (937,100) were attending public four-year or two-year institutions, whereas a much smaller portion (156,800) were in private institutions.

Retention   Retention, sometimes also referred to as *academic persistence,* is the ability to remain in school and matriculate toward degree completion. Latina/o students' persistence unfortunately is subject to "the revolving door syndrome" (Haro, Rodriguez, and Gonzalez, 1994). This phenomena constitutes a cycle where Latina/o students enter the educational system, drop out, and are subsequently replaced by new Latina/o students. As a result, the illusion of a stable set of students is created because the numbers remain constant. In fact, the Latina/o student dropout rate at U.S. four-year institutions and universities has exceeded 50% over the past few years (NCES, 2002). The enrollment of Latina/o students at four- and two-year institutions has improved over the past several years; however, the matriculation rates of this population still remain very low. The retention rate of Latina/o college students in postsecondary institutions remains lower than for White students and is lower than that of African Americans (Wilds & Wilson, 1998). Moreover, over 50% of Latina/o students who enroll in college do not graduate (Baltimore, 1995).

Degrees Conferred

The examination of college participation and degree conferrals verifies that Latina/os are an underrepresented group in higher education. Despite increasing enrollment statistics, the number of degree conferrals are adversely affected by attrition and nonpersistence. For example, the number of bachelor's degrees awarded between 1976 and 1987 rose less than 1% for Latina/o students. Similarly, because of noncognitive indicators (e.g., campus climate, support networks, programming), the prospects for Latina/os to complete their higher educational degrees remains lower when compared to Whites (Heller, 1984; Sudarska, 1987). For the 1994–95 academic year, Latina/os received a dismal 5% of all the undergraduate degrees; this added to the slow growth in higher education attainment (U.S. Department of Education, 1995). Carter and Wilson (1996), however, reported an 11% increase in the numbers of bachelor's degrees earned in 1993 and solid progress in all degree categories. Despite the increases, Latina/os remain underrepresented in the number of degrees conferred, with only 6% earning associate degrees and 4% earning bachelor's degrees.

An examination of Latina/o graduation rates can provide a better understanding of these students' progress in attaining undergraduate degrees. The 1997 National Collegiate Athletic Association (NCAA) graduation report provides a thorough look at the 1990–91 graduation rates for the entering cohort of 1983–84 through 1990–91. The report indicated a discrepancy between Latina/o and White students' graduation rates. It was found that the average percentage of graduation is 56%, with Latina/os reporting 49% and Whites 59% at all institutions. Review of public institutions' data showed that Latina/os have a 41% graduation rate, whereas Whites constitute 56% of the graduating population. Large public institutions graduate 46% of the Latina/o population and 59% of the White student population. Small public institutions graduate 28% of Latina/o and 45% of White students. All private postsecondary institutions graduate 65% of the Latina/o students and 72% of the White students; large private institutions graduate 68% of Latina/os and 73% of Whites, whereas small private institutions graduate 57% of Latina/o students and 68% of the Whites. This careful examination highlights the marked disparity between Latina/o and White graduation rates in higher education at every type of postsecondary institutions; this difference ranges from 6% to 17%. Moreover, the 15% difference in Latina/o and White graduate rates at public universities is important to acknowledge considering the imperative role of such institutions in relation to access.

As a result of low enrollment, nonpersistence, and subsequent low graduation rates, there is a need to examine the factors affecting the Latina/o undergraduate experience. Research can directly impact university administrators to develop academic and social programs that help retain Latina/o students. The next section of this chapter will take a noncognitive approach (Gloria & Rodríguez, 2000) to understanding the factors impacting the retention of Latina/o students in their educational pursuits.

Major Factors Affecting the Retention of Latina/o Students

The underrepresentation of Latina/os in higher education and their limited retention continues to impact the opportunities for learning and overall quality of education for all students (Gloria, Riechmann, Rush, 2000). Soon to be the numerical majority in the United States, it critical that higher education institutions be accountable for understanding, recruiting, retaining, and matriculating Latina/o students. In doing so, factors that must be considered are cultural and background variables, socioeconomic status, academic and acculturative stress, family support, campus climate and cultural congruity, and faculty mentorship.

Cultural and Background Variables

Numerous cultural and personal indicators have been identified throughout the literature as key factors that contribute to the achievement and retention of Latina/o undergraduates in higher education. For example, limited English proficiency, living in single-parent homes, irregular attendance patterns, and quality of prior education all play a significant role in the retention of ethnic minorities in college (Rendón & Hope, 1996). Moreover, descriptors such as irregular "low grades," and "academic deficiencies" were associated with Latina/o attrition (Reyes & Valencia, 1993). The type and quality of education prior to college has also been shown to be a predictor for college success. Discrepancies in the school system with outdated books and unequal access to technological equipment and quality teachers exacerbate the problem.

Parental education of Latina/o students is also a factor. Latina/o adolescents are considered at-risk for academic failure given that their parents are unfamiliar with the requirements and challenges of the education system in the United States (Gloria & Segura-Herrera, in press). A large percentage of Latina/o parents have low education levels and received their education in their homelands. Consequently, they are unfamiliar with the process of attaining a higher education in the United States and unable to provide direction and support to their children attending college (Gloria & Segura-Herrera, in press). Throughout Gloria's work, she has found that the support of mothers and the availability of educational resources within the home provides "best" indicators of subsequent educational performance.

Socioeconomic Status

Having limited financial means has also been associated with higher attrition rates for Latina/os. Quintana et al. (1991) found that Latina/os tend to experience greater levels of stress associated with financial concerns than White students. Most of the studies concerning college stress focus on the high levels of financial stress for Latina/o undergraduates. For example, Sánchez, Marder, Berry, and Ross (1992), in a study of 124 Latina/o students who had dropped out or were academically dismissed from a university found that the major reasons for dropping out were due to personal and/or economic concerns. The students reported that family and related financial obligations, as well as the need to take on adult roles, were the key variables in the decision to drop out for most students. Similarly, Young (1992) found that the number of hours worked weekly by Chicana/o students impeded them from graduating on time and/or dropping out. In a classic study, Muñoz (1986) found that higher education produces higher amounts of stress for Chicana/o students than for Whites. More specifically, the primary source of strain for Chicana/o students was financial because they come from lower socioeconomic background and their parents cannot contribute to their education.

Academic and Acculturative Stress

Aside from experiencing normal academic stress, Latina/o students are further impacted by their minority status, intimidation by the campus climate, and limited positive academic role models (Gloria & Robinson Kurpius, 1996). Quintana et al. (1991) found that compared to Whites, Latina/o students scored higher on academic and financial stress, and on valuing education measures. The concerns for academic stress included participants' perceptions of stress that resulted from approaching teachers, taking tests, writing papers, producing the quality of scholarship required by teachers, and failing to meet academic expectations. Quintana et al. (1991) assumed that the higher levels of academic stress that Latina/o students experience is most likely related to having attended economically disadvantaged secondary schools.

Similarly, Smedley, Myers, and Harrell (1993) found that minority status was another major source of stress relevant to the persistence of minority students in higher education. That is, ethnic minorities students' concerns as "minorities" were heightened by the negative expectations of their White peers and faculty. These students' minority status undermined their academic confidence and resulted in them questioning the peculiar demands of attending a highly competitive university. In contrast, the White students questioned their academic strength because of the stigmatized "special status" as minority students were viewed as the beneficiaries of affirmative action decision, despite their individual accomplishments.

Family Support

Macias-Wycoff (1996) reminds us of the deep feeling for family that permeates the Latina/o culture. In the social organization of Latina/os, family is considered the single most important institution. It is through the family and its activities that many Latina/os relate to significant others in their lives and learn to interact with greater society. Latina/os place special emphasis, sentiment, and value on the family, when compared to the U.S. population in general (Álvarez Jr., 1994). Family is an important resource for Latina/o students. Although it has been documented that Latina/o families provide limited financial support, emotional support from the family often allows students to work toward their fullest academic potential (Gloria, 1999). Thus, due to the importance of family in Latina/o cultures, it is critical to examine the role of family support when considering the educational arena, specifically academic persistence, among Latina/os.

In examining factors that contribute to the academic success of Latina/o university students, Arellano & Padilla (1996) reported the powerful effect of parental influence on students' academic success. Each respondent referred to the critical importance of parental support and encouragement. It is difficult to express the emotion with which the respondents described the role their parents' support played in making their success possible. Several of the respondents said that their parents were the most influential motivating factor and continued to be the main force for succeeding in their university studies. The majority of the parents provided strong emotional support in the form of encouragement to succeed in their academics. Likewise, Flores (1992) reports that continuous encouragement toward educational endeavors by both mothers and fathers increases the likelihood that the Latina/o students will persist in college. Gloria (1997) reported the importance of family support in ensuring a Chicana/o student's persistence until graduation. Specifically, she examined the extent to which nonpersistence decisions of Chicana/o undergraduates were influenced by the university and perceived support from family. Given the family's key role in Chicana/o culture, Gloria suggested that parents and family should be included in the university community. She called for the integration of family into the educational experiences of Chicana/o students. In particular, the importance of a university-based community, which integrates Chicana/o families, in facilitating the growth and persistence of Latina/o students in suggested.

Campus Climate and Cultural Congruity

Understanding perceptions of the environmental context and subsequent academic comfort of racial and ethnic minorities in higher education is particularly important when studying persistence (Gloria, Robinson Kurpius, Hamilton, & Wilson, 1999). Gloria et al. (1999) found that confronting negative contexts could result in decisions not to persist, particularly for racial and ethnic minority students at predominantly White institutions, who often perceive the environment as unwelcoming and intolerant of their presence on campus. Latina/o students tend to have more negative perceptions of the campus climate than White students (Hurtado, 1992; Loo & Rolison, 1986). Skinner and Richardson (1988) found that the social environment of large predominantly White universities has been problematic, even for minority students with strong academic preparation.

Hurtado and Carter (1997) found that Latina/o students' perceptions of a hostile climate directly affect their sense of belonging in their colleges. They reported that students who described their campus environments as characterized by racial-ethnic tension tended to have much lower levels of a sense of belonging. Further, Latina/o students were more likely to perceive less appreciation by the faculty and administration (Hurtado, 1994). As a result, Latina/o students had a difficult time dealing with the academic and social environment of the university. Moreover, the challenge was further impacted by the students' perceptions of a lack of adequate support from the university.

The academic environment is often discouraging for Latina/o students, because there is a paucity of Chicana/o faculty and administrators in higher education who can serve as role models or mentors (Gloria, 1998). Second, the problem is magnified because Latina/o students often experience cultural incongruity in the university setting. Thus, the problem becomes one of conflict in knowing how to balance participation in two different cultures finding balance of home and university values (Gloria & Robinson Kurpius, 1996). Identifying additional challenges, comparative studies have found that Latina/os report higher discrimination encounters on campus than their White counterparts (Hurtado, 1996; Nettles, 1990; Nora & Cabrera, 1996). Discrimination reports were associated with feelings of alienation among Chicana/o students (Oliver, Rodriguez, & Mickelson, 1985; Hurtado, 1994). Hurtado (1994) found that even though there is a relatively high amount of interaction across racial/ethnic groups, more than one in four Latino students reported substantial campus racial conflict.

Faculty Mentorship

Mentors perform a number of functions including the roles of teacher, counselor, guide, and sponsor. Mentoring, as a function of educational institutions, can be defined as a one-to-one learning relationship between an older person and a younger person that is based on modeling behavior and extended dialogue between the two (Decoster & Brown, 1982). A mentor is readily able to provide students with opportunities for advancement and the encouragement to take advantage of those opportunities (Healy, 1997). In addition, mentors propel protégés to their potential and elicit their commitment to achievement. Mentors contribute to the academic persistence of students helping them recognize their potential and providing opportunities in their field of interest.

Students who experience a high degree of faculty interaction take a more active role in their own education than other students (Cole & Anaya, 2001; Decoster & Brown, 1982). Tinto (1993) reported that frequent contact with the faculty is a particularly important element in student persistence. Students who are mentored or have faculty interactions are often more interested in pursuing their education and are more actively engaged in using their university's resources. Furthermore, this is true when the student-mentor contact extends beyond the formal boundaries to various informal settings.

Such informal contacts are strongly associated with continued academic persistence. For Latina/o students, the importance of role models and mentors cannot be underestimated. While it is important that all faculty take the responsibility to mentor all students (Gloria & Pope-Davis, 1997), the sheer presence of Latina/o faculty who have navigated and succeeded within the educational system proves to Latina/o students they can also succeed academically (Gloria & Rodriguez, 2000; Verdugo, 1995). Latina/o mentors can aid Latina/o students by providing them with guidance, accessing support systems, knowing about different academic or financial opportunities, and believing in their personal potential within the academic environment (Gloria, 1998).

The availability of mentors has been considered an essential component of educational institutions that facilitates retention (DeFour, 1991). However, due to the dearth of Latina/o faculty, mentorship continues to be a vital concern within academia. Because Latina/os represented only 2.4% of all full-time faculty in 1995 (Wilds & Wilson, 1998), it continues to be difficult to provide Latina/o students with Latina/o mentors.

Summary

Statistics support that the number of Latina/o students participating in American higher education institutions is growing. Unfortunately, the increase is not proportional to the current representation or population growth of Latina/os. Although the Latina/o population has increased, retention and matriculation rates remain dismal. An examination of the literature supports that various noncognitive factors contribute to the retention of Latina/o undergraduates. In attempting to provide improved academic and social support of Latina/o students in higher education, an understanding of the multidimensional components of their educational experience is warranted. It is imperative that the individual, environmental/social context, and the role of culture be considered in assessing institutional programs designed to enhance Latina/o student success. In conclusion, the successful retention of Latina/o students in higher education is not unlike other underrepresented groups. It is therefore important that Latina/o students feel a sense of academic security, environmental comfort, and support from positive role models. Further research is needed to help university administrators develop academic and social programs that help retain Latina/o students to graduation.

References

Álvarez, Jr., R. R. (1994). Changing patterns of family and ideology among Latino cultures in the United States. In T. Weaver. (Ed.), *Handbook of Hispanic Cultures in the United States: Anthropology* (pp. 147–167). Arte Público Press.

Anaya, G. & Cole, D. G. (2001). Latina/o student achievement: Exploring the influence of student-faculty interactions on college grades. *Journal of College Student Development, 42*(1), 3–14.

Arellano, A. R., & Padilla, A. M. (1996). Academic invulnerability among a select group of Latino university students. *Hispanic Journal of Behavioral Sciences, 18,* 485–507.

Baltimore, L. W. (1995). Collaboratives: Helping Hispanic students succeed. *NEA Higher Education Journal, 11*(2), 67–83.

Brown, S. V. (1992). Minorities in the graduate education pipeline: An update. In S. V. Brown (Ed.), *Minorities in graduate education: Pipeline, policy and practice.* Princeton, NJ: Graduate Record Examination Board, Educational Testing Service.

Carter, D. J., & Wilson, R. (1996). *Minorities in higher education: Fifteenth annual status report.* Washington DC: American Council on Education.

Decoster, D. A., & Brown, R. D. (1982). *New Directions for Student Services: Mentoring-Transcript Systems for Promoting Student Growth* (pp. 5–16). San Francisco: Jossey-Bass.

DeFour, D. C., & Palude, M. A. (1991). Integrating scholarship on ethnicity into psychology of women course. *Teaching of Psychology, 18*(2), 85–90.

de los Santos, A., Jr., & Rigual, A. (1994). Progress of Hispanics in American higher education. In M. J. Justiz & R. Wilson (Eds.), *Minorities in Higher Education,* 173–194. Pheonix, AZ: Oryx Press.

Flores, J. L. (1992). *Persisting Hispanic America college students: Characteristics that lead to baccalaureate degree completion.* Paper presented at the annual meeting of the American Educational Research Association, San Francisco, CA, April 20–24, 1992.

Gloria, A. M. (1997). Chicana academic persistence: Creating a university-based community. *Education and Urban Society, 30*(1), 107–121.

Gloria, A. M. (1998). *Comunidad: Promoting the educational persistence and success of Chicana/o college students.* JRSI Occasional Paper #48, The Julian Samora Research Institute, Michigan State University, 1–7.

Gloria, A. M., & Kurpius Robinson, S. R. (1996). The validation of the cultural congruity scale and the university environment scale with Chicano/a students. *Hispanic Journal of Behavioral Sciences, 18*(4), 533–549.

Gloria, A. M., & Pope-Davis, D. B. (1997). Cultural ambience: The importance of a culturally aware learning environment in the training and education of counselors. In D. B. Pope-Davis & H. L. K. Coleman (Eds.), *Multicultural counseling competencies: Assessment, education and training, and supervision* (pp. 242–259). Thousand Oaks, CA: Sage.

Gloria, A. M., Robinson Kurpius, S. E., Hamilton, K. D., & Willson, M. S. (1999). African American students' persistence at a predominantly White university: Influences of social support, university comfort, and self-beliefs. *Journal of College Student Development, 40,* 257–268.

Gloria, A. M., Riechmann, T., R., & Rush, J. D. (2000). Issues and recommendations for teaching an ethnic/culture-based course. *Teaching of Psychology, 27*(2), 102–107.

Gloria, A. M., & Rodríguez, E. R. (2000). Counseling Latino university students: Psychosociocultural issues for consideration. *Journal of Counseling and Development, 78,* 145–154.

Gloria, A. M., & Segura-Herrera, T. M. (in press). Ambrocia and Omar go to college: A psychosociocultural examination of Chicanos and Chicanas in higher education. In R. J. Velasquez, B. McNeill, & L. Arellano (Eds.). *Handbook of Chicana and Chicano psychology.* Lawrence Erlbaum.

Gonzales, R. & Ortiz, F. I. (2000). Latino high school students' pursuit of higher education. *Aztlan, 25*(1), 67–107.

Haro, R., Rodriguez, G., & Gonzalez, J., L. (1994). *Latino persistence in higher education: A 1994 survey of University of California and California State University Chicano/Latino students.* Paper presented at the Latino Issues Forum, San Francisco.

Healy, C. C. (1997). An operational definition of mentoring. *Diversity in Higher Education, 1,* 9–22.

Heller, S. (1984). Reaffirm drive for integration, colleges urged. *Higher Education and National Affairs Newsletter,* March 26, p. 3.

Hernandez, J. C. (2000). Understanding the retention of Latino college students. *Journal of College Student Development, 41*(6), 575–588.

Hurtado, S. (1992). The campus racial climate: Contexts for conflict. *The Journal of Higher Education, 63*(5), 539–569.

Hurtado, S. (1994). The institutional climate for talented Latino students. *Research in Higher Education, 35*(1), 21–41.

Hurtado, S., & Carter, D. F. (1997). Effects of college transition and perceptions of the campus racial climate on Latino college students' sense of belonging. *Sociology of Education, 17,* 324–345.

Hurtado, S., Carter, D. F., & Spuler, A. (1996). Latino student transition to college: Assessing difficulties and factors in successful college adjustment. *Research in Higher Education, 37*(2), 135–157.

Hurtado, S., Kurotsuchi, K., Briggs, C., & Rhee, B. S. (1996). Differences in college access in choice among racial/ethnic groups: Identifying continuing barriers. Paper presented at AIR 1996 36th Annual Forum, Paper: P46 May 1996, Albuquerque, NM, 397–733.

Hurtado, S., Milem, J. F., Clayton-Pedersen, A. R., & Allen, W. R. (1998). Enhancing campus climates for racial/ethnic diversity: Educational policy and practice. *The Review of Higher Education, 21*(3), 279–302.

Levine, A. (1989). *Shaping higher education's future.* San Francisco: Jossey-Bass.

Loo, C. M., & Rolison, G. (1986). Alienation of ethnic minority student at a predominantly White university. *Journal of Higher Education, 57*(1), 58–77.

Macias-Wycoff, S. E. (1996). Academic performance of Mexican American women: Sources of support that serve as motivating variables. *Journal of Multicultural Counseling and Development, 24,* 146–155.

Muñoz, D. G. (1986). Identifying Areas of Stress for Chicano Undergraduates. *Hispanic Student Achievement,* 131–156.

Nettles, T. M. (1990). Success in doctoral programs: Experiences of minority and White students. *American Journal of Education, 98*(4), 494–522.

Nora, A., & Cabrera, A. F. (1996). The role of perceptions in prejudice and discrimination and the adjustment of minority students to college. *Journal of Higher Education, 67*(2), 119–148.

Olivas, M. A. (1986). *Latino college students.* New York: Teacher College Press.

Oliver, M. L., Rodriguez, C. J., & Mickelson, R. A. (1985). Brown and Black in White: The social adjustment and academic performance of Chicano and Black students in a predominantly White university. *Urban Review, 17*(1), 3–23.

Progress in the achievement and attainment of Hispanic students. The Condition of Education 1995. Retrieved on December 12, 2001, from http://www.ed.gove/pubs/CondOfED_95/0vw2.html

Quintana, S. M., Vogel M. C., & Ybarra, V. C. (1991). Meta-analysis of Latino students' adjustment in higher education. *Hispanic Journal of Behavioral Sciences, 13*(2), 155–168.

Rendón, L. I., & Hope, R. O. (1996) *Educating a new majority: Transforming America's educational system for diversity.* San Francisco: Jossey-Bass.

Reyes, P., & Valencia, R. R. (1993). Educational policy and the growing Latino student population: Problems and prospects. *Hispanic Journal of Behavioral Sciences, 15*(2), 258–283.

Rodriguez, A. L., Guido-DiBrito, F., Torres, V., & Talbot, D. (2000). Latina college students: Issues and challenges for the 21st century. *NASA Journal, 37*(3), 511–527.

Sánchez, J., Marder, F., Berry, R., & Ross, H. (1992). Dropping out: Hispanic students, attrition, and the family. *College and University, 67,* 145–150.

Skinner, E. F., & Richardson, R. C. (1988). Resolving access/quality tensions: Minority participation and achievement in higher education. Paper presented at ASHE Annual Meeting.

Smedley, B. D., Myers, H. F., & Harrell, S. P. (1993). Minority-status stresses and the college adjustment of ethnic minority freshmen. *Journal of Higher Education, 64*(4), 434–53.

Sudarska, N. (1987). Racial and cultural diversity is a key part of the pursuit of excellence in the university, *Chronicle of Higher Education,* p. 42, February 25, 1987.

Tinto, V. (1993). *Leaving college: Rethinking the causes and cures of student attrition* (2nd ed.). Chicago: The University of Chicago Press.

U.S. Census Bureau, U.S. Department of Commerce. (2000). *Overview of race and Hispanic origin*. Washington DC: Government Printing Office.

U.S. Department of Education. (1992a). *Digest of education statistics, 1992*. National Center for Education Statistics, Department of Education, Office of Educational Research and Improvement. Washington, DC: Government Printing Office.

U.S. Department of Education. (1992b). *Dropout rates in the United States, 1991*. National Center for Education Statistics, Department of Education, Office of Educational Research and Improvement. Washington, DC: Government Printing Office.

U.S. Department of Education. (1995). *Mini digest of education statistics, 1995*. National Center for Education Statistics, Department of Education, Office of Educational Research and Improvement. Washington, DC: Government Printing Office.

U.S. Department of Education, National Center for Educational Statistics. (1994). *State comparisons of statistics, 1969–70 to 1993–94*. U.S. Census Bureau, 1997. Washington, DC: Government Printing Office.

U.S. Department of Education, National Center for Education Statistics. (1995). *Digest of education statistics, 1995*. Washington, DC: Government Printing Office.

U.S. Department of Education, National Center for Education Statistics. (1995). *The condition of education, 1995*. NCES 1995-273. Washington, DC: Government Printing Office.

U.S. Department of Education, National Center for Education Statistics. (2002). *The condition of education, 2002*. NCES 2000-025. Washington, DC: U.S. Government Printing Office.

U.S. Department of Education, National Center for Education Statistics. 2000. *Digest of education statistics, 2000*. Washington, DC: Government Printing Office.

Verdugo, R. R. (1995). Racial stratification and the use of Hispanic faculty as role models. *Journal of Higher Education, 66*(6), 669–686.

Weaver, T. (1994). The Culture of Latina/os in the United States. In T. Weaver. (Ed.), *Handbook of Hispanic Cultures in the United States: Anthropology* (pp. 15–38). Arte Publico Pres.

Wilds, D. J., & Wilson, R. (1998). *Minorities in Higher Education: Seventeenth Annual Status Report*. Washington, DC: American Council on Education.

Young, G. (1992). Chicana college students on the Texas-Mexico border: Tradition and transformation. *Hispanic Journal of Behavioral Sciences, 14*, 341–352.

Victoria-María MacDonald

Victoria-María MacDonald received her degrees in American History and the History of Education from Wellesley College and Harvard University. She is Associate Professor of History and Philosophy of Education at the Florida State University. Her specialty areas include History of Latinos and Education, History of Education in the South and the History of American Teachers.

Teresa García

Teresa García is a doctoral student in the College of Education at the University of Iowa in the social foundations program. Her research interests include the history of Mexican American education, Chicanas and Chicanos in the Midwest, and higher education.

Ms. García received a 2002 research grant from the State Historical Society of Iowa and has presented her research at meetings of the American Educational Research Association, American Educational Studies Association, and Midwest History of Education Society.

She holds a Bachelor of General Studies degree from the University of Iowa and a Juris Doctor degree from Creighton University. She previously served as director of the Upward Bound Project, a federal TRIO program at the University of Iowa, and as a staff attorney for Kansas Legal Services at the Legal Aid Society of Topeka. She is active in university and community issues related to campus cultural centers and the development of archives on the lives of women of color in Iowa.

2

HISTORICAL PERSPECTIVES ON LATINO ACCESS TO HIGHER EDUCATION, 1848–1990

Victoria-María MacDonald
and Teresa García

In *A Darker Shade of Crimson* Rubén Navarrette, Jr. (1993) recalls his first days at Harvard College in 1985:

> Of an entering class of just over 1,600 freshmen, I was one of only 35 Mexican-Americans . . . Was this the browning of the academy that affirmative action critics on Sunday morning talk shows foretold so ominously? Furthermore, aside from the low numbers, it was impossible not to notice the "quality" of those who had made it through Harvard's half-opened door. We had been carefully chosen it seemed. We were valedictorians, star athletes, class presidents, and National Merit Scholars. We were, in short, the *crema* of the Mexican crop. (p. 56)

Contemporary post-affirmative action discussions concern the loss of policies that brought large numbers of underrepresented groups into higher education during the last half of the twentieth century (Lindsay & Justiz, 2001; Ibarra, 2001). However, as an educational research community we have barely constructed an adequate history of the relatively recent entrance of some of these groups, particularly Latinos, Asians, and Native Americans into postsecondary education. The 2000 U.S. census suggests that growth of the Latino population will continue unabated throughout the twenty-first century. Resultantly, researchers have scrambled to fill in the holes of our sparse knowledge of the Latino population—one that is hardly new but dates back to sixteenth-century colonial America (MacDonald, 2001). This essay provides a social and historical backdrop designed to frame and explain the long and uneven historical trajectory of Latino access and participation in higher education from the nineteenth century through the 1980s. Of critical importance for understanding collegiate participation are the deeply rooted barriers of segregation and discrimination that have generally accompanied the Latino elementary and secondary experience. Numerous scholars including Nieto (2000), Donato (1997), Moreno (1999), San Miguel, Jr. (2001), and others have examined facets of these historical barriers to schooling. A comprehensive examination of those works is outside the scope of this chapter. However, one key to understanding higher education is to realize that the pipeline to college for Latinos has generally been blocked at the lowest levels of schooling, often prior to high school. As a result it was not until the last quarter of the twentieth century that Latinos entered higher education in significant numbers. Their political fight for access during the 1960s forced the academy and federal government to confront the issues and potential of a large and underserved population.

Historians of higher education have virtually ignored the presence of Latino students and faculty. In the only journal specifically devoted to this topic, *The History of Higher Education Annual,* not one article on Latinos has appeared in almost twenty years of publication. Commonly used texts in higher education foundations and history courses provide only passing reference to Latinos (Lucas, 1994; Goodchild & Wechsler, 1997). Donato and Lazerson (2000, p. 11) pointed out these inadequacies in the literature: "We still know little about how peoples of color were limited in their use of higher education and the ways they advanced through it, issues that are central to current debates over affirmative action and the outcomes of schooling." Scholars of Chicano or Puerto Rican studies have pioneered the majority of research on the historical relationship between Latinos and higher education. Aurora Levins Morales argues that "the role of a socially committed historian is to use history, not so much to document the past as to restore to the dehistoricized a sense of identity and possibility" (1998, p. 1). This essay brings to light the history of Latinos in American higher educational history through an examination of five major eras.

The first period, "Southwestern Class Exceptionalism, 1848–1920s," illustrates how Latino collegiate participation waxed and waned in the Southwest from the mid-nineteenth through the early twentieth century. Historians have documented the social and economic decline of Mexicans after the 1848 Treaty of Guadalupe Hidalgo. Promised the preservation of Spanish land grants, citizenship, and language rights, Mexicans encountered instead a series of discriminatory measures which resulted in significant socioeconomic decline (Pitt, 1966; Alonzo, 1998; Menchaca, 2001). Opportunities for higher education, linked closely to social class status during this era, subsequently also declined.

The second focus, "Imperial Conquests: The Case of Puerto Rico, 1898–1920," examines imperialistic policies imposed upon the newly acquired Puerto Rican lands in 1898. The University of Puerto Rico's creation during this era provided an important avenue of upward mobility for later generations of Puerto Ricans. During Puerto Rico's era of colonial tutelage, 1898–1948 (Carrión, 1983), however, appointed American educators narrowly defined the form of higher education Puerto Ricans should receive. On both the island and mainland Puerto Ricans were slanted towards narrow industrial education and normal school curricula.

In the third stage, "Slipping in the College Gates: 1920s–1950s," several factors, including the role of philanthropical organizations and the GI Bill are examined to explain the first generation of working-class Latino college students who entered higher education. This generation, entering against the odds, became role models for the student activists of the 1960s and 1970s.

In the fourth era, "El Movimiento in Higher Education, 1960–1980," the critical role of Latino youth in demanding higher educational access, curriculum, and faculty/staff recruitment is explored. This era was clearly the watershed of the entrance of Latinos into higher education.

The fifth and last period, "The Federal Government Steps In—the 1980s and 1990s," explores how the activism and demands of the previous generation is co-opted into federal policy. The important lobbying efforts of the Hispanic Association of Universities and Colleges, for example, resulted in the federal designation of Hispanic Serving Institutions (HSIs).

The complex history of Latina and Latino access to higher education corresponds to the complexity of contemporary issues related to Latina and Latino access and success in higher education. Diversity of national origin and generation in the United States, gender, socioeconomic status, and other factors impact a broad array of issues in higher education. This brief overview thus offers a foundation for understanding Latina and Latino access to higher education from a historical perspective that may inform efforts to examine and address contemporary issues.

Trajectories of Minority Higher Education

Minority groups have pursued pathways to higher education specific to their linguistic, political, racial, and socioeconomic position in American history. For example, federal policies concerning forced relocation, assimilation, and reservation schooling of Native Americans shaped the late twentieth-century passage of the 1975 Indian Self-Determination and Education Assistance Act and subsequent Tribally Controlled Community College Assistance Act in 1978 (Olivas, 1982/1997; Adams, 1995). In contrast, federal higher educational policies for African Americans emerged earlier in U.S. history. After the Civil War, the U.S. government and religious missionary organizations sent money and personnel to rebuild the South. Furthermore, African Americans themselves demanded and pooled resources for educational opportunities (Anderson, 1988).

From that era came the genesis of our Historically Black Colleges and Universities (HBCUs). The U.S. government founded Howard University in 1867. Dozens of private Black colleges such as Tuskegee, Morehouse, and Spelman arose during this era. Because Blacks were denied access to White colleges and universities in the American South, HBCUs received federal funds from the Second Morrill Land Grant Act of 1890, which provided monies for segregated Black state universities (Brown & Davis, 2001). In the twentieth century the War on Poverty, Title III of the 1965 Higher Education Act stipulated aid for "Strengthening Developing Institutions." HBCUs were well positioned to take advantage of these additional federal resources.

The Latino experience is distinct from both that of Native Americans and African Americans. Neither the federal government nor missionary organizations created historically Hispanic colleges. The rise of what Black intellectual W. E. B. DuBois called the "Talented Tenth," a college-educated elite from which to draw leaders, was thus absent among most Latino communities until after World War II. The post-1980 era witnessed the fastest growth among minorities in general. Lee (2002) pointed out that Asian, Black, Hispanic, and Native Americans were only 18% of all enrolled undergraduates in 1980 and increased to 27% by 1995. This chapter explores historical factors shaping the relative newcomer status of one of these groups, Hispanic Americans, within the context of rising minority participation in higher education during the latter part of the twentieth century.

Identity issues and census classification pose considerable challenges to historians of the Latino experience. The word "Latino/a" is utilized here to collectively denote the diversity of peoples including Mexican Americans, Puerto Ricans, Cubans, and Latin Americans who are linked to U.S. history through immigration, acquisition of lands, or political upheavals. The counting and labeling of Latinos, however, generally did not occur until the late twentieth century, posing difficulties for historians (Oboler, 1995; Rodríguez, 2000). Securing reliable data on the numbers of Latinos in postsecondary institutions prior to 1980 is problematic. Federal and state governments generally did not create a census classification for Hispanics until the 1970s (NCES, 1980).

As a result, many pre-1970 case studies that exist are based upon estimated counts of Hispanic surnames. The difficulties with this methodology include an undercounting of Latinos who possess Anglo surnames and an inclusion of South American or Iberian Spanish foreign students as U.S. Latinos. Despite these limitations, primary and secondary sources supplement statistical data to create a historical portrait of Latino higher education participation.

Southwestern Class Exceptionalism, 1848–1920s

As a result of the Treaty of Guadalupe Hidalgo (1848) the United States acquired the vast territories that include modern-day Arizona, Colorado, California, New Mexico, and Texas. The terms of this Mexican-American War treaty provided several rights to Mexicans who elected to remain in the United States. These rights included citizenship, preservation of former land grants, and Spanish language rights. The Gold Rush of the 1840s and early 1850s, with accompanying land grabs and a rapid influx of Anglo settlers to the West resulted in the erosion of these rights for the *Californios* (early Mexican settlers in the Northern New Mexico region known as California) and *Hispanos* (settlers in New Mexico and Colorado who claimed pure Spanish ancestry). Higher education participation during this era thus arose in a context in which the rights and status of many Southwestern Hispanics were eroding (León & McNeill, 1992; Menchaca, 2001; Weinberg, 1977). Historians have pointed out that the more resilient economic and political strength of Hispanos in New Mexico and Colorado protected bilingual traditions and equitable educational access well into the twentieth century (Donato, 1999; Getz, 1997). In contrast, conditions for Mexican Americans in Texas and California were more difficult, negatively impacting higher education access.

The possession of a college degree or even collegiate participation in mid-nineteenth-century America was rare for anyone regardless of race, gender, or ethnicity. Geiger (2000) concluded that college graduates represented only one percent of the male workforce before the Civil War. The small number of Latinos in nineteenth-century colleges were thus drawn from among the most privileged classes in the new territories as well as families from northern Mexico who sent their sons to receive a bilingual education (McKevitt, 1990/91). State universities in the Southwest provided one pathway for students seeking higher education during this era. The University of California opened its doors in 1869 with forty students. The university quickly found itself in a situation familiar to many nineteenth-century institutions—few students were adequately prepared for collegiate-level work. As a result, the university opened a preparatory department called the Fifth Class. Standards for admission were lower and during its brief existence from 1870 to 1872 the Fifth Class enrolled almost two dozen Mexican-born and *Californio* students. Furthermore, two Latino students passed the entrance examination and proceeded to the freshman class (León & McNeil, 1992). The abolition of the preparatory department in order to "raise standards" two years later resulted in the "virtual disappearance of Spanish surnamed students from the University of California" (León & McNeil, p. 194). Although some Latino students attended the Berkeley campus at the University of California during the next one hundred years, it was not until after 1970 that the Latino student was more than a rarity.

In Texas, the flagship campus opened in the fall of 1883. Kanellos (1997) pointed out that a Manuel García was the first Mexican American to graduate from the University of Texas in 1894. Little is know about other Latinos in the Texas university system during this early era. When researchers began counting Hispanic-surnamed students in the Texas university system in 1928, only 57 undergraduates (1.1%) at UT-Austin possessed Hispanic surnames out of a total of 5,390 enrollees. Only one Hispanic-surnamed graduate student enrolled that year out of 465 (0.2%) (Carter, 1970). (See Table 2.1.) Latino participation in late-nineteenth-century higher educational institutions in Arizona, Colorado, and New Mexico has received very little attention, but the sociohistoric context suggests participation may have been higher than Texas or California. Kanellos (1997, p. 45) noted that Mariano Samniego was appointed a member of the first board of regents for the University of Arizona in 1886; his presence may have encouraged Latino access among the student population during an era in which Latinos still maintained political power.

The role of Catholic higher educational institutions in providing access during this first era appears to yield promising answers to where Latinos found easier pathways to college. The emerging Anglo public schools of California and Texas quickly enacted English-only laws, forbidding the Spanish language. Furthermore, the Catholic religion and culture was denounced in the Pan-Protestant curriculum of primary and grammar public schools. In contrast, Catholic schools and colleges were more accepting of Hispanic bilingual and Catholic traditions (San Miguel, Jr., & Valencia, 1998).

Table 2.1 Enrollment of Spanish-Surname Students and Total Number of Students at the University of Texas at Austin for Selected Years

Year	Total No. of Undergrads	Spanish-Surname Undergrads	% Spanish-Surname Undergrads	Total No. of Graduate Students	Spanish-Surname Graduate Students	% Spanish-Surname Graduate Students	Total No. of Students	Spanish-Surname Total Students	% Spanish-Surname Total Students
1928–1929	5,390	57	1.1	465	1	0.2	5,855	58	1.0
1938–1939	10,103	152	1.5	818	3	0.3	10,921	155	1.4
1948–1949	16,356	395	2.4	2,177	37	1.7	18,533	432	2.3
1958–1959	15,533	518	3.3	2,229	49	2.2	17,762	567	3.2
1966–1967	22,559	634	2.8	4,786	126	2.6	27,345	771	2.8

Source: Carter, Thomas P. 1970. *Mexican Americans in School: A History of Educational Neglect.* p. 30.

For example, McKevitt (1990/91) documented the popularity of Santa Clara College (now university) in California as a choice for Hispanic college attendance. Between 1851 and 1876 almost four hundred Hispanic-surnamed students had attended. By 1867 one-quarter of the student population was Spanish-speaking. McKevitt (1990/91, p. 322) argues that the Jesuits in charge "actively recruited Spanish-speaking students" through the publication of a Spanish language catalogue. Similarly, in nearby Notre Dame College for women, the student population was largely Hispanic and even report cards and bills were printed in Spanish. By the late 1850s Notre Dame offered parallel courses in English and Spanish. Additional scattered references in local histories mention the presence of Latinos at institutions such as St. Mary's Catholic College in San Francisco in the late 1800s and the College of San Miguel in Santa Fe, New Mexico (Kanellos, 1997, p. 44).

Further research into the early state universities of the southwest territories and Catholic institutions will provide a fuller portrait of early Latino participation. The little that is known about these early students suggest that their socioeconomic positions allowed them entry to college. As the status of many Latinos declined in the late decades of the nineteenth century, collegiate participation among Latinos may have also dropped (Pitt, 1996). Unlike the African American experience, specific racial codes did not formally prohibit Hispanics from White universities and colleges, yet their numbers remained miniscule except perhaps in Catholic colleges. The political status of Latino youth, as demonstrated in the next section, also shaped their educational offerings. Anglo American's limited expectations for the youth of newly acquired Puerto Rico impacted participation of Puertorriqueños on the mainland during colonialism.

Imperial Conquests: The Case of Puerto Rico, 1898–1950

Over one hundred years ago, U.S. acquisition of Puerto Rico in the Spanish-American War of 1898 resulted in the introduction of American schools and the English language in Puerto Rico. A massive Americanization campaign in the Puerto Rican schools extended to the university level. In 1903, the University of Puerto Rico was created and emphasized normal (teacher training) and industrial departments. The university's emphasis upon teacher training for American assimilation, and agricultural and mechanical arts rather than classical studies, resembled that of many post-Civil War institutions on the mainland for African Americans and Native Americans (Anderson, 1988; Adams, 1995).

One form of Americanization involved sending youth to mainland colleges to become inculcated with American values. The colonial government sponsored approximately forty-five "poor young men of robust constitution and good conduct" per year between 1901 and at least 1907 to attend colleges in the United States. The colonial legislation (Section 73) narrowly specified the institutions available; "The colleges or institutions designated to which the said students shall attend are Hampton Institute, Hampton, Va., and Tuskegee Institute, Tuskegee, Ala., and such other similar educational institutions as the commissioner of education may from time to time specify (U.S. Commissioner of Education Report, 1907, p. 331).

Tuskegee and Hampton, African American industrial education colleges, were also the recipients of advanced students from Native American reservations (Lindsey, 1995). A loophole in the legislation enabled the commissioner to permit some Puerto Rican scholarship students to attend institutions with broader academic missions than Tuskegee and Hampton. For the school year 1903–04, the Commissioner of Education in Puerto Rico reported eighteen students in their third academic year at institutions as varied as Haverford, Rutgers, Cornell, Wesleyan, MIT, University of Michigan, University of Maryland Medical School, and Lehigh University (U.S. Commissioner of Education Report, 1905, p. 333). By 1905, almost five hundred Puerto Ricans were attending American institutions as a means of building pride in the United States and educating officials to staff the colonial government (Rodríguez-Fraticelli, 1986).

The University of Puerto Rico in Río Piedras was opened in 1903 and was typically free for students pledging to teach in Puerto Rico. However, financial and logistical difficulties often blocked access to higher education. The case of Ana Peñaranda Marcial illustrates the perseverance required of Puerto Rican students desiring a postsecondary education. Peñaranda Marcial began her baccalaureate degree at the University of Puerto Rico in 1921. Like many of her teaching colleagues, she could only take classes on Saturdays. The university created centers in rural areas where Peñaranda Marcial and other teachers could have more access. It was not until 1943, however, that she finally completed her degree (Sánchez-Korrol, 1994).

Serious socioeconomic conditions resulting from colonization spurred migration from the island to the mainland during the 1940s and 1950s. (Sánchez-Korrol, 1994). Puerto Ricans arrived in New York and Chicago and worked in low skill jobs (Padilla, 1985). Even teachers with B.A. degrees and teacher certification from Puerto Rico were unable to utilize their full economic potential on the mainland. Few Puerto Rican educators could pass the speech test required by New York City's Board of Examiners (Sánchez-Korrol, 1994). Furthermore, Puerto Rican children arriving to the mainland were often placed in classes for slow learners and one or two grades below their level because of lack of fluency in English. As a result, few went on to secondary school and completed the requirements necessary for college. Puerto Rican associations in New York lobbied on behalf of bilingual education during the 1930s through 1950s but received little government support (Sánchez-Korrol, 1994). Except for some unusual cases, access to higher education was deferred for a later generation of Puerto Rican youth who had migrated to the mainland.

Slipping in the College Gates, 1920s–1950s

> I assumed that there were other Mexicans like me on campus, and occasionally I would notice a Spanish surname, perhaps in some school publication. However, with the exception of some professors, the only other Hispanic I ever met at Berkeley in four years [1949–1953] was an Argentine student whom I dated for a short while. (Francis Esquivel, in Twyoniak & García, 2000, p. 163)

Frances Esquivel Tywoniak's recollection of growing up in California's Central Valley and entering the University of California at Berkeley in 1949 with an academic scholarship captures a little-known but significant era in Latino higher education. Historians have often referred to adult Mexican Americans of the 1930s through the 1950s as the Mexican American Generation. (García, 1989; Sánchez, 1993). García defines this group as "the first extensive bilingual, bicultural cohort of Mexican Americans in the United States" after 1848, when Mexico was conquered (Twyoniak & García, 2000). The Mexican American Generation's relationship to higher education remains shadowed.

The history of Midwestern Latino higher education within this era is also limited. Valdés (2000), a leader in this field, noted that in St. Paul, Minnesota's Mexican colonia of 3,000 inhabitants "not a single person" entered college until 1941. The young woman who broke the mold attended Duluth State Teacher's College (now University of Minnesota–Duluth). In Chicago, home to the second largest Puerto Rican population after New York, by the 1960 census only one percent of Puerto Rican men and women had attended four years of college. The median number of school years completed was only 7.9 (male) and 7.2 for women (Padilla, 1987). How many other Latino men and women attended the newly opened state and two-year institutions that accompanied the rapid expansion of public higher education in the mid-twentieth century is still undocumented. While knowledge about specific institutions such as that available for the University of Texas at Austin since 1928 provides some information, it is only a partial portrait because Latino youth of this era were most likely entering the college gates at smaller, less prestigious and more teaching-oriented schools.

What is apparent, however, is that during these decades an increasing number of Mexicans in the Southwest and Midwest; and Puerto Ricans in Chicago and New York began entering the college gates after two decades of minimal participation. Philanthropy, increasing numbers of middle-class Latinos and the GI Bill were major contributors to this shift. These twentieth-century pioneers, often the only Latinos in their classes, provided leadership and talent for the formation of the Chicano/Puerto Rican civil rights movement of the 1960s and 1970s.

The college-going pioneers in the years between 1930s and 1950s were clearly exceptional. Unlike the late nineteenth-century participation of Latinos from older, elite Hispano families, students from middle- and working-class families were finally entering higher education. The barriers to high school graduation (or even entrance) for Mexican Americans in particular, were formidable. In some areas of the Southwest Mexican children were segregated into either separate schools or classrooms based upon their accents, skin color, or surname (Donato, 1997). Lack of enforcement of school attendance laws, language difficulties, immigration, classroom harassment, and racism resulted in few Mexican American children even reaching eighth grade (Valdés, 2000). The pipeline to higher education was thus choked off early in most Latino children's lives. Despite these obstacles, which impeded most Mexican Americans from collegiate participation prior to the 1960s, at least four factors contributed to the few who broke through the barriers.

First, community and charitable organizations became involved. During the Great Depression of the 1930s the Protestant Young Men's Christian Association (YMCA) in Los Angeles committed $30,000 to work with Mexican American youth. The YMCA hired role model and social worker Tom García to head this project. García created boys' clubs, organized the first Mexican Youth Conference, and provided training and leadership to adolescent boys (Muñoz, 1989). Significantly, YMCA officials provided contacts with leaders in higher education. Scholarships, admissions information, and important networks were opened to Latino male youth. As an offshoot of the YMCA club, Mexican American students at UCLA created the first Latino student organization called the Mexican-American Movement (MAM). Under the direction of student Felix Gutierrez, the first Latino college student newspaper, *The Mexican Voice*, was in operation at UCLA from 1938 until 1944. After 1944 the title was changed to *The Forward* and the tone of the paper changed as it focused on war-time activities of members of MAM (Navarro, pp. 49–50).

A second factor opening access to higher education from non-elite Latino families involved what Muñoz (1989, pp. 24–25) described as the "active support of individual teachers, clergy, or social workers that were sympathetic and in a position to identify youth with exceptional intelligence." For example, Frances Esquivel secured a UC Berkeley alumni scholarship through the efforts of her high school history teacher, Miss Helen Grant, a UC Berkeley alumna (Twyoniak & García, 2000). Similarly, the writer and scholar Ernesto Galarza entered Occidental College in 1923 and then became the first Mexican American to enter Stanford through the active assistance of interested teachers (Muñoz, 1989).

Third, the passage of the Servicemen's Readjustment Act of 1944 (the GI Bill), also assisted in expanding higher education access in the mid-twentieth century. Muñoz (1989, pp. 48–49) argued that "among the thousands of returning Mexican American veterans who took advantage of this opportunity to pursue a higher education were Américo Paredes, Octavio Romano V; and Ralph Guzmán. They were destined to become . . . significant contributors to Mexican American intellectual life." Both Muñoz (1989) and Navarro (1995) concluded that post-World War II Chicano students were "studious," and "self-oriented" rather than active contributors to larger goals of social activism.

Other researchers portray a less passive role for Latino World War II veterans. Donato (1999) demonstrated how Hispano veterans in Colorado demanded local access to higher education and were responsible for creating the San Luis Institute, a public two-year college. One San Luis veteran recalled, "I remember that almost all of us who discharged from the military went to college." (p. 138). According to Donato, "the sense of camaraderie among San Luis students who went on to Adams State" eased their access and retention at a four-year institution (p. 139). The creation of the American G.I. Forum in Texas in 1948, an activist group designed to protect the civil rights of returning Mexican American GIs further suggests that veterans were not uniformly interested in individual success (Allsup, 1982).

Fourth we must look to Latino communities themselves for efforts resulting in increased college participation during the 1920s through the 1950s. The League of United Latin American Citizens (LULAC) was founded in 1929 and worked to improve conditions for Mexican Americans. This largely middle-class Texas organization provided college scholarships and challenged educational segregation (San Miguel, Jr., 1987). In New Mexico, the continued political strength of Hispanos was evident in the 1909 founding of the Spanish-American Normal School at El Rito. The legislature charged the institution to educate "Spanish-speaking natives of New Mexico for the vocation of teachers in the public schools of the counties and districts where the Spanish language is prevalent" (New Mexico Department of Education, 1917–18, p. 30). The school enrolled over one hundred students by 1918. In the 1930s the bilingual state teacher training college was still open and eventually absorbed into the New Mexico higher education system (Getz, 1997).

The 1920s through the 1950s also witnessed the entrance of Latino faculty into higher education. Anecdotal evidence suggests that prior to the 1940s Hispanic-surnamed faculty at White colleges and universities were generally from Spain and clustered in the Romance Language and Literature Departments (Twyoniak & García, 2000). Key role models and intellectuals who trained the leaders of the Chicano generation include George I. Sánchez, first at the University of New Mexico in the 1930s and then from 1940 until his death at the University of Texas at Austin. Historian Carlos Castañeda was also a significant figure at UT–Austin. He devoted his life's work to documenting and correcting Latino history as a professor in the Department of History (García, 1989). The pioneers on the faculty of White colleges most likely shared the limelight with peers at normal schools, two-year colleges, and Catholic institutions at mid-century. After these "firsts" and "greats" in Latino history, in stepped Latinos no longer content with the status quo, bringing their activism and energy with them.

El Movimiento in Higher Education, 1960–1980

> It is a fact that the Chicano has not often enough written his own history, his own anthropology, his own sociology, his own literature. He must do this if he is to survive as a cultural entity in this melting pot society which seeks to dilute varied cultures into a gray upon gray pseudo-culture of technology and materialism. The Chicano student is doing most of the work in the establishment of study programs, centers, curriculum development, and entrance programs to get more Chicanos into college. This is good and must continue, but students must be careful not to be co-opted in their fervor for establishing relevance on the campus. Much of what is being offered by college systems and administrators is too little too late. [Manifesto of El Plan de Santa Barbara, 1969. In Muñoz (1989, p. 200)]

The pioneers of the pre-1960 era demonstrated that Latino youth could succeed in college if they attained access. Furthermore, the first generation of Latino faculty appearing on campuses served as role models. Civil rights activism, anti–Vietnam War protests, and all forms of antiauthoritarianism converged in the 1960s and 1970s on U.S. campuses. This era brought unprecedented numbers of Latinos into academe and clearly represents a watershed in higher educational history. No longer isolated individuals and small groups on campus, the new Puerto Rican and Chicano college students across the nation organized to demand their rights.

The parallel Chicano and Puerto Rican activism emerged with a concrete agenda to change the role of Latino students on campus as other than privileged exceptions. These radicalized youth demanded a broad range of services aiding access and retention for Chicano and Puerto Rican students. Often connected to organizations that pushed for reform in K–12 schools and community improvements, the Latino student youth movement nonetheless had its own leadership and momentum. The histories of the Chicano (Mexican American), and Boricuan (Puerto Rican) movements in the 1960s will be examined separately, since regional and sociohistoric contexts varied these experiences.

The early 1960s were a period of identity development for many Mexican Americans as they looked to inspiration from their indigenous roots rather than pathways of assimilation. As the Black civil rights movement for access to White colleges and universities gained visibility in the national media, Latino students examined their own status and numbers in the academy (Navarro, 1995). Available data suggest that on the eve of the turbulent 1960s Latino students were still on the margins of academe. Valdés (2000, p. 159) noted that in 1960 Michigan, 40% of all seventeen- to twenty-four-year-olds in the state were attending some form of postsecondary institution, compared to only 7% of its Mexican population. In Houston, Texas, only 3% of Mexican American adults older than twenty-five had completed four years of college in that same year (de León, 2001). Researcher Herschel T. Manuel found in 1958 that only 5.7% of freshmen in 146 southwestern colleges had Hispanic-surnames (Carter, 1970, p. 31). By the mid-1960s however, numbers had increased to 12.8% (see Table 2.2). Finding strength in numbers, they organized *el movimiento*. One of the issues which engaged students was the small number of Latino faculty.

At the beginning of the movimiento's heyday (1968–1973), Muñoz (1989, p. 142) pointed out that "fewer than one hundred scholars of Mexican descent held doctorates in the United States. Of these, most held doctorates in education (Ed.D.s), which located them in a distinctly different research network with a very different emphasis from those scholars holding a Doctor of Philosophy." The low number of faculty who might be interested in teaching or researching Latino issues was a principal issue addressed in the youth movement's conferences and lists of demands.

Several simultaneous external events also sparked the creation of a militant Chicano movimiento that spread through the Southwest. The national attention given to Cesar Chávez and the farmworkers' movement, the politicization of Latinos through Viva Kennedy clubs, and a growing desire to take advan-

Table 2.2   Spanish-Surname Student Population at a Selection of Colleges and Universities, 1966–1967

Class	Total	Percent*
Freshman	1,006	12.87
Sophomore	652	8.34
Junior	810	10.36
Senior	759	9.71
Graduate school	631	8.07

*Percentages are based on the authors' calculations with estimated total enrollment of 7,816.

Source: Adapted from Carter, Thomas P. 1970. *Mexican Americans in School: A History of Educational Neglect*, p. 31. The enrollment of Spanish-surname students is the combined enrollment of University of Arizona, University of California at Riverside, University of Colorado, California State College at Los Angeles, Northern Arizona University, The University of Texas, and New Mexico Highlands University.

tage of federal War on Poverty programs contributed to the formation of student groups. The fall of 1967 witnessed the birth of several Mexican American student organizations. The Mexican American Youth Organization (MAYO) began at St. Mary's College in San Antonio, Texas, and then at UT–Austin. In Los Angeles the United Mexican American Students (UMAS) formed several chapters in area institutions including UCLA and Loyola. At the large East Los Angeles Community College, the Mexican American Student Association (MASA) was formed (Muñoz, 1989, p. 58). Frustrated with the lack of attention to Latino demands for more faculty and relevant courses, the students engaged in a series of conferences and protests to change the academy.

The Chicano movement received inspiration and training from African American organizations, particularly the Black Panther Party and the Student Non-Violent Coordinating Committee (SNCC) (Navarro, 1995, p. 86). Campus dynamics between Chicano and Black protest organizations were often tension-filled, however. Both Muñoz (1989) and Olivas (1982) note that Chicanos often felt slighted by an overemphasis on the recruitment of Black students. As a result "bitter and intense conflicts between Mexican Americans and Blacks on several campuses, [made] viable coalition politics difficult, if not altogether impossible" (Muñoz, 1989, p. 85).

The first Latino protest activity on a college campus occurred at San José State College (CA) in 1968. Approximately two hundred graduating seniors and members of the audience walked out of commencement exercises to protest the underrepresentation of Chicano students and lack of bilingual and cultural training for professionals (teachers, social workers, and policemen) who worked in Latino communities. The San José State walkout was the beginning of a series of conferences and strikes that changed the image of Mexican Americans as "passive" to that of a visible and militant group. Dolores Delgado Bernal's study of the East Los Angeles blowouts also illustrates the significant leadership roles of Chicanas in the movement (1998).

Among the many conferences and strikes which students engaged in, the conference in 1969 at University of California at Santa Barbara holds the most significance for Latino higher educational history. Emerging from the conference was El Plan de Santa Barbara; the plan represented the clearest and most detailed articulation of the demands of Latino college youth. Although El Plan Spiritual de Aztlán, created at the National Chicano Youth Liberation Conference in Denver in March of 1969 was a pivotal "magna carta" of the general Chicano movement, El Plan de Santa Barbara specifically concerned higher education.

The Chicano Coordinating Council on Higher Education, a coalition of students, faculty, and staff from California institutions of higher education organized the Santa Barbara conference to develop a unified platform for higher education reform in the area of Chicano studies programs, access, and retention. The conference resulted in the call for individual student groups to forego their current names and become the Movimiento Estudiantil Chicano de Aztlán (MEChA). Many groups joined MEChA, others retained their individuality. The manifesto "El Plan de Santa Barbara" focused on three key areas. First, it emphasized the obligation of college and university Chicanos to maintain ties with the barrio community. Second, it stressed the importance of changing institutions of higher education to open their accessibility to Chicanos. The hiring of Chicano faculty, administrators, and staff was viewed as a key step in achieving this objective. Lastly, the Santa Barbara plan called for the alteration of traditional European White interpretations of history, literature, and culture to incorporate Third World viewpoints and particularly Chicano perspectives (Navarro, 1995; Muñoz, 1989; Valdés, 2000). El Plan de Santa Barbara served as a model that was circulated throughout the nation as Chicanos and Puerto Rican students not only entered academe in the 1960s and 1970s in significant numbers but also worked to change academe itself.

While Chicano students on the West Coast and in the Southwest forged a largely Chicano identity on campuses, Puerto Rican students in the urban Northeast and Midwest also joined with community-based groups or created their own organizations. The population of Puertorriqueños swelled in the mid-twentieth century. In New York, the Puerto Rican population rose tenfold from 70,000 in 1940 to 720,000 in 1961. The work of ASPIRA ("aspire" in Spanish) for bilingual and bicultural educational programs in New York City set the groundwork for future militancy. Founded by educator and leader

Antonia Pantoja in 1961, ASPIRA focused on raising educational levels and preparing Puerto Rican youth for leadership. At the time of its founding, few Puerto Ricans were graduating from high school, and among those who did graduate few received academic diplomas (Pantoja, 1998). For example, in 1963 only 331 of 21,000 Puerto Rican high school graduates in New York earned academic diplomas. (Sánchez-Korrol, 1994, p. 230). The numbers of Puerto Rican students in the city colleges were correspondingly low. Traub (1994, p. 44) found that in 1964 City College, although located in Harlem, did not enroll more than 2% of its students from the Black community and "a much smaller number of Puerto Ricans."

The Puerto Rican youth movement did not arise in a vacuum but built upon decades of Puerto Rican American associations that had raised awareness of deficiencies in the community and local governments' response to Puerto Rican poverty, discrimination, and lack of bilingual assistance (Sánchez-Korrol, 1994). Similar to Mexican American youths who had shifted their identities to embrace both the spiritual homeland and signify a new activist stance, Puerto Ricans chose "Boricua" as a symbolic term. The name "Boricua" appears in the titles of numerous 1960s student organizations, the founding of Boricua College in New York City in 1973 and Universidad de Boricua (a university without walls founded by Antonia Pantoja). Boricua, explained Santiago (1995, p. xviii), stands for the word "Borinquén" or "Land of the Brave Lord," which the Arawak Indians called the island prior to Columbus's arrival. In contemporary times, Boricua is a term of endearment used among the Puerto Rican community. In the 1960s and 1970s Boricua served as a rallying cry for activist youth.

The radicalization of Puerto Rican youth is attributed to the small increase of college students as a result of early 1960s programs such as City University of New York (CUNY)'s SEEK (Search for Education, Elevation, and Knowledge), College Discovery, and SUNY Educational Opportunity Programs (EOP) (Serrano, 1998). These pioneer students created several organizations including the Puerto Rican Student Movement (PRSM) for ASPIRA members in the CUNY system. In addition Puerto Ricans for Education Progress (PREP) was a network of private college students who worked to get more students into prestigious private schools such as Princeton and Yale (Serrano, 1998). Although these early organizations were not long-lasting, they provided early leadership for the more radical movement that followed.

The pivotal turning point in the Puerto Rican student movement was the successful fight for open admissions at City College, generally considered the flagship campus of the CUNY system. In 1969 conditions were ripe for a showdown between minority students and administrators. Black and Puerto Rican students organized a strike and campus shutdown. The controversial Open

Admissions policy at CUNY resulted in a flood of Puerto Rican and Black students. By 1975 Puerto Rican undergraduates had increased to 18,570 or 8.3% of the population. In 1969 Puerto Rican students had only numbered 5,425 or 4%. (Rodríguez-Fraticelli, 1986). Similarly, at Brooklyn College students from the Black League of Afro-American Collegians (BLAC) and the Puerto Rican Alliance (PRA) occupied the president's office and issued a series of demands. Throughout the greater New York area public and private colleges experienced demonstrations and strikes during the tumultuous years of 1969 and 1970 as underrepresented students fought their way into college (Serrano, 1998).

In addition to increasing college enrollment for Puerto Rican, then Dominican, and other Latino groups in the greater New York area during the 1970s and beyond, the movement created Puerto Rican research centers critical to the rewriting and reinvigoration of a Puerto Rican history and culture. In 1971 after two years of battles, CCNY finally approved the creation of a Department of Puerto Rican Studies. Dr. Frank Bonilla of Stanford was brought to assist in the design of the program. Furthermore, CCNY agreed to open an office of Puerto Rican Development to increase Latino admissions and bolster retention rates. At Hunter College the Puerto Rican Student Union (PRSU) facilitated the creation of the Centros for Estudios Puertorriqueños in 1972, an archival and scholarly research center with a continuing presence in the research community.

Students at the Chicago Circle campus of the University of Illinois (now UIC) successfully fought for the inclusion of a Latino curriculum and assisted in the creation of Rafael Cintrón-Ortiz Latino Cultural Center. Similarly, the Center for Chicano-Boricua Studies at Wayne University in Detroit was founded in 1971 and continues its presence as a Midwestern research center (Valdés, 2000, p. 200). The peak of the Puerto Rican student movement was reached between 1969 and 1973. After 1973 many student organizations declined in numbers and militancy. The end of the open admissions experiment at CUNY in 1975 impacted Puerto Rican youth. The combination of new tuition charges—the first ever in the institution's history—and the general economic recession of the 1970s led to a decline in the steady Puerto Rican enrollment growth of the early 1970s (Traub, 1994).

Throughout the country, the student youth movement began to wane as government programs, private foundations, and institutions implemented many of their demands. Affirmative action initiatives among many institutions of higher education in the 1970s brought Latinos into colleges, many of whom are now faculty members (Keller, Deneen, & Magallán, 1991). In the long continuum of Latino higher educational history, the 1960s and 1970s was a permanent watershed, although Latinos remained clustered overwhelmingly in public two-year institutions (see Table 2.3). Although Mexican Americans and

Table 2.3 Percentage of College Students Enrolled in Different Types of Institutions, by Racial or Ethnic Group, Fall 1978

| Racial or Ethnic Group | Public Institutions | | | Private Institutions | | |
	Universities, %	Other Four-Year Institutions, %	Two-Year Colleges, %	Universities, %	Other Four-Year Institutions, %	Two-Year Colleges, %
Whites	19.7	24.8	33.2	6.5	14.6	1.3
Blacks	9.7	30.6	39.3	4.3	13.5	2.7
Hispanics	8.6	25.0	53.3	4.1	7.9	1.1
Native Americans	12.5	22.4	53.0	2.9	7.1	2.1
All students	18.4	25.2	34.5	6.4	14.1	1.4

Source: Brint, Steven, and Jerome Karabel. 1989. *The Diverted Dream: Community College and the Promise of Educational Opportunity, 1900–1985,* p. 128.

Puerto Ricans had not been previously barred from White colleges and universities on account of racial policies, their participation prior to the mid-1960s was negligible. The Latino student movement introduced the possibility not only of access to White institutions, but the creation of uniquely Hispanic colleges. The U.S. government's growing acknowledgment in the 1970s that "minority" was not only African American had a significant impact on subsequent state and federal court rulings and policies. President Richard Nixon's O.M.B. Statistical Directive 15 of 1973 finally created a separate federally identified group. As the controversial Richard Rodriguez wrote in *Brown, The Last Discovery of America* (2002), the result of this federal directive was that "several million Americans were baptized Hispanic" (p. 95). The intervention of the federal government in shaping policies towards Hispanic higher education is the subject of the next chapter.

The Federal Government Steps In, 1980s and 1990s

> While the increase in Hispanics pursuing a postsecondary education is significant, it is insufficient to assure parity in the workforce. From 1973 to 1994, the overall number of high school graduates enrolled in a four-year institution doubled, from 16 to 31 percent. College-bound Hispanics in four-year institutions, however, only increased from 13 to 20 percent. Plainly, postsecondary Hispanic student enrollment and graduation rates are not keeping pace with the Hispanic American presence in the general population nor with the available pool of Latino high school graduates. (President's Advisory Commission on Educational Excellence for Hispanic Americans, 1996)

The most recent discernible stage in Latino higher educational history recognizes the controversial and critical role of the federal government as a stakeholder in identifying and actively participating in Latino issues. The surging Latino population of the 1980s and 1990s with accompanying predictions of becoming the "largest" minority—and yet the least educated—caught the attention of the federal government. The creation of the term "Hispanic" in 1973 as OMB Statistical Directive 15 was received with skepticism from many scholars and activists. The "homogenization" of diverse peoples with individual social and historical ties to the United States raised debate and concerns (Oboler, 1995). From the longer historical perspective, however, the counting and documentation of Hispanics signaled unprecedented recognition and attention. In particular, Hispanics joined Blacks, Asians, and Native Americans as ethnically identifiable groups. This status permitted not only visibility but also a larger share of public funds. The combination of federal recognition of Hispanics as a separate minority group, and advocacy from the Hispanic Association of Colleges and Universities, the National Council of La Raza, the Puerto Rican Legal and Defense Fund, and others brought postsecondary needs and concerns from the preliminary inroads of the student movement to permanent recognition and status.

The year 1980 represented another turning point in Latino history. Latinos were the fastest growing minority group in the United States according to the U.S. census and the 1980s were heralded as the "Decade of the Hispanics." Sheer numbers alone, however, could not alter the almost stagnant postsecondary enrollment. The 1980 census revealed that while 20% of Californians were Hispanic, only 2.7% possessed college degrees. Nationally Latinos received only 2.3% of all baccalaureate degrees in 1980–81 yet earned 3% of all doctorates (U.S. Congress, 1985, p. 3). Detailed examination of these statistics revealed that the majority were clustered in community colleges. With the exception of Native Americans, Latino college students since 1980 have not fared well compared to African Americans and Asian Americas (see Figure 2.1). Furthermore, Puerto Rican students

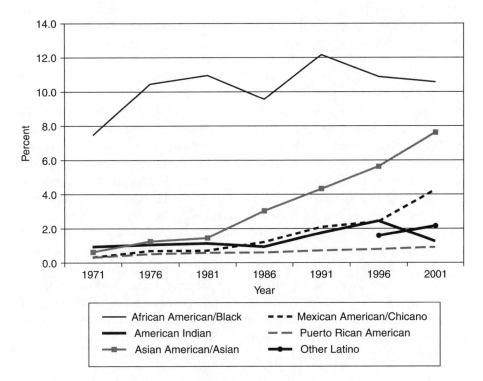

FIGURE 2.1   Minority representation of students in four-year colleges, 1971–2001.

Data courtesy of Linda J. Sax, Director, Cooperative Institutional Research Program and Associate Professor-in-Residence, University of California, Los Angeles.

enrolled in universities on the island of Puerto Rico were counted along with Latinos in the United States, creating a misleadingly high figure of collegiate participation (U.S. Congress, 1985, p. 4). Most disturbing in the early 1980s was the decline in gains made in the 1970s. The percentage of Hispanic high school graduates attending college for example, decreased from 35.4% in 1975 to 29.9% in 1980 (Olivas, 1986, p. 2). As a result of the severe disconnect between Latino educational achievement, the size of its population, and its relative underachievement compared to other ethnic groups, a series of steps were taken in the 1980s to regain advances begun in the 1970s.

Michael Olivas, through his supervision of the influential National Center for Education Statistics report, *Condition of Education for Hispanic Americans* (NCES, 1980), spurred reform in Hispanic education. Chairman of the Subcommittee on Postsecondary Education Paul Simon initiated the Hispanic Access to Higher Education Project after reviewing Olivas's work (U.S. Congress, 1985, p. 1). A series of hearings on the topic of Hispanics and higher education subsequently took place on several campuses during 1982 and 1983. Simon introduced H.R. 5240, The Higher Education Act Amendments of 1984, which recommended several reforms to aid Hispanic access and retention. These included the modification of Title III to provide direct aid to institutions with high concentrations of Hispanic students; specific monies for Hispanic students in the TRIO Programs;[1] a special emphasis on Teacher Preparation (Title V) programs to train teachers for Hispanic populations; and increased monies for the Graduate and Professional Opportunities Program (G*POP) to channel more Latinos towards graduate and professional schools. Although H.R. 5420 was not approved, subsequent legislation adopted the bill's key points. Furthermore, publication of the Staff Report on Hispanics' Access to Higher Education (1985) provided data to support future reforms.

The creation of the Hispanic Association of Colleges and Universities (HACU) in 1986 brought together Hispanic leaders in business and two- and four-year colleges and universities with large numbers of Latinos into one powerful advocacy organization. The mission of HACU, to improve the access and quality of college education for Hispanics, has been carried out through offices in San Antonio, Texas, and Washington, D.C. (Laden, 2001). HACU's most successful victory was the establishment of Hispanic Serving Institutions (HSIs) as a federally recognized category. Hispanic Serving Institutions, unlike HBCUs or Tribal Colleges, do not necessarily have a specific historic mission towards

---

[1]The name "TRIO" refers to a set of three federal outreach programs funded under Title IV of the Higher Education Act of 1965. The programs expanded beyond the original three—Upward Bound, Talent Search, and Student Support Services—but the name TRIO persists.

Latino education. Instead, the Department of Education defines HSIs as post-secondary institutions with at least 25% Hispanic full-time equivalent enrollment and also 50% or more low-income students. Laden (2001) credits HACU with successfully having HSIs recognized in the reauthorization of Title III of the Higher Education Act of 1992, thus securing eligibility for federal funds. Furthermore, in the reauthorization of the Higher Education Act of 1998, HSIs were included with Tribal Colleges and HBCUs under Title V, allowing them a larger slice of the federal pie.

The specific developments accompanying federal categorization received increased visibility in numerous private and publicly sponsored commissions created to examine the Latino educational condition at all levels. For example, President William Jefferson Clinton signed Executive Order 129000, "Educational Excellence for Hispanic Americans" in 1995. The order created a special task-force "to advance the development of human potential, to strengthen the nation's capacity to provide high-quality education, and to increase opportunities for Hispanic Americans to participate in and benefit from federal education programs (President's Advisory Commission on Excellence, 1996, p. 8.). The National Council of La Raza (Fisher, 1998) also sponsored a major study on education that differentiated achievement levels between the numerous Latino groups. The 1990s also witnessed emergence of a new field of studies called Latino Critical Theory and more attention to gender issues within the Hispanic experience (García, 1997; de la Torre & Pesquera, 1993; Valdés, 1997; and Stefancic, 1997).

Conclusions: 2000 and Beyond

The reality to many Latinos is that affirmative action did not cure all of their problems. For instance the income and education gap between Latinos and Euro Americans has increased dramatically in the last two decades. At the same time, however, the Mexican American middle class has expanded significantly since 1965. Undoubtedly, affirmative action along with the Voting Rights Act of 1965 played a role in this expansion . . . As a result, today more Mexican Americans attend universities than at any time in our history, something that would not have happened without the environment created by affirmative action. Affirmative action gave us the justification for our being at the university, and the right that administrators listen to our demands. (Acuña, 1998, pp. 1–2)

The long trajectory of Latino higher educational history does not suggest an ever-upward linear path of progress. Latinos in the middle and late nineteenth century enrolled in state and private, particularly Catholic, colleges. The declining social and economic status of Latinos after the turn-of-the-19th century appears to have negatively influenced postsecondary enrollment. Nevertheless, the creation of the University of Puerto Rico in 1903 established an historical legacy of higher education on the island that has not extended to mainland Puerto Ricans (Rodríguez-Fraticelli, 1986). By the mid-twentieth century, only middle-class or exceptional working-class Mexican Americans and Puerto Ricans had entered higher education. The GI Bill and private organizations including the YMCA and LULAC provided support for some of these post-World War II students.

The 1960s and 1970s were the watershed years for Latinos in higher education. The successful mobilization of student groups who targeted goals to enhance Latino college access and retention resulted in a permanent presence in academe. Universities, foundations, and state and federal governments created policies, centers, and curricula designed to meet student demands. Unfortunately, successes of this era lost momentum in the economic recessions of the 1970s and into the 1980s.

The 1990s witnessed a political backlash against Latinos and affirmative action. For example, California voters approved the California Civil Rights Initiative of 1996, commonly referred to as Proposition 209, which ended affirmative action programs in the state. Proposition 209 occurred in a climate in which affirmative action was likewise being challenged in the courts. Conflicting decisions in cases such as *Hopwood v. State of Texas* (Fifth Circuit, 1996) and *Smith v. University of Washington* (Ninth Circuit, 2000), respectively repudiating and permitting the use of race in admissions, called into question the future of affirmative action programs as well as the future of *Bakke v. Regents of University of California* (1978), the US Supreme Court decision permitting the use of race in college admissions.

Researchers point to future agendas impacting Latino higher education. One development concerns lawsuits filed to stop the use of Advanced Placement (AP) courses for admissions to college. The American Civil Liberties Union contends that many students in California and Texas simply do not have these offerings at their schools and should not be punished for unequal school resources (Chapa, 2002).

A further issue concerns undocumented Latino college students. Many students were raised in the United States but their parents did not have them naturalized; as a result they are being rejected from college admissions and financial aid packages. The complicated legal status of these students was brought to the attention of legislators, who introduced the Development, Relief, and Education for Alien Minors Act (DREAM Act) in the summer of 2002. The bill would grant legal residency to undocumented students with no criminal records who have been U.S. residents for at least five years and graduated from an American high school or received a GED (Torrejón, 2002).

Lastly, although promising gains have been made in higher education enrollment among Latinos, recent studies note that students continue to drop out at high rates for financial reasons. Furthermore, Latinos remain clustered in two-year colleges (40 percent) compared to 25% of White college students (Fry, 2002). Overall, researchers predict that Latinos will be underrepresented by 500,000 students by the middle of the twenty-first century, a devastating loss of human potential.

The perilous political climate of the late 1990s for affirmative action and other programs such as bilingual education suggests that Latino higher education may again cycle backward instead of forward. As this narrative has highlighted, numerical dominance of Latinos as the largest minority group in the United States does not *readily* translate into equity. History teaches us that an equitable higher education for Latinos in the future requires vigilance and activism today.

References

Acuña, R. F. (1998). *Sometimes There is No Other Side: Chicanos and the Myth of Equality.* Notre Dame, IN: University of Notre Dame Press.

Adams, D. W. (1995). *Education for extinction: American Indians and the boarding school experience 1875–1928.* Lawrence, KS: University Press of Kansas.

Allsup, C. (1982). *The American G.I. Forum: Origins and evolution.* Austin: Center for Mexican American Studies, The University of Texas at Austin: Distributed by the University of Texas Press. Monograph / Center for Mexican American Studies, The University of Texas at Austin, No. 6.

Alonzo, A. C. (1998). *Tejano legacy: Rancheros and settlers in south Texas, 1734–1900.* Albuquerque: University of New Mexico Press.

Anderson, J. (1988). *The education of southern Blacks, 1860–1930.* Chapel Hill: University of North Carolina Press.

Brown, M. C., & Davis, J. E. (2001). The historically Black college as social contract, social capital, and social equalizer. *Peabody Journal of Education, 76,* 31–49.

Carrión, A. M. (1983). *Puerto Rico: A political and cultural history.* New York: W.W. Norton.

Chapa, Jorge. (2002). Affirmative Action, X Percent Plans, and Latino Access to Higher Education in the Twenty-first Century. In M. Suárez-Orozco and M. M. Páez. (Eds.), *Latinos Remaking America,* pp. 375–388. Cambridge, MA: David Rockefeller Center for Latino American Studies, Harvard University and Berkeley: University of California Press.

Carter, T. P. (1970). *Mexican Americans in school: A history of educational neglect.* New York: College Entrance Examination Board.

de la Torre, A., & Pesquera, B. M. (1993). *Building with our hands: New directions in Chicana studies.* Berkeley: University of California Press.

de León, A. (2001). *Ethnicity in the sunbelt: Mexican Americans in Houston.* College Station, TX: Texas A&M University Press.

Delgado Bernal, D. (1998). Grassroots leadership reconceptualized: Chicana oral histories and the 1968 East Los Angeles school blowouts. *Frontiers: A Journal of Women Studies, 19*(2), 113–142.

Donato, R. (1997). *The Other Struggle for Civil Rights.* Albany, NY: State University Press of New York.

Donato, R. (1999). Hispano education and the implications of autonomy: Four school systems in Southern Colorado, 1920–1963. *Harvard Educational Review, 69* (2), 117–149.

Donato, R., & Lazerson, M. (2000). New directions in American educational history: Problems and prospects, *Educational Researcher, 29* (8), 4–15.

Fisher, M. (1998). National Council of La Raza, "Latino Education Status and Prospects: State of Hispanic America 1998."

Fry, R. (2002). *Latinos in higher education: Many enroll, too few graduate.* Pew Hispanic Center Research Report. *www.pewhispanic.org*

García, M. T. (1989). *Mexican Americans: Leadership, ideology & identity, 1930–1960.* New Haven: Yale University Press.

Geiger, R. L. (2000). New themes in the history of nineteenth-century colleges. In Geiger, R. L. (Ed.), *The American college in the nineteenth century* (pp. 1–36). Nashville: Vanderbilt University Press.

Getz, L. M. (1997). *Schools of their own: The education of Hispanos in New Mexico, 1850–1940.* Albuquerque: University of New Mexico Press.

Goodchild, L. F., & Wechsler, H. (Eds.). (1997). *ASHE reader in the history of higher education.* (2nd ed.).

Ibarra, R. A. (2001). *Beyond Affirmative Action: Reframing the Context of Higher Education.* Madison: University of Wisconsin Press.

Kanellos, N. (1997). *Hispanic firsts: 500 years of extraordinary achievement.* Detroit, MI: Visible Ink Press.

Keller, G. D., Deneen, J. R., & Magallán, R. J. (1991). *Assessment and Access: Hispanics in Higher Education.* Albany, NY: State University of New York Press.

Laden, B. V. (2001). Hispanic-serving institutions: Myths and realities. *Peabody Journal of Education, 76* (1), 73–92.

Lee, S. M. (2002). Do Asian American faculty face a glass ceiling in higher education? *American Educational Research Journal, 39,* 695–724.

León, D. J., & McNeil, D. (1992). A precursor to affirmative action: Californios and Mexicans in the University of California, 1870–72. *Perspectives in Mexican American Studies 3,* 179–206.

Lindsay, B., & Justiz, M. J., (Eds.). (2001). *Quest for equity in higher education: Toward new paradigms in an evolving affirmative action era.* Albany: State University Press.

Lindsey, Donal F. (1995). *Indians at Hampton Institute, 1877–1923.* Urbana, IL: University of Illinois Press.

Lucas, C. J. (1994). *American higher education: A history.* New York: St. Martin's Press.

MacDonald, V.-M., (2001). Hispanic, Latino, Chicano, or "Other"?: Deconstructing the relationship between historians and Hispanic-American educational history, *History of Education Quarterly, 41* (Fall 2001), 365–413.

McKevitt, G. Hispanic Californians and Catholic higher education: The diary of Jesús María Estudillo, 1857–1864, *California History 69* (Winter 1990–1991), 320–331, 401–403.

Menchaca, M. (2001). *Recovering history, constructing race: The Indian, Black, and White roots of Mexican Americans.* Austin: University of Texas Press.

Morales, Aurora Levins. (1998). The Historian as Curandera. JSRI Working Paper No. 40. East Lansing, MI: Julian Samora Research Institute.

Moreno, J. F., (Ed.). (1999). *The Elusive Quest for Equality: 150 Years of Chicano/Chicana Education.* Cambridge: Harvard University Press.

Muñoz, C. (1989). *Youth, identity, power: The Chicano movement.* London: Verso Books.

National Center for Education Statistics [NCES]. (1980). *The condition of education for Hispanic Americans.* Washington, DC: Government Printing Office.

Navarrette, R. (1993). *A Darker Shade of Crimson: Odyssey of a Harvard Chicano.* New York: Bantam Books.

Navarro, A. (1995). *Mexican American youth organization: Avant-garde of the Chicano movement in Texas.* Austin: University of Texas.

New Mexico Department of Education. (1917–1918). *Annual Report of the State Superintendent of Instruction.* Albuquerque, NM: Printing Co.

Nieto, S. (Ed.). (2000). *Puerto Rican Students in U.S. Schools.* Mahwah, NJ: Lawrence Erlbaum.

Oboler, S. (1995). *Ethnic labels, Latino lives: Identity and the politics of (re)presentation in the United States.* Minneapolis: University of Minnesota Press.

Olivas, M. (1982/1997). Indian, Chicano and Puerto Rican Colleges: Status and Issues. In L. F. Goodchild & Wechsler, H., (Eds.), *The History of Higher Education* (2nd ed.) 1997.

Olivas, M. (1986). Research on Latino College Students: A Theoretical Framework and Inquiry. In M. Olivas, (Ed.), *Latino College Students* (pp. 1–25). New York: Teachers College Press.

Padilla, F. M. (1985). *Latino ethnic consciousness: The case of Mexican Americans and Puerto Ricans in Chicago.* Notre Dame, IN: University of Notre Dame Press.

Padilla, F. M. (1987). *Puerto Rican Chicago.* Notre Dame: University of Notre Dame Press.

Pantoja, A. (1998). Memorias de una vida de obra (Memories of a life of work): An interview with Antonia Pantoja. *Harvard Educational Review, 68* (2), 244–258.

Pitt, L. (1966). *The decline of the Californios: A social history of the Spanish-speaking Californians, 1846–1890.* Berkeley, Los Angeles, and London: University of California Press.

President's Advisory Commission on Educational Excellence for Hispanic Americans. (1996). *Our Nation on the Fault Line: Hispanic American Education.* Washington, DC: GPO.

Rodríguez, Clara E. (2000). *Changing Race: Latinos, the Census, and the History of Ethnicity in the United States.* New York: New York University Press.

Rodriguez, R. (2002). *Brown: The last discovery of America.* New York: Viking Press.

Rodriguez, R. (October 6, 1994). Black/Latino relations: an unnecessary conflict. *Black Issues in Higher Education, 11,* 40–42.

Rodríguez-Fraticelli, C. (1986). *Education and imperialism: The Puerto Rican experience in higher education, 1898–1986.* Centro de Estudios Puertorriqueños Working Paper Series. Higher Education Task Force. Hunter College, New York.

San Miguel, Jr., G. (1987). *"Let All of Them Take Heed:" Mexican Americans and the Campaign for Educational Equality in Texas, 1910–1981.* Austin: University of Texas Press.

San Miguel, Jr., G. (2001). *Brown, Not White: School Integration and the Chicano Movement in Houston.* College Station, TX: Texas A & M University Press.

San Miguel, Jr., G., & Valencia, R. (1998). From the treaty of Guadalupe to Hopwood: The educational plight and struggle of Mexican Americans in the Southwest. *Harvard Educational Review, 68,* 353–412.

Sánchez, G. J. (1993). *Becoming Mexican American: Ethnicity, culture and identity in Chicano Los Angeles, 1900–1945.* New York: Oxford Press.

Sánchez-Korrol, V. (1994). *From colonia to community: The history of Puerto Ricans in New York City.* Berkeley: University of California Press.

Santiago, R. (Ed.). (1995). *Boricuas: Influential Puerto Rican writings—An anthology.* New York: Ballantine Books.

Serrano, B. (1998). Rifle, Cañón, y Escopeta! A Chronicle of the Puerto Rican Student Union. In Torres, A. & Velásquez, J. (Eds.), *The Puerto Rican Movement: Voices from the Diaspora* (pp. 124–143). Philadelphia: Temple University Press.

Stefancic, J. (1997). Latino and Latina Critical Theory: An Annotated Bibliography. *California Law Review, 85,* 1509–1581.

Torrejón, V. (2002, July 18). Residency urged for some kids of entrants. *Arizona Daily Star,* p. B8.

Traub, J. (1994). *City on a hill: Testing the American dream at City College.* New York: Addison-Wesley Publishing.

Tywoniak, F. E., & Garcia, M. T. (2000). *Migrant daughter: Coming of age as a Mexican American woman.* Berkeley: University of California Press.

U.S. Commissioner of Education. *Annual reports of the secretary of education, department of Porto Rico.* (1901–1910). Washington, DC: Government Printing Office.

U.S. Congress. Committee on Education and Labor. (1985). Staff Report on Hispanics' Access to Higher Education. 99th Congress, 1st Session. Serial No. 99-K. Washington, DC.

Valdes, Francisco. (1997). Under Construction: LatCrit Consciousness, Community and Theory. *California Law Review. 85,* 1087–1142.

Valdés, D. (2000). *Barrios Norteños: St. Paul and Midwestern Mexican Communities in the twentieth century.* Austin: University of Texas Press.

Weinberg, M. (1977). *A Chance to learn: The history of race and education in the United States.* Cambridge, UK: Cambridge University Press.

PART ONE

UNDERGRADUATE EXPERIENCES AND RETENTION

Amaury Nora

Amaury Nora is Professor of Higher Education and Associate Dean for Research and Faculty Development in the College of Education at the University of Houston, in Houston, Texas. His research focuses on college persistence, the role of college on diverse student populations across different types of institutions, the development of financial aid models that integrate economic theories and college persistence theories, graduate education, and theory building and testing. His inquiries have not only contributed to traditional lines of research on college persistence but have opened research on women and minorities in community colleges. Nora has been a Visiting Professor at the University of Michigan at Ann Arbor (Summer 1990) and Penn State University (Summer 1991). As Associate Professor of Higher Education at the University of Illinois at Chicago, Dr. Nora also served as Research Associate for the National Center on Postsecondary Teaching, Learning and Assessment (NCTLA), funded by the U.S. Department of Education. He has also served as consultant to the American Council of Education, the Ford Foundation, Hispanic Association of Colleges and Universities, U.S. Department of Education, and is currently a reviewer for the National Research Council in Washington, DC.

Dr. Nora has served on the editorial boards of *Research in Higher Education, The Review of Higher Education, The Journal of Higher Education,* and *The Journal of College Student Retention: Research, Theory, and Practice,* and as Program Chair for the 1999 Annual Meeting of the Association for the Study of Higher Education (ASHE). He was the recipient of ASHE's 1991 Early Career Scholar Award and the College of Education's, 2000 Research Excellence Award. Dr. Nora has published numerous book chapters and articles in refereed journals, including *The Review of Higher Education, The Journal of Higher Education, Research in Higher Education, Higher Education: Handbook of Theory and Research, Community College Review, Education and Urban Society, Journal of College Student Development,* and *Educational Record.*

3

ACCESS TO HIGHER EDUCATION FOR HISPANIC STUDENTS

REAL OR ILLUSORY?

Amaury Nora

As we enter the twenty-first century, one of the most hotly debated issues is that of the educational preparation of students (specifically of underrepresented groups) for the new technological world we will face in the near future, if it is already not upon us. There are those who would have us believe that great strides have been made with regard to the representation of minorities in all aspects of higher education, that a larger number of minorities are graduating from high school and attending college. There are those who propose that access to higher education should be based simply on merit and that present interpretations of Affirmative Action and college admissions policies embrace equality and equity for all involved. And then there are those who put forth the notion that the increases in number of students of color in postsecondary institutions are a testament to true access. Is this access to higher education for underrepresented groups a reality or merely an illusion? Darder, Torres, and Gutierrez (1997, p. xiii) make note that ". . . despite thirty years of educational reforms, Latino students continue to lag behind students from the dominant culture. . ." and that ". . . the proportion of Latino students enrolled in colleges and universities and those who graduate from high school prepared for admission to higher education remains low. As a body of scholarly research

47

begins to evolve, it appears that these [facts] have been chronic over at least the past thirty years."

Let us begin by examining the graduation rates from high school for Hispanics and non-Hispanic Whites as a beginning source of misinformation. While graduation rates as high as 68% have been reported for Hispanics (Wilds & Wilson, 1998), a closer examination of the data reveals that these rates represent the retention of students beginning at the twelfth grade and ending at graduation. However, the number of Hispanic students who graduate from high school must be examined within the context of overall attrition rates beginning in the transition from middle school to high school and those reported from the beginning of ninth grade to graduation. The attrition rate for Hispanic students from eigth grade to ninth grade is between 46% and 50% (Nora, 2002; Rendón & Nora, 1997). Moreover, the bad news does not stop there. For Hispanic students, an additional 50% percent are lost between the beginning of high school and the twelfth grade, with a few more dropping out before they finish the twelfth grade. Why the lengthy discussion on the dropout rates of Hispanic students in middle and high schools? Simply because despite the dismal number of Hispanics graduating from high school, an even more depressing fact is the number of graduating students who apply and enroll in higher education institutions. Only a third (35%) of Hispanic students who manage to traverse the K–12 educational system immediately go on to college after graduation. When an additional two years are added as a starting point for college-going rates, Marks (SREB Fact Book, 2000/2001) reports a 17% college-going rate for Hispanics compared to 28% for Blacks and 35% for Whites. Once more we must ask: Why do so few of our Hispanic students enroll in college? Carrasquillo (2000, p. 35) proposes:

> Hispanic students are highly under-represented in college preparatory and gifted and talented programs. Hispanic students are encouraged to take fewer years of course work in mathematics, physical sciences, and social studies than non-Hispanic white students. Even in subjects in which the years of course work are similar, the content of the courses differs substantially. For example, although Hispanic high school students are as likely as non-Hispanic white students to have taken three years or more of mathematics, they are less likely to have taken algebra, geometry, trigonometry, or calculus and more likely to have taken general and business math.

College Participation Rates

Table 3.1 displays the enrollment rates for first-year, degree-seeking minority students in 1984 and 1995 (College Board News, 1999).

The data presented in Table 3.1 shows that increases in minority enroll-ments for those who want to pursue a baccalaureate or associate degree had risen only 6% between 1984 and 1995. These figures, however, represent all minority groups in the United States. In 1997 the American Council on Educa-tion reported that Hispanic and African American students were enrolling in college at a rate of 35%, while non-Hispanic Whites were enrolling at a college-going rate of 44%. What is even more depressing is the fact that Hispanics are not evenly distributed among non-selective, selective, and highly selective insti-tutions. While 47% of all minority students are in two-year colleges, Hispanics represent 36% of the total community college enrollments (President's Advisory Commission, 1996) and represent 56.4% of all Hispanics enrolled in college (SREB Fact Book, 2000/2001). To conclude, national transfer rates from two-year colleges to four-year universities are a mere 22% (College Board News, 1998). For Hispanics, transfer rates may be as low as 10%, although educa-tional aspirations reported for this group reveal that 85% of Hispanic students attending a community college see that institution as the beginning step to the undergraduate degree (Rendón & Nora, 1997).

Degree Attainment

Perhaps a better beginning point for this issue should focus on the importance of higher education for social advancement (Nora, 2002) and its contribution to the improvement of personal well being (Astin, 1982; Pascarella & Teren-zini, 1991). With benefits from the attainment of an undergraduate degree in mind, it is no small wonder that higher education in the United States has become a cynosure for efforts to improve the condition of economically and socially disadvantaged subpopulations. What is most ironic is that the present condition of Hispanics (and other groups) is due in no small measure to the fact that in the past higher education's service as an instrument for social mobility was seldom indiscriminate. America's racial and ethnic minorities have been and continue to be grossly underrepresented in higher education and, subsequently, in those occupational fields that require a college education

Table 3.1 Minority Enrollment: Percent of Degree-Seeking
First-Year Students

	1984	1995
Four-year institutions	13.8	20.2
Two-year institutions	15.9	18.0

(Astin, 1982; Rendón, Jalomo, & Nora, 2000). As a consequence, these groups do not enjoy equitable participation in the larger society's social, economic, and political life.

One racial minority that has been particularly underserved by American higher education by both four- and two-year institutions is the Hispanic population (see Table 3.2).

By extrapolating from the figures in Tables 3.2, the rate of associate degree attainment in the majority population was more than 11.77 times the rate in the Hispanic subpopulation alone and more than 16.85 times for baccalaureate degree attainment. Data as far back as twenty years (Brown, 1981) tend to confirm the link between social and economic advancement and college graduation. Relative to the total population, Hispanics are overrepresented in lower level, poorer paying occupations such as service workers, craftsmen, operators, farm laborers, and non-farm laborers. On the other hand, they are underrepresented in more prestigious, better paying occupations including professional and technical workers, managers and administrators, and farmers and farm managers.

While the relatively low percentage of Hispanic students graduating from college is attributable in part to high attrition rates at the elementary and secondary school levels—which effectively decrease the number of individuals eligible for college attendance—and to the failure of a substantial number of high school graduates from the subpopulation to enroll in college (ACE, 1998; The Chronicle of Higher Education Almanac, 1998; College Board News, 1998), it is also due to the failure of many Hispanic students once enrolled in an institution of higher education, to persist to degree completion. Numerous studies involving national (National Center for Teaching, Learning, and Assessment, 1991/1995; College Board News, 1998), state (Tierney & Hagedorn, 2002) and institutional (e.g., Nora, 2002; Nora & García, 1999) data have shown that even within an extended time frame—five to six years—Hispanic students

Table 3.2   Associate and Baccalaureate Degrees Earned by Ethnicity

	Two-Year Institutions, % of Earned Degrees	Four-Year Institutions, % of Earned Degrees
Hispanic	6.60	4.67
African American	8.70	7.52
Asian American	3.80	5.21
White	77.70	78.73

Source: The Chronicle of Higher Education Almanac, 1998.

graduate from college at a rate that is from one and a third times smaller than the rate for Anglo students and one and a half times smaller than the rate for Asian American students. Within a normal time frame (fours years), the discrepancy is even more pronounced. To emphasize the point once more, there have been no substantial gains in graduation rates over the last twenty to thirty years. Tracking until 1980 students who entered college in 1971, Astin (1982) found that about 55% of the Anglos but only about 40% of the Mexican Americans in his national sample had achieved baccalaureate degrees during a nine-year period (see Table 3.3).

Attrition Rates in Two- and Four-Year Colleges

The exceedingly low degree attainment rates of Hispanics in higher education are attributable to the corresponding exceedingly high attrition rates among that group. High dropout rates of Hispanic students can be identified in three major aspects: first- to second-year persistence rates in community colleges, first- to second-year persistence rates for native students (those students enrolled in a four-year institution without transferring), and first- to second-semester persistence rates for transfer students.

Table 3.4 discloses the fact that attrition rates for Hispanic students are 1.3 times larger than those of non-Hispanic White students and almost 1.5 times larger than for Asian American students. Attrition rates for Hispanic students in

Table 3.3 Graduation Rates of Different Ethnic Groups within Six-Year Period

	Graduation Rates, %
Hispanic	41
African American	32
Asian American	63
White	56

Table 3.4 Dropout Rates of Different Ethnic Groups in Higher Education

	First- to Second-Year Attrition Rates, %
Hispanic	54.4
African American	63.3
Asian American	37.2
White	41.5

Source: National Center for Urban Partnerships (Rendón & Nora, 1997).

community colleges range from 60% to 80% for first-time college students. For Hispanic transfer students, the dropout rate from the beginning of their first year at the receiving institution to the second year ranges from 65% to 75%. All three junctures within the higher education system reflect a high degree of dropout behavior among Hispanic students. Collectively (and additively) all three result in a less than satisfactory degree attainment rate and unacceptable withdrawal rates.

The Seamless Web: Tears in the Fabric

The K–12 through 16 educational system has often been called an "educational pipeline" or, as more currently known, a "seamless web." The notion in using these metaphors is that the educational experiences of students can be perceived as one long, smooth continuum beginning in preschool and culminating in undergraduate degree attainment. Using a database representing actual enrollment figures from preschool to high school, and extrapolating dropout figures from the literature, it is possible to see that this seamless web is full of tears in its fabric with regard to Hispanic students.

The most telling feature in Table 3.5 is the realization of the cumulative effect of withdrawal at the different junctures in the pipeline. In this example, if a total of 2,856 Hispanic students entered in preschool only 4.2% (121) of those students will have earned an associate degree fourteen years later. Of that same total, a mere 1.6% (45) would have graduated from a four-year institution having earned an undergraduate degree. Of those students that managed to graduate from high school (762), the 121 students that graduated with an A.A. or A.S. degree would represent 16%. At the four-year college level, those 45 students that graduate with a B.A. degree would represent only 6% of those who graduated from high school. Even in the best of all circumstances, the 121 students represent 53% of those students who managed to enroll in a community college while the 45 students represent 20% of first-time-in-college students.

The argument posited in response to the dismal number of Hispanic students earning an undergraduate degree is that we have open admissions to higher education through the two-year sector and that an educational/training experience is available to all. Moreover, technical/proprietary schools are abundant and no one is being denied an education. However, no matter how palatable that argument is for the simple-minded, the truth is that equal representation in those sectors of society where the decision makers play cannot be attained without professional or graduate degrees. With so few minorities earning the means to advance to higher levels within our educational system,

Table 3.5 A Profile of Leakages within the Educational Pipeline

Total PreK Entering Students	Number of Students Entering 9th Grade	Number of Students Enrolled at Beginning of 12th Grade	Number of Graduating Seniors	Number of College-Going Students	Two-Year Graduation
2,856	1,428 (50% of total)	855 (60% of 9th graders)	762 (After 11% attrition)	229 (30% of graduating class)	121 (4.2%) (16%) (53%)
					Four-Year Graduation
					45 (1.6%) (6%) (20%)

53

Table 3.6   Degree Attainment at Doctoral Level

	Ph.D.s Earned, %
Hispanic	2.18
African American	3.19
Asian American	4.49
Native American	.31
Foreign nationals	26.65
White	60.42

equality in representation and participation cannot be achieved. Table 3.6 displays the total number of Hispanics earning Ph.D.s in 1994 (Casper Database, 1994). Of the 43,261 doctoral degrees awarded in that year, only 946 were received by Hispanics. In other words, 2.18% of all doctorates were awarded to Hispanic graduate students.

One startling revelation in the data is the high percentage rate in doctoral degree attainment for foreign nationals (26.65%). Even if we were to add the percentages of all minorities in the United States, foreign nationals are awarded more doctoral degrees than Hispanics, African Americans, Asian Americans, and Native Americans combined.

Barriers to Access: From Preschool to Graduate School

A discussion on the access to higher education for Hispanics that simply focuses on college entrance seriously distorts the issue. At the time that Hispanic students make it to the twelfth grade it is already too late to affect college eligibility (Rendón, 1997). Access to higher education is wrought at an early stage in a student's life. Hispanics are faced with multiple barriers at every stage of their schooling experiences.

Precollege Barriers

Based on existing conditions, Hispanic students lag behind other groups from elementary to middle school. These deficits are reflected in reading, mathematics, and science proficiency (President's Advisory Commission, 1996). Systemic barriers that affect Hispanic achievement include educational imbalances between affluent and less affluent school districts. Inequities in tax-based funding remains one of the major issues affecting the academic progress of students in K–12 (Kozol, 1991). Grade retention and suspensions from school adversely affect dropout behavior. Tracking in schools diverts Hispanics into general education courses that satisfy only the basic high school requirements. The fact that Hispanic students do not take college prep courses has damaging corollaries. The lack of academic preparation limits access to college and further disqualifies Hispanics for entry-level jobs in high-tech industries. Schools where the majority of Hispanic students are found operate with inappropriate curricula, lack computer technology, and employ uncertified teachers (Rendón & Hope, 1996).

Undergraduate Barriers

College affordability is key to access. An examination of economic trends in the middle to late 1980s and throughout the 1990s indicates that college became less accessible (affordable) to Hispanics (Orfield & Ashkinaze, 1991). Federal Pell grants, once the main source of meeting the costs associated with attending college, increased at a much slower level than the cost of college tuition during that time period. "To exacerbate matters, the share of family income required to pay for college costs has gone up most for those who occupy the bottom tier of the economic ladder. Low-income families have no reserves to draw on and are reluctant to secure loans that will exacerbate family debt" (Rendón, 1997).

Even when first-generation Hispanic students manage to graduate from high school and enroll in college, dropout rates are equally as high at this juncture. Time and again, these students find an invalidating and intimidating college environment, coupled with a faculty that is predominately White with little understanding of minority cultures, a Euro-centered curriculum, racism, and fiercely competitive learning environments. In a recent study, Padilla, Trevino, González, and Trevino (1997) found that minority students feel culturally or racially isolated on campus. The lack of minority role models and mentors, the lack of minority issues or materials in the curriculum, and the lack of noticeable minority support programs has led to adverse conditions that must be faced by Hispanic undergraduate students. As a consequence of these conditions, Latino students are less likely to successfully negotiate the transition from high school to college or to become involved in institutional life on campus, which itself leads to attrition.

Multiple barriers exist that operate against access opportunities for Hispanic students. To sustain true access, both structural and attitudinal transformations need to be instituted throughout the educational continuum.

Factors Affecting Hispanic College Persistence and Degree Attainment

As previously mentioned, the issue of access must ultimately focus on college completion or degree attainment. A discussion of those factors that have been determined to have an impact on persistence and subsequent graduation is necessary in discourse on access to higher education for Hispanics. Nora (1993) concluded that these factors fell within four major groupings:

1. Educational goal commitments (or educational aspirations)
2. Financial assistance
3. Social integration or experiences
4. Institutional commitments (or institutional fit).

Additional research by Nora and associates (1994, 1995, 1996, 1997, 2000, 2002) has identified other factors just as instrumental as those previously cited. Those factors include:

1. Environmental pull factors
2. Perceptions of prejudice and discrimination
3. Academic performance
4. Support and encouragement by parents
5. Academic and intellectual development while in college
6. Pre-college psychosocial experiences
7. Attitudes related to remediation
8. Mentoring experiences
9. Student resiliency
10. Spirituality on the part of students

The following Model of Student Engagement incorporates theoretical perspectives from different sources (e.g., Tinto, 1993; Braxton, 2001; Nora, 2002) and findings from empirical studies (e.g., Nora and associates, 1993, 1996, 2001, 2002; Pascarella & Terenzini, 1991). The model (Figure 3.1) consists of six major components: (1) precollege/pull factors, (2) sense of purpose and institutional allegiance, (3) academic and social experiences, (4) cognitive and non-cognitive outcomes, (5) goal determination/institutional allegiance, and (6) persistence.

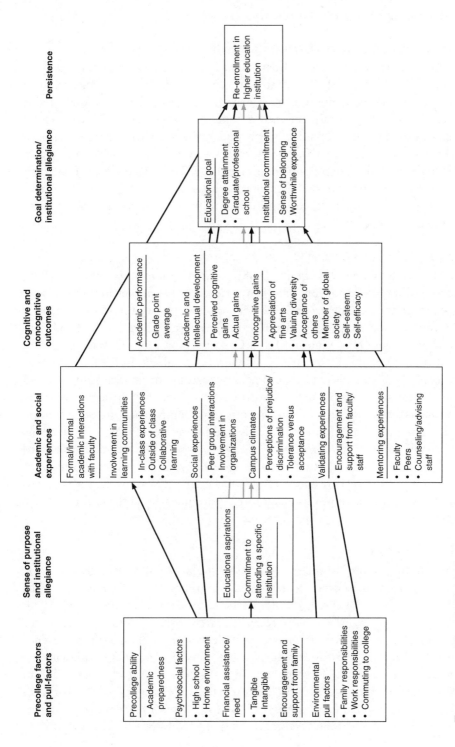

FIGURE 3.1 Theoretical framework.

57

Educational Aspirations

In two separate studies, Nora, Castañeda, and Cabrera (1992) and Cabrera, Nora, and Castañeda (1993) established that the educational dedication of Hispanic college students are prominent in affecting the intentions of this group of students to return for their second year in college, as well as actual persistence behavior. Hispanic college students possess the desire to earn an undergraduate degree and further pursue a professional or graduate degree that they bring with them upon entering college. These high educational aspirations are formed as early as elementary school (Rendón & Nora, 1997) and remain high in spite of their lopsided enrollment in two-year institutions (Nora & Rendon, 1990).

Financial Assistance

Past studies (Stampen & Cabrera, 1988; Cabrera, Stampen, & Hansen, 1990; Cabrera, Nora, & Castañeda, 1993) have validated the importance of financial assistance in the persistence process. Cabrera et al. (1990) found that financial aid creates an equal playing field among recipients (mostly minorities) and non-recipients (largely non-minorities) and Cabrera, Nora, and Castañeda (1993) revealed an intangible factor associated with financial aid. In their 1993 study, Cabrera et al. distinguished between actual awarding of financial aid (referred to as the tangible component) and attitudes associated with having received financial assistance (referred to as the intangible component). In those studies, both components were found to directly and indirectly influence the decisions of Hispanic students to remain in college. It is assumed that the intangible component is not only a reflection of stress reduction that comes from being able to pay for college-related expenses but that it may also represent a student's commitment to their respective institution, centering around the notion that the institution provided the financial means to remain in college.

Social Experiences

Although the majority of the research on the influence of social experiences on minority student persistence centers on the informal contact between students and faculty (e.g., Pascarella, 1985; Iverson, Pascarella & Terenzini, 1984; Smart & Pascarella, 1986), more recent research focuses on the impact of this factor on the adjustment of students to college and not simply on persistence (Nora & Cabrera, 1996; Cabrera, Nora, & Castañeda, 1993). Although the express influence of social experiences on persistence has mostly been found to be minimal for minorities, Nora's (1987) research on Hispanics at two-year institutions establishes that its presence is felt on the student's academic performance and, to a limited extent, on persistence decisions (Nora & Cabrera, 1996).

Commitment to a Respective Institution

Studies by Nora and Cabrera (1993), Nora, Castañeda, and Cabrera (1992), Allen (1988), and Braddock (1981) all found that the student's commitment to an institution exerted a positive effect on a minority student's decision to remain enrolled in college. Nora and Cabrera (1996) tested the influence of a minority student's commitment to his or her institution separately from those of non-minority students. The results point to this commitment as a driving force for non-minority students in their decisions to re-enroll. However, this factor was not significant in influencing persistence decisions for minorities. While a sense of belonging at an institution largely affects non-minorities, other cognitive and noncognitive factors are much more powerful in affecting minority students' retention.

Environmental Pull Factors

The influence of environmental pull factors on the persistence of college students was examined by Nora and Wedham (1991). In that analysis the authors identified three constructs that exerted a pulling-away effect both on the student's decision to remain enrolled in college and on his or her social and academic integration on campus. Those three factors included: family responsibilities such as taking care of a sibling, grandparent, or an entire family; working off-campus while enrolled in college courses; and commuting to college every day. The authors confirmed that those students that had familial responsibilities or were having to go to work off-campus could not fully integrate socially and academically and ultimately had to leave higher education altogether. Similar results were substantiated by Nora, Cabrera, Hagedorn, and Pascarella (1996), who found that minorities who had to leave campus to work were 36% more likely to drop out of college and minority women who had to deal with taking care of a family member were 83% more likely to withdraw from college. The sample consisted of both Hispanic and African American college students. As a final pull factor, having to commute to college was found to affect student decisions to remain enrolled, although there were no differences found between minorities and non-minorities.

Perceptions of Prejudice and Discrimination

In a study by Nora and Cabrera (1996), the authors found that Hispanic students were more prone to sense discrimination and prejudice in the classroom and on campus and that those perceptions were subsequently found to affect their academic performance, their academic experiences with faculty, their social experiences on campus, their academic and intellectual development, their commitment to an institution, and indirectly, their decisions to remain in college. Almost every aspect of a Hispanic college student's life was touched by these perceptions of discrimination and intolerance by the institution and others. In all cases, the effect was negatively felt. Hispanic students' grade point averages, their interactions with faculty and their peers, and their development as students were moderated by a sense of prejudice on campus and in their classrooms.

Support and Encouragement by Parents

In their research, Nora and Cabrera (1996) focused on three factors that heavily weighed on Hispanic students' decisions to remain in college. Those three factors included: encouragement and support by parents, academic performance, and the student's own sense that he or she was developing academically while in college. The authors found empirical evidence indicating that while "perceptions of discrimination and prejudice on campus negatively affected the adjustment to college and several college-related outcomes, much of the negative influence was negated by the student's perceptions that his or her family was supportive and provided encouragement while they were enrolled in college." Furthermore, Nora and Cabrera tested the contention that "successful adjustment to college included severing previous ties with family, friends, and past communities." Such links to significant others were instrumental for the successful transition from high school to college among Hispanics. Moreover, parental encouragement and words of support were found to exert a positive effect on students' integration into college, on their academic and intellectual development, on their academic performance and commitments, and finally, on their decisions to remain enrolled in college. In several studies on Hispanic and African American two- and four-year college students (e.g., Nora, 1987; Cabrera, Nora, & Castañeda, 1993; Nora & Cabrera, 1996; Nora & Rendón, 1990; Nora, Kraemer, & Itzen, 1997), this single factor has been found to significantly impact on the determination of minority students to persist. It is believed that the influence of family and community in the persistence process is due the interrelations between Tinto's (1993) transition phases and different sources and forms of encouragement and support from significant others (Nora, 2001). In a qualitative study, Rendón (1994) coins the phrase "validating experiences" in an examination of the behavior of faculty toward minorities in the classroom. She notes that when Hispanic two-year college students perceive an air of acceptance and faculty behavior that validates their worth in the class, those students tend to participate more fully in classroom discussions, interact more effectively with faculty, and reconsider their decisions to drop out.

Academic Performance and Academic and Intellectual Development

Possibly the most influential factor bearing on Hispanic students' withdrawal decisions is their academic performance during their first year in college. While course grades were found to influence the decisions of non-minorities to drop out of college, this factor was three times more influential for Hispanics (Nora & Cabrera, 1996). For Latinos, their academic achievement and corresponding perceptions that cognitive gains had or had not been made while attending college were the most prominent factors in deciding to remain enrolled in college. The authors note that, for Hispanic college students, their sense of belonging in college and their perceptions of possessing academic capital (the ability to earn a college degree) is seriously questioned whenever they experience a lower than expected academic performance. While most majority students may be able to "shake-off" a bad semester or even a year, it may be more devastating for Hispanic students. Perhaps an environment that they perceive as intolerant of minorities contributes significantly to their perceptions that they cannot overcome these setbacks, thereby overly influencing their decisions to drop out.

Precollege Psychosocial Experiences

More recently, Nora and Lang (1999) found that skills and attitudes developed prior to enrollment in higher education have an impact on a student's transition to a college environment and a student's decision to remain enrolled in college or drop out. Previous studies (e.g., Cabrera, Nora, Hagedorn, Terenzini, & Pascarella, 1999) that incorporated precollege factors as conceptualized by persistence theories and found limited influences on a student's academic and social adjustment and on his or her re-enrollment may have misspecified the conceptualization of these precollege factors. Nora and Lang (1999) believed that precollege high school experiences were more conceptually represented by a student's anticipatory view of future academic performance in college, leadership and involvement in high school activities, parental support and encouragement, and a sense of academic and social self-efficacy.

The results of Nora and Lang's (1999) study indicate that four major areas of intervention and support systems are highly influential in nurturing students through their first year in college and fostering the skills necessary to become involved in the college process and persisting to completion. These four areas focus on: (1) mentoring services, (2) faculty and staff development, (3) student activities/residence hall programming and (4) counseling initiatives. Mentoring programs staffed by both students and faculty, could develop strategies that focus on successfully engaging the student in positive academic experiences, alleviating fears that students might have with regard to their ability to succeed during their first year, and providing realistic feedback to students so that they can make informed decisions. Coupled with these strategies are efforts to provide an early systematic approach at identifying students who are in need of counseling, either personal or academic. Anticipatory fears, unrealistic self-expectations, and alienation are very real to students (particularly minority students) and a sense of isolation or not belonging has been found to negatively affect persistence (Cabrera & Nora, 1994; Nora & Cabrera, 1996). Counseling initiatives must be carefully planned by administrators, counselors, and faculty that not only address these issues but also are identified early on in the student's first year.

Remediation Anxiety

One of the most disturbing characteristics prevalent among first-time-in-college Hispanic undergraduates is the excessively high representation in remedial courses. Placement into developmental coursework rather than reform in the curriculum or teaching approaches has become the norm. Advocates of remediation believe that institutional efforts provide several benefits to developmental students, including the impact on persistence (Brattin, 1993; England, 1993; Boylan, Bonham, & Bliss, 1994; Wyatt, 1992). In spite of some evidence that remediation works, there is evidence that remedial courses may only be preparing students for subsequent developmental courses, that they do very little to prepare students to handle non-remedial courses, and that the attrition rates of these students once they are in college-level courses remains high (Nora, 1998). The reasons why developmental education may or may not have the effect that is sought may be linked more to the perceptions, attitudes, and values that those students labeled as "remedial" have with regard to remediation. Researchers (Boylan, Bonham, & Bliss, 1994; England, 1993; Heerman & Maleki, 1994; Morawski & Brunguber, 1993; Wyatt, 1992) have failed to uncover whether enrollment in remedial classes fosters student perceptions that affect not only their academic progress in developmental courses but their persistence to graduation as well.

Nora and Garcia (1999) examined the influence of attitudes and perceptions held by developmental students on dropout behavior. The researchers identified several components related to beliefs and values associated with remediation:

- *Placement in remediation.* This component examined whether Hispanic students acknowledge or reject the need for remediation and whether they perceive their remediation placement to be accurate or not.

- *Value of remediation.* This component took into consideration the degree to which Hispanics perceive that developmental education will prepare them to take college-level courses in the mainstream college environment.

- *Precollege preparation.* This component considered the extent to which their precollege academic preparation and precollege curriculum choices allowed them to develop the competencies necessary to succeed in college, an indication of how much confidence Hispanics believe they have to engage in college-level work.

- *Personal attributes and skills.* This component measured the degree to which Hispanics perceived personal characteristics, attributes, and skills contributed to their success in remedial courses.

- *Feelings of discrimination.* This component examined the perceptions of Hispanic developmental students that non-developmental students view them as having a "special status" because of their inclusion in remedial courses, encompassing the view that developmental students are discriminated against in the classroom and on campus by faculty and peers.

- *Validating experiences.* This component investigated the degree to which Hispanics perceived that experiences in the classroom and on campus with faculty, staff, and peers provided a sense of validation of developmental students as individuals and as college students.

- *Plans for degree attainment.* This component measured the degree of confidence that is engendered through remediation that students will reach a particular goal (degree attainment) in higher education.

Nora and Garcia (1999) concluded that Hispanic college persistence is impacted by a multifaceted set of interactions and integrations among institutional and personal factors. The model verified that factors external to the institution play a role in the college persistence process, as do organizational and personal variables.

Spirituality and Hispanic Student Persistence

Recently, the concept of religiousness or "religiosity/spirituality" has been employed as a noncognitive factor that influences undergraduate persistence (Zern, 1987; Forbes, 1998; Low & Handal, 1995; Thames, 1997; Crosby, 1985;

Crymes, 1987; Cogan, 1992). Nora and Anderson (2003) targeted the effects of religiosity on Hispanic students enrolled in a four-year, open enrollment, commuter, theologically conservative religious institution by exploring two types of religiosity: personal- and other-oriented. Hispanic students who experienced satisfaction with the development of their religious philosophy of life were more likely to persist, perhaps because of their desire for additional growth in that area. With regard to other-oriented religiosity factors, treatment of others (expressed through such acts as forgiveness of others, positive attitudes and behaviors toward others, and trust of others) influenced Hispanic students to continue in their undergraduate experience.

Concluding Remarks

Access to all sectors of higher education for Hispanic students is largely influenced by the academic and social experiences of this group early on in schools, by environmental and social circumstances prior to and during their enrollment in the K–12 educational system, and by parental influences. If one assumes that such experiences aid in shaping educational aspirations, desires, and postsecondary prospectives, real access to those sectors that demand a professional or graduate degree (where Hispanics are unreasonably underrepresented) cannot be addressed simply by concentrating on admissions into undergraduate programs. Moreover, true access cannot be reduced to guidelines that merely open the doors for Hispanic students but do nothing to provide those experiences vital for them to remain enrolled until graduation. Issues such as curriculum reform, faculty and staff development with regard to diversity issues, retention polices and programs, transfer from two-year to four-year institutions, articulation between K–12 and postsecondary institutions, and financial aid and choice of college have been minimized in important discussions centered around access. Discussions on minorities and higher education must not lose sight of the holistic nature of access. This discourse must also focus on building collaboratives across different racial and ethnic groups and must put emphasis on achieving a more diverse society specifically as it is mirrored in higher education. With prevailing attitudes questioning what constitutes "fairness" and "color-blindness," these access-related efforts may be the only means by which affirmative action, equity, and institutional tolerance can be achieved.

References

Allen, W. R. (1988). Improving Black student access and achievement in higher education. *Review of Higher Education, 11,* 403–416.

Astin, A. (1982). *Minorities in American higher education*. San Francisco: Jossey-Bass.

Boylan, H. R., Bonham, B. S., & Bliss, L. B. (1994). Who are the developmental students? *Research in Developmental Education, 11* (2).

Braddock, J. H. (1981). Desegregation and Black students. *Urban Education, 15,* 43–418.

Brattin, T. H. (1993). *The impact of mandatory placement and remediation on persistence and academic achievement: A study of the Texas Academic Skills Program at a state technical college*. Unpublished doctoral dissertation. University of Houston, Houston.

Braxton, J. M. (2000). *Reworking the student departure puzzle*. Nashville: Vanderbilt University Press.

Brooks, J. (1981). Academic performance and retention rates of participants in the college work study program and recipients of national direct student loans. *Dissertation Abstracts International, 41,* 3440A.

Cabrera, A., Nora, A., Hagedorn, L., Terenzini, P., & Pascarella, E. (1999). Campus racial climate and adjustment of students to college: A comparison between white students and African American students. *Journal of Higher Education, 70,* 134–160.

Cabrera, A. F., & Nora, A. (1994). College students' perceptions of prejudice and discrimination and their feelings of alienation. *Review of Education, Pedagogy, and Cultural Studies, 16,* 387–409.

Cabrera, A. F., Nora, A., & Castañeda, M. B. (1993). College persistence: Structural equation modeling test of an integrated model of student retention. *Journal of Higher Education, 64*(2), 123–137.

Cabrera, A. F., Nora, A., Castañeda, M. B., & Hengstler, D. (1992). The convergence between two theories of college persistence. *Journal of Higher Education, 63*(2), 143–164.

Cabrera, A. F., Stampen, J. O., & Hansen, W. L. (1990). Exploring the effects of ability to pay on persistence in college. *Review of Higher Education, 13*(3), 303–336.

Carrasquillo, A. L. (2000). *Language minority student in the mainstream classroom*. Clevedon, England: Multilingual Matters Limited.

Carter, D. J., & Wilson, R. (1997). *Minorities in higher education: Fifteenth annual status report*. Washington, DC: American Council on Education.

Center for the Study of Community Colleges. (1995). [Transfer rates]. Unpublished data. Los Angeles.

The Chronicle of Higher Education Almanac. (1997, August 29). [Special Edition], Volume XLIV, Number 1.

College Board News. (1999). *Reaching the top*. New York: The College Board.

Darder, A., Torres, R. D., & Gutierrez, H. (1997). *Latinos and education: A critical reader*. New York: Routledge.

England, D. C. (1993). *The impact on the success of high-risk students of placement policies established by Texas higher education institutions in the implementation of the Texas academic skills program* [CD-ROM]. Abstract from: ProQuest File: Dissertation Abstracts Item: 9329691

Goldberg, C. (1997, January 30). Hispanic households struggle as poorest of the poor in U.S. *New York Times,* pp. A1, D8.

Heerman, C. E., & Maleki, R. B. (1994). Helping probationary university students to succeed. *The Journal of Reading, 37*(8), 654–661.

Ibarra, R. A. (1996). *Enhancing the minority presence in graduate education VII: Latino experiences in graduate education: Implications for change.* Washington, DC: Council of Graduate Schools.

Iverson, B. K., Pascarella, E. T., & Terenzini, P. T. (1984). Informal faculty-student contact and commuter college freshmen. *Research in Higher Education, 21,* 123–136.

Jalomo, R. (1995). *Latino students in transition.* Unpublished doctoral dissertation, Arizona State University, Tempe, AZ.

Karabel, J. (1996, April 3). At a fork in the road of fairness. *Los Angeles Times,* Sec. B, p. 9, Col. 1.

Kozol, J. (1991). *Savage inequalities.* New York: Crown Publication.

Morawski, C. M., & Brunhuber, B. S. (1993). Early recollections of learning to read: Implications for prevention and intervention of reading difficulties. *Reading Research and Instruction, 32*(3), 35–48.

National Center for Education Statistics Statistical Analysis Report. (1996). *Remedial education in higher education institutions in fall 1995* (NCES Publication No. 97-584). Washington, DC: U.S. Department of Education.

National Center for Teaching, Learning, and Assessment. (1991/1995). National Center on Higher Education funded by the U.S. Department of Education, 1991–1995.

Nora, A. (1987). Determinants of retention among Chicano college students: A structural model. *Research in Higher Education, 36,* 31–59.

Nora, A. (1993). Two-year colleges and minority students' aspirations: Help or hindrance? In J. Smart (Ed.), *Higher education: Handbook of theory and research,* IX, 212–247.

Nora, A. (2002). A theoretical and practical view of student adjustment and academic achievement. In W. G. Tierney & L. S. Hagedorn (Eds.), *Increasing access to college: Extending possibilities or all students.* Albany: State University of New York Press.

Nora, A. (2001–2002). The depiction of significant others in Tinto's "Rites of Passage": A reconceptualization of the influence of family and community in the persistence process. *Journal of College Student Retention, 3*(1), 41–56.

Nora, A. (2002, November). *The impact of mentoring experiences on withdrawal behavior among first-year college students at a two-year institution.* Paper presented at the annual meeting of the Association for the Study of Higher Education.

Nora, A., & Anderson, R. G. (2003, April) *The role of religiosity as a determinant of persistence for minority and nontraditional college students: A logistic regression analysis of a theoretical model of student persistence.* Paper presented at the annual meeting of the American Educational Research Association.

Nora, A., & Cabrera, A. F. (1996). The role of perceptions of prejudice and discrimination on the adjustment of minority students to college. *Journal of Higher Education, 67*(2), 119–148.

Nora, A., & Garcia, V. (1999, April). *Attitudes related to remediation among developmental students in higher education.* Paper presented at the annual meeting of the American Educational Research Association.

Nora, A., & Lang, D. (1999, November). *The impact of psychosocial factors on the achievement, academic and social adjustment, and persistence of college students.* Paper presented at the annual meeting of the Association for the Study of Higher Education. San Antonio.

Nora, A., Rendón, L. I., & Cuadraz, G. (1999). Access, choice, and outcomes: A profile of Hispanic students in higher education. In A. Taskakkori & S. H. Ochoa (Eds.), *Readings on equal education, education of hispanics in the United States: Politics, policies, and outcomes,* Vol. 16, 175–200.

Nora, A., Cabrera, A. F., Hagedorn, L. S., & Pascarella, E. T. (1996). Differential impacts of academic and social experiences on college-related behavioral outcomes across different ethnic and gender groups at four-year institutions. *Research in Higher Education, 37*(4), 427–452.

Nora, A., Castañeda, M. B., & Cabrera, A. F. (1992). *Student persistence: The testing of a comprehensive structural model of retention.* Paper presented at the annual conference of the Association for the Study of Higher Education, Minneapolis, MN.

Nora, A., Kraemer, B., & Itzen, R. (1997, November). *Factors affecting the persistence of Hispanic college students.* Paper presented at the annual meeting of the Association for the Study of Higher Education, Albuquerque, NM.

Nora, A., & Rendón, L. I. (1990). Determinants of predisposition to transfer among community college students: A structural model. *Research in Higher Education, 31*(3), 235–256.

Nora, A., & Wedham, E. (1991, April). *Off-campus experiences: The pull factors affecting freshman-year attrition on a commuter campus.* Paper presented at the annual meeting of the American Educational Research Association, Chicago.

Olivas, M. A. (1996, March 29). The decision is flatly, unequivocally wrong. *The Chronicle of Higher Education, 42*(29), B3(1).

Orfield, G., & Ashkinaze, C. (1991). *The closing door: Conservative policy and Black opportunity.* Chicago: University of Chicago Press.

Padilla, R. V., Trevino, J., Gonzalez, K., & Trevino, J. (1997). Developing local models of minority success in colleges. *Journal of College Student Development, 38*(2), 125–135.

Pascarella, E. T. (1985). Students' affective development within the college environment. *Journal of Higher Education, 56,* 640–663.

Pascarella, E. T., & Terenzini, P. T. (1991). *How college affects students.* San Francisco: Jossey-Bass.

President's Advisory Commission on Educational Excellence for Hispanic Americans. (1996). *Our nation on the fault line: Hispanic American education.* Washington, DC: Government Printing Office.

Rendón, L. I. (1994). Validating culturally diverse students: Toward a new model of learning and student development. *Innovative Higher Education, 19*(1), 33–52.

Rendón, L. I., Jalomo, R., & Nora, A. (2001). Minority student persistence. In J. Braxton (Ed.), *Rethinking the departure puzzle: New theory and research on college student retention.* Nashville: Vanderbilt University Press.

Rendon, L. I., & Nora, A. (1997). *Student academic progress: Key data trends.* Report prepared for the National Center for Urban Partnerships, Ford Foundation, New York.

Rendón, L. I. (1997, September). *Access in a democracy: Narrowing the opportunity gap.* Paper prepared for the Policy Panel on Access of the National Postsecondary Education Cooperative, Washington, DC.

Rendón, L. I., & Hope, R. (1996). *Educating a new majority.* San Francisco: Jossey-Bass.

Rendón, L. I., & Nora, A. (1997). *Student academic progress: Key data trends.* Report prepared for the National Center for Urban Partnerships, Ford Foundation, New York.

Smart, J. C., & Pascarella, E. T. (1986). Socioeconomic achievement of former college students. *Journal of Higher Education, 57,* 529–549.

Southern Regional Education Board. (2001). SREB *Fact book on higher education: Texas featured facts (2000/2001).* Atlanta: Southern Regional Education Board.

Stampen, J. O., & Cabrera, A. F. (1988). Is the student aid system achieving its objectives: Evidence on targeting and attrition. *Economic of Education Review, 7,* 29–46.

Tinto, V. (1993). *Leaving college: Rethinking the causes and cures of student attrition.* Chicago: University of Chicago Press.

Wilds, D. J., & Wilson, R. (1998). *Minorities in higher education, 1997–98: Sixteenth annual status report,* 1–2.

Wyatt, M. (1992). The past, present, and future need for college reading courses in the U.S. *The Journal of Reading, 36,* 10–12.

Alberta M. Gloria

Alberta M. Gloria received her doctorate in Counseling Psychology from Arizona State University and is currently an Associate Professor at the University of Wisconsin–Madison. Her primary research encompasses psychosociocultural factors for Chicano/Latino and other racial/ethnic students in higher education and issues of cultural congruency for these students within the academic and cultural environment. Other areas of research include academic support and cultural congruity for racial and ethnic minorities and professional development issues for counselors in training. Her work has appeared in journals such as *Cultural Diversity and Ethnic Minority Psychology, Hispanic Journal of Behavioral Sciences,* and *The Counseling Psychologist.* She currently is a Senior Editor for the *Journal of Multicultural Counseling and Development.* As an active member of APA, she has served as the secretary and membership chair for the Section for Ethnic and Racial Diversity for Division 17 and is currently the Chair-Elect for this section. She was awarded the Women of Color Psychologies Award from Division 35 in 1999 and the Emerging Professional Award from Division 45 of APA in 2002.

4

LATINA/O AND AFRICAN AMERICAN STUDENTS AT PREDOMINANTLY WHITE INSTITUTIONS

A Psychosociocultural Perspective of Cultural Congruity, Campus Climate, and Academic Persistence

Alberta M. Gloria and Jeanett Castellanos

The educational experiences of college students has long been a topic of discussion. However, the differential experiences of ethnic/racial minority students—Latina/os, African Americans, American Indians, and Asian Pacific Americans—attending predominantly White institutions (PWI) present unique challenges for understanding the educational system as a whole. In that the representation of ethnic/racial minority students within the educational system does not parallel national demographics (Aguirre & Martinez, 1993; Wilds & Wilson, 1998, Wilds, 2000), an evaluation of

The authors thank Derek Iwamoto and Cecilia Nepomuceno for their assistance with this chapter. Correspondence should be referred to Alberta M. Gloria, University of Wisconsin, 349A Education Building, 1000 Bascom Mall, Madison, WI 53706-1398 or Agloria@mail.soemadison.wisc.edu higher education policies is warranted. Specifically, ethnic/racial minorities have struggled to enter an educational system that is based on White or European American culture and values (Okibar, 1994). As such, higher education has historically excluded ethnic/racial minorities from equal educational access and opportunity (Feagin, Vera, & Imani, 1996; Justiz, Wilson, & Björk, 1994). Today, ethnic/racial minorities remain undereducated and underrepresented despite their progress in access to and graduation from American institutions of higher education (Wilds and Wilson, 1998), which in turn effects their economic and social mobility, perpetuating a cycle of unemployment and underemployment (Nevárez-La Torre & Hidalgo, 1997; Wilds, 2000).

In an effort to understand the low graduation rates of ethnic/racial minorities, cognitive indicators (e.g., standardized test scores) have been scrutinized (Sedlacek, 1998; Young & Sowa, 1992). Despite the misperception that cognitive indicators provide an unbiased assessment of student potential (Milem & Hakuta, 2000), sociopolitical and sociocultural aspects of environmental and cultural contexts are overlooked. Scholars have subsequently argued for comprehensive and contextual-based investigations for ethnic/racial minority students (Sedlacek, 1998; Wohl & Aponte, 1995). The influences of self-beliefs and perceptions, social interactions and supports, cultural influences, and environmental contexts, therefore, need to be considered in assessing ethnic/racial minority student persistence (Gloria & Pope-Davis, 1997; Gloria & Rodríguez, 2000).

Two groups of particular interest are Latina/o and African American college students, given their low enrollment, retention, and graduation rates (Wilds, 2000). Latina/os are not equally represented in the educational system, despite being the fastest growing and youngest racial and ethnic group in the United States (U.S. Department of Education, National Center for Education Statistics [NCES], 2000c). Specifically, Latina/o children comprise a large percentage of the elementary and secondary school-aged children (NCES, 2000b), yet in high school and college their educational presence is not proportionally reflected by their entry into secondary and higher education (NCES, 1998b; 2000c). African Americans also have long endured discriminatory and unequal educational access (Feagin, Vera, & Imani, 1996). Powell (1998) described the educational system in which "[t]he gains by African Americans have, more often than not, been made in the face of powerful resistance, sometimes violent intimidation, discrimination, indifference, and benign neglect" (p. 97).

In light of these concerns, the purpose of this chapter is to discuss Latina/o and African American student educational experiences at PWIs. In creating a structure from which to discuss these varied educational experiences, the chapter is organized into five different sections. First, a brief review of current educational statistics for Latina/o and African American college students will be provided. Second, research trends and patterns of the educational experiences and academic persistence of Latina/o and African American students are reviewed. Third, the conceptual basis of this chapter (i.e., a psychosociocultural (PSC) framework, Gloria & Rodríguez, 2000) will be discussed relative to issues and concerns encountered by Latina/o and African American students. Fourth, within the PSC framework, the specific constructs of campus climate, cultural congruity, and role models and mentors will be addressed. In this discussion, voices of current Latina/o and African American undergraduates are interwoven within the discussion of the chapter's main constructs, highlighting navigation and coping methods used to "manage" the university setting and providing "real-life" educational experiences and perspectives. The student voices were compiled through the process of written feedback, where students were provided with open-ended questions regarding their educational experiences. Finally, the chapter concludes with implications for research and recommendations for improving the current practice of university administrators, faculty, and staff in providing a more conducive environment for Latina/o and African American students.

Although a multitude of factors and individual variables influence educational perceptions of Latina/o and African American students (e.g., ethnic and racial identity, worldview, age, sexual orientation, college-generation status, socioeconomic status), this chapter will only focus on several central discussion points. Similarly, given the large heterogeneity among and between different ethnic/racial minority students, the educational interactions and experiences and of all Latina/o and African American students will not be the same. As such, the information presented here is intended as a framework for conceptualizing and understanding individual student realities.

Educational Descriptives of Latina/o and African American College Students

Ethnic/racial minority students continue to account for only a small percentage of all college students despite enrollment gains (Wilds, 2000). In 1976, 16% of the college population were ethnic/racial minorities, as compared to 27% of the college population in 1997 (NCES, 2000a)—a dismal 11% increase. Increased enrollment for both men and women of color has recently been reported in 1996–1997 (3.2% and 4%, respectively), however, these increases remain below that of the registration numbers from the previous decade (Wilds, 2000). Despite higher enrollments for ethnic/racial students as compared to White students, they continue to be underrepresented at every level of education.

Examining early educational trends, most elementary and secondary schools continue to be racially segregated (Gay, 2001). Although there are schools that have high student of color representation, students of color are not necessarily attending school with ethnically or racially similar peers. In contrast, school personnel (i.e., teachers, administrators, and policy makers) within most schools are White (Gay, 2001). Similarly, many students of color contend with lower academic expectations, educational tracking, misplacement into special education, fewer educational resources, lack of teachers of color, and teachers who have not been trained in integrating cultural traits and values into classroom curriculum (President's Advisory Commission of Educational Excellence for Hispanic Americans, 1996; Valencia, 1991). "Together these situations increase failure rates and the chances that the affected students will become school dropouts" (Gay, 2001, p. 200). This increased failure is reflected in the low high school graduation and college enrollment rates of both Latina/o and African American students (NCES, 1998b; 1999; 2000c).

Regarding college enrollment, more Latina/os enroll part-time (45%) as compared to African Americans (40%) and Whites (39%). As a result, Latina/os (35%) are more likely than African Americans (32%) and Whites (25%) to take more than six years to earn a baccalaureate degree (NCES, 1996). Further, Latina/o and African American students have the lowest enrollments at Research I and II Universities than any educational institutions (e.g., Baccalaureate Colleges I and II, Associate of Arts Colleges) (NCES, 2000c).

According to the most recent annual report by the American Council on Education, Latina/os had the largest enrollment gain of the four major ethnic/racial groups (23.2%), whereas African Americans had the smallest enrollment gain (10%) over the past five years (Wilds, 2000). Specifically, Latina/os have experienced little change in their college graduation rates since the early 1990s while African Americans experienced the greatest increase in college graduation rates between 1992 and 1997. Although African Americans have an 8.3% increased enrollment rate since 1993, this increase is less than half the rate of all other ethnic/racial minority student populations (Wilds, 2000). Similarly, African American student enrollment has fluctuated over the past 20 years (NCES, 2000a).

A practical aspect of college entry is finance. Because high school graduates from lower income families are typically not as prepared for college as their counterparts from middle- and upper-income families, their admission into a four-year college is less likely (NCES, 2000c). It is important to note, however, that students from lower income families are just as likely as middle-income families to enroll in a four-year or postsecondary institution within two years of graduation from high school (NCES, 1998a). For Latina/o students, half of the incoming freshmen come from families with incomes less than $20,000, with 50% receiving financial aid; two out of every five students (40%) receive some form of federal aid; and 15% receive institution-specific aid (O'Brien 1993). Similarly, African American students receive a substantial amount of financial aid (Patterson Research Institute of the College Fund/UNCF, 1997). For example, 66.3% of African American students at four-year colleges and universities receive financial aid, with slightly more African American women receiving financial aid than do their African American male counterparts. Although monies can pay for school, financial support generally does not consider the family in need and as a result many students delay or discontinue their educational pursuits to help their families meet other financial obligations (Pappas & Guajardo, 1997; Quintana, Vogel, & Ybarra, 1991). For example, there are substantially more African American females who are financially independent with financial dependents (23.3%) than African American males who are financially independent with financial dependents (15.0%) (Patterson Research Institute of the College Fund/UNCF, 1997).

Finally, when examining the number of degrees conferred, Latina/os earning bachelor's degrees more than doubled whereas African Americans had only a small growth in the number of bachelor's degrees earned for 1997. Specifically, Latina/os students made up 9% of all undergraduate students in 1997 yet earned only 5.3% of all bachelor's degrees. Similarly, African Americans made up 11.2% of all undergraduate students in that same year yet earned only 8.1% of all undergraduate degrees (Wilds, 2000).

Review of Select Journals

Based on a brief overview of current educational statistics of Latina/o and African American college students, it is evident that educational process and outcome studies are needed. Similarly, the low Latina/o and African American student representation in higher education and its subsequent impact on social mobility and the national economy (Milem & Hakuta, 2000) warrants greater emphasis within the current literature. To examine the current literature base, four journals were reviewed over a ten-year period (between 1990 and 2000). The review included two general journals regarding college student and higher education (*Journal of College Student Development* and *Journal of Higher Education*) and two specialty journals (*Hispanic Journal of Behavior Sciences* and *Journal of Black Psychology*). The first inclusion criterion was that a study investigated some aspect of the psychological, social, or cultural educational experience of Latina/o and African American college students relative to academic persistence. Next, studies for which a college population was the focus of investigation were included, however, those studies conducting research with a convenience sample of college students were not included. This second criterion eliminated many studies from this review, however, this process allowed specific studies to be examined.

The two general education journals differed substantially in the number of articles regarding Latina/o and African American college students' academic persistence. In the *Journal of Higher Education* nine articles were identified whereas 57 articles were identified in the *Journal of College Student Development*. For the *Journal of Higher Education* the focus of the research was adjustment and racial or campus climate. The majority of the studies were quantitative, with an even split in the study of Latina/o and African American college students. The range of the topics found in the *Journal of College Student Development* was broader, with cultural aspects focusing on racism, identity (e.g., racial and ethnic), and overall campus climate. Social issues focused on alienation and social relationships (e.g., with peers and faculty). Psychological aspects most frequently included topics related to self-concept.

When examining the specialty journals, the *Journal of Black Psychology* had six data-based articles on African American college students and the *Hispanic Journal of Behavior Sciences* had 13 data-based articles on Latina/o college students. For the former, issues of racial identity or general identity (e.g., imposter syndrome) were the focus of examination. For the *Hispanic Journal of Behavior Sciences*, there were 13 articles, of which 12 were quantitative and one that was qualitative. Of the 12 quantitatively-based articles, one study was a meta-analysis of previous research. In contrast, the focus of the studies was related to stress (e.g., adjustment, academic, social) and social support (e.g., family).

The majority of the research examined one of the three constructs (i.e., psychological, social, or cultural), however, relatively few studies provided a contextually based investigation by examining all three construct areas. For example, an assessment of Latina/o students' self-perceptions (psychological), faculty or staff perceptions of Latina/o students (social), and the university setting (cultural) could more clearly reveal the complexities of student interactions. That is, a more complex investigation of student experiences is needed. Instead, negative assumptions and biases held against Latina/o students would be contextualized within the unwelcoming university climate (Wilds, 2000), providing insight to students' decisions to withdraw or separate from university activities. The examination of variables such as age, gender, college-generation status, sexual orientation, financial status (e.g., independent with dependents), disability, and other moderating variables could also be examined contextually, rather than simply serving as descriptive or nominal student attributes. Such studies went for a more contextualized understanding of Latina/o and African American students' educational experiences, while allowing for individualized variables to be considered (e.g., ethnic and racial identity, acculturation, gender identity, perceptions of discrimination).

Taking a Holistic Approach to Educational Persistence

Although each of the three constructs (i.e., psychological, social, and cultural aspects) merits attention individually, a more integrative or holistic approach creates a collective and contextualized assessment of ethnic/racial minority student college experiences. The result of such comprehensive investigations would allow for the intentional direction of student policy and procedure, and would hold universities accountable for creating inclusive learning environments for all students. This is relevant since the entire context of student development and persistence needs to be a central aspect of educational research (Allen, 1992; Wohl & Aponte, 1995).

Recently, Gloria and colleagues (Gloria, Robinson Kurpius, Hamilton, & Willson, 1999; Gloria & Ho, in press; Gloria & Robinson Kurpius, 2001) empirically tested a psychosociocultural (PSC) approach to assessing the academic nonpersistence decisions of ethnic/racial minorities. The framework takes a multidimensional approach to the educational experiences of different student populations. That is, psychological (e.g., self-beliefs), social (e.g., impact of relationships), and cultural (e.g., values and environmental context) dimensions are considered simultaneously to have accurate perspectives about the educational interactions and decisions of racial and ethnic minority students attending PWIs. Addressing student issues devoid of PSC dimensions is equivalent to asking for students' feedback about university climate but then refusing to listen or integrate students' feedback into the subsequent programming.

Although the framework was originally created to direct student counseling services for Latina/o students (Gloria & Rodriguez, 2000), it inherently addresses ethnic/racial minority student development concerns. Influences of cultural factors (e.g., values and working assumptions, environmental context), social support systems (e.g., faculty mentors, family support), and psychological issues (e.g., self-perceptions or belief in skills and abilities to succeed) on the overall psychosociocultural well-being cannot be dismissed. Most importantly, addressing the dynamic and interdependent relationships of these constructs must be considered in providing context-specific student interventions. The following areas of campus climate, cultural congruity, and role of mentors provide those areas for discussion relative to the PSC framework. Also, student voices poignantly illustrate the concepts and educational experiences. It is important to note that the student voices presented are not intended to speak for entire cultures, but rather to illuminate the individual educational realities and contexts encountered.

Campus Climate: Why invite me here if you really don't want me here?

> I lack a sense of belonging here, a feeling of an outsider. (African American female)

Studies have examined and highlighted the challenges of racism, prejudice, and interracial tensions that both Latina/o and African American students experience on predominantly White campuses (D'Augelli & Hershberger, 1993; Miville, Molla, & Sedlacek, 1992). In addition, several studies indicate a resurgence of hostility against ethnic/racial minority students (Nora & Cabrera, 1996; Springer, Terenzini, Pascarella, & Nora, 1995). For example, Gloria (1997) found that Latina/os feel unwelcomed and overlooked on college campuses. Research has similarly found that African Americans described their campus climates as hostile and uninviting (Mack, Tucker, Archuleta, De Groot, Hernández, & Oh Cha, 1997). Unfortunately, the issues of campus and racial climate are consistently overlooked when examining academic persistence or explicitly addressing the creation of ethnic/racial minority student programming (Hurtado, Milem, Clayton-Pederson, & Allen, 1998).

Student responses to being "tolerated" on PWI campuses are often that of alienation or marginalization (Ponterotto, 1990). For example, one student indicated an all too familiar response,

> I try to adjust to it the best I can, but mostly I just mind my own business and keep to myself. (Latino male)

The alienation described above, a common and self-protective response to coping within an unwelcoming environment, suggests experiences of powerlessness, normlessness, and social isolation. Students often experience powerlessness in the university setting as they feel a lack of control over their educational situations (Steward, Germain, & Jackson, 1992), particularly as many ethnic/racial minority students are "constantly reminded that they do not belong" (Carroll, 1998, p. 83). As a result, many students choose to drop out or feel pushed out of the academy as a function of the unwelcoming environment. For example, one student expressed her difficulty in the environment.

> At my last school (another four-year university), I felt there were fewer opportunities for African American students. It was hard to fit in and find my niche. This was one of the main reasons I left and transferred to this institution. As an African American student, there was nothing for me, as a student yes, but not as an African American student. Here things are a little better. (African American female)

Similarly, the encounter of gender and ethnic/racial based stereotypes within the educational setting are also micro-aggressions (Carroll, 1998) or direct and indirect interactions that convey disregard or contempt. That is, students and their abilities are deemed invisible (Franklin & Boyd-Franklin, 2000) or are negatively perceived (Carroll, 1998). For example, two students identified the perceptions attributed to them as a function of gender and ethnicity, which in turn discounted them as students of success and ability. That is, they encounter,

> the stereotypes of being passive individuals, wanting to be a house-wife, getting married, wanting kids and not wanting an education or a profession. (Latina)

> ethnic bias in education, in other words a stereotype that women should stay home only. (Latina)

Because the academy typically does not have large ethnic/racial minority representation and ethnic/racial enclaves are small, Latina/o and African American students often encounter culture shock (Fiske, 1988; Gloria & Pope-Davis, 1997). One student identified her difficulty of finding culturally-similar peers and its effect on her interactions.

> It is taking a lot for me to adjust and feel part of this campus. The student body is not adequately represented culturally. There are only a few minorities. It was extremely difficult adjusting to this culture shock, because I didn't feel like I could relate to many people here. (Latina)

As indicated by Hurtado, Milem, Clayton-Pederson, & Allen (1999), campus demography must change to reflect increased diversity to provide welcoming and inclusive learning environments. In addition to the low numerical representation, many African American students experience social isolation (Steward, Germain, & Jackson, 1992) as they are made to feel separate from the university culture and alone in the system. One student addressed the isolation felt as a result of few African American peers.

> There are not very many classes that address African American culture. When there are, we all flood the class. I walk in the classroom and say, wow! Look at all these Black people, and there are only five of us. (African American female)

Similarly, one student addressed the issue of separateness from the overall university culture, yet identified the importance of social supports and continued need for university interactions.

> The campus climate is not always inviting to the minority student so minorities stay in clusters to gain the support and relationships that are needed to endure the sometimes cold climate. However, this does not stop me from participating in activities that may interest me but are not related to my culture. (African American female)

Research has indicated that African Americans attending PWIs experience greater levels of overt racism than do their counterparts at predominately Black colleges (Feagin et al., 1996). Further, both Feagin et al (1996) and Cokley (1999) found that the nature of the environment (e.g., forcing assimilation of the student to the cultural values) impacts the interaction of African American students with others. This perceived racism is subsequently related to increased feelings of marginalization and social isolation (Lang & Ford, 1992). Unfortunately, negative university social experiences have been identified as primary reasons for African American students to make academic nonpersistence decisions (Gossett, Cuyjet, & Cockriel, 1998). Given Saddlemire's (1996) findings that White students often hold inaccurate understandings of African American culture, it is critical to increase the interactions that would allow African American students to feel comfortable, welcomed, and celebrated at PWIs.

Poignantly stated, one student indicated her simple yet highly sophisticated assessment of the university cultural climate.

> Sometimes I ask myself "Are we succeeding because of the university setting or in spite of it?" (Latina)

Cultural Congruity: Do I belong here, or is it really a question of belonging?

A closely related construct to campus climate is that of cultural congruity. Cultural congruity has been defined as the cultural fit or match between one's internal values and those of the university environment (Gloria & Robinson Kurpius, 1996). An assessment of the climate is central to determining different levels of tolerance or hostility directly or indirectly manifested as cultural values or behaviors on campuses. One student stated,

> I don't utilize the values of the university. (African American female)

The degree of cultural fit or congruity is such that students do not enculturate or attempt to assimilate the dominant sociocultural system. One student identified how she views her fit in the university and her subsequent response.

> My cultural values and those of the university are not quite congruent. Because (name of student organization) is Latina-based, I gather a lot of support and encouragement from its members. I cannot say that I feel like I belong in the university setting, but because my goal is to get an education, belonging has become less significant. (Latina)

Most PWIs expect that Latina/o and African American students integrate into the cultural mold of the university setting (Feagin et al., 1996; Cokley, 1999). The ramifications of such reshaping allow the university to maintain a status quo and require students to manage or navigate the balance of personal and environmental values (Gloria & Robinson Kurpius, 1996). Ultimately, the attempt to assimilate students to a single model of value and behavior inherently does not value or respect diversity and individual differences (Gloria & Pope-Davis, 1997). For example, Cervantes (1988) interviewed Latina/o and African American students and found that they often felt the need to hide themselves culturally or to separate from White students and faculty in order to survive the setting. This separation of self is reflected as a current student poignantly stated:

> I split in half. There is my fake half and my real half. I have learned to use each half properly. (Latino male)

The splitting of self directly addresses the difficulty of cultural congruity, which in turn relates to academic nonpersistence decisions for both Latina/o and African American college students at PWIs. Specifically, decreased cultural congruity was associated with increased nonpersistence decisions for Latina/o students (Gloria & Robinson Kurpius, 1996). A similar relationship between cultural congruity and academic nonpersistence decisions has also been found for African American students (Gloria et al., 1999).

There are several interrelated aspects to consider in addressing cultural congruity for Latina/o and African American college students. The cultural values and assumptions of PWIs are generally that of independence, individualism, and competition (Feagin et al., 1996). For Latina/os and African American, many of whom value collaboration and collective communities, the incongruity is likely to be high. As a result, many students must balance and often suppress their normative values and behaviors for those of the larger environment. Although university personnel and the larger educational structure may call for students to integrate into the current socioenvironmental context, students must balance the values of competition versus collaboration, individualism versus collectivism, and formality of relationships versus personal and collegial relationships. As such, educational integration is often tantamount to cultural cleansing as students are expected to strip away their own values and culture, allowing for the status quo of the university culture and environment. One student described the difficulty of such a cultural balance.

> Trying to manage both cultures has proven to be difficult. I try to balance my time by doing school during the week and my culture and family on the weekends. Both put a lot pressure on me to commit to one or the other, but I am slowly incorporating both into my life. (Latina)

As students navigate the balance, it is also important to highlight that students must work hard to maintain their cultural identities in the process of education. For example, two students stated,

> I try to unite with as many peers as possible and not to hide my ethnic background from others. (Latina)

> I stick to my cultural values, regardless of what others say or think. Sometimes it is hard to do this, because the university environment is so different, but I tend to hold on to my values. (Latino male)

Role Models: If you can do education, so can I—or— How can I do education if I don't see others like me "doing" education?

In balancing the cultural differences inherent in academia, the role of mentors for ethnic/racial minorities is imperative. For example, ethnic/racial minority role models motivate students and also provide "a group that is a natural sounding board for many problems" (Verdugo, 1995, p. 669). Same ethnicity/race mentors also introduce a culturally based perspective to the environment and can assist ethnic/racial minority students with their educational experiences and maintenance of cultural identity. Unfortunately, there is a paucity of Latina/o and African American faculty: although their numbers increased until 1976, their percentages have dropped since then. Specifically, Latina/o faculty declined from 1.7% to 1.4% and African American faculty declined from 4.4% to 4.0% between 1977 and 1984 (Washington & Harvey, 1989). More recently, the Hispanic Association of Colleges and Universities (1995) reported a 1 to 76 Latino faculty-to-student ratio in contrast to a 1 to 55 African American faculty-to-student ratio. Latinos comprised 3% of full-time faculty, and African Americans represented 5% of all full-time faculty in 1995 (NCES, 2000a).

Student-faculty interactions positively relate to educational outcomes (Pascarella & Terenzini, 1991) and thus an increase in faculty diversity is mandatory. For example, Nora and Cabrera (1996) reported that faculty interaction with Latina/o students had a positive effect on the student experience, where students perceived less discrimination in the classroom and on campus. Similarly, African American students who were mentored perceived the university environment more positively, had greater cultural congruity, and were more likely to make academic persistence decisions (Gloria et al, 1999).

It is important to note, however, that Latina/o and African American students continue to experience racist attitudes from faculty and to feel uncomfortable interacting with faculty (Allen, 1981; Mingle, 1987). A student addressed the issues of few same-race faculty mentors and the importance of more ethnic/racial minority faculty representation.

> I can't say I have a significant mentor. This could be because of the lack of African American faculty. I feel less comfortable approaching those people not like me. (African American female)

Locating and establishing mentoring relationships with Latina and African American female faculty is also a relevant concern for women of color. The challenge of finding an ethnic/racial woman faculty member is a well-documented issue, as there are fewer ethnic/racial women faculty than other faculty group in academia (Kezar, 1999). Indeed, the need for role models and mentors who can advocate for and help guide students through issues of racism and sexism is necessary for educational success (Carroll, 1998). One female student plainly identified an educational challenge of finding a gender and ethnically/racially similar mentor. She stated,

> Finding faculty who are minority females to help guide me through the academic arena is a big issue. (African American female)

> The first thing that I did when I got here was to find someone who was like me. Even though [Latina faculty member] was not the same

> as me, I felt safe that she could understand me and that she had gone through some of same things that I was. (Latina)

Although some students may select same-ethnicity/race mentors, it is important that *all* faculty take responsibility for the mentoring of *all* students (Gloria & Pope-Davis, 1997). Faculty-student interaction is particularly relevant as the effect of frequent faculty interaction has been found to increase grade point average, intellectual development, and personal development (Pascarella & Terenzini, 1991). One student underscored the need for basic support, regardless of the ethnicity or race of the faculty member.

> I always look for faculty support. When I find someone who is understanding I try to stay close to that professor/faculty. (Latino male)

Because of the limited number of Latina/o and African American faculty on PWIs, older siblings and student peers often serve as primary role model. That is, more senior students often help incoming students to "learn the ropes" and find other sources of support (e.g., helpful or friendly faculty and university staff) (Gloria, 1999). Two students identified the importance of accessing students who have more educational experiences to help them succeed.

> I try to find professors who are caring, fair and approachable. Also I talk to many students who are upper division and graduate students. These people tend to give me good advice on how to succeed in school. (African American female)

> I have the support of my mother and older sister. My older sister is two years ahead of me and has just graduated from university. She is my good friend and a helpful guide to school. (Latina)

Family members or community persons can also fulfill the role of mentor or primary role model for many Latina/o and African American students (Gloria & Rodriguez, 2000). Importantly, family support and encouragement have a direct effect on culturally-appropriate social integration and persistence for Latina/o and African American students, particularly as the value of family is central for both (Gloria, 1999). Also, the role of community, in particular church, is a crucial social support. Two students identified the role of family and church communities.

> Most of my role models are outside the university. They are in the community and in my church. (African American female)

> The church, my community, my family (extended and nuclear), and my friends are the main facets to a basic stable support system. Weekends,

in particular, are my days to regain momentum with my self, my spiritual needs, and my family commitments. (African American female)

I am at school because of my family and my community. Without them, I couldn't and wouldn't be here. (Latina)

Not previously identified in the literature but evident in student voices is the role of community leaders on student's achievement and persistence. For example, having a role model or a community icon to provide indirect support is central to students' culture and education. Many Latina/o students identify with Cesar Chávez, who emphasized education of the community, the poor, and the underrepresented. In addition, Che Guevarra was identified as an inspirational academic source for one student. For example,

Whenever I write a paper, I always put on my Che T-shirt to inspire me. In fact, the first paper I wrote when I wore that T-shirt—I got an A. Ever since, I have continued to wear the shirt for a good grade. (Latino male)

Similarly, reading about famous African Americans educationally encouraged one student.

It's important that I revisit the work of Martin Luther King and Malcolm X as they represent our people, our struggles, and goals. I carry a button of Dr. King with me to remind me when I get caught up and look to him for strength. (African American male)

Cultural icons and community leaders are liaisons between the ethnic/racial student's cultural background and education. Ultimately, knowing that others (e.g., community leaders, faculty, family members, peers) have educationally succeeded provides hope and guidance for Latina/o and African American students that they too can succeed educationally (Carroll, 1998; Gloria, 1999; Gloria & Rodriguez, 2000).

Implications for Theory and Practice for All University Personnel

The university must assume an active leadership role to enhance the academic experiences of Latina/o and African American college students. As student voices have expressed educational challenges, social isolation, and feelings of marginalization, it is evident that an increase in university cultural sensitivity and inclusion must be addressed. Specifically, academic units and student affairs must work in tandem to address relevant issues of campus climate, retention of ethnic/racial minority students and faculty, and the impact of cultural values on the current setting (e.g., curriculum).

Although most academic units have traditionally relied upon student services to effect recruitment, retention, and student programming, it is imperative that the responsibility of diversifying university campuses falls to both units. First, academic units must actively recruit and retain ethnic/racial minority faculty (Gloria & Pope-Davis, 1997). This charge can be headed by academic chairs, who can institute small structural changes to influence the larger campus community. For example, it is recommended that academic units include questions on infusion of diversity within the curriculum and establish a culturally welcoming classroom setting. That is, departments need to hold faculty accountable for creating inclusive classroom learning environments. Faculty can also re-evaluate their curricula and personally examine their own cultural biases (Gloria, Reickmann, & Rush, 2000). Finally, creating a departmental norm in which service is part of the advancement for tenure will provide both internal and external support for increased understanding and sensitivity of faculty toward all students.

Student affairs professionals play an essential role on university campuses. As student advocates, they must actively improve the current campus climate at PWIs. In particular, student affairs professionals should evaluate the representation of ethnic/racial minority staff, the campus climate, the overall African American and Latina/o student experience, multicultural sensitivity of all employees on campus, and the university's initiative and commitment to multicultural issues. For example, student affairs professionals can conduct cultural audits or create diversity initiative groups to strategize with students how the university can provide a more culturally inclusive environment. In addition, a multicultural retention council can be established to monitor and improve the persistence and retention of ethnic/racial minority students. Finally, coordinating a community/university partnership can help to establish working relationships and mutual support of both systems (Gloria, 1997). When community leaders come to campus and address current issues encountered by Latina/o and African American communities and their families, the university's cultural climate improves and cultural congruity is enhanced for all students and university personnel. Further, knowing the institutional climate and psychosociocultural aspects of the student communities is warranted in providing ethnic/racial minority-based programming (Cokley, 1999). In short, university personnel need to understand how the college environment impacts the social and psychological functioning of ethnic/racial minority students in providing inclusive learning environments (Cokley, 1999).

University counseling centers also have a vital role in the successful change of campus climate for Latina/o and African American students at PWIs (Gloria & Rodriguez, 2000). On-campus counseling centers can collaborate with academic and student affairs units in increasing assessment efforts. As industrial/organizational psychology attempts to evaluate corporate cultures and their organizational climates, psychologists trained in interpersonal skills can help with this initiative. Counseling center professionals can provide consultation in the form of cultural assessments of university departments and units. Furthermore, they can direct and guide those who resist the inclusion of differences or refuse to address diversity. Another recommendation is for counseling center staff to provide psychoeducational support for Latina/o and African American students (Gloria, 1999). These groups can address campus-related issues while also identifying student recommendations for improving campus climate and culture-specific student services. In supporting Latina/o and African American students, counseling center staff need to become active participant-observers of the educational processes (e.g., student interactions, campus climate, university programming) to increase cultural inclusion and help students navigate the current environment.

Latina/o and African American students also have the responsibility to contribute to their educational experiences. Students must be active participants in their education and seek opportunities to enhance their experiences. As university and community leaders, students must educate the university community about their educational challenges and experiences. That is, students need to voice their opinions and provide constructive feedback to educate university personnel. Through campus involvement and self-expression, campus officials can actively address student needs and challenges. Specific examples include students writing about their educational experiences or providing opinion articles for school newspapers. Similarly, students can develop anthologies (which are currently being written at some PWIs) in an effort to document and validate ethnic/racial minority students' observations and experiences. Creative and experiential writings can help Latina/o and African American students understand that they are not alone in their educational challenges, thereby creating support for continued education. Similarly, students can work with university officials (e.g., student affairs professionals, multicultural center staff, and faculty) to set ethnic/racial minority student goals each academic year. Such strategies can empower students, create effective support systems, and provide a vehicle for individuals in the university (i.e., faculty, staff, and students) to ensure the academic persistence of all students. Finally, regardless of campus involvement and individual variables of students (e.g., age, ethnic identity, college-generation status), all students need to actively secure mentoring or support from student peers, faculty, and family/community to aid their educational pursuits. In doing so, Latina/o and African American students can secure the specific and individualized psychological, social, and cultural supports that they need to succeed educationally.

The examination of Latina/o and African American college student experiences must be consistent, comprehensive, and intentional. Specifically, programmatic research that addresses psychological, social, and cultural components of each individual and the university system is warranted. In these investigations, it is necessary to emphasize the mechanisms students use to survive and thrive in the university environment, while not compromising their values and practices. Despite encountering culture shock, lack of cultural reflection in values and numerical representation, the students highlighted in this chapter and many other Latina/o and African American students continue to persist academically. To continue the current trend of increased enrollment and graduation, all university systems and subsystems (e.g., academic departments, student counseling centers, student organizations, university community) must actively become part of the educational process in working toward inclusive visions and goals—allowing all voices to be heard and valued.

References

Aguirre, A., Jr., & Martinez, R. O. (1993). *Chicanos in higher education: Issues and dilemmas for the 21st century.* ASHE-ERIC Higher Education Report No. 3, Washington, DC: The George Washington University, School of Education and Human Development, 17–51.

Allen, W. A. (1981). *Black student characteristics, experiences and outcomes in the U.S. system of higher education.* Ann Arbor, MI: University of Michigan Press.

Allen, W. R. (1992). The color of success: African-American college student outcomes at predominantly White and historically Black public colleges and universities. *Harvard Educational Review, 62,* 26–34.

Carroll, G. (1998). *Environmental stress and African Americans: The other side of the moon.* Westport, CT: Praeger Publishers.

Cervantes, O. F. (1988). The realities that Latinos, Chicanos, and other ethnic minority students encounter in graduate school. *Journal of La Raza Studies, 2,* 34–41.

Cokley, K. (1999). Reconceptualizing the impact of college racial composition on African American students' racial identity. *Journal of College Student Development, 40,* 235–246.

D'Augelli, A. R., & Hershberger, S. L. (1993). African American undergraduates on a predominantly White campus: Academic factors, social networks, and campus climate. *Journal of Negro Education, 62,* 67–81.

Feagin, J. R., Vera, H., & Imani, N. (1996). *The agony of education: Black students at White colleges and universities.* New York: Routledge.

Fiske, E. B. (1988). The undergraduate Hispanic experience: A case juggling two cultures. *Change, 20*(3), 29–33.

Franklin, A. J., & Boyd-Franklin, N. (2000). Invisibility syndrome: A clinical model of the effects of racism on African-American males. *American Journal of Orthopsychiatry, 70,* 33–41.

Gay, G. (2001). Educational equality for students of color. In J. A. Banks & C. A. McGee Banks (Eds.), 4th ed., *Multicultural education: Issues and perspectives* (pp. 197–224). New York: John Wiley and Sons.

Gloria, A. M. (1997). Chicana academic persistence: Creating a university-based community. *Education and Urban Society, 30*(1), 107–121.

Gloria, A. M. (1999). Apoyando estudiantes Chicanas: Therapeutic factors in Chicana college student support groups. *Journal for Specialists in Group Work, 24,* 246–259.

Gloria, A. M., & Ho, T. A. (in press). Environmental, social, and psychological experiences of Asian American undergraduates: Examining issues of academic persistence. *Journal of Counseling and Development.*

Gloria, A. M., & Pope-Davis, D. B. (1997). Cultural ambience: The importance of a culturally aware learning environment in the training and education of counselors. In D. B. Pope-Davis & H. L. K. Coleman (Eds.), *Multicultural counseling competencies: Assessment, education and training, and supervision* (pp. 242–259). Thousand Oaks, CA: Sage.

Gloria, A. M., Rieckmann, T., & Rush, J. D. (2000). Issues and recommendation for teaching an ethnic/culture-based course. *Teaching of Psychology, 27*(2), 102–107.

Gloria, A. M. & Robinson Kurpius, S. E. (1996). The validation of the University Environment Scale and the College Congruity Scale. *Hispanic Journal of Behavioral Sciences, 18,* 533–549.

Gloria, A. M., & Robinson Kurpius, S. E. (2001). Influences of self-beliefs, social support, and comfort in the university environment on the academic persistence issues for American Indian undergraduates. *Cultural Diversity and Ethnic Minority Psychology, 7,* 88–102.

Gloria, A. M., Robinson Kurpius, S. E., Hamilton, K. D., & Willson, M. S. (1999). African American students' persistence at a predominately White university: Influences of social support, university comfort, and self-beliefs. *Journal of College Student Development, 40,* 257–268.

Gloria, A. M. & Rodriguez, E. R. (2000). Counseling Latino university students: Psychosociocultural issues for consideration. *Journal of Counseling and Development, 78,* 145–154.

Gossett, B. J., Cuyjet, M. J., & Cockriel, I. (1998). African Americans' perception of marginality in the campus culture. *College Student Journal, 32,* 22–32.

Hispanic Association of Colleges and Universities (1995). *Closing the Hispanic faculty gap*, January–February Newsletter, 1, 7.

Hurtado, S., Milem, J. F., Clayton-Pederson, A. R., & Allen, W. R. (1998). Enhancing campus climates for racial/ethnic diversity through educational policy and practice. *The Review of Higher Education, 20th Anniversary Edition, 21*(3), 279–302.

Hurtado, S., Milem, J. F., Clayton-Pederson, A. R., & Allen, W. R. (1999). Enacting diverse learning environments: Improving the campus climate for racial/ethnic diversity in higher education. *ASHE/ERIC Higher Education Report Series, 26*(8), Washington, DC: The George Washington University, Graduate School of Education and Human Development.

Justiz, M. J., Wilson, R., & Björk, L. G. (Eds.). (1994). *Minorities in higher education*. Phoenix, AZ: Oryx Press.

Kezar, A. J. (1999). Higher education trends (1997–1999): Faculty. ERIC Clearinghouse on Higher Education, Washington, DC.; George Washington Univ., Washington, DC. Graduate School of Education and Human Development.

Lang, M., & Ford, C. A. (Eds.). (1992). *Strategies for retaining minority students in higher education*. Springfield, IL: Charles C. Thomas Publishers.

Mack, D. E., Tucker, T. W., Archuleta, R., DeGroot, G., Hernandez, A. A., & Oh Cha, S. (1997). Interethnic relations on campus: Can't we all get along? *Journal of Multicultural Counseling and Development, 25*, 256–268.

Milem, J. F., & Hakuta, K. (2000). Special focus: The benefits of racial and ethnic diversity in higher education. In D. J. Wilds (Ed.), *Minorities in higher education 1999–2000: Seventeenth annual status report* (pp. 39–64). Washington, DC: American Council on Education.

Mingle, J. (1987). *Focus on minorities: Trends in higher education participation and success*. Denver, CO: Education Commission of the States and State Higher Education Executive Officers.

Miville, M. L., Molla, B., Sedlacek, W. E. (1992). Attitudes of tolerance for diversity among college students. *Journal of the Freshman Experience, 4*(1), 95–110.

Nevárez-La Torre, A. A., & Hidalgo, N. M. (1997). Introduction. *Education and Urban Society, 30*, 3–19.

Nora, A., & Cabrera, A. F. (1996). The role of perceptions of prejudice and discrimination on the adjustment of minority students to college. *Journal of Higher Education, 67*(2), 119–147.

O'Brien, E. M. (1993). Latinos in higher education. *Research Briefs, 4*(4), 1–13. (ERIC document reproduction service #ED 383790.)

Okibar, F. E. (1994, November). *Multiculturalism in the university curriculum: Infusion for what?* Paper presented at the Regent Conference on Diversity and Multiculturalism in the University Curriculum, Manhattan, KS.

Pappas, G., & Guajardo, M. (Eds, 1997). Ethnic diversity as a measurement of quality in higher education. *Latinos in Colorado: A profile of culture, changes, and challenges, 5,* 19–22. (ERIC document reproduction service #ED 412314.)

Pascarella, E. T., & Terenzini, P. T. (1991). *How college affects students: Findings and insights from twenty years of research.* San Francisco: Jossey-Bass.

Patterson Research Institute College Fund/UNCF. (1997). *The African American education data book, Volume I: Higher and adult education.* Washington: Author.

Ponterotto, J. G. (1990). Racial/ethnic minority and women students in higher education: A status report. *New Directions for Student Services, 52,* 45–59.

Powell, M. H. (1998). Campus climate and students of color. In L. A. Valverde & L. A. Castenell (Eds.), *The multicultural campus: Strategies for transforming higher education* (pp. 95–118). Walnut Creek, CA: AltaMira Press.

President's Advisory Commission of Educational Excellence for Hispanic Americans (1996). *Our nation on the fault line: Hispanic American education.* A report to the President of the US, the nation and the Secretary of Education. Washington, DC: Department of Education.

Quintana, S. M., Vogel, M. C., & Ybarra, V. C. (1991). Meta-analysis of Latino students' adjustment in higher education. *Hispanic Journal of Behavioral Sciences, 13(2),* 155–169.

Saddlemire, J. R. (1996). Qualitative study of white second-semester undergraduates' attitudes toward African American undergraduates at a predominantly White university. *Journal of College Student Development, 37(6),* 685–691.

Sedlacek, W. E. (1998). Special focus: Admissions in higher education: Measuring cognitive and noncognitive variables. In D. J. Wilds & R. Wilson (Eds.), *Minorities in higher education 1997–1998: Sixteenth annual status report* (pp. 47–66). Washington, D.C.: American Council on Education.

Springer, L., Terenzini, P. T., Pascarella, E. T., Nora, A. (1995). Influences on college students' orientations toward learning for self-understanding. *Journal of College Student Development, 36(1),* 5–19.

Steward, R. J., Germain, S., & Jackson, J. D. (1992). Alienation and interactional style: A study of successful Anglo, Asian, and Hispanic university students. *Journal of College Student Development, 33(2),* 149–157.

U.S. Department of Education, National Center for Education Statistics [NCES]. (1995). *The educational progress of Hispanic students.* (Office of Educational Research and Improvement, No. 4, NCES 95-767). Washington, DC: U.S. Government Printing Office.

U.S. Department of Education, NCES. (1996). *The condition of education.* NCES 1996-304. Washington, DC: U.S. Government Printing Office.

U.S. Department of Education, NCES. (1997). *Enrollment in higher education: Fall 1995*. NCES 1997-440. Washington, DC: U.S. Government Printing Office.

U.S. Department of Education, NCES. (1998a). *Access to postsecondary education for the 1992 high school graduates*. NCES 1998-150. Washington, DC: U.S. Government Printing Office.

U.S. Department of Education, NCES. (1998b). *Racial and ethnic differences in participation in higher education*. NCES 1998-012. Washington, DC: U.S. Government Printing Office.

U.S. Department of Education, NCES. (1999). *The condition of education 1999*. NCES 2000-009. U.S. Government Printing Office.

U.S. Department of Education, NCES. (2000a). *Digest of Education Statistics 1999*. NCES 2000-031. U.S. Government Printing Office.

U.S. Department of Education, NCES. (2000b). *Racial and ethnic distribution of elementary and secondary students*. NCES 2000-005. Washington, DC: U.S. Government Printing Office.

U.S. Department of Education, NCES. (2000c). *The condition of education 2000*. NCES 2000-062. Washington, DC: U.S. Government Printing Office.

U.S. Department of Education, Office of Educational Research and Improvement. (1995). *Digest of education statistics*. Washington, DC: U.S. Government Printing Office.

Valencia, R. R. (1991). The plight of Latino students: An overview of schooling conditions and outcomes. In R. R. Valencia (Ed.), *Chicano school failure and success: Research and policy for the 1990's* (pp. 3–26). London: Falmer Press.

Verdugo, R. R. (1995). Racial stratification and the use of Hispanic faculty as role models. *Journal of Higher Education, 66*(6), 669–686.

Washington, V., & Harvey, W. (1989). Affirmative rhetoric, negative action: African-American and Hispanic faculty at predominantly White institutions. ERIC Clearinghouse on Higher Education, Washington, DC (ED316075).

Wilds, D. J. (2000). *Minorities in higher education 1999–2000: Seventeenth annual status report*. Washington, DC: American Council on Education.

Wilds, D. J., & Wilson, R. (1998). *Minorities in higher education 1997–1998: Sixteenth annual status report*. Washington, DC: American Council on Education.

Wohl, J., & Aponte, J. F. (1995). Common themes and future prospects. In J. F. Aponte, R. Y. Rivers, & J. Wohl (Eds.), *Psychological interventions and cultural diversity* (pp. 301–316). Boston: Allyn and Bacon.

Young, B. D., & Sowa, C. J. (1992). Predictors of academic success for Black student athletes. *Journal of College Student Development, 33*, 318–324.

Guadalupe Anaya

Guadalupe Anaya received a B.A. in Psychology and an M.S. in Counseling Psychology from Indiana University, Bloomington. She received the Doctor of Philosophy in Education from the University of California, Los Angeles. She has conducted numerous evaluations of college student programs and has extensive experience working with undergraduate students and student organizations. Dr. Anaya has taught graduate courses in Educational Psychology at the University of Illinois, Urbana-Champaign; Educational Leadership at Indiana University, Bloomington; and Social and Comparative Education at the University of California, Los Angeles. She conducts research on student learning and development, on the validity of alternative indicators of learning, and on the educational experiences and achievements of African American and Latina/o students.

Darnell G. Cole

Darnell G. Cole received his doctorate in higher education administration and educational psychology from Indiana University and is currently an assistant professor at Marquette University in Milwaukee, Wisconsin. His primary research interests include the college experiences of racial/ethnic minorities on predominantly White campuses, faculty-student interactions, and sociocultural factors impacting college student development. Other areas of research interest include the impact of multicultural education on preservice teachers. His work has appeared in the *Journal of College Student Development, Teaching and Teacher Education, Journal of Classroom Interaction, Journal of Creative Behavior* and the *Journal of Hispanic Higher Education.* He is a member of ACPA, NASPA, and ASHE and annually serves as AERA session chair, discussant, and/or reviewer. *Urban Education* and *Educational Foundations* are among national journals for which he has reviewed article submissions. In the summer of 2000, he received the Best Teacher award from Marquette University.

5

ACTIVE FACULTY INVOLVEMENT

MAXIMIZING STUDENT ACHIEVEMENT EFFORTS

Guadalupe Anaya and Darnell G. Cole

Greater numbers of Latina/o students are graduating from high school and attending college yet only 22% of Latina/o high school graduates attend college, while 30% of African American and 41% of White students do so (Devarics, 2000). Latina/o students are actually only 5% of college graduates (Wilds & Wilson, 1998) and there is much more that can be done to increase college matriculation, academic performance, and graduation rates. The task of improving the academic achievement of Latina/o students requires state, policy, and institutional efforts; however, an examination of the role that faculty play is indispensable. This is not a simple matter, as the task involves an understanding of Latina/o students and their professors, and most importantly of their interactions and relationships. There is a small but growing body of research on undergraduate student-faculty interactions and it includes a few but important studies on minority and Latina/o students. A research-informed foundation can be established and utilized to develop strategies that actively involve faculty in the maximization of Latina/o students' learning efforts and educational outcomes. To this end we offer the reader an overview of relevant literature.

In this chapter, the key elements influencing Latina/o student-faculty interactions are outlined to underscore the active role that faculty can take in maximizing students' efforts to reach their educational potential. The first section, Student-Faculty Interactions, begins with a review of relevant literature and of important problems associated with understanding the impact that faculty can have on students. This literature has not adequately addressed the fact that American universities are the product of and part of a multiracial society. Nor has the literature taken into account the fact that students and faculty interact in a racially saturated social milieu. Factors critical or unique to the experiences of racial minorities are often absent in the educational research literature on college students. Because of these limitations we turned to studies on minority students, on African American students, and on Latina/o students. The second section, Minority Students in a Multiracial Society, consists of a sample of the work of social and counseling psychologists that focus on race, the minority experience, and on the nature of interracial and cross-cultural interactions. This literature can help us understand the nature of the student-faculty interactions of minority and Latina/o students. We include a brief discussion of conceptual frameworks from interracial and cross-cultural research. In the third section, Minority Student Experiences with Faculty, we present research on minority and Latina/o college student experiences with faculty. This literature incorporates race, not as a categorical variable, but as a complex aspect of the student experience and thus has made very valuable and unique contributions to the literature on student-faculty interactions. In the fourth section, Latina/o Student Achievement, we provide a summary of our recent research on Latina/o student-faculty interactions. We examine the impact on achievement of different types of interactions and of the quality of contact with faculty. Finally, we conclude the chapter with recommendations for active faculty involvement in the maximization of the efforts that students make to reach their educational goals.

Student-Faculty Interactions

Student development and learning are in part a function of the motivation and effort of the individual, and in part are linked to students' college experiences and the educational opportunities made available by the university. Within the university, a variety of educational environments provide unique and specific social contexts that can influence student learning and development. Professors are an integral aspect of the college environment, as are their interactions with students. Early research indicates that frequent interactions with faculty contribute to a variety of developmental and educational outcomes (Astin, 1977) as well as academic performance (Pascarella, Terenzini, & Hibel, 1978). In early studies student academic outcomes were reportedly influenced in particular by student-faculty discussions of intellectual matters, course-related issues, and student career goals (Pascarella, Terenzini, & Hibel, 1978). Endo and Harpel (1982) found that the progress made by students toward their intellectual goals was enhanced when students perceived their professors as being helpful. Furthermore, student-faculty interactions appeared to have a greater impact on the overall academic development of college seniors (Terenzini & Wright, 1987). Apparently, the developmental readiness of the student also played significant role. The early research suggests that a variety of student-faculty interactions can enhance educational outcomes and academic performance, that the quality of the interactions matters, and that perhaps certain students (college seniors) obtain greater benefits from their interactions with their professors. A comprehensive review of the literature indicates that despite the use of a variety of definitions and measures of these interactions as well as of student academic development, they consistently reported on the educational benefits of student interactions with faculty (Cole, 1999).

Given that multiple measures had been used in earlier research Anaya (1992) compared the use of several measures of student performance, including college undergraduate grades and student reports of academic or learning gains. Although the undergraduate grade point average (GPA) has been the measure of choice in research on student achievement, the validity of GPA and self-reported learning gains has been questioned. Critics contend that the validity of the grades and the GPA is threatened by the fact course grades typically do not take into account the student's performance level at the beginning of the course; they are normative rather than criterion-based indicators of academic performance. In other words, critics of these measure maintain that grades do not actually measure academic progress. Also used in the early research are student-reported measures of educational and developmental outcomes; this method has become increasingly popular. Basically, students are asked to estimate the degree of cognitive change or learning over a stated period of time. Here again, regardless of the type of learning measure used in student achievement and retention studies, similar results are reported in the literature (Anaya, 1992). In fact, recent methodological studies have reported as valid each of three measures of college student learning: GPA, student-reported learning, and standardized test performance (Anaya, 1992, 1999). More importantly, these studies report that student-faculty interactions enhanced academic achievement. In sum, a variety of student-faculty interactions do indeed play an important role in student achievement (Anaya, 1992, 1999; Astin, 1993; Pascarella & Terenzini, 1980; Terenzini & Wright, 1987). Faculty and institutions wishing to examine the impact of student-faculty interactions on the educational outcomes of Latina/o students can select from a variety of learning outcome indicators. The student-reported method of examining the impact of faculty on student learning is attractive from a practical perspective. It presents a uniform measure for use in between-college or between-program comparisons. It is also fairly inexpensive to survey and to ask Latina/o students to report on their contact with faculty, on the quality of the contact, on their satisfaction with faculty, as well as how much they have changed or learned over a given period of time. We now turn to a discussion of research and literature that could be particularly useful in understanding the nature and potential role of faculty in the educational outcomes for Latina/o students.

Minority Students in a Multiracial Society

The research generally has not examined the impact of student-faculty interactions on the educational outcomes for minority students. In fact, very few studies on this topic have focused on African American students and even fewer include Latina/o students' experiences. Notable among these is Fleming's (1984) landmark social psychological study on African American students, which shed much light on the complex nature of the college experience for minority students. In this comprehensive study she interviewed, surveyed, and tested students at several universities. She reported that students at predominantly White institutions (PWIs) had very limited contact with their professors outside of the classroom in comparison to their peers at historically Black colleges and universities (HBCUs). However, more recent data on non-HBCUs suggests that similar proportions (35%) of Latina/o and White students (Nora & Rendón, 1990), and similar proportions (36% and 32% respectively) of African American and White students (Cole, 1999) interact with faculty outside of class. Approximately one third of the students in each of these groups report interactions with faculty outside of class. Thus, the logical question that follows is: are similar benefits accrued by all students? Turning again to Fleming's research (1984), she found that relatively smaller intellectual gains were attained among African American students at PWIs in comparison to both their peers at HBCUs and to White students at PWIs. This is a finding that has been supported by subsequent research. Allen (1992) and Davis (1991) observed relatively larger gains in undergraduate grades for White students than for African American students as a result of contact with faculty. If the same proportion of African American and White students, one third, interacts with professors, are they having different types of interactions? Is the nature of student relationships with faculty qualitatively different for African American students? If so, could this difference account for differences in accrued academic benefits? A potential source of difference in the experiences of minority students stems from racial and cultural factors.

Interracial Interaction

For African American, Latina/o and other racial minority students interactions with faculty are generally interracial interactions, but for White students they are, more often than not, same-race interactions. Social and counseling psychologists have hypothesized the effects of a multiracial social context on individual development (Cross, 1987; Garza & Lipton, 1982; Hall, Cross & Freedle, 1972; Helms, 1990; Keefe & Padilla, 1987; and Ramírez, 1977) and on the experiences and interactions of individuals (Helms, 1985; Ramírez, 1977). Prejudice, racism, and discrimination contribute to differences in individual development, differences between groups, and can shape interactions amongst members from different racial groups (Allport, 1954; de Anda, 1984; Helms, 1985). College student and faculty experiences may vary as a function of differences in race-related experiences, awareness of race, ability to deal with racial diversity, and differences in understanding of racial issues. Consequently, student and faculty perceptions and evaluations of their interactions with each other may vary. Because interracial interactions reflect the experiences of the individuals involved, they can shape the course of student-faculty interactions, which hypothetically are associated with student educational outcomes. The following discussion of Helms' (1985) work on the effects of race on counseling and of de Anda's (1984) work on bicultural socialization illustrates potential variations of minority student interactions with university faculty, counselors, and staff.

Helms' work focuses on the development of a healthy racial identity and on the role that racial identity plays in student-counselor relationships. The latter can be of use for understanding Latina/o student-faculty interactions. Helms (1985) posits that an individual may have a healthy or an unhealthy racial identity. Within these two broad categories she describes several levels of identity development. For purposes of the present discussion, we refer only to the two broad categories. Given the possible combinations of identity statuses in a student-counselor relationship, Helms undertakes an analysis of the counseling process and makes predictions for counseling outcomes. The relationship classification schema is based on the developmental status (racial consciousness and identity) of the student and of the counselor. The student's racial consciousness may be less developed than that of the counselor, resulting in a "progressive" counseling relationship in which the counselor is able to lead the student towards healthier development. Or, the student and counselor may have the same level of racial consciousness, a "parallel" counseling relationship, which would result in a developmental impasse because the counselor may not be able to guide the student towards a healthier development. If the counselor is at an earlier developmental stage than the student, to the degree that racial issues are important, the relationship may end because the counselor is unable to enter the student's frame of reference: this would be a "regressive" counseling relationship. This model differentiates types of racial relationships and specifies developmental outcomes for students and provides scenarios for the relationship. The outcomes depend on a complex set of psychological characteristics and processes that may be operating during interracial interactions (Helms, 1985). In other words, perceptions of student-faculty interactions may be due to factors associated with interracial interactions. For instance, the racial consciousness of each may be very different as a result of differences in socialization and differences in race-related experiences. The expression of racial consciousness in attitudinal and behavioral modes is affected by the role played in a relationship: superior or subordinate. Thus, Latina/o students and their professors might have positive experiences and continue their interactions; alternately one or the other may experience dissatisfaction or frustration and quickly terminate student-faculty contact.

Cross-Cultural Interaction

Models of bicultural development focus on an individual's ability to operate in distinct cultural settings. De Anda's (1984) work on bicultural socialization takes into account racial and cultural psychological characteristics and processes that can shape the experiences of minority students and their interactions with faculty and staff of the same or different race. In brief, she takes into account six critical factors: the overlap or commonality between racial groups or cultures; availability of cultural translators; feedback from each cultural group; cognitive and behavioral approaches and the mesh with the dominant group; degree of bilingualism; and degree of dissimilarity of physical appearance. For purposes of this chapter, we limit our discussion to de Anda's (1984) proposition that there are three types of agents that can facilitate the educational socialization process for minority students: cultural translators, mediators, and models. Translators are members of the individual's minority group who have successfully undergone the dual or bicultural socialization process. They are posited as possibly the most effective in assisting minority students because they are familiar with the convergence and divergence of the two sociocultural worlds that a minority student experiences. Models provide behavioral and attitudinal patterns that students can emulate. The model must be a minority for purposes of assisting the student to learn to operate in the culture of the minority group; but for learning mainstream behavior the model can be a member of either group. Members of the mainstream culture can serve as mediators by providing behavioral guides and serving as formal socialization agents. The feedback provided by socialization agents can guide students towards learning the norms of the university and appropriate attitudinal and behavioral modes. However, inappropriate negative feedback can be disruptive, can cause undue stress, and lead to student disengagement from the socialization task. De Anda (1984) suggests that bicultural development is facilitated when socializing agents provide corrective feedback that is specific, and when they identify positive aspects of student performance.

Minority Student Experiences with Faculty

Frequently minority college students face race-related assumptions about their academic ability, ambition, and high school preparation, as well as more general faculty perceptions of minority students. These factors can hinder student-faculty relationships (Kraft, 1991). Regardless of ability level, minority students may experience limited accessibility to faculty (Arnold, 1993; Turner, 1994). One in six high-achieving Latina/o college students perceive that White students had more faculty access and support (Hurtado, 1994). And once access is gained, both high-achieving and average minority students often relate poignant personal narratives about the lack of guidance and support from faculty (Feagin, Vera, & Imani, 1996; Arnold, 1993). But there is also research evidence that inspires optimism: some minority students have very good or unique relationships with university faculty and staff and therefore also enjoy academic benefits. African American, Mexican American, Native American and White students who had contact with professors or staff whom they saw as role models tended to have high grades (Mayo, Murguía & Padilla, 1995). However, in the same study, the researchers found that meetings with faculty outside of class for help or advice only enhanced the academic performance of African American and White students. The complex nature of interracial interactions can vary from one minority group to another and, may be an important factor that shapes—in different ways for each group—the quality of interpersonal interactions with their professors as well as student educational outcomes. Research and theory on interracial interactions can help us understand the potential nature of these interactions and illuminate the influence that student-faculty interactions might have on educational outcomes for various minority students.

The research and theory discussed thus far indicates that minority students' experiences with their professors can vary considerably. De Anda's and Helms' conceptual frameworks allow for an analysis of minority student relationships with counselors, faculty, and staff as well as educational outcomes for Latina/o students. The educational research discussed at the beginning of the chapter indicated that the same proportion of African American, Latina/o, and White students interact with their professors. However, the research on minority college students points to differences in perceptions of faculty accessibility, guidance, and support and to possible differences in the developmental and learning benefits derived by minority students (as compared to those obtained by White students). In an effort to move the research forward, a recent set of studies examined the nature of student-faculty interactions for African American and Latina/o students and the benefits, if any, they might obtain from these interactions (Anaya and Cole, 2001; Cole, 1999; Cole and Anaya, in progress). In these studies the authors examine information provided by students at numerous campuses across the country, compare the results with previous research, discuss the nature of student-faculty interactions, and propose a classification system.

Cole (1999) and Cole and Anaya (in progress) identified four types of student-faculty interactions reported by African American and White undergraduates. First, a student engages in general contact with a professor. Generally, students seek information or advice—for example, they may request course information or discuss coursework. The second form of interactions focuses on academics. In this type of interaction a student and professor might discuss a critique of coursework, writing assignments, or class-papers. This interaction is class-specific and project-focused, emerging primarily from faculty feedback. The third type is primary-interpersonal interactions in which a student spends time with a professor socializing, having coffee, coke, or snacks, or discussing the student's personal problems and career ambitions, or they may be interactions resulting from student collaboration with faculty research projects. This latter form of interaction suggests a student-faculty relationship that extends well beyond academic issues, is more interpersonally engaging, and is likely to be initiated and definitely encouraged by the professor.

The last aspect is a student's perception of the quality of student-faculty interactions; it reflects student satisfaction with faculty contact and relationships. Students assess the quality of faculty contact regardless of the type of contact experienced. Thus, students who only experience general contact with professors may be as satisfied with their faculty relations as students who have had primary-interpersonal faculty contact. In the next section we discuss the potential impact of a variety of student-faculty interactions on the academic achievement of Latina/o students.

Latina/o Student Achievement

A recent cross-sectional study of Latina/o undergraduates attending thirty different colleges across the country examined the potential influence of a variety of student-faculty interactions on academic achievement (Anaya and Cole, 2001). Student interactions with their professors were characterized as (1) general, (2) academically related, and (3) primary-interpersonal contact. As in earlier studies, 36% of the students reported frequent and brief after-class interactions with their professors. This general yet purposeful contact can be a precursor to more meaningful and rewarding interpersonal interactions. General interactions occur most frequently, followed by student-faculty interactions of an academic nature. As might be expected, primary-interpersonal interactions occur least frequently. In fact, even the academically oriented interactions reported by Latina/o students were rather superficial, most often regarding general course information and less often involving in depth discussion of the student's work. Finally, with respect to more meaningful student-faculty interactions, very few students (less than 20%) reported primary-interpersonal interactions. The authors attributed the low rate of these interactions to the fact that 46% of the Latina/o students in this study see their professors as neutral, and 12% see them as remote and unsympathetic (as opposed to approachable and helpful). The data from this study is consistent with studies reporting that minority students experience constrained or unsatisfactory interactions with faculty (Arnold, 1993; Fleming, 1984; Feagin, Vera, & Imani, 1996; Hurtado, 1994; Turner, 1994). This may be due, in part, to interracial and cross-cultural aspects of the student-faculty interactions of Latina/o students. Unfortunately, Rendón and Valadez (1993) have noted faculty resistance to structural and psychological changes that might enhance cultural understanding and possibly accommodate culturally diverse student populations.

The second part of the study examined the potential impact of student characteristics, educational environments, and faculty on Latina/o student achievement (Anaya and Cole, 2001). While the focus of this chapter is on the role that faculty can play in enhancing student achievement, it is prudent to acknowledge that student characteristics such as background, motivation, and behavior can play a significant role. For example, having college-educated parents, having high educational plans, and the amount of time spent on school-work contribute to achievement. However, the latter student factor, academic behavior, has the greatest impact of the three (Anaya and Cole, 2001). Also an important consideration is the educational environment. The type of college attended by a student provides a general indicator of the educational environment, as does the student's major. For example, students attending research universities tend to have lower college grades than those attending doctoral-granting colleges and comprehensive colleges. Additionally, research on college students has consistently shown that many educational benefits ensue from living on campus (Astin, 1993; Pascarella & Terenzini, 1991). However,

Anaya and Cole (2001) reported that Latina/o students living on campus obtained no academic advantages (63% of the students in the study lived on campus). Thus, in the study on Latina/o student achievement, the researchers took these factors into account before examining the impact of contact with faculty.

Anaya and Cole (2001) incorporated ten measures of student-faculty interactions in the study to determine what, if any, influence there might be on student achievement as measured by undergraduate GPA. After controlling for student characteristics, seven of the student-faculty interaction measures were statistically significant. However, once campus factors were also taken into account, only three of the measures were significant. In other words, if student factors are equal (motivation, behaviors, etc.), seven of the student-faculty interaction measures are associated with academic achievement, suggesting that professors influence the academic performance of all students. College environments (experiences and activities) also contribute to student perform-ance, thus their influence is also taken into account. And, after taking both student and college influences into account three student-faculty interaction measures remained statistically significant: (1) visited informally after class with a professor, (2) frequency of speaking with a professor, and (3) the stu-dent's perceptions of the quality of their relationships with professors. The authors concluded that the after-class visits are associated with student per-formance because this particular measure is moderately associated with the other interaction measures (correlations range from .3 to .5). Thus, a variety of student-faculty interactions are likely to contribute to student performance: discussing course work, working with a professor on a research project, and discussing career plans. On the other hand, the authors found minimal evi-dence that informal contact with faculty (having coke, coffee, or snacks with professors) facilitates academic achievement. However, as suggested in the lit-erature on minority college students, quality is a very important aspect of interactions with professors. Student achievement, as measured by undergrad-uate grades, is enhanced when Latina/o students perceive professors to be approachable and helpful (Anaya and Cole, 2001).

Recommendations and Summary

To the degree that the social milieu of a college campus is malleable, students, faculty, staff, and administrators can all play a critical role in maximizing stu-dent achievement by creating and facilitating activities and programs in which faculty can engage Latina/o students outside the classroom. Academic perform-ance is facilitated by environments in which students actively engage in the learning process and by those that provide learning opportunities in a variety of settings (Anaya, 1996, Cole, Sugioka, & Yamagata-Lynch, 1999). In other words, engaging students in educationally related and distinctly intellectual interactions with professors enhances student achievement. Thus, faculty and staff wishing to direct attention and energy towards student academic progress could incorporate a three-part strategy: increase and promote student-faculty interaction, provide opportunities for interactions that complement classroom learning, and attend to the quality of student-faculty interactions.

First, simply promote and increase the frequency and type of student-faculty interactions: general contact, academic interactions, and primary-interpersonal interactions. Perhaps the most common interactions are general in nature. When general contact targets the needs of Latina/o students in a culturally relevant manner, they can begin to lay the foundation for more meaningful academic and primary-interpersonal interactions. For example, professors typically participate in orientation programs. Given that a large proportion of Latina/o students are first-generation college students, the role that parents play can also be enhanced. Many of the parents of this group of Latina/o students are unaware of the expectations and demands placed on their college child. A bilingual parent track could be incorporated in orientation activities. Well-designed orientation programs can facilitate the transition of first-generation Latina/o students to college life and contribute to the academic socialization process. As Latina/o students persist beyond the first year, faculty and staff can continue to develop and implement culturally relevant programs and activities for continuing students.

A second strategic element entails interactions that complement classroom learning. Recall that the research discussed earlier indicates that Latina/o student involvement in educationally related and distinctly academic interactions with professors, rather than social interactions, promote student achievement. Academic departments and student services units can enhance students learning and achievement through academically relevant forums, debates, and workshops on international, national, regional and campus issues of interest to minority students in general and Latina/o students in particular. Careful attention should be paid to the quality of the interactions, because student achievement can also be enhanced when professors are perceived as accessible and supportive.

The third element of a three-part strategy consists of institutional and faculty efforts designed to facilitate nurturing and mutually satisfying interactions. Given that Latina/o students' interactions with faculty may be described as interracial and as cross-cultural, this may be the most challenging aspect of a deliberate strategy. The discussion in this chapter on interactions in a multiracial society provides a minute glimpse of relevant literature. Given the possibility that cultural and racial factors may contribute to the nature of students' interactions with faculty, they should be addressed and incorporated in professional development programs for White and minority faculty. Thus, under the right interpersonal circumstances the quality of Latina/o student-faculty relationships can be enhanced. As a result, fewer and fewer Latina/o college students may perceive faculty as neutral, remote, or unsympathetic. General and academic student-faculty interactions could begin to be much more mutually satisfying. Primary-interpersonal interactions could thus be more readily facilitated through, for example, Latina/o-oriented tournaments, field days, and collaborative student-faculty research programs (sponsored or hosted by academic units, cultural centers, Latina/o student organizations, residence halls, or student unions). The research on the academic performance and achievement of Latina/o students underscores the need for creating rewarding quality learning environments.

In tandem with policy and programs to enhance educational outcomes for Latina/o students, further research is needed to improve our understanding of their experiences and needs. Research efforts should, in addition to examining more closely the nature of student-faculty interactions, make a determination of students' perceptions of the quality of each of these interactions. More investigations are needed on individual and institutional factors that influence interracial and cross-cultural interactions. Additionally, in light of distinctly different educational performance and attainment profiles of Mexican American and Puerto Rican students (Pennock-Roman, 1990) an even closer examination of within-group differences may also prove fruitful.

In sum, although the frequency of interactions with faculty is low, Latina/o college students tend to have favorable perceptions of the faculty. At the same time, a significant portion of Latina/o students view faculty as neutral, remote, or unsympathetic. Thus, the most challenging task for faculty and staff is to increase the frequency and type of student-faculty interactions for Latina/o students while ensuring engaging and supportive interactions. The research also suggests that the role of faculty is critical if educational outcomes—academic performance, achievement, graduation—are to improve. Professors can elect to make the first move, respond to the initiative of an individual student, or to participate in formal efforts presented by administrators and student affairs professionals. In any of these permutations, the academic benefits associated with student-faculty interactions would be secured for increasing numbers of Latina/o college students.

References

Allen, W. R. (1992). The color of success: African-American college student outcomes at predominantly White and historically Black public colleges and universities. *Harvard Educational Review, 62* (1), 26–44.

Allport, G. W. (1954). *The nature of prejudice.* Cambridge: Addison-Wesley.

Anaya, G. (1992). *Cognitive development among college undergraduates.* Unpublished dissertation.

Anaya, G. (1996). College experiences and student learning: The impact of academic and non-academic activities. *Journal of College Student Development, 37*(6), 1–12.

Anaya, G. (1999). Accuracy of student-reported test scores: Are they suited for college impact assessment? *College and University: Journal of the American Association of Collegiate Registrars and Admissions Officers, 75*(1).

Anaya, G., & Cole, D. (2001). Latina/o student achievement: Exploring the influence of student-faculty interaction on college grades. *Journal of College Student Development, 42*(1), 3–14.

Arnold, K. D. (1993). The fulfillment of promise: Minority valedictorians and salutatorians. *The Review of Higher Education, 16*(3), 257–283.

Astin, A. W. (1977). *Four critical years revisited.* San Francisco: Jossey-Bass.

Astin, A. W. (1993). *What matters in college? Four critical years revisited.* San Francisco: Jossey-Bass.

Cole, D. G. (1999). *Faculty-student interactions of African American and White college students at predominantly White institutions.* Unpublished doctoral dissertation, Indiana University, Bloomington.

Cole, D., & Anaya, G. (in progress). *Exploring distinctions in types of faculty-student interactions of African American and White college students.*

Cole, D., Sugioka, H., & Yamagata-Lynch, L. (1999). Supportive classroom environments for creativity in higher education. *Journal of Creative Behavior, 33*(4), 277–293.

Cross, W. E., Jr. (1987). A two-factor theory of Black identity: Implications for the study of identity development in minority children. In J. S. Phinney & M. J. Rotherman (Eds.), *Children's Ethnic Socialization: Pluralism and Development.* Newbury Park, CA: Sage Publications.

Davis, R. B. (1991). Social support networks and undergraduate student academic-success-related outcomes: A comparison of Black students on Black and White campuses. In Allen, W. R., Epps, E. G., & Haniff, N. Z. (Eds.), *College in Black and White: African American students in predominantly White and historically Black public universities.* Albany, NY: State University Press of New York.

de Anda, D. (1984). Bicultural socialization: Factors affecting the minority experience. *Social Work, 39*(2), 101–107.

Devarics, C. (2000). Hispanic serving institutions make impressive strides. *Black Issues in Higher Education.* Sept. 28, 32–35.

Endo, J., & Harpel, R. (1982). The effect of student-faculty interaction on students' educational outcomes. *Research in Higher Education, 16*(2), 115–138.

Feagin, J. R., Vera, H., & Imani, N. (1996). *The agony of education: Black students at White colleges and universities.* New York: Routledge.

Fleming, J. (1984). *Black in college.* San Francisco: Jossey-Bass.

Garza & Lipton (1982). Theoretical perspectives on Chicano personality development. *Hispanic Journal of Behavioral Sciences, 4*(4), 407–32.

Hall, W. S., Cross, W. E., Jr., & Freedle, R. (1972). Stages in the development of Black awareness: An exploratory study. In R. L. Jones (Ed.), *Black Psychology.* New York: Harper and Row.

Helms, J. E. (1985). Toward a theoretical explanation of the effects of race on counseling: A Black and White model. *The Counseling Psychologist, 12*(4), 153–165.

Helms, J. E. (1990). *Black and White facial identity: Theory, research, and practice.* J. E. Helms (Ed.). New York: Greenwood Press.

Hurtado, S. (1994). The institutional climate for talented Latino students. *Research in Higher Education, 35*(1), 21–41.

Keefe, S. E., & Padilla, A. M. (1987). *Chicano Ethnicity.* Albuquerque: University of New Mexico Press.

Kraft, C. L. (1991). What makes a successful black student on a predominantly white campus? *American Educational Research Journal, 28*(2), 423–443.

Mayo, J. R., Murguía, E., & Padilla, R. V. (1995). Social integration and academic performance among minority university students. *Journal of College Student Development, 36*(6), 542–552.

Nora, A., & Rendón, L. I. (1990). Determinants of predisposition to transfer among community college students. *Research in Higher Education, 31*(3), 235–255.

Pascarella, E. T. (1980). Student-Faculty informal contact and college outcomes. *Review of Educational Research, 50*(Winter), 545–595.

Pascarella, E. T., & Terenzini, P. T. (1991). *How college affects students.* San Francisco: Jossey-Bass.

Pascarella, E., Terenzini, P., & Hibel, J. (1978). Student-faculty interactional settings and their relationship to predicted academic performance. *Journal of Higher Education, 49,* 450–463.

Pennock-Roman, M. (1990). Test validity and language background: A study of Hispanic American students at six universities. New York: College Entrance Examination Board.

Ramírez, M. III. (1977). Recognizing and understanding diversity: Multiculturalism and the Chicano movement in psychology. *Chicano psychology.* New York: Academic Press.

Rendón L. I., & Valadez, J. R. (1993). Qualitative indicators of Hispanic student transfer. *Community College Review, 20*(4), 27–37.

Terenzini, P. T., & Wright, T. M. (1987). Influences on students' academic growth during four years of college. *Research in Higher Education, 26*(2), 161–179.

Turner, C. S. (1994). Guests in someone else's house: Students of color. *The Review of Higher Education, 17*(4), 355–370.

Wilds, J. D., & Wilson, R. (1998). *Minorities in higher education: Twelfth annual status report on minorities in higher education.* Washington, DC: American Council on Education.

PART TWO

STUDENT VOICES

Raymond "Ramón" Herrera

Raymond "Ramón" Herrera is a Ph.D. candidate in counseling psychology at Washington State University. He is also the academic coordinator for the McNair Achievement Program. He earned his masters in counseling and has worked extensively in the area of Multicultural Student Services. He is the past coordinator of the Multicultural Student Mentor Program, a program recognized nationally for its innovative approaches to retaining students of color in higher education.

6

NOTES FROM A LATINO GRADUATE STUDENT AT A PREDOMINANTLY WHITE UNIVERSITY

Raymond "Ramón" Herrera

We will change the academy, even as the academy changes us. And more and more of us will experience academic success—with few, if any regrets.

—Laura Rendón, 1992

The Four Choices

I'd always hoped for an opportunity to tell my story of being a Latino Ph.D. student at a predominantly White university located in a rural community in the middle of a wheat field. While the experiences and perspectives are mine, it is my hope that my story will provide lessons for fellow students, faculty, and family. What I share in this chapter are some ideas about recruiting, retaining, and graduating Latino graduate students. My story is one of many, but unfortunately most go unheard.

My journey toward the Ph.D. began in the guidance counselor's office when I was in high school. However, it is not the heart-warming story of a caring counselor going above and beyond the call of duty to compassionately guide the student toward life's promises via academic and career opportunities and everyone lives happily ever after. Not close. I remember I was in fourth period (Science), and the teacher received a phone call from the counselor's office. The teacher hung up the phone and motioned me to the front of the class. As I approached him, he told me that the counselor wanted to see me right away. Upon hearing this news, my mind began to race as to what I could have possibly done wrong to warrant a visit to the counselor's office, or more likely, of what was I being wrongfully accused.

My walk to the counselor's office was silent except for the heartbeat in my ears. I walked into his office and he told me to have a seat. I still didn't know why I had been summoned. "So Ramón, what are your plans?" he asked. "For what?" He looks, apparently at me as puzzled as I felt, and said, "After you graduate?" Even though I had no plans, I was relieved when I realized that I was not in trouble. So after taking a deep breath, I remarked, "I'm not sure. Maybe I'll go to City College." Sensing my lack of conviction and assuredness about attending community college, the counselor looked at me for a long, uncomfortable moment and said, "What if I give you four choices?" I thought to myself, "Sure, probably four choices I didn't have already." I replied to him in a small, but inquisitive voice, "O.K." To this, he proudly offers, "Army, Navy, Air Force, or Marines?" Now, these four choices really caught me off guard for I had not considered the military as an option. The military seemed so foreign to me, something my grandfather did during World War II, something my father protested during the Vietnam War, but nothing me or others of my generation really considered as an option post graduation, and definitely not as a career. With my mind racing again, but this time with the romantic notions of traveling the world and getting paid to wear a slick uniform, I started to consider the military as a real possibility.

That night I went home to tell my mother about my meeting with the counselor. She reacted initially with some worry, but this worry dissolved into a sense of relief and pride that I had not seen from her in quite some time. Recently divorced and now raising three children, I knew my mother was anxious about my graduation and my future plans, or lack of, for my life after high school. She knew that the world was not a welcoming place for a young Latino without a college education or marketable skills. My new options seemed to provide an answer for her. Sensing a weight had been lifted from her shoulders and gaining her approval, I decided to join the Marines, as other Chicanos my age who enlisted in the military tended to do. The reasons for this choice seems to stem from some faulty messages we had received somewhere in our formative years, that by joining the most physically and psychologically demanding of the services, we were proving our manhood and other anglicized notions of machismo. (But that's for another chapter.)

As in many ethnically diverse schools across the country, most of the teachers and administrators at my high school were White. It was not until later did I realize that I had been tracked into a vocational path primarily because I was Latino. The guidance (or lack thereof) provided by this particular counselor is all too common. The limiting of options by this particular gatekeeper proved to be the first of many motivating factors for me to pursue a higher education in order for me to be equipped with the tools necessary to make systemic changes to institutions that have shortchanged, cut off, and even destroyed the potential of Latina/os since their founding. When I discovered that I had been had, my belief at the time was that the more education I would attain, the less I would encounter such institutional racism. (I'm still waiting for less institutional racism.)

Like many young people of color and working-poor Whites, the military provided the promise of opportunities that I would have not had otherwise. And while I did benefit from some of these opportunities, not shared with me in the television commercials or in the recruiting office was the fact that these opportunities would come with a price. And that price was staying silent when confronted with injustice, furthering the imperial practices of the good ole U.S. of A. Another potential price was losing yourself in the myths of equality of our country if you do not keep your psychological guard up. My experiences of being tracked into the military planted the seeds for me to question every social, global, and interpersonal interaction I would ever be a part of. I realized very quickly after enlisting that I did not want to make the military my life's work. It became clear that I would be spending the next four years of my young adult life in an institution that did not value the real, total me, but rather pieces of me—as in, my labor to meet its needs, my mind to solve its problems, and my skin color to improve its image. This experience would prepare me well for my pursuit of a Ph.D.

Note on the Next Generations

First-generation college students who come from migrant backgrounds and speak English as their second language have written many of the inspirational real-life stories about Latina/o college students persevering in the cold realities of academia. But that isn't my reality. That is my father's story. Even though I am a second-generation college student, who spoke English as my first language and was fortunate to not have to toil in the fields like so many do, I still experienced many of the same difficulties that first-generation Latina/o college students experienced a generation ago. I thought it was supposed to get better, easier for us. While many first-generation college students are continuing to come to the academy, there are more second-generation college students as well. This greater representation is a prime example of the increasing diversification of the Latina/o community at large, and in higher education. Yet attrition is also a prime reality for second-generation Latina/o college students in higher education. Such factors must be taken into account when attempting to recruit, retain, and graduate Latina/o graduate students.

Self-Doubt

I remember the exact moment when I found out I was accepted into the Ph.D. program. I was having lunch in the Chicana/o Latina/o Student Center at Washington State University when a professor from one of the programs I had applied to entered the Center and motioned me to come over and speak with him. My initial thoughts were, "I must have forgot something in my application packet and this will disqualify me from being considered." As I moved closer to him, he began to smile. When I was in front of him he put out his hand to shake mine and said, "Congratulations on being accepted into the program." I let out an uncharacteristic, "Oh my God!" I hugged the professor and thanked him profusely. Now, I had never been accused of being overly excited about anything, ever! But at this time and place, in the Center with a professor who came and sought me out, it just happened. So after thanking the professor, I ran outside looking for someone to tell, someone to share my good news with. Not finding anyone I knew, I was a bundle of energy and began walking through the center of campus, not sure what to do or say or how to contain myself, or even knew where I was walking to, just walking, moving, and emoting.

Shortly, self-doubt began to creep in. Maybe, they made a mistake? Maybe, they meant to admit the other Raymond Herrera? Maybe, they misread my GRE scores and as soon as they figure out my real scores they'll call me and rescind their offer? Questions like these still surface to this day. I have completed all of my coursework with a respectable grade point average. I have passed my preliminary examinations. I have earned my master's degree. I have completed my pre-doctoral internship at one of the most sought-after sites in the country. I am currently writing my dissertation. Yet, in spite of all these accomplishments, the questions and self-doubt persist. The thoughts and feeling I had when asked to write this chapter are a prime example of this. The sequence is: Elation—apprehension—self-doubt—resolve to complete (repeat often).

Accepting the Reality and Telling the Family

For a few weeks after I was notified of the wonderful news that I would be going to graduate school and earning a Ph.D., my mood was celebratory, as was the mood of those around me who had been a strong support network for me through some difficult times. I was so proud to inform my family that I was going to be a graduate student. While they had an idea that this was as good thing, they didn't really know what it meant for me or for them, particularly in terms of sacrifice, hard work, and perseverance. I remember one of my relatives saying, "Graduate school? But I thought you just graduated?"— not understanding that "graduate" now meant something different. But my father understood. He was the first in our family to go to college, and the only one to attend until myself. While congratulatory, his concerns were more pragmatic, as he asked me what type of job I could get with a degree in counseling psychology. He was concerned that I be able to provide for myself and some day a family. I knew he was proud, but I also sensed he was concerned for my future.

Hanging On to Me

Along with the anxiety, self-doubt, and lack of knowledge of the forthcoming journey, came the dynamic experience of being me, and understanding who I really am in graduate school. It has been difficult hanging on to me, because "me" keeps changing. Part of this change has been the negotiation between the two worlds that Dr. Rendón (1992) discusses in her inspiring work entitled, "From the Barrio to the Academy: Revelations of a Mexican American 'Scholarship Girl.' " A Latina graduate student gave this article to me when I was feeling particularly disillusioned about my experiences in my program and academia in general. Have you ever read something that spoke to your mind and heart and by the end of the reading you felt empowered to do anything you decided to do? For me, it has been "From the Barrio to the Academy . . . "

The changes within were apparent to my family. There was this tension between being proud of me and feeling awkward that we were living very different lives. When I would return home for the holidays, it was rejuvenating in some ways, and sad in others. I was rejuvenated with the love, foods, laughter, tears, and all things shared among families. But I was saddened because I always had to leave them, and there was a growing disparity in our education levels, views of the world, and goals for life. I did not want these things to separate us the same way the miles did. And so far, they haven't. As funny as it sounds, the physical distance has brought us closer to one another.

I was comforted by Dr. Rendón's words, knowing that I was not the first Latina/o graduate student to experience the unique challenges I have highlighted. I was inspired to continue on my journey toward the Ph.D. I believe that things happen for a reason and in this instance, I was meant to read her article at that particular point in my life so that I could keep hanging on to me.

Climbing into the Ring

The journey of this Latino graduate student at a predominantly White institution introduced unique challenges. A major factor in deciding to stay at the same institution for my graduate work was the solid financial package I was offered. This four-year package was a collaborative effort of the department, the graduate school, and the Office of Multicultural Student Services (MSS). On top of the tuition and fees being covered, I would be paid to work as a graduate assistant for MSS, coordinating a mentoring program for students of color, the same program I had the good fortune of being apart of as an undergraduate. I was excited about this work, and the expectations to produce a quality product were high. I didn't realize how much of a time commitment it would require to coordinate such an endeavor. And then there were the classes I was to take! This was a case where some academic mentoring would have been appropriate.

As for the actual coursework and academic rigor, I was not adequately prepared. It took me a while to figure out how to study, how to write, how to engage in class at the graduate level. While I did receive some wonderful mentoring in the application process, the next phase of the journey I'd have to go alone, or at least until I was able to make connection with my next mentor. I noticed that the most of the other students did not seem to be as lost or overwhelmed by the coursework. My peers seemed to be rolling along, challenged, but not overwhelmed. They talked the language of the professors, understood their jokes, and it seemed that they had known each other for years. Did I miss something? Was there an orientation session or reception that I missed? Was there a "how to" guide that I hadn't received? Later in my first semester, I attended the annual Multicultural Convocation and the keynote speaker spoke of a way of knowing that people of color were not aware of and didn't have access to. He asked, "Do you ever get that feeling in class that White students and professors know something that you don't know? You're not sure what it is but you know it's there?" I answered to myself, "all the time." The language was different, the humor was different, and the praise was different. It felt like I was witnessing the class taking place, but not included as a rightful participant.

The heavy load of graduate work and the challenge of coordinating a program really tested my resilience and my belief in myself. Self-doubt has been so close by that it should have received admittance into the program as well;

it was everywhere I turned. It was apparent rather quickly that the farther I was to go in higher education, the fewer Latina/os there would be. Why was I chosen to continue? What was it about me that set me apart from others? Again, I was feeling like the program maybe had made a mistake in admitting me. As I talked with other students of color in my program about what I was experiencing, they communicated that they were having many of these same thoughts and feelings. Thinking that we were going to be discovered as frauds, I felt we did not belong. The imposter phenomenon is defined as the internal experience of intellectual phoniness (Clarence & Imes, 1978). Now, I didn't feel phony, but I did feel there was so much I needed to learn before I would be academically on par with my White counterparts. I also felt a pressure of being the representative for the entire Latina/o community. This pressure did not appear because of some official appointment by the governor or because I had been voted in by the community. But it was implied. Particularly when professors would ask me, "So Ramón, how does the Latina/o community view this particular issue?" Now, all eyes were on me.

Exacerbating this self-doubt and pressure to represent my entire ethnic group were rumblings among some White students in the program that I was admitted into the program primarily because I was Latino and not for my intellectual capabilities, nor my potential to be an effective counseling psychologist. While my program has done and excellent job in recruiting and retaining graduate students of color, the climate in classes and around the program still needs a great deal of work. Numbers are one thing, but the quality of the experience for those students who are admitted is quite another.

With so many factors contributing to my graduate experience, the novelty of attending class faded quickly. Each time I would go to class, I felt like I was climbing into a boxing ring, about to do battle. Going to class with your fists up takes a great deal of energy. One of the factors that kept me in the system was the supportive people who love and care for me and wanted me to succeed. This support network has been invaluable. It's a cliché, but I would not be here without them—literally! Like those folks in a boxer's corner who each have their function—a trainer, a cut man, a dietician, and a masseuse—all there for me to be my best. No one does it alone. When I win, we all win.

Attending a predominantly White university presents other challenges outside of the classroom. If you put yourself out there as someone who is committed to transforming the institution, you will most likely be called upon to serve on various task forces, search committees, advisory boards, etc. Initially, I was flattered to be asked to serve in these capacities, but the lesson learned here was that time and energy are precious commodities and if you don't guard them vigilantly, they will dissipate. Before agreeing to write this chapter

I had to do a cost/benefit analysis with my time and energy. I am grateful and blessed to have been asked to participate in this publication, but it is yet another responsibility.

Something that I did not expect to happen to me as a result of attending a predominantly White university is that I've learned more about Chicanismo and indigenous ways than when I lived in the very diverse San Francisco Bay Area. One reason for this is that for most students, college in general is a time of self-discovery. But for myself, being isolated away from a Chicano community, from family, and from everything other than the culture of a rural White university and farming community, left me longing for things that I had previously taken for granted. While traditions, music, and foods became more important to me, what I missed dearly were the cultural ways of my home community—e.g., familismo, personalismo, and collectivism—and being able to get lost and become inconspicuous in a large crowd of people of color.

A result of this yearning for culture was my assisting in the organizing of CAMARADAS, a Chicana/o Latina/o graduate student association. As I and other Latina/o graduate students spoke to one another across campus, three themes seemed to resonate for all of us:

1. A need for a social support network
2. A need for mentoring (for ourselves and for undergraduates)
3. A need for graduate students to be proactive on behalf of the Latina/o community on campus and around the state

While my journey may not have been a smooth ride, I was saddened to hear of others who had it much worse than I did in their programs. Many of the founding members of CAMARADAS were pushed out of their programs and sought refuge in other, less destructive ones.

My experience is directly connected to and influenced by the experience of others. If they are suffering, I can feel it too. If they succeed, I also feel a sense of accomplishment. The academic world is individualistic and this does not lend itself well to those who identify with community first. This idea of being responsible for others is often looked upon by faculty and even many graduate students as a weakness, as being co-dependent, and not in the best interests of anyone involved. Many CAMARADAS did not share with their programs that they were members of the group out of fear that they would be "advised" to quit the group due to time constraints. The programs failed to recognize that CAMARADAS was the best retention effort being made at the university for Latina/o graduate students. And, the students were doing it themselves. We kept each other in graduate school.

Unfortunately, there was a consequence to maintaining my support network. This newfound sense of belonging and connection with other Latina/o graduate students took time and energy from my academic work. I was receiving the support and validation in CAMARADAS that I was not receiving from my program. I wanted to spend time with my new network of friends, share meals and stories of home. They provided me with the Latina/o vitamins and minerals that kept my mind, body, and spirit healthy. In her chapter, Mentoring Chicana/o and Latina/o Students for Careers in Academia: From CAMARADAS to Encuentros, Lucila Loera (2000) eloquently states:

> Although these experiences develop interpersonal, leadership and communication skills, and while they can be psychologically and spiritually invigorating, these multiple roles and responsibilities often take their toll, as academics and other areas suffer. (p. 19)

It became apparent to at least one faculty member on campus that I was dedicating some of my resources to activities outside of my studies. In his effort to provide guidance, he implied that I needed to spend more time with my head in the books and less time with student organizations and other social happenings as this involvement might jeopardize my retention in the program. From my perspective, the opposite was true. I believe that it is because of these extracurricular endeavors that I am still in graduate school, for they provided me (and continue to do so) what I needed to sustain myself in a department that is devoid of these elements. Although the organization is currently in hiatus, I have experienced so many wonderful things, have made lifelong relationships, and learned about myself in ways than I ever imagined. My fellow Latina/o graduate students and CAMARADAS alumni who are new professors provide me with a great sense of pride and hope that I need to continue and to finish.

Notes on Recruitment, Retention, and Graduation

My experiences are not unique. There have been many who have come before me, and more who will follow me (hopefully, many more). Reliving these hard lessons, I have considered some ways in which my experience could have been smoother, more fulfilling, better at instilling hope and preparing for life after graduate school. Many of these suggestions are centered on promoting a healthier program climate and providing a genuinely nurturing environment for students to prosper. I recognize that there are financial and logistical considerations that could hinder the implementation of some of these proposals.

Some are as simple and basic (and inexpensive) as a phone call or even an e-mail to check in with a student. Others present logistical difficulties or have monetary costs attached. But, as they say in medicine, "an ounce of prevention . . . "

The best recruitment tools you can have are the students who are currently in your program. If the students are constructively challenged, valued for their intellectual perspectives, and genuinely appreciated for their multicultural experiences, they will speak highly of the program and all of its great offerings to prospective students. While a solid financial package is extremely attractive in recruiting students, money alone will not get students through. I think many programs make the assumption that if a student is funded, is passing classes, and making progress toward his or her degree, that there is nothing left to attend to. Not at all close. A student can have all of these, but still feel unvalued, used, and unfulfilled. This will be communicated to those prospective students, as well. Students will speak the truth to other students.

Recruitment, Retention and Mentorship

Like many Latina/o students around the country, they were seen as competent members of their respective graduate cohorts, but not as future colleagues who were worthy of the mentorship needed to ensure those futures. (Pizarro, 2000, p. 10)

Of all the factors associated with the recruitment, retention and graduation of Latina/o graduate students, I consider mentoring to be the most critical. Many of my fellow Latina/o graduate students comment on how important a good mentor, a bad mentor, or no mentor is to their persistence and degree completion. I witnessed other students being mentored almost immediately after admittance into programs. Mentorship often takes the form of the student being invited to be a member of a research team, attending conferences with faculty, and being introduced to others in the field who have similar research interests. These are just some of the mentoring activities that can propel students toward careers they would have not had otherwise.

With mentoring, as with all relationships, communication is crucial. The faculty mentor/graduate student dynamic can be intimidating to the student at times and may not always lend itself to open lines of communication. It is the responsibility of both parties involved to ensure that these lines remain open and mutually useful. However, the mentor, given her/his position of authority, should make the initial and ongoing genuine efforts to create a comfortable space for the relationship to begin and grow.

After much struggle, I recognized that I needed to seek mentoring from outside of my program. I have been fortunate to meet a number of Latina/o and non-Latina/o faculty at conferences, meetings, and on internship who have offered to help me in any way they could to ensure that I complete my degree. Mentoring goes beyond the nuts and bolts of academic writing, but into all facets of being a Ph.D. candidate and beyond. As I get closer to graduation, it becomes more apparent that being politically savvy can do wonders for a career in academia. I've seen this, but I've also had this explained to me by a faculty member from another institution. Financial management is another area I've received some guidance in. All of this is mentoring. The knowledge you need to thrive as a professional that is not taught in the classroom is often transmitted through mentoring. When the time comes, I will be sure to return the favor by offering to mentor graduate students who need the compassionate guidance necessary to finish their degree and move into their careers more smoothly.

Notes to Fellow Graduate Students

It sounds like a lot of gloom and doom, but it has also been rewarding. When times are the toughest, I draw upon my life experiences before coming to graduate school, and then things do not seem so bad. Here are a few things to keep in mind:

- Be protective of your time and commitments, but do not be selfish. When I was an undergraduate, I knew of a few Latina/o graduate students on campus but was never afforded the opportunity to learn from them. I spent a great deal of time at the Chicana/o Latina/o Student Center and rarely saw a graduate student come into the center, let alone interact with undergraduates. This could have been because of time limitations or because they wanted to maintain some professional distance (they may have been the instructors for some undergraduates). However, your interaction with undergraduates will have a profound effect on them and on yourself. You will be modeling for undergraduates that Latinas/os do indeed go to graduate school and succeed, and in turn, you will be re-energized by their enthusiasm and willingness to better themselves by continuing their education. A little mentoring of undergraduates by a graduate student can go a very long way for all parties involved.

- Self-assessment at different times in your program is a must. At some point you have to ask yourself, "Is this what I really want to do, my passion? Can this program deliver what it said it can, at least to a minimal degree?" You may realize that your passion lies in another field of study and may ask yourself, "Do I really want to go to law school?" Better to figure it out and plan accordingly than to suffer through a program you're unhappy with.

- There will be a time when you are seen as a veteran graduate student in your program. You may be asked to help orient new graduate students to the program. It is your responsibility to offer your knowledge and past experiences to those coming behind you. Be honest about your program. Talk about its strengths, and its areas for growth. Every program has both.

- Get mentoring where you can. Talking with other Latina/o graduate students has convinced me that mentoring is in short supply. Having multiple mentors may be ideal. One mentor may not meet all of your needs and you may have to seek others away from you program to provide you with what you are looking for. Conferences and other large meetings are great for meeting faculty and establishing mentor/mentee relationships.

- Graduate. We are needed desperately by our community and society at large.

Notes to Undergraduates

- If you have remotely considered graduate school, consider it more, resolve to apply, and bring a friend along. Like a friend of mine once said, "If Ramón can make it, anyone can." While humorous, there is truth in this statement. If you haven't been told yet, you are capable, you are deserving of the opportunity, and you are needed in graduate school.

- Participate in programs that will prepare you for graduate school, such as the Ronald E. McNair Achievement Program (Trio). It is never too early to start thinking and preparing for graduate school. We had a saying in the Marines, "The more you sweat in peace time, the less you bleed in war." Gruesome, but the message gets to the point.

- When researching graduate programs, talk with current and former students of the program to get a more complete picture of the program. Graduate colleges and program faculty, while perhaps well-intentioned, may exert more energy and dedicate more resources to the recruitment aspect of the triad, and not so much to the other two prongs—the quality of retention efforts and ensuring that students graduate.

- When you see Latina/o graduate students on campus, inquire about their program, their progress, and what they do for fun. If they seem tired, stressed out, and/or in a hurry, give them some encouragement to continue to do well. Ask them about applying to graduate school, ask for whatever advice they can give you.

- Take the time to explain to your family what you are about to undertake when you become a graduate student. For many families, your undergraduate graduation means not only that you have finished college, but also that you will be returning home to them (if indeed you moved from home to attend school). Take time in preparing them for possibly being away for a few more years. Highlight for them the benefits of graduate school.

Notes to Family and the Support Network

- Please be patient with us. Provide us the love and support (and cooking) that only you can. You may not always understand what we're talking about because I know we don't, but that's ok. Listen and provide the encouragement and cariño that has sustained us for this long. Ask questions about what we're doing. Stay in contact with us. Learn how to use e-mail. Visit us at least once if you can.

- Spouses, fiancés, partners, and good friends: this will be a challenging time. As I'm sure you're aware, the rates of divorce and relationship breakup during graduate school are very high. The nature of the relationship will change given the time and energy required of graduate study. But, loving, nurturing, and fulfilling relationships are possible (and I can vouch for this. Thank you, Lulu.).

Notes to Faculty and Program Administrators

- Be honest about what you can offer, who you are, and your limitations. If mentoring is not your strength, provide the student with this truth so that she/he can seek others who can fulfill these needs. Many students, like me, won't know to ask about mentoring and assume that mentoring is a formalized function of the program and will wait to be assigned a mentor. I waited for a faculty member to approach me, and I'm still waiting. Refer and defer to others when you can't offer what the student needs or wants. A team mentoring approach can be very rewarding for all parties involved. Advising is not the same as mentoring. If you meet with your student once or twice a semester to see if he/she registered for classes, that is not mentoring.

- It is important to recognize the heterogeneity among Latina/os. It is important that these variations are seen as complimentary, not as an inconvenience. This is not to be confused with the corporate notions of "kumbaya" multiculturalism, which are too often adopted by universities as a way to solve a problem, but in fact trivialize our complexities, as individuals and as a group.

- As long as going to graduate school costs money, funding will always be an issue. Let's move beyond the short-term solutions of providing a full ride for the first year only to leave the student scrambling to stay in school for the remaining years.

- Recruit more recent Latina/o graduates to become faculty in your program. The excuse "there aren't any out there" is a myth. I see and know of many who want to diversify graduate programs but are not afforded the opportunities.

What Next?

My partner and I half-jokingly sing through our apartment the love song from the Broadway musical, West Side Story, "There's a place for us, somewhere a place for us." I say "half-jokingly," because we often feel like there really isn't a place for us after I graduate. I pursued a graduate degree in large part to afford myself more choices in life, including where to live. But no place really jumps out at me as a welcoming, hospitable place to work, live, play, and raise a family. Being at a predominantly White university for so long has taken its toll on my soul. It has been difficult to say the least, but I have made it this far and will continue until the completion of all requirements for the degree of doctor of philosophy. Nietzsche said, "What does not kill me makes me stronger." I am strong today. With my hard work, my folks in my corner, and my adopted mentors, there is no stopping this Latino Ph.D. candidate. Next stop—graduation day. And you're all invited to attend.

References

Clarence, P. R., Imes, S. A., (1978). The imposter phenomenon in high achieving women: Dynamics and therapeutic intervention. *Psychotherapy: Theory, Research, and Practice, 15*, 241–247.

González, K. P., Marin, P., Pérez, L. X., Figueroa, M. A., Moreno, J. F., & Navia, C. N. (2002). Understanding the nature and context of Latina/o doctoral student experiences. *Journal of College Student Development, 42*, 563–579.

Loera, L. (2000). Mentoring Chicana/o and Latina/o students for careers in academia: from CAMARADAS to Encuentros. In Pizarro, M. (Ed.), *Chicana/o and Latina/o Studies for the 21st Century: New Perspectives on Mentorship and Research (pp. 17–26)*. Pullman, WA: Washington State University.

Pizarro, M. (2000). The encuentros series: Chicano/Latino empowerment from theory to praxis. In Pizarro, M. (Ed.), *Chicana/o and Latina/o Studies for the 21st century: New Perspectives on Mentorship and Research (pp. 9–15)*. Pullman, WA: Washington State University.

Rendón, L. I., (1992). From the barrio to the academy: Revelations of a Mexican American "scholarship girl." *New Directions for Community Colleges, 20*, 55–64.

Veronica Orozco

Veronica Orozco received her B.A. in Psychology from the University of California, Irvine, in 2002 and is currently a graduate student in the Counseling Psychology Department at the Ohio State University. Her research interests are aligned with issues affecting the Latino population. For example, as a McNair research scholar, she investigated Latino scores on the MMPI-2, specifically, the validity of the Hypochondriasis (HS) scale among Latino college students. As a student in the Honors in Psychology Program, her senior thesis entitled "Latinas' Well-being in Higher Education: Navigating Their Educational Challenges," which examined the coping strategies most commonly employed by Latina undergraduate students to overcome their challenges in higher education. Upon graduation, she was awarded the Order of Merit Service Award for her involvement in the community.

7

LATINAS AND THE UNDERGRADUATE EXPERIENCE

¡NO ESTAMOS SOLAS!

Veronica Orozco

When I first came to the university, I was uncertain of myself and whether I could succeed. I wondered if I could manage the cultural and social challenges of the academy. I wondered if I could succeed in a way that would make my family and me proud. I often wondered if I was alone in my questions and uncertainty.

In this chapter, some of the psychological, social, and cultural factors affecting Latinas and their undergraduate experiences at institutions of higher education will be introduced. In doing so, I will share my story as a Mexican American female pursuing higher education, referring to those experiences that have facilitated my success or have impeded my progress. Additionally, literature pertaining to experiences of Latinas in higher education that parallel my personal experience will be integrated into this narrative.

Latino and Latina Student Experiences in the United States

Latinos and Latinas will represent the largest minority group in the United States in 2010 (Haro, Rodríguez, & Gonzáles, 1994), nonetheless, they are underrepresented in institutions of higher education (Zea, Jarama, & Bianchi, 1995). The number of students enrolling in American colleges is consistently increasing, yet the number of students obtaining a degree before leaving college is decreasing, particularly among minority students (Strage, 1999). The Chronicle of Higher Education Almanac (1997) additionally illustrates the declining number of Latino students pursuing higher education, with the number of Latina students decreasing. Interestingly, Latinas earn better grades in college, but their persistence to graduation is lower than their male counterparts (Gloria, 1997; Vasquez, 1982).

Remembering Where I Come From

As a first-generation Mexican American female, I had the experience of living in both the United States and my parents' homeland. As a consequence of living in Mexico for seven years, I was immersed in the Mexican culture. Spanish is my native tongue and it was in Michoacán, Mexico, that I engaged in the typical daily routines of a townsperson, which included hand-making tortillas and tending farm animals. To the townspeople of San Lorenzo, obtaining a higher education was a rare, if not unheard of, occurrence. For example, my mother's formal education ends at first grade and my father never went to school.

Accordingly, I resigned myself to the idea of conforming to the standards of my community, which included limited education, marriage, and a family. In fact, I did not question the norm and I envisioned myself married at a young age, with a limited education, and children. To my surprise, in 1988 my family moved to the United States hoping to lead a comfortable life; this gave me the opportunity to obtain an education. Although unsure of the educational process, my parents knew they did not want me breaking my back working the fields as they had done. Much like the findings of Quintana, Vogel, and Ybarra (1991), my parents understood the value of a college degree, in particular to secure a well-paying job.

Coming from a traditional working-class family and living in a city overwhelmed by gang influences, there were already several circumstances that were working against my advancement in the United States; I did not speak a word of English, and I lived in an inner-city community, in poverty. In addition, despite my parents understanding the value of an education, they did not understand its demands. Given the circumstances of having parents of low educational levels, occupational positions, and income, it has been proposed that students are more likely to perform poorly in academics (Vásquez, 1982), and as a result do not persist to graduation. In direct contrast, it was those same circumstances that fueled my desire to persevere—to live the "American Dream," to live in a safer community, and to help my parents economically.

A Newfound Opportunity

College was never spoken of at home. It was an opportunity that neither my parents nor I knew about. As a result, going to college never crossed my mind. It wasn't until my oldest brother left for college that I felt I had a chance. The consideration that weighed most heavily for me, however, was whether I would leave home to go away to college. The traditional Latino culture is family and community oriented, where the collective and not the individual is stressed (Quevedo-García, 1987). Consequently, major life decisions, such as college attendance, are made with the consent of family members (Quevedo-García, 1987). Accordingly, if I did anything or went anywhere, it was with the consent of my parents. As a female, they also consistently advised me to learn how to cook and clean so I could appropriately provide for a husband and family.

Because Chicanas (Mexican American females) are often the first generation to enter higher education, they often experience stresses as a result of sex-role conflicts (Gloria, 1997; Vásquez, 1982). The traditionally high value placed on family often produces a struggle between pursuing education and the traditional roles of wife and mother, which may result in additional educational stress. Not only did I have specific gender roles to fulfill at home, but as a female, the idea of leaving the household before marriage was considered highly unacceptable. Yet there I was, considering the "culturally unacceptable" event of leaving home for school.

Although I never directly asked my parents for permission to go to college (an event that was contrary to what I had been used to), I knew that if they said that college was not an option or that I could not go, I would not attend. As I began sending out completed college applications, my parents were unaware of what I was doing. Acceptance letters from different colleges began coming and I told my parents, but they did not understand what it meant. I told my parents I was going away to school and in disbelief my mother said, "*Dios que te acompañe*" (May God bless you). When I told her I was going to study in Indiana, however, in her astonishment she objected, "*No, no te vayas hasta allá. ¿Qué vas a hacer tan lejos?*" (No, don't go all the way over there. What are you going to do so far away?) Although she had no idea where Indiana was, she knew it was not California.

My father advised me to attend the University of California, Irvine (UCI), not because it was a Research Type I Institution, or because of the majors offered, or because it was in keeping with my personal educational and career goals—but because my brother was there. As a female, my parents were concerned for my safety. With my brother at the same school and UCI less than one hour away from home, my family was relieved when I revealed my decision to attend my top-choice school, UCI.

I welcomed the upcoming transition to college. Having graduated from high school and feeling prepared, I was ready and willing to begin my career at a four-year university. After all, I had graduated with superior grades. Little did I know that much was about to change.

On the Verge of Dropping Out

My first year at the university was an educational catastrophe! I entered UCI as a Biological Sciences major. After a few C–, D+, and Fs, it was not only evident that my strengths were not in biology, but I realized how poorly prepared I was for college. Looking back, I realize that I am one of the many Mexican Americans students in the educational pipeline that were not adequately prepared for admittance into institutions of higher education (Kavanaugh & Retish, 1991). Accordingly, I questioned the quality of my high school education. Further affirming this realization, others cringed when I revealed which high school I attended. For example, peers jokingly asked how many tattoos I had and what was the percentile of my SAT scores—perhaps to covertly question my acceptance to UCI. Although I had no tattoos, my SAT scores were in fact poor. I was embarrassed, lost, and confused in my educational surroundings. Not knowing I could drop classes or where to go for academic guidance, I doubted my abilities to succeed educationally. After being placed on academic probation, which I remained on for the entire academic year, I finally found the academic counselors.

As if the threat of dismissal from the university was not enough, the culture shock that I experienced impacted me tremendously. This shock took the form of the limited ethnic minority representation on campus. My high school was mostly made up of minorities, with Latinos representing the largest proportion. In my new university setting, however, Latinos represented approximately 12% of the student population. The most recent student data report indicates that in January 2001, Latino undergraduate students represent 11.5% of the total UCI undergraduate population (Common Data Set for UC Irvine, 2001; 2,045 out of 17,723). As a result, I actively looked for other students who physically appeared Latino. Although I did not necessarily interact with them (e.g., talk with them), their presence comforted me.

It was the lack of a sense of connection, of having numerical representation, and an environment in which I was visible and comfortable that also added to my culture shock. In considering minority dropout rates, the issue of campus climate is a central and informative issue (Hurtado & Carter, 1997; Gloria & Rodriguez, 2000). Campus climate refers to the academic, social, and interpersonal comfort experienced by racial and ethnic minorities on university or college campuses. Although campus climates can be both positive and negative, it is most often the negative influences that serve to alienate or isolate Latino students from the mainstream of campus life (Green, 1988). This alienation often serves as a one of the primary reasons for not remaining in school. I too encountered some of the same experiences, feeling alone and unwelcomed.

Family

Adding to my sense of alienation in higher education were my interactions with my parents about my educational experiences. My parents knew that my grades were awful. However, given their educational levels, it was difficult for them to provide the kind of support that I needed from them with regard to my education (Kavanaugh & Retish, 1991). They did not understand the repercussions of my grades and I really wished that they did. In order for my mother to understand the effect of a 'minus' on a grade, I would explain to her that a C– was like a D. Also, when I showed her my graded tests with big red Fs she would simply tell me to try to do better. Although I wanted and needed more advice, I knew it was the best and only advice she could offer. Throughout high school, I longed to be commended for my educational success. Now in college, I longed to be reprimanded by them for the lack of success; I wanted to be able to share my experience with them.

To my dismay, family and school were two separate entities; like water and oil, they never mixed—they seemed to repel one another. If parents are unaware of the demands and workings of the educational system, they often are unable to value their children's efforts or provide the type of support and encouragement needed to influence goal achievement and academic attainment (Gloria, 1997). This same phenomenon was happening for me. Although it was difficult to accept that my parents were unable to be involved in my academic life as much as I would have wanted and needed them to be, I understood that we had different appreciation levels and understanding of academics. Regardless of their limited involvement, it was of most importance that they did not discourage my efforts.

Emotionally, my parents did not know I felt alone and alienated and that my feelings were intensified when I could not go home because of the demands of my schoolwork. As a result of trying to manage my family and school demands, I was unmotivated and I very much disliked my situation. Because I realized that it had been my choice to pursue higher education, despite its being different from what I was accustomed to, I refused to give up. When my parents visited me in the dorms and brought *carnitas* (fried pork meat) with jalapeño chili peppers and warm tortillas, it was then that I knew they cared—and that was reinforcing of me to stay in school.

The various academic, work, and social responsibilities prevented me from often returning home to visit. The White cultural values of rigid schedules, a competitive nature, individual achievement, autonomy, although not universally accepted (Ponterotto, 1990), were clearly reflected in the university and I had no option but to abide by them. My parents too now acknowledged the demands of school and waited for me to contact them—they rarely called me. It was when I would call my mother overwhelmed and frustrated wanting to go home, that she would say, "*Pues vente*" (Then come), which was her way of comforting me and alleviating my desire to return home. Unfortunately, as a student, I had to neglect either my family or my studies, which was not a simple decision when I was trying to obtain an education to better my family. All I could think of were the deadlines quickly approaching, so I would postpone going home.

Determined to Stay in School

I was determined to remain at UCI. Thus, when I was assigned an African American male academic counselor, I was unwavering on making the most of the academic relationship. We met periodically; he reviewed my grades, and suggested tutoring sessions, which I sought because they were paid for by their services. Finally, I felt that someone at the university cared about my academic success or in my case, failure. At that point, I had some guidance and felt a sense of hope. Over the next two years, I concentrated solely on raising my grade point average. Soon, I discovered that my passion lied in the field of psychology; it was then that my grades escalated.

Throughout my undergraduate career, I worked. Like other Mexican American students, I mainly relied on a financial aid package, which primarily included grants and loans (Lango, 1995). Despite these monies, it was essential that I worked, knowing that my father (a mill operator) and mother (a housewife) could not provide for me financially. My work, however, conflicted with my studies in my freshman year, which has been found to negatively affect Latina students' academic progress (Lango, 1995). Once I made academics my priority and learned to manage my time, working prompted better study habits. As I realized that working too many hours could be detrimental to my grades, I rarely worked more than 12 hours a week.

In reflecting on my early educational experiences, it was my need to succeed and my desire to give my parents a better life and provide encouragement and guidance for my younger siblings that motivated me to persist in higher education. Although the road to higher education was difficult, I kept a positive outlook. For example, in comparison to my parents, I thought of myself as being fortunate for having the opportunity to better my life through education. And even though my loans kept increasing, the amounts did not deter me as I am certain that some day I will be able to repay them. Ultimately, it was my mindset of being fortunate, my sense of responsibility for my family, and the realization that my situation could be worse that impelled me to strive forward.

Acclimating to the University Through Social Support

It took me three years to emerge as the student that I knew I could be. After one year spent in failure, and two years spent marinating in academics, and university values and culture, I was finally prepared to take on challenges that had previously intimidated me and caused me to regress.

Mentorship

It was not until the summer after my junior year, when I was accepted into an intense research program at UCI, that I felt my undergraduate career began. The attention, encouragement, and guidance I received from faculty and staff, including Dr. Caesar D. Sereseres, during the Summer Academic Enrichment Program (SAEP) was critical in my involvement that following year. Most importantly, I realized faculty and social networks would support me for the rest of my undergraduate career—unlike my first academic counselor who was only temporary—and that made a great difference.

Furthermore, I procured a mentor, Dr. Jeanett Castellanos, who provided the opportunity for my intellectual growth, facilitated my advancement as an undergraduate student, and acquainted me with the organizational values, culture, specific actors, and provided advice and support. It was this type of information and faculty interaction with a Latina faculty member that allowed me to participate fully in the academy (Laden, 1999). The mentoring relationship enabled me to make connections with other supportive faculty connections, such as with Dr. Thomas A. Parham. Although I received the majority of my academic support from minority faculty, it was unnecessary for my mentor and I to have a similar racial and ethnic background in order for a productive and effective mentoring relationship to develop (Gloria & Rodríguez, 2000). Regardless of ethnic and racial backgrounds, it was the negative perceptions from faculty that somehow I lacked the determination to reach my desired educational goals that were damaging to my motivation and sense of comfort in the university. As a Mexican American female, it was clear that encouragement from parents, faculty, and peers was a significant factor in my path to succeed educationally (Vásquez, 1982).

Student Organizations

Joining a Latina-based sorority, Sigma Lambda Gamma, in which the majority of the members were Latinas, helped fill the void of not being able to visit my family. In other words, it was my way of coping being away from my family. As a Latina student also in pursuit of higher education, I quickly identified with this group. It was the dynamic interaction and identification that allowed me to persevere emotionally and psychologically in the face of adversity. Sharing my concerns regarding family and culture and struggles encountered in the university allowed me to cope. The sorority members, whom I considered my family away from home, were the single most important system in the university that provided me emotional support. Hurtado and Carter (1997) report that although students' participation increased from the second to the third year, students' sense of belonging significantly increased only when they belonged to religious organizations and to sororities and fraternities compared to non-members. I similarly found that my experience with being affiliated with a Latina sorority was beneficial.

Although I did not belong to a religious organization, prayer and faith as a means of coping was always on my mind. For example, I clearly remember and hold to a phrase that was offered by a friend, "God never gives you anything you can't handle." The saying was sufficient in easing my anger and distress at a time when both academics and my family were vying for my attention. Ultimately, learning how to cope with the various educational situations and struggles encountered throughout my undergraduate years was important as I consistently and successfully navigated college.

A Fulfilling Undergraduate Experience

Considering that my early academic career was filled with personal and academic challenges, I doubted I would graduate. Through persistence and continuous familial, peer, and faculty support, I graduated UCI with Honors in Psychology. Furthermore, I was accepted and would attend my top choice school for graduate study—The Ohio State University. That decision created a new area of potential conflicts for my family and me. My father wanted me to get a job, which would have meant quitting school. My mother did not want me to move so far away, yet she understood my ambition and did not hold me back. I realized that distance, finances, and academic responsibilities would prevent me from visiting home often, yet both my parents and I understood the sacrifice as a result of my choice to pursue higher education. Despite the distance and sacrifice, my parents supported me and my decision.

Recommendations

The transition into higher education can be a difficult and alienating one. There may exist programs targeting Latino students in general, however, I encourage early outreach programs specifically targeting incoming Latina students. Such efforts would welcome Latina students, allowing them to feel comfortable in the campus environment, with peers, faculty, and staff. Further, it would be helpful to introduce incoming Latina students to those Latinas who are currently attending the university, either through a formal or informal peer-mentoring program. Doing so would allow them to ask questions, see someone who is "succeeding," have a reference group, and have someone to "show them the ropes." Additionally, meeting Latina students would allow incoming students to inquire about more personal matters—including the balance between traditional family expectations and the pursuit of higher education. Recruitment efforts may initially work well, yet are meaningless when they are not offered consistently throughout the first year. Latina students must feel included in the university system, particularly when they are the first to attend college and have parents who have limited formal education, as they are likely to drop out of school.

Ultimately, Latina students need to be encouraged to seek a support system within the university. For example, a support group targeted for incoming Latina students can provide a comfortable and relaxed atmosphere where they can openly discuss their struggles as a result of pursuing higher education and familial influences and expectations (Gloria, 1999). Furthermore, Latina students who have been in the university can offer their support by informing them where they can find academic support services, financial aid office, and other offices commonly used. Latina students already in the university can help to ease the transition and other eminent culture shocks.

University-based efforts to retain Latina students must include family. Although typically not well-recognized by the university, family greatly influences and is of critical importance to Latina students (Gloria & Rodríguez, 2000). Therefore, in recruitment seminars and orientation programs, the family needs to be included and informed about the higher education experience. Parents may need reassurance that their daughters will be safe and taken care of at the university. Having a Spanish-speaking Latino faculty member with whom the family can communicate and have their questions answered is one way in which to reassure parents about their daughters at college. In particular, parents may need to be informed about how to support their child, especially when they have a limited education and are unable to engage with the student about their academics. When the family is involved, the encouragement and support provided is of great support for Latina students and helps them to have positive experiences and successfully complete college.

Latina students should be able to expect a fulfilling undergraduate career when they are involved in the university. A mentor can help to make the difference between a positive and negative higher education experience. Accordingly, faculty mentors are essential to a Latina's undergraduate experience. Mentors can validate their acceptance and provide the guidance and support to encourage them to succeed and further their education. Because Latina students may prefer a mentor of their ethnic/racial background, schools need to increase their efforts to hire and retain faculty/staff of Latino background.

Overall, Latina students need continual support and encouragement when higher education is a new facet in their lives. The university needs to be more attentive and involved in the needs of Latina students when they are more likely to drop out, even when their grades are better than their Latino counterparts. The university in its entirety may not be able to make one great change that will facilitate the experience of Latina students; however, modifying or creating programs for Latinas can increase retention rates and ensure a more fulfilling experience in higher education.

The Educational Journal Continues

As a result of successfully navigating and graduating with my undergraduate degree, I have a more sophisticated understanding of how to manage and cope in graduate school. Although there are aspects of undergraduate and graduate school that are substantially different, I am able to similarly mobilize my social supports of peers, faculty mentors, and connections with my family to facilitate my educational journey. As the pull between family and school continue to challenge me, I realize my ability and confidence to honor and succeed in and for both.

References

Chronicle of Higher Education: Almanac Issue. (1997, August 29), p. 23.
Common Data Set for UC Drive. (2001). http://www.oas.uci.edu/cds/

Gloria, A. M. (1997). Chicana academic persistence: Creating a university-based community. *Education & Urban Society, 30*(1), 107–121.

Gloria, A. M. (1999). Apoyando estudiantes Chicanas: Therapeutic factors in Chicana college student support groups. *Journal for Specialists in Group Work, 24*(3), 246–259.

Gloria, A. M., & Rodríguez, E. R. (2000). Counseling Latino university students: Psychosociocultural issues for consideration. *Journal of Counseling and Development, 78*(2), 145–154.

Green, M. F. (Ed.). (1988). *Minorities on Campus: A Handbook for Enhancing Diversity.* Washington, DC: American Council on Education.

Haro, R. P., Rodríguez, G. J., & Gonzáles, L. J. (1994). *Latino persistence in higher education: A 1994 survey of University of California and California State University Chicano/Latino students.* San Francisco: Latino Issues Forum.

Hurtado, S., & Carter, D. F. (1997). Effects of college transition and perceptions of the campus racial climate on Latino college students' sense of belonging. *Sociology of Education, 70*(4), 324–345.

Kavanaugh, P. C. & Retish, P. M. (1991). The Mexican-American ready for college. *Journal of Multicultural Counseling and Development, 19*, 136–144.

Laden, B. V. (1999). Socializing and mentoring college students of color: The Puente Project as an exemplary celebratory socialization model. *Peabody Journal of Education, 74*, 55–74.

Lango, D. R. (1995). Mexican American female enrollment in graduate programs: A study of the characteristics that may predict success. *Hispanic Journal of Behavioral Sciences, 17*(1), 33–48.

Ponterotto, J. G. (1990). Racial/ethnic minority and women students in higher education: A status report. *New Directions for Student Services, 52*, 45–59.

Quevedo-García, E. L. (1987). Facilitating the development of Hispanic college students. *New Directions for Student Services, 38*, 49–63.

Quintana, S. M., Vogel, M. C., & Ybarra, V. C. (1991). Meta-analysis of Latino students' adjustment in higher education. *Hispanic Journal of Behavioral Sciences, 13*(2), 155–168.

Strage, A. A. (1999). Social and academic integration and college success: Similarities and differences as a function of ethnicity and family educational background. *College Student Journal, 33*(2), 198–205.

Vásquez, M. J. T. (1982). Confronting barriers to the participation of Mexican American women in higher education. *Hispanic Journal of Behavioral Sciences, 4*(2), 147–165.

Zea, C. M., Jarama, L., & Trotta Bianchi, F. (1995). Social support and psychosocial competence: Explaining the adaptation to college of ethnically diverse students. *American Journal of Community Psychology, 23*(4), 509–531.

Sylvia Hurtado

Sylvia Hurtado, associate professor and director of the Center for the Study of Higher and Postsecondary Education, conducts research on understanding diverse college contexts for the success of diverse college students. Her roles include research and teaching at University of Michigan's Center for the Study of Higher and Postsecondary Education (since 1992).

She was a University of California Presidential Postdoctoral Fellow for the Sociology Department and research analyst for the Higher Education Research Institute and the Center for the Study of Evaluation at UCLA. Other administrative experience includes: assistant to the dean, Division of Graduate Studies and Research at the University of California, Santa Cruz (1983–1986); special assistant to the director of admissions at Massachusetts Institute of Technology (1982–1983); and assistant regional director of admissions at Princeton University (1980–1982). She obtained a Ph.D. in education from the University of California, Los Angeles (1990), an Ed.M. from Harvard Graduate School of Education (1983), and an A.B. in sociology from Princeton University (1980).

Dr. Hurtado has published articles and research reports related to her primary interest in student educational outcomes, campus climates, and diverse students in higher education. Her recent books are *Enacting Diverse Learning Environments* (Jossey-Bass, 1999), and a co-authored book entitled *Intergroup Dialogue: Deliberative Democracy in School, College, Community, and Workplace* (University of Michigan Press, 2001). She has written numerous articles on student transition to college, access, and on creating campus climates for learning among diverse peers. She also serves on the editorial boards of the *American Educational Research Journal, Journal of Higher Education* and *Sociology of Education,* and was Associate Editor of the *Review of Higher Education.*

Mark Kamimura

Mark Kamimura is a Ph.D. student in Higher Education concentrating in Public Policy at the University of Michigan, Ann Arbor. He received his Masters from Columbia University and is currently a Research Assistant for the Diverse Democracy Project. His current research interests are in the area of public policy development, and implementation, specifically looking at its affects on communities of color. He would like to explore further the triangular relationship of K–12, higher education, and public policy and the effects they have on each other, and how this affects society.

8

LATINA/O RETENTION IN FOUR-YEAR INSTITUTIONS

Sylvia Hurtado and Mark Kamimura

Of the over 1.3 million Latina/o students enrolled in higher education at the turn of the century, only 40% were enrolled in four-year institutions (NCES, 2001). This figure represents the lowest level of four-year participation of *any* of the other racial/ethnic groups in the country. The fact that Latina/os are least likely to take a direct path to the baccalaureate degree has been the case for over three decades without change. This suggests that significant attention must be devoted to educating Latina/o students in four-year colleges and universities in terms of providing access, assisting in their transition to colleges, and retention through graduation if we hope for them to achieve more advanced degrees that will ensure the economic viability and leadership needs of Latina/o communities. The purpose of this chapter is to identify some of the important principles of practice derived from educational research that will enhance Latina/o student retention at four-year institutions. Student voices are added to illustrate the principles from a recent set of focus groups collected at ten public universities in student discussions about their experiences on these campuses.

In order for Latina/o students to succeed in college, we must understand that retention is contingent on numerous structures of institutional support and student experiences in college. Many times we do not address the systematic challenges Latina/o students face when they enter higher education. The principles outlined in this next section aim to address these challenges and provide strategic directions for administrators and faculty in an effort to increase retention rates of Latina/o students at four-year colleges and universities.

Principle 1: Increase Participation Rates to Create a Latina/o Presence on Campus

The need to increase Latina/o participation is essential in order to increase the retention of Latina/os at colleges and universities. Latina/o enrollment rates in four-year institutions have not kept pace with the demographic growth of college-age Latina/os, and some argue that the gap between White and Latina/o college participation rates have actually increased in comparison to 20 years ago (Heller, 1997). It can be argued that a significant Latina/o presence on campus, or the development of a critical mass, can diminish stereotyping and provide more opportunities for students to begin to feel a sense of belonging at the institution. A study of high-achieving Latina/o students revealed that students tended to perceive a less hostile and more inclusive climate at predominantly White institutions with relatively higher Latina/o student enrollments (Hurtado, 1994). The increased representation of Latina/os and other students of color provide a community for historically underrepresented students, allowing them to develop networks of support with other Latina/os and students who share similar transition and precollegiate experiences.

Adopting aggressive recruitment strategies to increase Latina/o participation rates can result in identifying students who might otherwise not consider a four-year institution. This means that recruiting efforts need to be focused in demographically Latina/o-concentrated areas, involving counselors and parents in the application process, and coordinating with early outreach programs in high schools. Aggressive recruiting of Latina/os also must include a focus on areas of study where they remain highly underrepresented, such as engineering and science programs. In some cases, Latina/o college students can become engaged in assisting with the recruitment process to increase their representation in various fields of study.

Principle 2: Assist Students in Navigating the Institution

Once Latina/os enroll in colleges, the challenge of surviving the rigor of college-level courses and adapting to a new environment can present many obstacles. Although students have fulfilled all of the requirements of the admission process, many Latina/os have been educated in primary and secondary school systems that do not prepare them because these schools lack the resources to offer advanced placement courses, honors courses, college preparatory curricula, college counseling, or information about what to expect in college. Some colleges and universities have summer programs for incoming students from disadvantaged academic and socioeconomic backgrounds that aim to close these gaps of high school preparation. Summer Bridge programs and state-funded programs like CAMP (California Alliance for Minority Participation) bring students to campus during the summer to attend classes, live in the residence halls, and work closely with faculty, administrators, and tutors in programs they will enter in the fall. These experiences help students navigate the campus and allow them to build peer networks, as well as identify resources among faculty and administrators at an early stage of their college career.

Many colleges have adopted general student orientation programs that are geared towards all students during their first week of college or the week prior to the beginning of classes. Although these programs may be effective and helpful to the general student body, they may not sufficiently meet the needs of Latina/o students who may be the first in their family to attend college. Some colleges and universities have established student of color orientation programs or programs focused on low-income and first-generation college students that may compliment the general orientation program. These programs are foundational for students of color and specifically for Latina/o students to meet advisors, become acquainted with other Latina/o college students who can help mentor them, and become involved in Latina/o cultural organizations. Latina/os who have come from primarily segregated communities may have never experienced being "the one and only" in a classroom or have never lived in an environment where they were the only Latina/o student or person. Having programs in place that help students maintain their cultural connections can alleviate "homesickness" and provide the tools to navigate the college experience through the first year of college. Previous research has shown that culturally specific programs are sometimes viewed as more welcoming, and provide an entry point for the use of many of the general services. For example, students who participated in culturally specific support programs tended to have relatively higher interaction with faculty and more frequent use of general support services (Hurtado, Milem, Clayton-Pederson, & Allen, 1999).

The size of an institution can affect the adjustment of Latina/o students in a number of different ways. Most immediate to students' experiences is the impersonal feeling of large introductory lectures and the lack of availability of professors; simply knowing where to go or whom to approach for help can be difficult. On smaller campuses, faculty tend to be more accessible and resources/services tend to be more centralized, at least by location, but the array of available services may be more limited. At larger institutions, appropriate resources and services may be more difficult to find and the small number of faculty of color cannot always provide guidance when they have multiple demands on their time. For this reason, high quality orientation programs that are student-centered and sensitive to the needs of a multicultural population are essential. Latina/o students who reported ease in "getting to know their way around" campus and perceptions of a welcoming climate for diversity tended to have an easier time adjusting to college academically, socially, and emotionally well into the second year of college (Hurtado, Carter, & Spuler, 1996; Hurtado & Carter, 1997).

One Latino student explained the difficulty in navigating a large campus and the value of orientation programs and academic support programs targeted to assist students of color:

> There are certain people on this campus that you've got to find. It's like a needle in a haystack. When you find those certain people, they'll help you in an institution like this. They make sure you graduate. . . . I was a [Summer] Bridge [program] student and they say you can come a semester before you start freshman year. You'll take seven credits worth of classes . . . Learn everything about the University, all your little connections that you can make, before fall starts. So when you come here in the fall, when you get that two weeks off before fall starts, you walk around here as a freshman in your fall semester knowing everything. [There is] another example of how CSP [the Comprehensive Studies Program held throughout the academic year] helps you out. They take students and accelerate them compared to regular incoming freshmen.

Principle 3: Monitor Adjustment for Retention

It is one thing to recruit underrepresented students and develop orientation programs with the hope that it will increase the graduation rates of Latina/o students and other students of color, but in order for this work to be successful there needs to more consistent monitoring of student progress. This principle aims to address the issue of monitoring Latina/o student adjustment to increase retention through three components:

1. Recognize academic problems early
2. Help students manage their time and resources
3. Encourage study groups and use of academic support services

Most of the higher educational research has established that the more engaged students are with the college experience, the more likely they are to be retained through graduation (Astin, 1993; Tinto, 1993). However, devoting the necessary time to academic tasks, participating in student organizations, balancing income-producing work schedules, and acclimating to the college environment and the surrounding community can be a stressful experience. Developing programs that monitor Latina/os and other students of color provide the opportunity for advisors to direct students towards services that can work with them to address issues that may inhibit their academic progress or social development. Recognizing academic problems early may at the same time allow students to become aware of issues they are dealing with simultaneously that are resulting in negative academic outcomes. Signs of disengagement (such as low class attendance, low levels of engagement in student activities, the fact that peer advisors do not see or know the student, and missed appointments) should be a red alert that the student may be well on his or her way to withdrawing from the institution. Establishing ways to engage Latina/o students on a regular basis in such activities as study groups, peer mentoring programs, and use of academic support programs allows students to "report in" about their progress to others who care about success.

One area where program administrators can also assist students is in managing their time and resources. This may include workshops on time management to develop efficient study habits, allocating more time to certain courses than was initially anticipated based on faculty expectations, and allocating time to discuss content with peers and/or tutors to acquire mastery over course material. Small tips—such as carrying a pocket calendar to make sure appointments are not missed and that exams and paper deadlines are anticipated in advance—allow students to begin to structure their time and organize their activities. Teaching students to establish priorities and shifting emphases to accomplish academic, social, and work goals are important. Students who begin to take on responsibility for organizing major activities (e.g., Hispanic Heritage Week), also learn to plan ahead, establish long-term working goals, manage and find resources—all of which can become valuable when also applied to academic and career-related planning activities. A related area is managing financial resources (earning and spending money), something that may be new to students who have never balanced a checkbook or difficult for students who have peers with much more discretionary income.

Students' ability to pay for college expenses and financial aid difficulties can prove to be an added source of stress. Financial decisions are not only made when students choose a college but are also re-evaluated each year they attend college, with research showing that aid decisions play a key role in the choosing the types of colleges students will attend and whether they will remain in the college they have chosen (St. John, 2000). In addition, family situations can change dramatically from year to year among students from the lowest incomes. It is not surprising to learn that some Latina/o college students were valued wage-earners for family income prior to college and their role may not diminish despite the new demands of college life.

Principle 4: Build Support from Peers: "It takes one to retain one."

When Latina/o students are asked who helped them most in their transition to college, the majority refer to a friend or peer and secondarily to support staff (Hurtado, Carter, & Spuler, 1996). Since Latina/o culture relies on a familial support system, students also tended to identify the support of family members during college as important. Yet, while this personal-emotional support is necessary, many family members do not understand many of the issues students face in college. If the majority of Latina/o students come from communities and families where they are first-generation college students, then the necessary support needed to deal with challenges they face may not exist because of the lack of "college knowledge." Latina/o students who found support from their peers, especially from experienced upperclassmen rather than fellow first-year students, tended to score higher on measures of academic and social adjustment in college (Hurtado, Carter, & Spuler, 1996).

Places that foster the building of these peer mentor support systems are cultural centers, Latina/o student organizations, diverse residence halls, and student of color orientation programs. The communities that develop around the aforementioned places provide Latina/os the immediate opportunity for peer support networks within the institution. Many student affairs and academic support programs can effectively use peer mentoring programs to help retain students in college. For Latina/o students, finding and establishing new support systems is key to building problem-solving skills and solutions to issues that may arise throughout their college career. This principle is dependent on whether peers can be found and engaged at the various stages of their college careers, underlining the importance of the previous principles because without representation there will be a definite lack of peer support.

A Latino student described a peer mentoring program at a large public university:

> [The program] was overseen by administrators, but it was run by students, by undergraduates, and it's called the Student Support Transitional Program, so it's targeted to minority freshmen and low-

income White [students], so we got the whole realm [of multicultural students] in there. And every year we randomly pick 100 students from this state and we put them in the same dorm and we track them through their first year through [peer] mentoring. We offer them workshops, we give them some financial assistance, and just let them know that they have an upperclassman there, you know, that they can work with, So ever since [participating] in that program, I'm still involved with them just to track [freshmen] throughout their year.

Principle 5: Increase Communication between Racial Groups

While Latina/o students and all students adjust to the college environment, they must also learn to interact with a wide range of cultures—peers from racial/ethnic groups that are different than their own. The previous principles focused primarily on Latina/os and their specific needs. This principle addresses the interaction of Latina/o students with students of other racial/ethnic backgrounds through three methods of increasing communication between racial groups:

1. Programs that seek to change intergroup dynamics
2. Formal educational activities around race and cultural understanding
3. Activities to increase the campus knowledge of the Chicana/o-Latina/o culture

Programs that facilitate intergroup dialogue can positively impact intergroup dynamics by allowing students of different racial/ethnic backgrounds to discuss their perceptions and misconceptions of each other in an effort to better understand their different experiences (Zúñiga & Nagda, 1993). Using structured programs to facilitate this dialogue allows Latina/o students to begin communication with other student communities and, in turn, build more support and networks with other students. While majority students learn much about Latina/o students and their heritage, Latina/o students also learn about other students' experiences to better reflect on their own college experience. The ability to understand their own experiences as Latina/o students in a White majority or multicultural context gives students a new perspective to better understand their own adaptation and responses when conflict arises.

Two Latina/o students spoke about an intergroup educational experience:

One of the programs that really helped me was the Leadership 2000 Program . . . last year I went and there's gay, lesbian, Mexican, Chicano, White, Black—any kind of person goes there and talks about the issues that they have [relating to] diversity and what they don't understand. I mean, I can tell you for me that [experience] really changed my life in regards to how I treat other people and view other people.

That's a really good program. You just learn so much about people and not just learning what their culture is, but learning what kind of problems they're having to face and that kind of helps you identify with them. Because a lot of those people are like "Wait, you know what? Yeah, I have the same problem. I face those same issues every day."

The formal educational activities around race/ethnicity include courses in the curriculum that concentrate on issues that affect different racial/ethnic populations, educational programs around specific issues of race, and inclusion of race/ethnicity as a topic in the general courses (also known as "curriculum integration"). The development of these curriculum-based educational activities allows more students the opportunity to learn about the dynamic of race/ethnicity in society. Addressing issues relevant to the Latina/o population in a curricular or classroom context can provide validation for Latina/os and their experiences. It also provides an opportunity for them to learn more about their own history, continuing social problems, and rich cultural traditions that have been neglected in prior schooling.

The third component of this principle is to provide activities that increase campus knowledge of the Latina/o culture in co-curricular contexts. The majority of Latina/o students feel that students at their colleges and universities know very little about the Latina/o culture and that this is a contributing factor to racial tensions across campus (Hurtado, 1994). Efforts to educate campuses on the culture of the Latina/o community typically occur during Hispanic Heritage Month, which is mostly celebrated through food, exhibits, and guest speakers. While these celebrations organized by students are important, educators need to provide intentional educational activities and facilitate discussions that focus on many of the key issues that affect Latina/os to truly begin to educate students about the Latina/o experience.

Principle 6: Employ Faculty and Administrators as a Form of Structural Support

At public and four-year colleges and universities, administrators of color represent 15% of all professional positions, while Latina/os only represent about 2.9%; for faculty of color they represent 14.5% of all research and instructional positions with Latina/os holding only 2.5% of these positions (NCES, 2001). The numbers of faculty and administrators who are Latina/o are keeping pace with the growing numbers of Latina/o students. As a result, the demands on these individuals are great because of the expectations placed on them by student communities of color and it is difficult for them to find a balance with the roles they hold in the university. Increasing faculty and administrators of color is only a one of many steps necessary to retain Latina/o students.

These individuals represent role models who have successfully overcome the challenges of being "one of the few" in postsecondary education. They serve as mentors in assisting Latino students to navigate the system and provide resources to enhance scholarship and academic achievement. However, in institutions that lack Latina/o administrative or faculty role models, students may not see successful leaders or scholars in the institution who look like themselves, represent their perspectives, and serve as resources for student retention. In order to increase the representation, we must attract and the promote them. The presence of Latina/o administrators and faculty positively affects the experience of Latina/o students in many ways (e.g., role modeling, mentorship, and cultural agents that help alleviate feelings of alienation, cultural incongruity, and marginalization). Core leadership support in central administration and high institutional priorities for diversity are key to developing a cadre of tenured minority faculty (Rowley, Hurtado, & Ponjuan, 2002).

Increasing the numbers of Latina/o faculty and administrators is an ongoing and sometimes slow process—but it remains absolutely vital. It is important to note that the quality of interactions that Latina/os have in all faculty and administrative contacts can have a strong impact on retention. Students of color were less likely to perceive racial tension on campuses where faculty and administrators were "student-centered" and demonstrated their attention to their personal and academic concerns (Hurtado, 1992). Interaction between faculty and students in the context of retention refers to developing quality relationships in the forms of advising and mentoring of students, assisting students in developing solutions to problems that may arise (e.g. financial, interpersonal), and acting when racial incidents arise. Many of these mentoring and advising relationships can be fostered through cultural centers where students have access to the faculty advisor of the center or support services programs. However, the responsibility for retention is not limited to one unit on campus nor should it fall on the shoulders on one administrator or faculty of color: *all* faculty and administrators must increase the quality interactions with students of color to get a better handle on the issues that affect retention and assist students well before they make a decision to leave the institution. Administrators and faculty need to be culturally sensitive and account for student concerns when developing policy, curriculum, campus planning, and other strategic planning initiatives for the campus (Hurtado, 1993; Hurtado, 2002). Retaining Latina/o students through faculty and administrative support means creating a general institutional climate that is inclusive of the Latina/o experience and builds support mechanisms around the challenges Latina/o students face at four-year institutions.

Principle 7: Understand Retention on Campus through Research

To better understand the issues surrounding both attrition and retention of Latina/os at four-year institutions, educators need to take on several investigative tasks. The institution needs to take a closer look at several dimensions that affect the climate for diversity, including their historical legacy (which may include practices that privilege some student groups over others), structural representation (number of Latina/o students, faculty and staff), the psychological climate (e.g., how do students perceive the climate?), and behavioral dimensions (e.g., the nature of interactions between students, faculty, and administrators)—all of these can affect the retention of Latina/os (Hurtado, 2002). Understanding these elements of an institution can paint a clearer picture of the climate Latina/os experience at four-year institutions. Retention efforts need to look more closely at the Latina/o transition to college to better identify the challenges and barriers Latina/os face during this transition period (Hurtado & Carter, 1997). Because nearly 56% of all Latinos are enrolled at 2-year institutions (NCES, 2001), better information is also needed about Latina/o transfer experiences. The transition from two-year institutions to four-year institutions has received very little research attention to date and it is incumbent on institutions to develop their own studies to improve this access point and their retention efforts for transfer students. Overall, it is important to collect information about Latina/o students and their experiences to understand issues that might impact their retention.

Conclusion

College campuses have much to learn about creating inclusive and multicultural learning environments, and difficulties in retaining Latina/o students are a prime signal that this is the case. We might expect Latina/o students to leave an institution when they have trouble adapting, but when one looks at the number of non-returning students, it is a sign that *the institution* has not yet adapted to educating this student population. If we wish to make a real difference in student retention, institutions have to find ways to adapt their practices to accommodate changing student populations. Some practices and policies may be outdated and faculty may be teaching to a vision of a student that no longer attends their college. Fortunately, most institutions are large enough that students may find a comfortable niche for adapting and developing their personal and academic goals, but we cannot leave such behavior to chance. It should not be "like a needle in a haystack" as one student described. For this reason, the seven research-based principles for retaining Latino students indicate actions that can be successfully employed by institutions.

Across the seven principles, it should be noted that many actors on campus have to take responsibility for retaining Latina/o students. One institution, for example, has a campus-wide student retention day where students, faculty, and staff can highlight programs, present studies conducted on campus, and invite guest speakers to engage more people in campus retention efforts. Overall, the seven principles indicate the need for more intentional coordination, resources for varied support programs geared to students at different stages of their college career, and attention to the design of activities that bring about the social and academic integration of Latina/o students on campus. Improving the overall climate for diversity and building a student-centered culture among faculty and administrators is an important direction that the seven principles encompass. Finally, listening to student voices about their concerns, difficulties, and successes in transition to the institution can be an informative way of identifying areas for further work or development in retention initiatives. As the growing Latina/o population reaches college age, campuses need to gear up for assisting students to navigate their way toward successful completion of the baccalaureate degree. Higher education institutions continue to play an important role in sustaining the economic development, citizenship participation, and leadership in growing Latina/o communities.

References

Astin, A. W. (1993). *What Matters in College*. San Francisco: Jossey-Bass.

Heller, D. E. (1997). Access to higher education, 1976–1994: New evidence from an analysis of the states. Ed. D., Harvard University, (November, 1997) DAI-A 58/05, p. 1611–1798.

Hurtado, S. (1992). The campus racial climate: Contexts for conflict. *The Journal of Higher Education, 63*(5), 539–569.

Hurtado, S. (1994). The Institutional climate for talented Latino students. *Research in Higher Education, 35*(1), 21–41.

Hurtado, S. (2002). Creating a climate of inclusion: Understanding Latina/o college students. In W. A. Smith, P. G. Altbach, & K. Lomotey (Eds.), *The Racial Crisis in American Higher Education: Continuing Challenges for the Twenty-First Century* (pp. 121–135). Albany, NY: State University of New York Press.

Hurtado, S. & Carter, D. F. (1997). Effects of college transition and perceptions of the campus racial climate on Latino college students' sense of belonging. *Sociology of Education 70* (October), 324–345.

Hurtado, S., Carter, D. F., & Spuler, A. (1996). Latino student transition to college: Assessing difficulties and factors in successful college adjustment. *Research in Higher Education 37*, no. 2, 135–57.

Hurtado, S., Milem, J. F., Clayton-Pederson, A., & Allen, A. (1999). *Enacting diverse learning environments: Improving the climate for racial/ethnic diversity in higher education.* ASHE-ERIC Report Series. San Franciso: Jossey-Bass.

National Center for Education Statistics [NCES]. (2001). Postsecondary enrollment, *Digest of Education Statistics, 2001.* Washington, DC: NCES.

Rowley, L., Hurtado, S., & Ponjuan, L. (2002). *Organizational rhetoric or reality?: The disparities between avowed commitment to diversity and formal programs and initiatives in higher education institutions.* Paper presented at the American Educational Research Association, New Orleans, LA.

St. John, E. P. (2000). The impact of student aid on recruitment and retention: What the research indicates. *New Directions for Student Services, 89,* 61–75.

Tinto, Vincent (1993). *Leaving college: Rethinking the causes and cures of student attrition* (2nd ed.). Chicago: University of Chicago Press.

Zúñiga, X., & Nagda B. A. (1993). Dialogue groups: An innovative approach to multicultural learning. In D. Schoem, L. Frankel, X. Zúñiga, & E. A. Lewis (Eds.), *Multicultural Teaching in the University* (pp. 313–333). Westport, CT: Praeger.

PART THREE

LATINA/O ADMINISTRATORS' EXPERIENCES AND RETENTION

Roberto Haro

Roberto Haro, a Mexican American scholar/activist, is a retired professor and university executive with career service at the University of California, California State University, State University of New York, the University of Maryland, and the University of Southern California. He earned his bachelors and two advanced degrees at the University of California, Berkeley. His doctorate is in Higher Education Administration and Public Policy. Haro received tenure at three universities and became an Assistant Chancellor at the University of California, Berkeley. Later, he headed the team that planned and developed the California State University, Monterey Bay Campus.

A regular contributor to the professional literature, Haro has written five monographs, over 76 articles in scholarly journals, and numerous chapters in books dealing with leadership, executive selection, and the role of governing boards and trustees in higher education. His recent publications have appeared in *The Chronicle of Higher Education* (Dec. 2001) and *Hispanic Outlook in Higher Education* (May 2002) and deal with presidential selection at selective colleges and universities. His chapter on Latino executive selection is in *Latinos in Higher Education,* edited by David Leon (London: Ablex Press, 2003).

Juan Francisco Lara

Juan Francisco Lara is Assistant Vice Chancellor at the University of California, Irvine; Director of the Center for Educational Partnerships (CFEP); Statewide Executive Director for the California Alliance for Minority Participation in Science, Engineering, and Mathematics (CAMP); and an adjunct professor in the UCI School of Social Sciences. Lara has an extensive background in teaching, undergraduate recruitment and retention services, precollege programs, research, public and community service, administration, fund raising, and scholarship development. He has been particularly successful in the design and development of K–12, community college, and four-year university educational partnerships. He has taught at junior and senior high schools and community colleges in Compton, East Los Angeles, and Pasadena as well as at UCLA and the Claremont Graduate School of Education. He currently teaches in the UCI School of Social Sciences.

Lara completed his Ph.D. in Higher Education Administration at UCLA in 1980, and concurrently earned a cognate specialization in Urban Planning from the UCLA School of Architecture and Urban Planning. He also has an M.A. in Urban Teaching from Occidental College, Los Angeles, and was a CORO Foundation Fellow. In addition, Lara has been a postdoctoral Fellow through the National Council of La Raza and a Scholar of the Tomás Rivera Center, a National Institute for Policy Studies affiliated with the Claremont Graduate School. He earned a B.A. in English from St. Mary's College in California, with minors in the Classics and World Literature, Theology, and Philosophy.

Recent awards include Educator of the Year from the 100 Black Men of Orange County (1996), the Rancho Santiago Community College District (1998), and the Orange County Hispanic Chamber of Commerce (2002).

Before coming to UCI in 1990, he held positions of Dean, Assistant Dean, and Assistant Professor of the Graduate School of Education and Assistant Provost of the College of Letters and Science at UCLA.

9

LATINOS AND ADMINISTRATIVE POSITIONS IN AMERICAN HIGHER EDUCATION

Roberto Haro and Juan Francisco Lara

The rapid increases in the Latino population across this country, especially among the ten to twenty-five years of age cohorts, has caused educators and researchers to examine closely their educational attainment. While the focus of most education-based research on this population group has been in the primary and secondary schools, a few studies have been done on their participation in higher education that includes status as students, and less so as staff, faculty, and administrators. The professional literature contains some important statistical and analytical studies on this minority population as students and non-teaching faculty, but very little has been done on their status as college and university administrators. The focus of this chapter, therefore, will be on Latinos and administrative positions in American higher education.

When the professional literature is reviewed, there were but a handful of studies prepared on Latinos[1] in leadership roles in American higher education. The two most often quoted are A. Esquibel's (1993) *The Career Mobility of*

---

[1] The terms Latino and Hispanic will be used interchangeably to avoid repetition. They will also refer to both females and males.

Chicano Administrators in Higher Education, and R. Haro's chapter "Held to a higher standard: Latino executive selection in higher education" in R. V. Padilla & R. C. Chavez (Eds.) (1995) *The Leaning Ivory Tower: Latino Professors in American Universities.*[2] Most of the available statistical data on the status of Latinos in administration at American colleges and universities come from the American Council on Education (ACE) compilation of statistics on minorities in higher education.[3] The data provided by ACE need to be disaggregated to better understand the actual status of Latinos in administration. The most recent information available on Hispanics in administrative roles reveals some important gains, along with some serious challenges (ACE, 2002).

The appointments of Tessa Martínez Pollack as President of Our Lady of the Lake University in Texas, and France Anne Catherine Dominique Córdova as Chancellor at the University of California, Riverside dramatically increases the number of Latino females serving as presidents or chancellors at four-year universities. These two top female executives join other Latino presidents and chancellors at universities in Michigan, New Mexico, New York, Texas, California, and Puerto Rico, and account for a slight increase in the number of new Hispanic presidents at four-year institutions. However, the greatest improvement in the number of Latino men and women presidents are at the two-year colleges. At community colleges, there is a steady increase in the appointment of Latinas and Latinos to presidencies and superintendencies, particularly in the Southwest. Later, a few thoughts will be shared that may help the reader understand why Hispanics are becoming leaders at these colleges. For the moment, however, only two Latinos have served as presidents of doctoral granting research universities, which are the flagship campuses in the respective university systems in Arizona and New Mexico: Manuel Pacheco, former president of the University of Arizona, and F. Chris García, President of the University of New Mexico. But before continuing, there are data about the Hispanic population, particularly those in the college-age cohort, that require comment.

An increasing amount of critical information gathered from reviews and research about Hispanics and American higher education is beginning to be disseminated. Several important reports have been published that deal with student demographics and particularly the steady increases in the Latino numbers within the traditional college-age cohort (Aguirre & Martinez 2002). These and numerous newspaper and other print materials continue to provide

---

[2]R. Haro's latest chapter on Latinos and leadership roles in higher education appears in David Leon (Ed.) (2002), *Latinos in Higher Education.* (London: JAI/Ablex Press).
[3]The most recent compilation of these data are in the American Council on Education 19th annual status report, (2002) *Minorities in Higher Education: 2001–2002.*

hard data on "who is going to college." In broad brush strokes, various organizations and demographers are stating that increasing number of "minorities, especially Hispanics" are preparing for and going to college. A few intrepid demographers, like Leo Estrada at UCLA, have prepared reports and papers that demonstrate an upward trend in the number of Latino men and women preparing for and entering college, mainly at two-year institutions. Moreover, the demographic studies now reveal those Hispanic students in the most populous states, California and Texas, are nearly 50% of the high school graduates in those respective areas. And this in spite of the fact that Latino students, especially males, have the highest drop out rates in K–12 (Armas, 2002).

The increase in the numbers of Latino students going to college, particularly at publicly supported two- and four-year institutions, raises several questions. First, what is the faculty composition (ethnic and gender) of these colleges and universities? Second, what is the status of Latinos in the support staff areas? Third, are Latinos making progress in gaining academic vice president/provost and president roles at these institutions? And finally, what is the representation (ethnic and gender) of members of the governing boards for these institutions, and how are they selected and appointed? Discussion on the fourth question will be reserved for a place later in this chapter. But what about the first three?

Studies (Hispanic Border Leadership Institute, 2002) done in several states with large and expanding Hispanic populations reveal that the number and percentage of Latino faculty (here are included only those in tenure track, full-time teaching positions) are increasing at the two-year colleges, barely gaining ground at four-year regional universities, and almost stagnant at the most selective research universities in the country. Comments about private, four-year liberal arts colleges will follow in different parts of this discussion. Ed Apodaca, Associate Vice President at the University of Houston in Texas, recently did a study (Apodaca, 2003) on the number of Latino faculty at four-year colleges and universities in Texas. His results are sobering, reflecting a concentration of most Hispanic faculty at seven colleges and universities. And finally, the number of Latino faculty at the private four-year liberal arts colleges and universities, especially the most selective ones, reveal no appreciable change in the number or percentage of Latino faculty in the last five years. The situation for Latino faculty at Ivy League institutions reveals very little change in the number of Hispanic faculty, especially among the domestic-born group. So, there are increases in Hispanic faculty at the publicly supported two-year colleges, and regional four-year universities, but very little change elsewhere. While more properly the subject of another piece, it is important to consider that the number of Latino graduates in doctoral programs is not increasing substantially, causing various highly regarded demographers and educational researchers considerable concerns about the future availability of qualified Hispanic Ph.D.s for faculty roles in American colleges and universities. Putting aside the issues of faculty, it is propitious to focus on the status of Hispanics in non-teaching capacities in American higher education.

Latinos in non-teaching, support staff positions, particularly in the traditional student services, are increasing in both numbers and percentages of administrators in these areas, particularly at the two-year colleges, and at publicly supported regional universities, especially in the Southwest. In fact, there are increasing numbers of Latino females and males in vice presidencies for student services, business affairs, and even a few in senior level fund raising roles. The career paths in these fields, especially at the publicly funded institutions, are providing important opportunities for Hispanic advancement into middle management and senior administrative jobs. A large percentage of Latinos in support staff leadership roles are at Hispanic Serving Institutions (HSI), not all of which are members of the Hispanic Association of Colleges and Universities (HACU). These institutions, with gradually increasing Latino student populations, are targeting qualified Latinos for leadership roles in the traditional student support services. But the improved climate for Latinos to serve in senior management roles in student services is not the case in academic administration.

The situation for Latinos seeking academic executive leadership roles is troublesome. There are less than a handful of Latinas and Latinos serving as directors of university libraries and information services. And after examining the pipeline in these academic specializations, the limited, if any, participation of Hispanics in graduate programs leading to these fields is not very promising. As for academic vice presidencies, and presidencies, Hispanics are gaining ground at the two-year colleges, gaining a few positions at the regional universities, and barely adding one or two persons to the ranks of provosts, chancellors, and provosts at research universities. The more selective the colleges or universities, the greater the challenge for Latinos to become provosts, the position from which most presidents are picked. The status of Hispanics in academic administrative positions at selective private four-year liberal arts colleges is distressing because of the very limited representation of Latino faculty, department chairs, and deans.

Considering the interrelationship of the information that has been shared raises several critical matters. An increasing number of Latino students—but with an important caveat for males—are graduating from high school and going to college (Fry, 2002, p. 4). Hispanic students, particularly in the Southwest, Puerto Rico, Florida, Illinois, and New York, will continue to increase their numbers and percentage among the college-age cohorts in our nation's population. Yet, many will never go to college, while others who do may well end up in terminal programs at two-year campuses. Meanwhile, the attrition rate for Hispanic students at many of the regional universities in the United States is staggering (Fry, 2002, p. 2). At some of the universities in California and Texas, the dropout rate in the first and second year is so high as to constitute a serious revolving door syndrome.[4] Who is teaching Latino college students? Currently, White men are the majority of faculty at most colleges and universities attended by Hispanic youth. There are increasing numbers of White women moving into the teaching faculty ranks at institutions serving or beginning to serve this minority population. While no reliable studies exist about the relationship of White women faculty to Latino students, considerable anecdotal information is surfacing about strained relationships between female faculty and Hispanics, especially male students. In some of the papers and conversations held at regional conferences, particularly in the Southwest, comments have surfaced about the "negative image" that faculty have about Latino students.[5] Such an attitude is most prevalent at highly selective institutions where faculty want to concern themselves with their research and interact only occasionally with the best and the brightest students. Most of the older faculty still consider Latino students somehow less well prepared or less intellectually capable than their Asian and White counterparts.

Considering the increasing numbers of Latino and other underrepresented students attempting to gain access to colleges and universities, particularly state-supported ones, the answer to recruiting and coping with them once on the campus has been the employment of minority staff to assist in attracting, socializing, and helping these newcomers matriculate. Consequently, campus administrators and faculty do not, for the most part, object to the appointment of minority support staff, even to management jobs in such capacities. These staffs provide invaluable services that range from recruiting Latino students, to helping them gain access to the institutions, and once admitted, they provide assistance in adjusting to the campus and matriculating successfully. Once Latinos are on the campus, most faculty do appreciate support staff, especially if they [the faculty] can send Hispanic students with adjustment issues and learning difficulties to academic support centers increasingly employing Latino staff. Moreover, an increasing number of Hispanics are employed in "outreach" positions by colleges and universities. In their assignments, staff work mainly off campus with high school counselors to provide

---

[4]The revolving door syndrome is that process by which colleges and universities recruit large numbers of Hispanic students each year to balance their high attrition rate in the first two years.
[5]Such comments were shared by participants at the "Pathways to College: Linking Policy with Research and Practice" conference in Albuquerque, NM (Sept. 17–18, 2002).

information on access to college, level of preparation required, and other matters like financial assistance. In many locations, outreach staff work closely with Hispanic students and their parents on how best to prepare for access to the college or university of choice. Most of these positions are usually located within the division of student services. Some, however, if they involve tutorials and academic skills' development for students, may lodge in another branch of the college or university's administrative structure. It is in outreach jobs, particularly in geographical areas where there are large concentrations of Hispanics, that Latino staff are gradually moving into administrative roles, and some into middle and upper management jobs in student services. At most community colleges with burgeoning enrollments of Hispanics (Fry, 2002, p. 6), a conscious effort is made to recruit Latinos to work closely with these and other minority students. Moreover, many of these institutions have initiated retention programs that are, for the most part, administered by Hispanic staff and designed to help Latino students do well in their classes and prepare them for transfer to a four-year college or university. This may help to explain the increasing numbers of Latino men and women gradually moving into administrative roles in the student services areas. And it may also account for the increases in Hispanic administrative personnel reported by groups such as the American Council on Education. But what about in other areas such as business, administrative services, and development functions?

Hispanic representation in management jobs within the ranks of the business and administrative services in higher education is growing. Advancement, however, tends to be slow because of low personnel turnover in middle and upper management jobs. Nonetheless, an increasing number of senior administrative positions in these fields, particularly at publicly supported two- and four-year colleges and universities, have been openly recruiting, with continuing efforts to encourage "qualified minorities from underrepresented groups" to apply. Meanwhile, if the increasing number of Hispanics hired at entry-level, and even supervisory-level jobs is any indication of future potential for advancement to administrative roles, the opportunities for Latino employees are encouraging. It must be understood that in these capacities—providing administrative, business, financial, and other forms of support services to the operations of a college or university—most faculty, senior academic administrative leaders, and even members of governing boards are inclined to accept qualified Latino employees. That hospitality, however, may not carry over to other kinds of leadership roles on the campus.

Perhaps the greatest challenge for Latinos is in the area of academic administration at colleges and universities. The career path to academic administration involves serving as a faculty member and gaining tenure (or security of employment as it is called at some institutions). It is from the faculty ranks, therefore, that the most important campus executives are usually drawn after serving in the capacity of department chair, dean, or director of an academic program (Haro, 1995a, pp. 194–196). It is important, therefore, to devote attention to the role faculty play in the preparation of academic executives.

Almost exclusively, presidents and provosts are drawn from the faculty ranks, usually having served as a department chair and then a dean. In Haro's research on Latinos and executive selection in higher education, there was a very limited representation, at regional universities, of presidents who came from jobs such as vice presidents for student services, the development office, or administrative services. Among the group he surveyed, none was a Latino (Haro, 1995). As for the most selective colleges and universities, a cursory review by Haro failed to identify any presidents who had come from anything other than a provost or other senior level academic role, i.e., vice president for research or dean of graduate studies. The appointment of senior academic administrators, particularly at the most selective four-year colleges and universities, has posed several major challenges for Latinos. Unless they are able to gain tenure, become a department chair, and then an academic dean or director, their chances to become an academic vice president/provost or president are slim, at best.

Who selects presidents, particularly at the private, liberal arts colleges and universities? It is done by the members of their governing boards. And who sits on these boards? A quick search revealed that only a handful of Latinas and Latinos serve on the boards of such institutions. The governing boards of private liberal arts colleges and universities have a way of socializing their members, perpetuating established values and belief systems, and inculcating them to new members in a relatively short time. Such private governing boards are mainly impervious to external influences that emanate from minority communities, unless the institution in question serves a predominant minority, religious, or a gender-based clientele. But this process also cuts two ways. When an HACU institution, which may be private, searches for a new president, the board may be very receptive to Latina and Latino candidates. The same is true for African Americans at HBCUs, and females at non-coed institutions. The situation is somewhat different for the two-year publicly supported colleges. Most of them have an elected board of trustees and find themselves responsible to an electorate with the power to remove them after their term expires, or in some cases, by recall. Consequently, in studies on presidential selection conducted by Haro (2002), at the two-year colleges, a correlation emerges between the number of minority trustees and the propensity to select a woman or minority, or both, as presidents for these institutions. Increasingly, the political process may tend to influence elected college trustees in a district with a large or growing population of minorities, particularly Latinos, to hire a minority. Definitely, more studies are needed to review this process.

But turning to the private liberal arts colleges and universities, especially the most selective ones, the members of the governing boards may be indifferent if not negatively disposed toward the selection of a Latino, female or male, for a top administrative role. This will be discussed in greater detail later. More important at this point is that the changing of attitudes and behavior on most governing boards is slow, if nearly glacial. It may appear as if governing boards at the most selective private colleges and universities tend to "clone" themselves. Why is this important? A substantial part of a board member's "indoctrination" is to become aware of and adhere to the traditions of the institution, and vote in keeping with those norms. For example, at a selective liberal arts college, nationally recognized for the high percentage of their graduates attending the most prestigious graduate programs and professional schools in the United States and England, the governing board has always selected White males for president. When the chairman of the board at this liberal arts institution was interviewed, he was asked if the college would ever offer the presidency to a Latino male or female. Pointing to the pictures of previous presidents at the college—who were all White males—he said, "We have a tradition of excellence at this campus, and our choice for the person to maintain those high standards will coincide with the qualities of those who went before" (Haro, 2002, Chapter 10). In brief, what he implied were that Blacks, Latinos, and other non-Whites, need not apply.

A development that may be influencing the activities of governing boards, particularly in the selection of a new president, is the increase in the number of ex-presidents recruited to serve on the boards of trustees of private institutions. In her article on this process, Julianne Basinger (2002, pp. A29–30) uncovered a small but important group of presidents turned trustees. These former presidents, mostly White men with a few White women, bring considerable experience and influence to a board. However, little is known, other than their own hiring practices, that sheds any light on how receptive they might be to the appointment of a Latino female or male for a presidency, especially at a highly selective private institution. It may be safe to assume that these ex-presidents will, for the most part, continue to consider presidential candidates from within their own circle of acquaintances. And within those academic circles there are few if any Hispanic academic vice presidents or provosts.

An intriguing perspective on the appointment of college presidents is what Clara M. Lovett refers to as the "dumbing down of college presidents." In her piece on presidential selection, Lovett (2002, p. B20) states that presidential aspirants must navigate a treacherous political process. The successful ones, she claims are articulate, photogenic, and skilled in the art of self-promotion. She goes on to say that sartorial correctness is required, and the goal is to look like a college president from central casting, where the image connotes a strong, attractive White male. Most Hispanic candidates do not, for the most part, fit such a mold. Moreover, it is not surprising to find subtle biases and stereotypes about Hispanics surface in conversations among groups that are called on to comment on presidential candidates. In addition, executive search consultants will often play an important role in steering a board of trustees into favoring a "safe" candidate to consummate the search expeditiously, and avoid confrontation or controversy with other groups like faculty, students, and local media (Lovett, 2002). Unfortunately, many promising Latino presidential aspirants do not fit the image of what selective, private liberal arts colleges and universities are seeking, and will not have the kind of support base, self-promotion, and external influential assistance (such as from an executive search firm) needed to gain the job of president.

But what about the selection of provosts and presidents at public four-year universities? Here it is essential to divide the institutions into two categories. First, the regional universities, which tend to serve a discrete geographical region, e.g., Northern Colorado University, and second, the major research universities which serve an entire state, and even consider themselves a national and international resource, e.g., University of Texas at Austin. Slowly, the appointment of minorities to academic vice presidencies and presidencies at regional universities is taking place. Again, there is an interesting correlation between the number and voice of Latinos in state legislative bodies and the appointment of Hispanics to executive level positions at state-supported regional universities. Even at the prestigious University of California, political pressure from the Lieutenant Governor's office and the Latino Caucus in the Legislature did help the appointment of a Hispanic woman as Chancellor at the Riverside campus. The President of the University of California and the newly appointed Chancellor at that campus both deny that political influence resulted in this appointment. It is, of course, understood that they must assume this posture in order to protect themselves from challenges within their system and campus, and from future political activities by community groups and elected officials. Much as scholars and academicians at Harvard University, the University of Pennsylvania, and the American Council on Education who studies executive selection decries the use of political pressure to appoint minorities to presidencies, it is well known that political influence has been used to appoint White men to university leadership roles, and most recently White women to presidencies. While White females were not part of the older, established political, or "good old boy" networks, within the last three decades, they have established formidable groupings and efforts to promote themselves into presidencies. This is a positive development in opening opportunities for women in leadership roles in the academy. However, some corresponding efforts to help Hispanic men and women achieve senior administrative positions in higher education is not yet in place.

Another intriguing factor in presidential selection involves choices between White women and minorities. Professor Evelyn Hu-DeHart from Brown University made some telling remarks about White women and minorities in the academy at a College Board Regional Conference (San Francisco, 1998). She posited that White males may prefer to approve the appointment of a White woman to an academic leadership role over a minority because she may be like their wife, daughter, or sister. And second, there may be an unintended competition between White female academic vice presidents/provosts and minority applicants where biases from different on- and off-campus elements toward a Hispanic candidate may weigh against a Latina or Latino. In studies conducted by Haro (1995b) on governing board attitudes and behavior, there are indications that some White women may not be well disposed toward Latino male applicants for executive level appointments. While not substantiated by sufficient research, there appears to be a tendency within the last few years for White decision makers on the faculty and on governing boards, particularly when they may feel compelled to appoint a Hispanic, to prefer a female. Additional research will be required to explore this supposition.

So why this concern with executive level appointments at colleges and universities and Hispanics? It is important to mention and stress the role a president of a selective liberal arts college, and the president or chancellor of a selective university play in conditioning attitudes and behavior between key policy and decision makers in our nation. Several older but still important works describe how critical decisions are made in high level policy groups and commissions that influence our society. *The Power Elite,* by C. Wright Mills (1956), and G. William Domhoff's *The Powers That Be* (1978), and similar studies, describe how leaders from the corporate, governmental, and not-for-profit sectors serve on the same boards or commissions, and play a very significant role in determining policies and practices that affect and condition our lives. The presidents of major colleges and universities often are asked to serve on these boards and commissions. So, when the increase in the Latino population begins to surface as a topic for consideration on the agenda of major boards and commissions in this country, who speaks for the Latino population? It must be realized that only a limited number of Latinos have attained top leadership roles in the major corporate and governmental arenas, with even fewer in the arenas of philanthropy and higher education. Therefore, when the time comes to carefully examine educational matters that affect Hispanic students and their families, less than a handful of Latino college and university leaders may be available to speak authoritatively on such concerns in these cameral settings. The reality is that Hispanics are not well represented in the higher circles and among the power elite in America. And it is a source of continuing disappointment for the Hispanic communities in this country.

It would not do to complete this discussion without offering some constructive suggestions for how to increase the number of capable Hispanics moving into administrative roles in higher education. There are several efforts underway to develop "leadership programs" for Latinas and Latinos. The Mexican American Legal Defense and Education Fund (MALDEF) has a youth leadership program, several Latina organizations have programs designed to encourage young Latinas to prepare for leadership roles in education, government, and the corporate world. The Hispanic Association of Colleges and Universities (HACU) also has a successful leadership program. However, new efforts are required to establish cohesive programs that identify and develop Latinos for leadership roles in higher education. Among the few programs that do exist, their goals are not, for the most part, focused on higher education, and they are limited in both scope and expected outcomes, particularly with regard to the preparation of leaders for the academy. There is a reliance by Hispanics on the American Council on Education Fellows Program, the old Woodrow Wilson Fellows effort, and the Harvard University Institutes for management training in higher education. While these short-term efforts do help to expose participants to desirable management skills and behavior, a cohesive, structured program—with long-term sustainability—is needed. Such a program will focus exclusively on Hispanics and will tap high potential Latino students early in their secondary school experience and prepare and target them for selective four-year colleges and universities where they will be paired with mentors capable of developing leadership potential and shepherding them to graduation with high achievement. These students will be recruited for successful matriculation at the best graduate or professional programs. Following that, a working network must be developed to identify and make available opportunities for postdoctoral training, providing a positive impetus for targeted Hispanics to achieve faculty roles at selective colleges and universities. They can proceed to follow academic administrative career paths eventually leading to presidencies at selective four-year liberal arts colleges and universities.

While what has been proposed above may seem ambitious, it is attainable and does represent a positive approach toward increasing the number and caliber of Hispanics prepared to assume administrative and top leadership roles in American higher education. The very rapid increases in the Latino population in this country, and especially the growing number of Hispanic students preparing for college, requires bold steps, among them the assurance of novel paradigms designed to prepare the kind of Latino leader needed in the years ahead. It will then be the mission of these new Hispanic leaders to serve as articulate spokespersons and change agents, committed to the harmonious blending of new methods to continue excellence while amalgamating underrepresented population groups into our best colleges and universities.

References

Aguirre, A., Jr., & Martinez, R. O. (2002). Resource shares and educational attainment. In D. Leon (Ed.), *Latinos in Higher Education* (pp. 37–55). London: JAI/Ablex Press.

American Council on Education. (2002). *Minorities in Higher Education, 2001–2002.* 19th annual status report. Washington, DC: Author.

Apodaca, E. (2003). *Texas Higher Education Hispanic Report Card.* Houston, TX: University of Houston.

Armas, G. C. (2002). Hispanic dropouts on the rise. *Concord Monitor Online.* Oct. 11, 2002, p. 17

Basinger, J. (2002, February 8). More presidents recruit ex-presidents for their institutions' boards. *The Chronicle of Higher Education,* pp. A29–30.

Domhoff, G. W. (1978). *The Powers That Be: Processes of Ruling Class Domination in America.* New York: Random House.

Esquibel, A. (1993). *The Career Mobility of Chicano Administrators in Higher Education.* Boulder, CO: Western Interstate Commission on Higher Education.

Fry, R. (2002). *Latinos in Higher Education: Many Enroll, Too Few Graduate.* Washington, DC: Pew Hispanic Center.

Haro, R. (1995a). Held to a higher standard: Latino executive selection in higher education. In R. V. Padilla & R. C. Chávez (Eds.), *The Leaning Ivory Tower: Latino Professors in American Universities* (pp. B32–33). Albany, NY: State University of New York Press.

Haro, R. (1995b, December 8). Choosing trustees who care about things that matter. *The Chronicle of Higher Education,* pp. 189–207.

Haro, R. (2002). Latinos and academic leadership in American higher education. In D. Leon (Ed.), *Latinos in Higher Education* (pp. 155–191). London: JAI/Ablex Press.

Hispanic Border Leadership Institute. (2002, March). *A Compromised Commitment: Society's Obligation and Failure to Serve the nation's Largest Growing Population.* Arizona State University: Author.

Leon, D. (Ed.). (2002). *Latinos in Higher Education.* London: JAI/Ablex Press.

Lovett, C. M. (2002, April 5). The dumbing down of college presidents. *The Chronicle of Higher Education*, p. B20.

Mills, C. W. (1956). *The Power Elite.* New York: Oxford University Press.

Padilla, R. V., & Chávez, R. C. (1995). *The Leaning Ivory Tower: Latino Professors in American Universities.* New York: State University of New York Press.

Kathleen Harris Canul

Kathleen Harris Canul is the University Ombudsman at the University of California, Irvine, where she has worked for the last ten years. Prior to her present role, she served as a clinical psychologist and taught courses in psychology, including courses in Chicano/Latino Psychology, at UCI. She conducts lectures on culture and psychology at the local, state and national level.

10

LATINA/O CULTURAL VALUES AND THE ACADEMY

LATINAS NAVIGATING THROUGH THE ADMINISTRATIVE ROLE

Kathleen Harris Canul

I did not know when I accepted my administrative position as an Ombudsman at a Research Type I institution that my personal experiences of gender and race discrimination would serve as valuable lessons to prepare me for this job. Today, I recognize that those incidents prepared me well for the daily fights for justice and equity. I also did not realize that having a hard-earned doctorate from a reputable institution still would not be enough for a Latina to be considered a true professional. Lastly, I did not know that when I would want to go across the hall or to another floor to visit another Latina administrator to share a story, talk about our children or husbands, family, that there would be no one there.

Latina/o Representation in Administrative Roles in Higher Education

Latina/os only represent a mere 2.5% of all full-time administrators in higher education in the United States. Most Latina/os hold administrative positions that are at the lower levels and the positions do not allow them to implement policy changes in higher education. For example, only 2.6% of all college and university presidents in the United States are Latina/o (de los Santos & Rigual,

1994). Verdugo (1995) suggests that racial stratification plays a major role in the low number of Latina/o in administrative positions, which further impacts the experience. Latina/o faculty and administrators are negatively affected by racial stratification in many ways: stereotyping, marginalization, tokenism, and alienation. Moreover, there is a common belief in higher education that Latina/o professionals do not possess the appropriate skills needed to be successful in the academy (Verdugo, 1995). Latina/o administrators are not present in large numbers in the academy and such challenges make for a unique experience in higher education.

Personal History

It has been almost three years since I began my tenure as University Ombudsman. I consider myself privileged to be in a position to advocate for fairness at a four-year research institution. As a daughter of a Mexican migrant farm worker mother and Russian Jewish father, I was raised with sensitivity to the realities of injustice and disparity in this world. I was also blessed with the richness of blended cultures, with the appreciation that each of us comes with us a legacy of our ancestry which gently and sometimes not so gently influences our personal ways of being.

If dealing with my mixed heritage was not enough, I also, by necessity, learned to cope with having a mentally ill mother who was not always able to fulfill her parental obligations. As a growing child, I was keenly aware that I was not quite like the others. Instead, I had an intimate awareness of human relations, a special appreciation for different coping mechanisms and solutions for problems. Not surprisingly, I became a clinical psychologist and developed a little more sophistication in my understanding of others. Simultaneously, I gained a special appreciation of the resilience of human nature when people are confronted with life's difficulties.

In the capacity of a cultural competency educator, I found myself frequently in the position of speaking and teaching on the "Psychology of Latinos." In such a capacity, I initially felt very uncomfortable being a spokesperson for a group of people whose psychologies are incredibly diverse and complex, but with time, I realized that it was not about teaching dominant society the secrets of Latina/os, but rather it was about sensitizing others to subtleties and nuances within and across cultures. Although as humans we are more alike than different, culture-specific values significantly shape our perception of the world and difficulties can and do arise when these views clash. These collisions may occur as a result of misunderstanding and misinterpretation across a wide array of interpersonal interactions and across many, if not all professional disciplines.

I must confess that thus far in my career, I have devoted countless hours to teaching and training other service providers about Latina/o cultural values in order to enhance the quality of services provided, yet I have never once applied the concepts to myself and my work style, and even less to my current profession. Hence, I have neglected to assess the role of my culture(s) and the influence on my administrative and managerial style. If I reflect upon my job performance, I can now clearly see both how my heritage facilitated my struggles and how my heritage assisted in my survival.

Latina/o Cultural Values and Administrative Work Style

The remainder of this discourse will focus on traditional Latina/o core cultural values as they relate to my experiences operationalizing my administrative role in academia. I offer these thoughts with caution, as the following is one Latina's perspective and it is my hope that the information is of help to other Latina/os who are finding themselves, at times, confused and disoriented in their professional lives. More specifically, I will address what I believe are several cultural values inherent to me. Other works in this area go to greater depth from a psychological perspective (Falicov 1996, 1998), but for the purposes of this chapter, I will briefly summarize each value (e.g., personalismo, respeto, and religion; Cuellar, Arnold, & Gonzalez, 1995; Santiago-Rivera Arredando & Gallardo-Cooper, 2002) and provide examples of how they have been be actualized in the administrative workplace for me in the role of Ombudsman.

Collectivism versus Individualism

Perhaps one of the greatest differences observed when comparing Latina/os to dominant culture regarding issues of identity is the collectivism-individualism dimension (Triandis, 1995). Latina/os value being a member of a community and family, and this membership takes priority over individualism. Latina/os raise children to be interdependent ("overly dependent" on each other, according to some services providers) and Latina/os believe that all behaviors affect the family and the greater community. In dominant culture, independence is considered a virtue. For example, there is much discussion in parenting literature on the importance of "teaching" three-month-old babies to sleep through the night, on their own. To the contrary, Latina/o culture emphasizes that we must accommodate to our children's needs, and we learn to teach our children to rely on their parents for survival. We learn that we must sacrifice for others and that our behaviors do not solely exemplify our individual personalities; rather our comportment reflects upon our entire community.

In my capacity as an Ombudsman, my first instinct is to work collaboratively with my team, ask questions of and encourage suggestions from my office mates, and not jump into a decision without consultation. My instinct to reach out to my colleagues has been viewed as passive, non-decisive, and too non-directive. The reality is that I do not see myself as independent from my colleagues or my staff. We are a team and my mission is to bring honor and pride to my office, not to myself, personally. Furthermore, when approached for a project or a report, I reflect on the greater benefit of my work, the report, and its contributions. Short- and long-term duties are processes and not simply projects to complete.

It has also become evident that as a Latina administrator with strong cultural values, I have encountered several unique challenges relative to social interaction and accountability. In order to survive in higher education, it has become very clear that the ability to publicize one's successes and to act in a manner consistent with self-promotion is vital. It is a difficult balancing act to both be true to my culture by maintaining a sense of modesty in the workplace, and at the same time to publicly take ownership for my accomplishments. Many Latina/os have also been at a disadvantage of being vulnerable to others who have had much more practice in assuming credit (even when unearned) for good work performed. Similarly, I have no difficulty asking for fair compensation and resources for my staff, but I cannot do the same for myself. From my Latina's eyes, I expect that my supervisors will value my hard work and accomplishments, and thus I will be rewarded. I should not have to point out how good I am; let my work speak for itself. In dominant culture, it is much more acceptable to ask for a raise or needed resources in contrast to Latina/os culture where we experience a sense of discomfort both in risking shame in receiving a negative response and in placing someone in an awkward position of potentially saying "no" to a request. It is my belief that as Latina/o professionals we are more likely to move on to another position where we may feel better appreciated than to ask for fair compensation that is clearly due.

Personalismo

Generally speaking, personalismo can be described as the value placed on building and maintaining personal relationships (Falicov, 1998; Paniagua, 1998; Santiago-Rivera, Arredando, & Gallardo-Cooper, 2002). Personalismo is the avoidance of conflict and emphasis on harmony and are qualities encouraged within Latina/o culture. Even in our professional relationships, we tend to be people- rather than task-oriented. A significant part of job satisfaction is related to interpersonal relationships. Without a doubt, job content and performance are important, but for Latina/os, interactions with colleagues provide a sense of belonging and also make the task at hand more manageable and rewarding. It is imperative that I establish good working relationships with my supervisors, colleagues, and staff. As a group, Latina/os, I believe, have a greater tolerance for individual differences and idiosyncratic behavior. This can be both positive and problematic. If I have a disagreement with a colleague, how can I express this in a manner that is indirect and non-confrontational? Also, there sometimes is the reality that when a woman is assertive, she is often perceived as aggressive. For many individuals inexperienced with Latina/o culture, the concept of an outspoken Latina is foreign and she may be treated much more harshly by a male-dominated administration for overstepping social and gender boundaries.

While Latina/os are often categorized as passive and non-assertive in our communication style, I must offer that mutual respect takes precedence over "petty" differences. People come first. An example I can offer is the invitation-to-lunch scenario. In dominant culture, the concept of separate checks or splitting the bill is common. In Latina/o culture, to discuss the financial transaction about lunch is inappropriate and cold. Usually, someone has invited another to lunch, and the person inviting pays the bill. Case closed. The practice of kindness and generosity—"simpatía"—are ingrained in our culture. What I have, I can share, if you have a need. Additionally, the ability to say "no" to a request has not been reinforced in Latina/o culture. If someone comes to you with a need, you must acknowledge that this individual has humbled him or herself and you must respect this request by accommodating it, to the best of your ability. Considering the importance of personalismo and simpatía, as both an employee and a supervisor, I often find myself in situations where because I do not feel I can say, "No, boss. I cannot work on that assignment over the weekend," or "No, Employee. You may not take the afternoon to celebrate your child's birthday." Consequently, I find myself with a significant workload and with a desire to be a manager who is responsive to the needs of her staff.

Respeto

Further impacting the Latina administrator's task to juggle various cultural values, Latina/os have strict cultural rules to follow. Our culture is hierarchical and not necessarily democratic when addressing interpersonal relationships. A significant degree of dutifulness (respeto) is demonstrated in all of our communications and interactions with our parents, the elderly, individuals in professional positions (doctors, educators, etc.), and anyone who is in a position of superiority. In the Spanish language, Latina/os even have a means of demonstrating respect by using the formal "usted" (sir or madam) instead of "tu" (you) when addressing a higher-ranking individual. One of the early messages I received as a child was to not question authority. As an ombudsman, how am I supposed to not question authority? Of course, I have learned to navigate through this dilemma. I do not directly question the authority of an individual or idea. In many cases, particularly in the conflict resolution arena, it is counterindicated. I am blessed with the cultural inheritance of having respect for another person's belief system ("Cada cabeza un mundo"; loosely translated, every mind lives in its own world), and at the same time I must rise to the challenge of offering another perspective. There is a difference in saying "you are wrong" and "With all due respect, I would like to offer another viewpoint." I also find it incredibly difficult to challenge a decision that has been made by my supervisor which affects me personally. If I am denied a vacation request, a promotion, or any personal benefit, I am not likely to fight it, but if these decisions jeopardize my personal or professional development, I am apt to seek other employment opportunities, rather than remain in a position where I feel disrespected or undervalued.

Marianismo

Gender roles are ascribed through socialization and cultural transmission. The Latina/o culture has pronounced gender roles when we discuss traditional Latina/o families. As a result, Latina women have been closely associated with passivity and superlative femininity (marianismo). America has magnified these traits, and many people stereotypically characterize Latina women as baby machines, uneducated, and poor. The contemporary/modern, acculturated Latina is an individual who speaks her voice, exchanges opinions, and is not submissive to a patriarchal system. Consequently, Comas-Díaz (1994) reminds us that Latina women who assume positions of responsibility are often overlooked. As a result of gender and ethnicity (the double minority effect), Latinas may experience depreciation in the work environment and can find themselves fighting gender stereotypes, sexism, and discrimination. In my experience, I have found myself in conversations with people who label me as "quite assertive for being Latina" and "pleased to see me speak up." Oftentimes, I sense people's disapproval of my self-assurance and vocal tendencies. In fact, I have even been punished for it (e.g., marginalization and exclusion of important decision-making processes).

Another challenge unique to being a Latina administrator is the balance between home and the academy. Reflecting on my experience, I have found myself countless times balancing my home, family, and work. Many times I have felt guilty for staying after hours to complete reports, meet deadlines, and prepare for presentation. In addition, I have found myself taking work home to ensure that I spent quality time with my family. Mainstream culture endorses the mobility of women in the workforce but does not embrace the practices of motherhood and parenting in a workday. For instance, I can recall numerous questioning curious glances while taking my children to work. For some Latinas, commitment to the job may be in question, because they may have chosen to attend a child's midday school event. It is challenging to disprove that one must be a good administrator or good mother. In my case, to stay consistent with my cultural values and to fulfill my job expectations, I manage the two.

Religion, Spirituality, and Fatalismo

It almost seems inappropriate to discuss religion and spirituality in reference to work or in relation to my administrative role, but most people have a faith; Latina/os tend to be Catholic. Our spiritual beliefs do influence our comportment in many aspects of our lives, including our jobs. The influence of religion for Latina/os is so significant that it is difficult to separate the influences of Catholicism from Latina/o culture itself. Latina/os are raised to accept God's destiny (Cuellar, Arnold, Gonzáles, 1995); this value is best expressed in the phrase "El hombre pone y Dios dispone," which translate as "Man proposes and God disposes." I remember countless conversations with my grandmother and mother where we would discuss our plans and dreams and the dialogue would end with "Si dios quiere," God willing. One cannot be so egotistical as to exclude God from our aspirations, according to traditional Latina/o beliefs. Coupled with our fatalistic nature that events are predetermined, it is difficult for some traditional Latina/os to be proactive in certain aspects of our lives. We are supposed to face challenges directly as they are character-building opportunities from God. In all frankness, I am not as Catholic as my mother would like, but it is also difficult to disengage from the pervasiveness of the fatalistic mentality (Falicov, 1998; Sue & Sue, 1990).

Conclusion

Are these experiences of gender and race inequity in the workforce something I should accept and welcome for educational purposes? Being passed over for a promotion or being minimized in one's professional role are events that are demoralizing, but should they be actively addressed? Of course my heart tells me that there is injustice in this world and in my life, but in many instances the fight is more costly than the initial loss. These cumulative educational experiences have certainly granted me skills that have allowed me to become who I am professionally. I believe that as a Latina administrator, I need to be highly selective in the battles I choose to fight. There is also still a sense of discomfort in taking a struggle solely for personal gain. It is much easier to come to the defense of others. I have learned to be tolerant by necessity and for my own professional survival.

In this brief chapter, I have attempted to introduce the relationship between several Latina/o cultural values and administrative work style. By no means is this a comprehensive review, rather it is one Latina administrator's perspective on the cultural influences integrated into the realities of her job. A further discussion on how one's ethnicity flavors one's leadership is certainly merited. Without a doubt, as Latina/os rise through the administrative ranks, it is an issue that will become even more salient and worthy of examination.

References

Comas-Diaz, L., & Greene, B. (1994). *Women of color: Integrating ethnic and gender identities in psychotherapy.* New York: Guilford Press.

Cuellar, I., Arnold, B., & Gonzalez, G. (1995). Cognitive referents of acculturation: Assessment of cultural constructs in Mexican Americans. *Journal of Community Psychology, 23,* 339–356.

de los Santos, A., Jr., & Rigual, A. (1994). Progress of Hispanics in American higher education. In M. J. Justiz & R. Wilson (Eds.), *Minorities in higher education,* 173–194. Pheonix, AZ: Oryx Press.

Falicov, C. J. (1998). *Latino families in therapy: A guide to multicultural practice.* New York: Guilford Press.

Falicov, C. J. (1996). *Mexican Families* In M. McGoldrick, J. K. Pierce, & J. Giordano, (Eds.), *Ethnicity and family therapy* (2nd ed.), pp. 169–182, New York: Guilford Press.

Paniagua, F. (1998). *Assessing and treating culturally diverse clients: A practical approach.* Thousand Oaks, CA: Sage.

Santiago-Rivera, A., Arredondo, P., & Gallardo-Cooper, M. (2002). *Counseling Latinos and la familia.* Thousand Oaks, CA: Sage.

Sue, D. W. & Sue, D. (1990). *Counseling the culturally different: Theory and practice.* New York: Wiley.

Triandis, H. C. (1995). Individualism & collectivism: New directions in social psychology. Boulder, CO: Westview Press.

Verdugo, R. R. (1995). Racial stratification and the use of Hispanic faculty as role models. *Journal of Higher Education, 66*(6), 669–686.

PART FOUR

LATINA/O FACULTY
EXPERIENCES
AND RETENTION

Raymond V. Padilla

Raymond V. Padilla is Professor, College of Education and Human Development, Department of Educational Leadership and Policy Studies, University of Texas at San Antonio. He developed the Student Success Model (SSM) to increase college graduation rates for minority and majority students; and promotes innovation and change in U.S. higher education to enhance educational opportunities for Latina/o students and faculty. Relevant publications include, *The Leaning Ivory Tower: Latino Professors in American Universities* (co-edited with Rudolfo Chávez Chávez), and *Debatable Diversity: Critical Dialogues on Change in American Universities* (co-authored with Miguel Montiel). Current interests include the application of qualitative research methods to the study of issues related to Latina/os and higher education. He is the developer of Hyper-Qual, a software program for the analysis of qualitative data. Dr. Padilla received a Ph.D. in higher education from the University of California, Berkeley.

nfluence of the "Educational Pipeline"

ady noted, accessing the professoriate through the hiring, tenure, and ion process occurs within the much broader context of the educational characteristic of the U.S. educational system (see Figure 11.1). Those knocking at the doors of the academy seeking entrance to the profes- already have been shaped, molded, and filtered by the educational in many significant ways (Ibarra, 2001; Romo & Falbo, 1996; Valen- ▶1; Valenzuela, 1999). Thus, only a relative few seek a life in the pro- te, even fewer are invited to join, and only the stalwart and the lucky anointed as tenured professors.

shown in Figure 11.1, the educational pipeline is really a segmented, iical system of educational institutions each geared to a specific stage levelopment of the individual. The system as a whole manifests the e of nineteenth-century thinking with its strong emphasis on rational- istrial models of human organizations. With weak links across seg- the transitions from one segment to another have historically been spots for Latino students, especially the transition from junior high o high school and from high school to college (Jalomo, Jr., 1995). His- , the K–12 segment has received the most attention in terms of public on and financing, followed by the postsecondary segment, especially

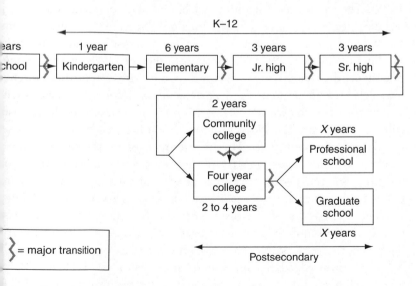

I.I   The educational system of the United States shown as a ed "educational pipeline."

180

The

As alr
promc
pipelir
who g
soriate
pipelir
cia, 19
fessori
becom

As
hierarc
in the
influen
ist, inc
ments,
trouble
school
torical
discuss

BARRIERS TO
THE PRO:

Ray

Issues related to Latina/o faculty in higher education ne
the complexity of the "educational pipeline" that exists
in the organizational dynamics that occur in highly bur
institutions (Oakes, 1985; Ovando & Collier, 1998; Sch
1998). The dynamics of institutional life involve langu
technical, economic, and other interactions that often
competition or clashes between various interests g
(Berliner & Biddle, 1995). With respect to the specific i
retention, the underlying structural complexity is
microlevel search committees, departmental, and colleg
a dynamic of their own (Padilla & Montiel, 1998), an
cultures which vary considerably across the multitiered
institutions (Tierney, 1990). This chapter focuses on th
faculty encounter in accessing the professoriate and on
after they gain access to it. Neither access nor success
understanding the nature of the difficulties is both chall

The main focus of the discussion will be on th
tenure, and promotion) and its impact on Latina/o f
higher education. First, the background influences of
will be acknowledged. Then a general framework for
which will be useful for understanding how Latina/os
suggesting ways in which Latina/o faculty can be more

X
Pre

Legen

FIGURE
segmer

after World War II. The emphasis on preschool is relatively recent, stemming largely from the impact of the Great Society program envisioned by President L. B. Johnson as a way to deal with the social frictions brought about by the civil rights movement of the 1950s and 1960s. The highest segment consists of graduate and professional schools, which are gateways to lucrative or prestigious careers and professions, including the professoriate.

With respect to Latina/o faculty, there are at least two important points to highlight with respect to the educational pipeline as depicted in Figure 11.1. First, there is ample empirical evidence to show that historically and as a whole, Latina/o students apparently achieve less than other students as they engage the various educational segments, and they seem to do worse as they progress from one segment to the next (Fisher, 1998; García, 2001). Secondly, the highest and most difficult to reach segment involves professional and graduate schools (Wilds & Wilson, 1998). Yet, it is precisely this level of education which is a prerequisite for admission into the professoriate. So while HTP is difficult and challenging for all individuals, Latina/os who have already experienced greater barriers and difficulties in the educational pipeline are bound to face additional problems and challenges in their efforts to enter and succeed in the professoriate. The nature of the "greater barriers and difficulties" experienced by Latina/os in the educational pipeline is beyond the scope of this chapter. However, they can be summarized as involving language and cultural issues, poverty, immigrant status, prejudice and discrimination, assimilationist modes of thinking, lack of political empowerment, deficit thinking about Latina/o students, etc. (Darder, Torres, & Gutíerrez, 1997; Moreno, 1999; Valencia, 1991, 1997). It is important to recognize these educational pipeline experiences not only because they have an impact on the number of Latina/os attempting to enter the professoriate, but also because they influence the interests and attitudes which Latina/os bring to the academy (Ibarra, 2001; Padilla & Chávez Chávez, 1995). The latter may be focal points for conflicts and incongruities with prevailing attitudes and interests on campus.

HTP as a Gateway and a Destination

Figure 11.2 shows a concept model of the hiring, tenure, and promotion process as typically implemented in postsecondary institutions in the United States. The top panel shows that HTP is multistaged and implicitly contained within a larger educational continuum that encompasses the educational pipeline already discussed and various post-tenure sequelae, such as post-tenure review and gaining professional stature (not shown in the model). The hiring stage determines whether Latina/os gain access to the professoriate,

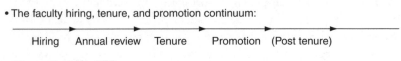

- The faculty hiring, tenure, and promotion continuum:

  ————————▶————————▶————————▶————————▶————————

  Hiring   Annual review   Tenure   Promotion   (Post tenure)

- Given rational for HTP:
  - To ensure the quality and integrity of the academic enterprise

- Achieved through:
  - Documentation and assessment of qualifications
  - Rational decision making: Expert judgment
  - Shared governance: Representation of diverse interests
  - Fairness

- Thus assuring that:
  - The competent will be hired and retained
  - The incompetent will not be hired or retained
  - Rules of fair play are followed

FIGURE 11.2   Nature and rationale for faculty HTP.

while annual reviews and the final tenure review determine whether these professors will be retained. Promotion to full professor signals successful career advancement and access to the more influential roles played by faculty in governance processes, as well as potential access to administrative roles, such as department chair, dean, provost, or president. So in many ways, the faculty hiring stage is a gateway to all of the key positions in academia. Faculty retention issues become apparent during annual reviews and final tenure review. It is during these performance reviews that institutional micropolitics become most relevant and where clashes between academic interests and attitudes (along with personal clashes) are most evident (Mindiola, 1995).

The received view of why HTP exists can be stated quite simply: it exists to ensure the quality and integrity of the academic enterprise. This objective can be achieved through various mechanisms, including the documentation and assessment of candidate qualifications, the use of rational decision-making involving expert judgment, the representation of diverse interests in the decision-making process, and the implementation of procedures that promote fairness in the review of applications. If all of these mechanisms work properly, then the expected results are that only the competent faculty will be hired and retained, the incompetent will not be hired or retained, and rules of fair play will be followed (Baez & Centra, 1995). In other words, the received view of HTP holds that only the best and the brightest are allowed into the professoriate, and of these only those who prove themselves get to stay.

• Decision-making logic:

	Decision	
Candidate	Qualified	Not qualified
Qualified	OK	False negative
Not qualified	False positive	OK

• Expected outcomes for decisions made by faculty:

	Decision	
Candidate	Qualified	Not qualified
Qualified	OK	Max. false neg.
Not qualified	Min. false pos.	OK

• Expected outcomes for decisions made by administrators:

	Decision	
Candidate	Qualified	Not qualified
Qualified	OK	Min. false neg.
Not qualified	Max. false pos.	OK

FIGURE 11.3   The logic of the HTP process.

This view of HTP is supported by a specific logic of the HTP process (see Figure 11.3). As shown in the top panel of Figure 11.3, during the hiring process a decision has to be made as to the fitness of each candidate for a faculty position. In logical terms, the candidate is either really qualified for the position or not. Likewise, a decision will be made by the hiring agent(s) as to whether the candidate is qualified or not. The object is to make correct decisions about each candidate. However, there is always the potential to render an incorrect decision. The two logical possibilities for error are that a candidate who is really qualified is considered not qualified (false negative), and a candidate who is not really qualified is considered qualified (false positive). Clearly, either of these errors can be detrimental to the academy. False positive decisions allow the incompetent to enter the professoriate, while false negative decision unjustly deny entrance to the competent.

To minimize decision errors, the hiring process usually includes decision making by both faculty and administrators. The logic of faculty decision making is shown in the second panel of Figure 11.3. Since the least desirable outcome for faculty is to have the incompetent hired, theoretically they are more susceptible to making false negative errors (i.e., qualified candidates will be turned down). However, this also minimizes the false positive errors. The logic of administrator decision making is shown in the bottom panel of Figure 11.3. Theoretically, administrators are in the best position to ensure that all candidates are treated fairly. Logically, this means that administrators are more likely to make false positive errors while minimizing false negative errors. In short, the combination of faculty expertise and administrative good judgment should result in competence and integrity in the professoriate, as espoused by the received view of HTP. Figure 11.4 summarizes the received view of HTP in relation to various issues and their conventional treatment in academia.

As shown in Figure 11.4, issues of quality, justice, and equity are addressed by the system of university governance that involves both faculty peer review (to deal with issues of quality) and administrative review (to deal largely with issues of equity and justice). Quality is maintained by minimizing the number of unqualified faculty hired, tenured, or promoted. Justice and equity are upheld by minimizing the number of qualified faculty not hired or denied tenure and promotion. Finally, equity is also maintained by minimizing discrimination on the basis of race, ethnicity, gender, etc., as is prominently asserted on most university job postings. In short, the received view holds that faculty HTP decisions are rendered within a system of checks and balances that makes decision making as effective and fair as possible (Figure 11.5). This desired state is achieved through the systematic use of faculty and administrative expertise each in its proper context.

The actual implementation of the HTP process requires multiple levels of decision making as a further check on quality and fairness (Figure 11.6). Faculty personnel committees are conjugated across the various levels of the orga-

---

• Quality, justice, and equity:
    • Peer review deals with quality issues
    • Administrative review deals with justice and equity issues

• Quality is maintained by:
    • Minimizing the number of unqualified faculty hired or retained
    • Minimizing the number of unqualified faculty who are tenured or promoted

• Justice is upheld by:
    • Minimizing the number of qualified faculty not hired or retained
    • Minimizing the number of qualified faculty denied tenure or promotion

• Equity is maintained by minimizing discrimination on the basis of:
    • Race
    • Ethnicity
    • Gender, etc.

FIGURE 11.4   Key issues in HTP and their conventional treatment.

nization, including typically the department, college, and university levels. Likewise, administrative levels involve the department chair, the college dean, the provost, the president, and ultimately the governing board of the institution. In theory, this vertically and horizontally differentiated decision-making system should result in fair and proper decisions about faculty HTP. In practice, various distorting influences can come into play which can threaten the integrity of the whole enterprise.

How HTP Goes Wrong

At the macro level, HTP is sensitive to the available supply of faculty. When there are faculty shortages (the period of the 1960s comes to mind) the qualifications for getting a faculty position may be relaxed. There are alternatives to relaxing qualifications, such as importing faculty from other countries, but there are many considerations, including cost, English language proficiency, etc., which favor the lowering of qualifications in times of faculty shortages.

At the micro level, there are quite a number of influences which can distort the ideal version of HTP. Personal networks have a strong influence on who gets hired among equally qualified candidates. It is instructive to examine the catalog of a college or university to see where its faculty obtained their degrees. Such an examination sometimes reveals that faculty are drawn from a specific university or a small set of universities. This shows that networks are in play for the purpose of landing a faculty job. Such networks may have more than one purpose, so that hiring faculty may be just one of their functions. They may

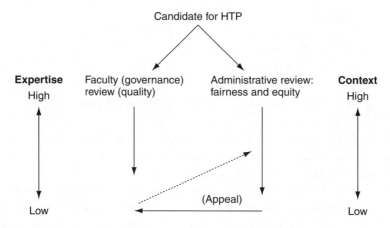

FIGURE 11.5   Theoretical HTP system of checks and balances.

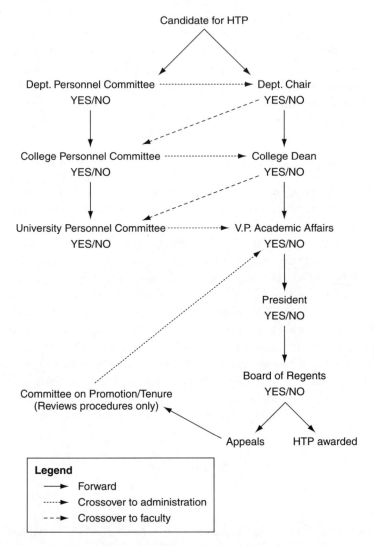

FIGURE 11.6   Typical HTP implementation process.

also serve to assist network members in getting published, obtaining grants, conducting accreditation reviews, recruiting students, getting papers accepted at national conferences, obtaining tenure and promotion, and so on.

Another microlevel influence is paradigm fit. Most research and scholarship is conducted within a specific theoretical and methodological framework. When theories or methods clash, camps will develop around specific theories or methods. These camps are not generally friendly toward each other (Guba, 1990; Reason & Rowan, 1981). If a junior professor espouses a theory or method that goes counter to the senior professors in the department or the college, the untenured professor runs the risk of bad reviews for tenure and promotion. The critical reviews are generally expressed in terms of concern for the quality of the work produced. But in reality, it is very difficult to distinguish between poor academic work and paradigm clashes. In general, the senior professors prevail, thus opening the way for distortions in HTP due to paradigm conflicts.

Besides paradigm clashes there are also personal clashes which can distort HTP. These personal clashes run the gamut of the human condition (including jealousy, envy, personality clashes, ambition, one-upmanship, egotism, etc.), and the political landscape (including gender issues, sexual orientation, race, ethnicity, religion, social class, etc.). Personal clashes are just one manifestation of the dynamics to maintain "personal turf" in the academy. Each faculty member strives to maintain an arena of influence which protects the faculty member's privileges, resources, and status. Who gets hired and fired are key decision points that help to shape the contours of a faculty member's personal turf. Personal turf is also apparent among university administrators. Administrative personal turf can distort HTP in a number of ways, including the rendering of favorable decisions for relatives, spouses, and friends (Mindiola, 1995), and making judgments that are consistent with the interests of powerful faculty members or groups, and sometimes even influential persons and power brokers in the outside community (Padilla & Montiel, 1998).

Personal turf is a way to describe the special interests that center around the individual professor or administrator. But there are also unit-level interests which on their own or in combination with personal turf can distort HTP. Each department or college has its own organizational dynamics and micropolitics. Hiring, tenure, and promotion decisions can be influenced by these unit-level micropolitics. Mindiola (1995) provides a classic example of how personal turf and unit interests at the department level conspired to produce tenure denial in his case. According to this author, his tenure was put in jeopardy because the spouse of a powerful faculty member in the department went up for tenure at the same time that he did. In order to enhance this well-connected faculty member's chances of getting tenure, Mindiola's tenure was denied at the department level under the belief that only one person would be given tenure at the university level. So by knocking out the competition, the spouse of the powerful faculty member would have a better chance of gaining tenure.

These and other distortions of HTP can affect any faculty member, majority or minority alike. However, for Latina/os and other minorities some of these distortions apply with particular virulence or in a form that is specific to minority faculty. The supply distortion, for example, is particularly salient among Latina/o faculty. So far, graduate and professional schools in the United States have not produced a sufficient number of Latina/o faculty to meet the need for such faculty (Wilds & Wilson, 1998). Faculty also have not been produced evenly across the various disciplines. There are severe Latina/o faculty shortages especially in the sciences, engineering, mathematics, and some of the professional schools, such as business administration and law. As a result of these shortages, in many cases Latina/os will not even enter the faculty applicant pools. In other cases, Latina/o faculty may be hired before they are ready, for example, before completing their dissertation.

Another distortion of HTP involves the academic interests that Latina/o faculty often bring to the campus. This problem is a variation of the paradigm clashes already discussed, but with an ethnic twist. Latina/o faculty, particularly in the social sciences, arts, humanities and some of the professions (such as education, health professions, public administration, etc.), often want to research issues and problems related to the Latino population. These interests can be seen as insignificant or irrelevant by non-minority faculty members (Ibarra, 2001; Reyes & Halcón, 1997) who presume that such ethnically focused research will not make fundamental contributions to the enhancement of legitimate knowledge within the established paradigms. When such ethnically focused research is presented for tenure review or promotion, it can be seen as low quality by the review committees, resulting in denial of tenure or promotion for the candidate. Now, it is entirely possible that such ethnically focused research could be of low quality. However, it can be almost impossible to distinguish between research that has been turned down because it is low quality and research that has been turned down because it is ethnically based and offended the interests of nonminority faculty involved in the review process. As with paradigm clashes in general, it is often the case that administrators reviewing tenure and promotion cases will go along with the interests of powerful faculty members who can write devastating critiques of academic work even when such critiques are self-serving. (For a parallel set of issues involving the hiring of Latino faculty, see the Addendum to this chapter).

For Latina/o faculty, HTP can also be distorted by what might be called the "obligation factor." Latina/o faculty often feel that they are obligated to accept onerous administrative assignments and service work with students and the local community (Ibarra, 2001; Padilla & Montiel, 1998; Reyes & Halcón, 1997). This administrative and service work takes away from the faculty member's efforts to conduct research, publish, and develop a record of teaching excellence. The service obligation factor is particularly devastating for untenured professors who are constantly under the microscope and expected to demonstrate that they deserve to be tenured. Instead of spending time in the laboratory, the library, gathering data in the field, or writing papers and books, Latina/o faculty—discharging an unrealistic service obligation—will be out recruiting students, getting involved with community issues, or providing service (and even mere window dressing) on too many university committees which need minority representation. Whether through personal inclination or organizational pressures, the obligation factor can cause considerable distortion of HTP for Latina/o faculty in ways that are difficult to discern by members of review committees who themselves may not have been subject to the obligation factor.

Distortions of HTP as they apply to Latina/o faculty also can be seen in terms of the quality and justice issues already discussed. Specific strategies and practices by hiring agents of a university can distort the claim of quality in HTP. Making "defensive hires" is one example of such practices. In this case, below average (or those not ready to be hired) Latina/o faculty are hired so that they can be eliminated during the annual performance reviews or the final tenure review. This practice allows an institution to fend off criticisms that it is not hiring Latina/o faculty while ensuring that those faculty who are hired will not be retained. In effect, a revolving door for Latina/o faculty is produced. Another practice, as already noted, is paradigmatic filtering. This practice may result in quality faculty, but only for those Latina/o faculty who are agreeable to prevailing academic perspectives, i.e., those who will not rock the academic boat. There is also the practice of "stacking the deck," where Latina/o faculty will be included in the short list of job applicants but only to show color on the short list. They will not be hired, even when well qualified, but they will be tallied up to dress up affirmative action reports.

In terms of fairness and justice, there are various practices which distort this aspect of HTP in relation to Latina/os. One such practice is "skimming the cream," where only the very top notch Latina/o faculty will be hired. While this practice will maximize the chances for getting tenure, it also eliminates from the professoriate Latina/os who have more modest, but nevertheless acceptable, levels of talent and preparation. There are plenty of examples of average professors among majority professors in academia, but this will never be the case for Latina/o professors in institutions which practice skimming the cream of Latina/o professors. Another distortion of fairness is the practice of "making non-offers" to Latina/o professors. In this case, a noncompetitive offer is made by the hiring agent as a means to dissuade a prospective faculty member from accepting a position. If the faculty member is inexperienced in negotiating faculty positions, or simply gets offended by the non-offer and withdraws from the position, the institution will hire someone else and the Latino community will have nothing to complain about since the candidate withdrew voluntarily. This tactic is particularly effective because academic job negotiations are always shielded from public scrutiny. It is most useful when there are other candidates still in the applicant pool who are more congenial to the hiring agent. Still another distorting practice is to delay the hiring process. The hiring agent can simply wait a long time to make an offer, hoping that the applicant in the mean-time will accept a job elsewhere. This tactic is particularly useful when the Latina/o candidate is the sole applicant left in a search. If the applicant goes elsewhere, the job search will be closed and perhaps reopened the following year when a different pool of candidates will be considered.

It is important to recognize that distortions of HTP, whether of quality or fairness, are extremely difficult to identify and document in particular cases. Even when HTP goes terribly wrong, the most likely outcome is that the wronged applicant will take his or her lumps and move on. But there are exceptions. When faculty hiring and tenure cases wind up in court, there is a rare opportunity to peek into the inner workings of HTP in academia. An example involving tenure was already mentioned in the Mindiola (1995) case. A good example of what can go wrong in the hiring of Latina/o faculty is the Acuña case. The Addendum to this chapter is a very small part of the thou-sands of pages generated by this celebrated case. Included in the Addendum is the testimony provided by Padilla, who was an expert witness for the plaintiff in this trial. A close reading of the testimony will demonstrate some of the dis-tortions to HTP already discussed. It also will reveal how subtle, overpower-ing, and devastating those distortions can be for an applicant.

Proactive Strategies for Latina/o Faculty Access and Retention

The robustness of the HTP system as already described, coupled with the sub-tlety and multiplicity of distortions to which it is susceptible, creates a profes-soriate that is very challenging for Latina/os to access, and once in, to move up in. Nevertheless, there has been considerable thought given to this problem by various policy makers, educational leaders, and constituency groups, start-ing as far back as the late 1960s (Aguirre, Jr., 2000; Aguirre, Jr., & Martínez, 1993; Astin, 1982; Chicano Coordinating Council for Higher Education, 1969; Olivas, 1979; Turner & Myers, Jr., 2000). The strategy of affirmative action, which was favored by the civil rights movement, seems to have lost support over the past thirty years. Under affirmative action, institutions of higher education receiving federal funds were required to take affirmative steps to hire minorities in proportion to their numbers in the various official job categories. However, since Latina/os were not proportionately represented in the various academic fields as faculty members, affirmative action was short-circuited from the start for this population. Colleges and universities were not required under the doctrine of affirmative action to produce Latina/o faculty in proportion to their numbers in the general population. So in spite of the harsh criticisms of affirmative action made by its critics, it seems that, at least for the Latina/o population, the program often was more effective as window dressing for institutions than as a means to produce more Latina/o faculty and to get them hired by colleges and universities.

In spite of these difficulties with affirmative action (Reyes and Halcón, 1997), as Latina/os became more involved with postsecondary institutions during the 1970s and 1980s, specific strategies aimed at influencing the HTP process did emerge. At the hiring stage of HTP, it was found that set-asides of faculty positions specifically designated for diversity hires did indeed lead to more hiring of Latina/o faculty. Another effective strategy was to include Latina/os in "target of opportunity" hiring programs, which are generally designed to bring outstanding faculty (typically non-minority) to a campus. Still another good strategy was to "grow your own" by providing incentives for departments to increase the supply of Latina/o faculty across the disciplines. All of these efforts to increase access to the professoriate within the framework of HTP required strong leadership and support both from high level university administrators and from Latina/o campus and community activists who needed to exert continuous political pressure on the universities to hire more Latina/o faculty.

At the tenure and promotion stage of HTP, at least two strategies were advocated for enhancing the tenurability and promotability of Latina/o faculty. One strategy was to enhance their research and publication productivity by designing structured ways to provide faculty release time, research assistants, seeds grants, etc., to Latina/o faculty, especially those who were untenured. The most sophisticated expression of this strategy involved the creation of various research centers or institutes specifically designed to focus on Latina/o research. Through assignment or affiliation with these research units, Latina/o professors could be given material and moral support to become productive scholars, even when their research focused on ethnic topics. When implemented diligently and with sufficient support from university leaders, this strategy does seem to increase the tenure and promotion chances for Latina/o faculty. However, the effectiveness of this strategy varies by discipline. The Latina/o research centers seldom encompass all of the fields typically found on a university campus, especially the natural and physical sciences, mathematics, engineering, and the like. Latina/o research centers which are usually geared to the arts, humanities, or social sciences (or their application), often have minimal impact on Latina/o faculty in other fields.

Another strategy that has been advocated for alleviating the problems of HTP for Latina/os is for senior administrators, such as provosts or vice presidents for academic affairs, to conduct ad hoc reviews of Latina/o tenure and promotion cases when it is suspected that negative recommendations by faculty review committees and lower level administrators have been rendered due to distortions of HTP. Although the author is aware of at least one large public university in the Southwest that agreed in principle to such ad hoc reviews, there doesn't seem to be even one instance in which the university actually conducted such an ad hoc review. Nevertheless, the idea of keeping an eye on HTP, given the known distortions to which it is susceptible in the case of Latina/o faculty, can still be carried out but in more informal ways. Two or three senior faculty members speaking informally to the provost or vice president for academic affairs can influence the outcome of tenure and promotion decisions, especially when there is evidence that HTP did not proceed smoothly in a particular case. Such informal advocacy has limits due to the secretive nature of tenure and promotion reviews. It also requires that senior Latina/o professors already be present in the institution and that these senior professors be willing to advocate for untenured professors or those going up for promotion.

Once Latina/o faculty are tenured or promoted, postsecondary institutions still have to struggle to retain those faculty. In academia, it is often the case that the best chances for salary increases and career advancement occur when a faculty member is offered a job by a competing institution. Naturally, it is not uncommon for many faculty members, including Latina/os, to test the waters by applying for faculty or administrative positions in other colleges or universities. When there are inherent faculty shortages, which is true for Latina/o faculty, a postsecondary institution that has managed to assemble a significant number of Latina/o faculty must guard against being raided by other campuses. An effective strategy against such raids is to make competitive counteroffers to faculty who have documented offers of employment elsewhere. Clearly, there are limits to this strategy because some Latina/o faculty will choose to leave for personal reasons, or the cost of keeping them is simply too high. Nevertheless, it is worth protecting an institution's investment in Latina/o faculty by making competitive counteroffers when other campuses try to lure them away.

Are there no alternatives to HTP? Alternatives that are more than the workarounds already discussed? Certainly one can conceive of a radical alternative to HTP, one that most likely would reshape the entire postsecondary educational landscape. Perhaps HTP should be removed entirely from colleges and universities and placed instead in the hands of a civil service type of system. HTP would be driven by examinations and review boards that would be independent of the unit hiring a faculty member. Such a system would remove the micropolitics and distorting special interests inherent in the current HTP process. Hiring units would be required to hire from an official list of qualified candidates. Such a system would not only be merit driven, but it would save institutions of higher education thousands of hours of faculty time which under the current system must be expended in search committees. This time could be spent more productively in teaching and research activities.

Such a radical proposal is unlikely to be implemented in the foreseeable future. Therefore, less radical proposals are needed that can influence HTP in its current form on behalf of Latina/os. What is needed is more flexibility in hiring, tenuring, and promoting Latino faculty. Such flexibility can be defended under the philosophy that postsecondary institutions must constitute themselves in a manner that reflects the diversity of populations, cultures, etc., present in the larger society that they serve. The concept of diversity goes beyond the idea of affirmative action. Affirmative action was designed to make amends for the effects of past discriminatory practices. Diversity is driven by a political understanding that in a democratic society every citizen has a voice and a vote. To privilege some citizens and to ignore others is not a sound policy for a public institution to follow. Sooner or later those who are being ignored will make their presence felt through the political process. When such political forces become large enough, public institutions will have to change anyway. It is a function of effective leadership to anticipate those political changes and take proactive steps to fall in line with new political configurations.

Figure 11.7 shows the key elements for creating flexibility to promote faculty diversity in postsecondary institutions. First, a policy framework for

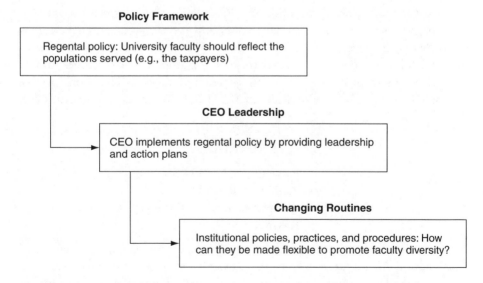

FIGURE 11.7   Creating flexibility to promote faculty diversity in public postsecondary institutions.

diversity must be created. Accomplishing this task is the responsibility of governing boards. Secondly, the highest levels of institutional leadership must design and implement action plans for faculty diversity. Finally, action plans must be implemented by the line units in the university. Throughout the university, institutional routines may have to be modified in order for diversity hiring practices to take hold. Otherwise, the inherent distortions to which routine HTP is susceptible will vitiate all attempts to diversify the faculty.

Summary

Although not discussed at length in this chapter, the influences of the educational pipeline on the ability of Latina/o faculty to access and succeed in the professoriate should not be underestimated and more research needs to be done in this area. Most likely the attitudes and experiences that Latina/os acquire while struggling through the educational pipeline create a particular mindset that influences how Latina/os approach the role of a faculty member and what they expect from academia. When these role perceptions and expectations are not congruent with those of majority faculty, conditions are created for conflict and disagreement that can impact the success of Latina/os as faculty members.

The logic and dynamics of HTP were discussed in this chapter, along with the various distortions that can occur and the strategies that have been used in the past to help Latina/os gain greater access and success in the professoriate. The hiring, tenure, and promotion (HTP) system currently operating in U.S. postsecondary institutions has deep roots and is very well entrenched. It is unlikely that major changes will be made to HTP in the near future, in spite of recent efforts by governing boards to look for alternatives to tenure and to require periodic post-tenure reviews of tenured faculty. Thus, prospective Latina/o faculty must learn to deal with the HTP system as currently instituted.

Addendum

November 21, 1994
RE: Acuña vs. Regents et al.
Complete Statement of Testimony
Raymond V. Padilla

I have been asked to give an opinion regarding the professional competence of Dr. Rodolfo Acuña, an applicant for appointment as a senior Professor with tenure in the Department of Chicano Studies at the University of California at Santa Barbara.

I. *Opinion.* My considered opinion is that Dr. Acuña is an authority on Chicano Studies, and that he is one of the top scholars in the field.

II. *Basis for the opinion.* In determining the stature of an academic, it is a customary practice in academic institutions to consider at least the combined weight of two sources of evidence: (1) the academic's contributions to his or her field of study, and (2) the national and international reputation of the academic.

A. *Dr. Acuña's academic contributions to the field of Chicano Studies.* The most important substantive contribution that Dr. Acuña has made to date is his book *Occupied America,* which has been in print for over twenty years. This publication represents a pioneering contribution to the field because it begins to define in academic terms the content, boundaries, and themes of Chicano Studies, particularly as seen through the theories and methods of an historian. *Occupied America* has become a part of the canon, or corpus, of scholarly literature that defines the field of Chicano Studies as an academic activity. In academia, for a work to be considered as a part of the canon of its field requires that the work make a fundamental contribution to the field such that thinking in the field be shaped by it, that it survive the critique of scholars in the field over a sustained period of time, and that new generations of scholars find valued insights and inspiration from the work even when newer scholarship has taken the field in new directions. *Occupied America* has all of these characteristics, an opinion that is shared by a number of the extramural reviewers who submitted review letters on Dr. Acuña's academic work.

B. *Dr. Acuña's national and international reputation.* There are at least three customary ways to determine an academic's national and international reputation: (1) from the opinions of experts in the academic's field of study, (2) from the academic's leadership in the field, typically as manifested through involvement in professional associations central to the field of study, and (3) through honors and awards that have been bestowed on the academic.

1. *The opinions of experts in the field.* The letters of extramural reviewers, a number of whom are themselves considered experts in the field of Chicano Studies, consistently and emphatically state that Dr. Acuña is one of the top academics in the field of Chicano Studies. For example, Dr. Juan Gómez-Quiñones, a full professor in the Department of History at the University of California at Los Angeles, says unequivocally that "Professor Rudy Acuña is among the top three senior professors in the field of Chicano Studies nationally." Professor Deena J. González, Associate Professor of History from the Claremont Colleges, holds the opinion that Dr. Acuña is "indisputably one of our highest-ranking academicians." Likewise, Dr. Arnoldo DeLeón, a well-published and acclaimed Professor of History, categorically asserts that "In the field of Chicano history, Professor Acuña is regarded as a foremost authority."

Other extramural reviewers express similar opinions. What is noteworthy in these opinions is the explicit and categorical manner in which recognized experts in the field of Chicano Studies give testimony to the the high reputation that Dr. Acuña has earned as an academic.

2. *Leadership in the field.* According to Dr. Acuña's curriculum vitae, he has made scholarly presentations at just about every meeting of the National Association for Chicano Studies (NACS), the flagship professional association for scholars interested in Chicano Studies. This has given Dr. Acuña's academic work a critical audience of specialists who can support or challenge his ideas. In addition, Dr. Acuña has been widely sought after over many years as a consultant in the design of Chicano Studies programs at dozens of colleges and universities which range from local community colleges to top tier universities such as the University of Michigan, Harvard University, the University of Wisconsin, and the University of California at Berkeley. Consultation at top universities normally requires that the consultant have a national reputation in his or her field. Finally, Dr. Acuña has been invited frequently to give lectures and keynote addresses to a wide range of academic and general audiences. This indicates not only that Dr. Acuña is held in high regard by specialists in the field, but also that he is able to communicate the key concepts of his speciality to the general public.

3. *Honors and awards.* Dr. Acuña has received significant honors and awards for his contributions to the field of Chicano Studies. The most notable of these are the Distinguished Scholar Award given by the National Association for Chicano Studies, the Homenaje (Honor) bestowed by the University of Guadalajara Feria Internacional del Libro for being the Outstanding U.S. Scholar of U.S.-Mexico Studies, and the Rockefeller Humanities Fellowship, among others.

C. *Assessment of contradicting evidence.* In reaching the opinion that I have expressed regarding the professional competence of Dr. Acuña, I have carefully considered the opinions of others, namely the extramural reviewers, the Chair of the Department of Chicano Studies (Yolanda Broyles-González), Provost David A. Sprecher, the members of the Ad Hoc Review Committee, and the members of the Committee on Academic Personnel as expressed in the various administrative memos and committee reports of record. Both the extramural reviewers and the Chair of the Department of Chicano Studies expressed opinions that are substantially consistent with my own regarding Dr. Acuña's professional competence. But there is a stark contrast between these emphatically positive opinions and the equally emphatic but negative opinions held by the Provost and the two committees mentioned above. Such diametrically opposed opinions require at least a brief comment.

1. *Arguments of the Ad Hoc Review Committee.* A key argument of this committee is that Dr. Acuña is a "cult professor." This claim is based on a single word that is found in one of the letters of the extramural reviewers. In the original source, the word is used oddly in reference to the book *Occupied America,* not to Dr. Acuña. Given that there are thousands of words that were written by the extramural reviewers, none of whom expressed the view that Dr. Acuña is a "cult professor", it is rather surprising that the Ad Hoc Committee chose to build a key argument on such a thin reed of evidence. In the original text, the word is used in a parenthetical expression which on close reading seems oddly out of context. Given that there is no similar expression used by any of the other outside reviewers, one has to at least consider the possibility that the four letter word is a typographical error, perhaps that the intent was to write "cultivated" instead of "cult" which would make much more sense in the context of describing a book that has been revised, improved, and cultivated over a period of some twenty years. The Ad Hoc Committee goes on to characterize Dr. Acuña as a "master spirit." This is a clear exaggeration that is not supported by the available evidence, but that plays on the committee's portrayal of Dr. Acuña as a purported cult leader. Along with the malignant powers attributed to Dr. Acuña by the committee, the committee also perceives the Chicano Studies faculty as naive innocents who would be mesmerized and overshadowed by the occult powers of Dr. Acuña.

This conjured scenario then gives license to the Ad Hoc Committee to arrogated unto itself a custodial responsibility for the Chicano Studies Department, which the committee characterized as a "trustee responsibility." This is an extremely odd role for such a committee given that most departments jealously guard their departmental autonomy, something which is normally protected by most university governance systems. But the Ad Hoc Committee reasoned that since the department was small and conflicted, neither of which characteristics are unique to the Chicano Studies Department, they should step in as the arbiters of personnel decisions. Given this committee stance, their fantastic characterization of Dr. Acuña as a "cult professor" then becomes, in the committee's opinion, a fatal flaw that should bar him from exercising leadership in the Chicano Studies Department.

In an effort to bolster its case, the Committee also argues that Dr. Acuña might, as the lone senior professor in the department, become "dictatorial." Yet, such a speculation is clearly contradicted by the opinions of the extramural reviewers who have known and worked with Dr. Acuña for many years. To wit: "For being a senior scholar, I find him [Dr. Acuña] to be actually quite humble" or "Professor Acuña is also known to many of his colleagues and students as an incomparable administrator" or "After two years as Chair, he [Dr. Acuña] initiated a rotating Chair program, playing a mentoring role in order to develop and encourage the emergence of leadership within the Department." These characterizations of Dr. Acuña from people who have known and worked with him are diametrically opposed to the characterizations of the committee which have no evidentiary basis.

The Ad Hoc Committee also argues that Dr. Acuña's scholarship is wanting, mostly because it does not, in their view, adhere to "solid, traditional history." Instead, they argue that his work "has a political agenda," and that it lacks the features of acceptable scholarship, namely "judicious, thoughtful reflection on the evidence." Yet, historian Juan Gómez Quiñones writes about the same work that it "is a reflective distillation of a very wide extensive reading of primary and secondary sources." Here again are two diametrically opposed conclusions, one from a committee of faculty with no expertise in Chicano Studies, the other from a senior professor in the same university who is a recognized expert in Chicano Studies. Another outside reviewer with expertise in Chicano Studies declares that Dr. Acuña's academic works continue to be regarded as "part of the bedrock which has provided guidance, critical appraisal, and theoretical rigor to many scholars." This comment is in stark contradiction to the Ad Hoc Committee's conclusion that Dr. Acuña is "an inveterate polemicist and pamphleteer who ignores the rules of evidence." Such a conclusion must be evaluated in the context of another extramural reviewer who noted that "Professor Acuña endeavored to have all unpublished manuscripts, theses, and dissertations cited in *Occupied America*." In like manner, the Committee concludes that Dr. Acuña "lacks the kind of reflective, theoretically sophisticated mind that every department needs." Yet, one of the expert extramural reviewers declares that "Acuña has written seminal studies of originality, conviction and rigor." As one encounters numerous contradictory positions along the same lines between the conclusions of the Committee, which had no Chicano Studies experts among its members, and the opinions of extramural experts in the field with personal knowledge of Dr. Acuña, I find that my own opinion is in agreement with the informed opinion of the extramural experts regarding the merits of Dr. Acuña's professional standing in the field.

The Ad Hoc Committee expresses reservations about Dr. Acuña on grounds other than the quality of his work or the nature of his character. One such reservation is that he "has never trained doctoral students." This appears to be factually true, but it is important to weigh this fact against the reality that the Chicano Studies Department to which Dr. Acuña seeks appointment does not currently offer a Ph.D. program and there do not seem to be any plans to offer one in the near future. Moreover, he has extensive experience guiding masters-level students. Since there are no doctoral students to chair in the department, one has to wonder about the relevance of this criterion for employment. Another concern is that Dr. Acuña would be the first full-time appointment in the Chicano Studies Department which would therefore preclude "periodic peer review in an established discipline and department." This criticism reflects not so much on Dr. Acuña's professional standing as it does on the Committee's view of the Chicano Studies Department as one that has to be watched over by faculty from other departments of the University. This custodial license is not normally given to personnel committees whose chief and customary function within the governance system of higher education is to review hiring procedures to ensure that they were properly followed by the hiring unit in reviewing candidates for faculty positions, and, to the extent that relevant expertise is available to the committee, to render an opinion regarding the applicant's qualifications. Finally, the Committee expresses reservations about Dr. Acuña because he only received affirmative votes from half of the Department faculty, the other half having abstained. The abstentions are considered "a most serious matter." Yet, the report of the Department Chair sheds light on the nature of these abstentions. Two faculty members who abstained expressed modest reservations about Dr. Acuña's colloquium presentation, and the third faculty member expressed reservations about his not being "in the forefront of gender issues." Such criticisms would normally appear in the statement of strengths and weakness of a candidate, but they can hardly be elevated to the status of "a most serious matter" that would seriously jeopardize a candidate.

In summary, the opinions expressed by the Ad Hoc Committee regarding the professional competence of Dr. Acuña are inconsistent with the opinions of outside experts with respect to the merit of Dr. Acuña's scholarly contributions. The Committee's characterizations of Dr. Acuña's personality traits, e.g. "cult leader," have no foundation in fact and are largely a fabrication of the Committee. Further, the abnormally expanded powers of the committee which allowed it to arrogate unto itself custodial powers over the affairs of the Chicano Studies Department constitutes a departure and misapplication of the principles of faculty governance on which such a committee is founded. Such committees customarily adhere to a fastidious regard for the autonomy of academic departments. And while the Ad Hoc Committee chose to "adopt the strictest kind of scrutiny" in the Acuña case, it failed to implement one important procedure designed to guide its work: "As the University enters new fields of endeavor and refocuses its ongoing activities, cases will arise in which the proper work of faculty members departs markedly from established academic patterns. In such cases, the review committees must take exceptional care to apply the criteria with suf-ficient flexibility" (Section 210-1d, Academic Personnel Manual). No such flexibility is evident in the committee's consideration of the Acuña candi-dacy. Taking all these considerations into account, I do not see compelling evidence in the work of the Ad Hoc Committee that would dissuade me from the opinion that I have given above regarding Dr. Acuña's professional competence.

2. *Arguments of Provost David A. Sprecher.* In recommending denial of appointment, Provost Sprecher argues that the research of Dr. Acuña is "not archival" and that "its nature differs from the quality of research expected of ladder faculty in the UC system." The first assertion is emphatically contra-dicted by the extramural reviewers as noted above. The second assertion is too vague to fathom its meaning. In reaching his conclusion about Dr. Acuña's academic competence, Provost Sprecher failed to properly weigh the opinion of outside experts because of his belief that "It is to his political activities rather than scholarly work that the letters are mostly addressed, and some of the support comes from writers without the expertise to assess the research. By and large the letters are not analytical." With respect to the first point, even a cursory reading of the extramural letters reveals that the majority of reviewers clearly focused on the significance of Dr. Acuña's scholarly works, as opposed to his extracurricular activities. The Provost's conclusion on this point is clearly in error. With respect to the second point, it is true that one or two of the reviewers expressed reservations about not being experts in Chicano his-tory. However, they are all established professors in their respective disciplines, and so their status is not different from the university faculty who participated in the two committees reviewing Dr. Acuña's candidacy, since no members of those committees are experts in Chicano Studies or Chicano history. Thus, to be consistent, the Provost would have had to dismiss the assessments of both review committees, something which he did not do. Finally, if indeed one or two reviewers were not competent to evaluate Dr. Acuña's scholarly accom-plishments, this would be a procedural problem that belongs to the university and not to the candidate since the candidate has little if any control over who is to be selected as an extramural reviewer. With respect to the final point, that the letters were not analytical, this is clearly a misreading of the majority of letters, some of which go into great detail analyzing the content, importance, and impact of Dr. Acuña's writing. Here again, the Provost is simply in error.

Another argument is that there "appears to be a lack of invitations to par-ticipate in scholarly meetings and to present papers, and the more general absence of participation in the profession." This conclusion is not supported either by the evidence provided in Dr. Acuña's curriculum vitae or in the reports of the extramural reviewers.

Another key argument is that there is not sufficient Departmental support and that the Department Chair "presents strong rhetoric in support of the case." Yet the original report of the Department Chair reveals a well-argued case for the appointment of a senior professor who will lead and guide the development of the Department into the twenty-first century. The support and lack thereof for the candidate by the Department faculty is carefully documented. Clearly, the Provost discounted the cogent arguments of the Department Chair in favor of his own view of the Department based on "conversations" with the Chair and the faculty.

Taking the above considerations into account, I did not find persuasive the Provost's critique of Dr. Acuña's professional competence, especially since he so grossly misread the letters of extramural reviewers.

3. *Arguments of the Committee on Academic Personnel (CAP)*. As a start, the CAP repeats the key negative arguments contained in the reports of the Ad Hoc Committee and the Provost. Since these arguments have been considered above, no further comment needs to be made on this portion of the CAP report. The independent comments of the CAP pertain to four areas: research, reviewers, teaching, and service. With respect to research, the committee concluded the following about *Occupied America:* "It is not however a scholarly monograph. It would in our judgment be problematic as to whether such a book would move a scholar to tenure in the absence of other scholarly work." As noted above, this conclusion about the importance of *Occupied America* to the field of Chicano Studies is totally contradicted by the expert opinions of the extramural reviewers. Since there were no Chicano Studies specialists in the CAP committee, greater credence has to be given to the opinions of the extramural reviewers.

With respect to the reviewers, the CAP report simply assembles a hodge-podge of quotes from the various reviews that do not constitute a cogent argument as to the professional competence or lack thereof of Dr. Acuña or of the reviewers themselves for that matter. Nor does the string of quotations illuminate or properly interpret or summarize the views of the various [external] reviewers. In tone, the collage of quotations tends to leave the reader wondering about what the reviewers think of Dr. Acuña's professional competence. In fact, the reviewers are emphatic about the high accomplishments that Dr. Acuña has achieved in the field of Chicano Studies. This fact is not properly reflected in the CAP summary.

The CAP report devotes exactly three sentences to Dr. Acuña's teaching ability. One of those sentences alludes to Dr. Acuña's lack of work with doctoral students. Clearly, the CAP failed to give proper weight to Dr. Acuña's stellar accomplishments in teaching as documented by the opinions of the extramural reviewers. This is a failure of omission that tended to disparage the candidate's accomplishments.

Finally, with respect to service, the CAP devoted exactly two sentences to this topic. Here again, the committee failed by omission. As in the case with teaching, this failure of omission tended to disparage the candidate's accomplishments in university and community service.

In the context of these failures of omission by the CAP, it is instructive to refer to the prime directive contained in the Academic Personnel Manual (section 210-1d) with respect to the criteria for appointment of professors: *"Superior intellectual attainment, as evidenced both in teaching and research or other creative achievement, is an indispensable qualification for appointment or promotion to tenure positions"* (emphasis in the original). It is difficult to imagine how the CAP could have conscientiously applied this prime directive when the topics of teaching and service were dispensed within a total of five sentences.

On the basis of the above considerations, it is clear that the CAP did a superficial job in reviewing Dr. Acuña's candidacy for appointment as a professor, and thus their arguments are not persuasive and so do not change the opinion that I have presented above regarding Dr. Acuña's professional competence.

III. *Summary.* I have presented my opinion that Dr. Acuña is an authority on Chicano Studies and that he is one of the top scholars in the field. I have given the basis for my opinion, which includes consideration of contradicting opinion and my rejection of it.

References

Aguirre, Jr., A. (2000). *Women and minority faculty in the academic workplace: Recruitment, retention, and academic culture.* San Francisco: Jossey-Bass.

Aguirre, Jr., A., & Martínez, R. O. (1993). *Chicanos in higher education: Issues and dilemmas for the 21st century.* ASHE-ERIC Higher Education Report No. 3. Washington, DC.: The George Washington University, School of Education and Human Development.

Astin, A. W. (1982). *Minorities in American higher education.* San Francisco: Jossey-Bass.

Baez, B., & Centra, J. (1995). *Tenure, promotion, and reappointment: Legal and administrative implications.* ASHE-ERIC Higher Education Report No. 1. Washington, DC: The George Washington University School of Education and Human Development.

Berliner, D. C., & Biddle, B. J. (1995). *The manufactured crisis: Myths, fraud, and the attack on America's public schools.* New York: Addison-Wesley.

Chicano Coordinating Council on Higher Education. (1969). *El plan de Santa Barbara: A Chicano plan for higher education.* Oakland, CA: La Causa Publications.

Darder, A., Torres, T. D., & Gutíerrez, H. (Eds.). (1997). *Latinos and education: A critical reader.* New York: Routledge.

Fisher, M. (1998). *Latino education. Status and prospects.* Washington, D.C.: National Council of La Raza.

García, E. (2001). *Hispanic education in the United States. Raíces y alas.* New York: Rowman & Littlefield.

Guba, E. G. (Ed.). (1990). *The paradigm dialog.* Newbury Park, CA: Sage Publications.

Ibarra, R. A. (2001). *Beyond affirmative action. Reframing the context of higher education.* Madison: University of Wisconsin Press.

Jalomo, Jr., R. (1995). *Latino students in transition: An analysis of the first-year experience in community college.* Unpublished doctoral dissertation, College of Education, Arizona State University, Tempe.

Mindiola, T. (1995). Getting tenure at the U. In R. V. Padilla & R. Chávez Chávez (Eds.), *The leaning ivory tower: Latino professors in American universities* (pp. 29–52). Albany, NY: State University of New York Press.

Moreno, J. F. (Ed.). (1999). *The elusive quest for equality: 150 years of Chicano/Chicana education.* Cambridge, MA: Harvard Educational Review.

Oakes, J. (1985). *Keeping track: How schools structure inequality.* New Haven, CT: Yale University Press.

Olivas, M. (1979). *The dilemma of access: Minorities in two year colleges.* Washington, DC: Howard University Press.

Ovando, C. J., & Collier, V. P. (1998). *Bilingual and ESL classrooms: Teaching in multicultural contexts* (2nd ed.). New York: McGraw-Hill.

Padilla, R. V., & Chávez Chávez, R. (Eds.). (1995). *The leaning ivory tower: Latino professors in American universities.* Albany, NY: State University of New York Press.

Padilla, R. V., & Montiel, M. (1998). *Debatable diversity: Critical dialogues on change in American universities.* Lanham, MD: Rowman & Littlefield.

Reason, P., & Rowan, J. (Eds.) (1981). *Human inquiry: A sourcebook of new paradigm research.* New York: John Wiley & Sons.

Reyes, M., & Halcón, J. (1997). Racism in academia: The old wolf revisited. In A. Darder, R. D. Torres, & H. Gutíerrez (Eds.), *Latinos and education. A critical reader* (pp. 423–428). New York: Routledge.

Romo, H. D., & Falbo, T. (1996). *Latino high school graduation: Defying the odds.* Austin: University of Texas Press.

Schmidt, Sr., R. (2000). *Language policy and identity politics in the United States.* Philadelphia: Temple University Press.

Spring, J. (1998). *Conflict of interests: The politics of American education* (3rd ed.). Boston: McGraw-Hill.

Tierney, W. G. (Ed.). (1990). *Assessing academic climates and cultures.* San Francisco: Jossey-Bass.

Turner, C. S. V., & Myers, Jr., S. L. (2000). *Faculty of color in academe: Bittersweet success.* Boston: Allyn and Bacon.

Valencia, R. R. (Ed.). (1991). *Chicano school failure and success: Research and policy agendas for the 1990s*. New York: The Falmer Press.

Valencia, R. R. (Ed.). (1997). *The evolution of deficit thinking: Educational thought and practice*. Washington, DC: The Falmer Press.

Valenzuela, A. (1999). *Subtractive schooling. U.S.-Mexican youth and the politics of caring*. Albany, NY: State University of New York Press.

Wilds, D. J., & Wilson, R. (1998). *Minorities in higher education, 1997–98: Sixteenth annual status report*. Washington, DC: American Council on Education.

Roberto A. Ibarra

Roberto A. Ibarra is special assistant for diversity, Office of the President, and associate professor of sociology, at the University of New Mexico. He is a social anthropologist and a nationally recognized expert on minority issues in higher education. He was recently appointed to direct and coordinate the University of New Mexico's (UNM) strategic diversity initiatives, and to help UNM achieve its diversity goals in attracting and retaining underrepresented faculty and staff.

From 1995 to 2001, Dr. Ibarra served as assistant vice chancellor for Academic Affairs at the University of Wisconsin-Madison. His responsibilities included supporting faculty initiatives for collaboration with historically Black colleges and universities, Tribal colleges, and Hispanic-serving institutions.

Prior to his most recent position, Ibarra was dean in residence for the Council of Graduate Schools in Washington, D.C. (1994–95), and chaired the CGS Committee on Minorities in Graduate Education (1995–96). He also previously served as assistant dean of the Graduate School, Office of Fellowships and Minority Programs at UW-Madison (1989–97); and as assistant dean of the College of Letters and Science also at UW-Madison, (1986–89).

He also was a legislative assistant, Wisconsin State Senate (1985–86); equal rights officer, Wisconsin State Personnel Commission, Madison (1984–85); employment opportunity specialist, Wisconsin State Division of Affirmative Action (1983–84); and, administrator, Mexican-American Migrant and Bilingual Education Programs, Arlington Heights, Illinois (1969–71). He also was an assistant and, later, associate professor of anthropology at Fort Lewis College, Durango, Colorado (1976–84).

Dr. Ibarra holds a Masters and a Ph.D. in social/cultural anthropology from the University of Wisconsin-Madison (1976). His latest book, *Beyond Affirmative action: Reframing the Context of Higher Education* (University of Wisconsin Press, 2001), is a study of Latino graduate students, faculty, administrators, and non-academics across the country. That research recovered a significant new multicontext design for diversity that is becoming recognized as a new paradigm for educational change.

12

LATINA/O FACULTY
AND THE TENURE PROCESS
IN CULTURAL CONTEXT

Roberto A. Ibarra

Academia continues to be the largest employer of Latinos and Latinas who hold doctoral degrees. Yet, the tenure rate for Latina/o full-time undergraduate faculty from 1989 to 1996 declined nearly 19%, the largest decline among all the underrepresented populations surveyed in higher education (Carter & Wilson, 1997, p. 35). For Latino males the tenure rate is about 44%, but for Latinas the rate is even lower, not quite 38% in 1996 (Carter & Wilson, 1997). This decline finally began to reverse itself in 1997 (Harvey, 2001). Even so, these statistics, coupled with a tight job market and fewer faculty retirements than expected during the 1990s (Bowen & Rudenstein, 1992), give more than a little credence to the impression that academia has ignored Latinos. It is crucial to understand the current circumstances before we develop solutions.

If they are to generate change in higher education, Latino faculty members need to achieve a critical mass in the U.S. professoriate. While some see optimistic trends in the increasing percentages of minority faculty (Schneider, 1997; Harvey, 2001), other evidence shows that the progress toward building a tenured Latino faculty continues to be very slow. For instance, data from the American Council on Education show that only 2.3% of all faculty in 1993

This chapter has been adapted from *Beyond Affirmative Action: Reframing the Context of Higher Education* (2001), with permission from The University of Wisconsin Press.

were Latino (Carter & Wilson, 1997). A recent report on faculty shows little has changed. According to the National Center for Education Statistics, Latinos still comprised only 2.6% of all faculty in 1997 (Roey, Skinner, Fernández, & Barbett, 1999, p. 11).

According to Alicea (1995), the highest percentages of Latino faculty are found among the growing number of lecturers and instructors, primarily adjunct teachers, on our campuses. Data from the Higher Education Research Institute (HERI) survey of nearly thirty-four thousand faculty show that among Latinos surveyed in 1996, which was about 2.2% of all faculty surveyed, fewer were above the rank of assistant professor, and more Latino faculty were clustered at the lecturer and instructor levels than any other minority group except American Indians (Astin, Antonio, Cress, & Astin, 1997). Twenty-six percent of all Latinos in the survey were adjuncts, and 30% of all Latinas were adjuncts. Quite simply, it appears that more Latinos (more than 32%) hold non–tenure track positions than almost any other minority faculty in the survey (Astin et al., 1997, p. 37).

Some of these figures could be attributable to a greater number of Latinos in the overall population. But this is not a major factor. The job market for tenure track positions was tight in the 1990s, but the percentage of new Latino doctorates during that time was also relatively flat. The HERI survey provides a partial explanation for the figures: a large number of Latinos are teaching in two-year institutions, which tend to hire instructors and lecturers. Almost 33% of all Latino faculty and 48% of all Latina faculty work at two-year institutions; only Native American faculty hold more appointments at two-year colleges, and they are almost invisible at four-year institutions and universities (Astin et al., 1997, p. 4). Unfortunately, whether they cluster at two-year institutions by choice or necessity is a topic that requires extensive analysis and is beyond the scope of this chapter.

Among the different Latino ethnic groups surveyed by HERI, the situation is even more tenuous. Mexican American/Chicano faculty, the largest ethnic population among Latinos, were also the largest cluster at the instructor level (40.6%). Forty-one percent of all Chicanos and 48% of all Chicanas in higher education are non–tenure track faculty (Astin et al., 1997, pp. 63, 89). By comparison, Anglo women surveyed by HERI hold about 26% of non–tenure track appointments, and Anglo men hold about 11% of those teaching jobs.

There is one bright spot. One quarter to one third of all Latinos in the HERI faculty survey, including Mexican Americans, were working on a doctoral degree. The question is whether the professoriate has enough full-time tenure track positions to absorb the potential increases. If colleges and universities continue to replace full-time faculty positions with part-time adjunct professorships, the future for more full-time, tenure track Latino faculty looks grim. This of course generates some conflict for Latino and Latina faculty across the country (Alicea, 1995; Garza, 1993).

The Latino Study and Faculty Issues

Why are so few Latinos and Latinas entering graduate education or the professoriate? Those were the primary issues explored among seventy-seven individuals, forty-one Latinos and thirty-six Latinas, whom I interviewed for a project for the Council of Graduate Schools (CGS) in 1994 and 1995. Portions of the research were published as a monograph entitled *Latino Experiences in Graduate Education: Implications for Change* (1996). The study focused on selected samples of Latino faculty, administrators, and graduate students working on master's or doctoral degrees. I also interviewed non-academics, individuals with doctoral degrees who had either left academe or never pursued an academic position.

Of the seventy-seven participants in the study, forty-six were Latinos and Latinas who had completed their graduate work and moved on to faculty, administrative, or nonacademic positions. Among that subset, there were twenty-six faculty members. Each participant was asked about the specific concerns of Latino faculty or administrators on campus. The responses were sorted into four general categories and listed in order of frequency of response: campus culture and climate issues; recruitment; tenure and research; and governance (Ibarra, 2001).

For the most part the responses reflect persistent stressors associated with minority faculty. Although the groupings are subjective, the categories subjects identified are not much different from those generated by other scholars (Moody 1997; Meyers and Turner 1995). Although this chapter concentrates mainly on tenure issues, the following are the top ten issues identified by the Latino and Latina faculty respondents in the CGS study by frequency of response:

1. Hiring problems—20
2. Gender issues—14
3. Minority burden (overcommitment to minority activities/teaching)—13
4. Tenure issues—11
5. Racism, classism, and tokenism—9
6. Retention issues—8
7. (Tie) Intracultural issues—5
    Lack of support groups—5
    Promotion problems—5

Latino and Latina Tenure Issues

Tenure issues pose vexing problems for Latinos around the country. It is probably not unreasonable to describe tenure as the Valley Forge of the academic cultural wars today. Most of those who teach at colleges and universities see tenure as their ultimate goal; it marks their arrival and acceptance into the ethnic group known as the professoriate. Yet minority faculty, in this case Latino faculty, recognize that tenure also is a political tool that can be used against them (Mindiola, 1995).

The patterns of declining tenure rates and few Latinos in tenure track positions confirm their concern. For instance, roughly 20% of the participants in my study complained bitterly about issues associated with academic activities like publication quotas and research priorities. But whether to continue tenure as a guarantee of "academic freedom" or to abolish it as an "insurmountable obstacle" in reforming higher education has been an ongoing (and sometimes heated) debate (Arnold, 1996; Chiat, 1997; Leatherman, 1996; Magrath, 1997; Perley, 1997).

Among the strongest advocates for tenure reform today is William Tierney (1990, 1997, 1998a). He and Estela Bensimon (1996) are authors of a controversial book that examines the current system of tenure and promotion and evaluates it against its effects on academic organizational cultures, especially women and ethnic minorities. They find the system no longer meets the needs of higher education. While the authors assume the original reason for tenure is still valid, whether tenure actually protects academic freedom is questionable (p. 27). The main reason is that not all faculty are tenured, and with the growing number of non–tenure- track positions held mainly by minorities, the system designed to protect academic freedom in this country is now counterproductive and outdated. Like Tierney and Bensimon, I found that the tensions and turbulence encountered by women and ethnic minority faculty are related to the entrenched system of academic tenure.

How did tenure affect the Latino and Latina faculty I interviewed? Ten people answered the question directly, but nearly all mentioned tenure during the interview. In reviewing the transcripts, I found many respondents discussed tenure in a variety of contexts. Although I discerned no patterns directly associated with ethnicity, I did find interesting differences related to gender. Table 12.1 shows that of twenty-six Latino and Latina faculty, almost evenly divided by gender, more women than men encountered problems at some point during their tenure process, but many of the men saw others run into tenure problems. Apparently none of the faculty I interviewed had been denied tenure themselves, yet this issue ranked high on their list of concerns

Table 12.1   Latino Study: Profile of Tenure Problems by Gender, 1994–95

	Left Academe	No Tenure Problems	Witness to Problems (none personally)	Had Problems	Not Yet Tenured
12 Males	0	5	3	2	2
14 Females	3	3	0	6	2
26 Total	3	8	3	8	4

and many discussed tenure as one of the more stressful experiences they encountered in higher education.

One interesting pattern about faculty members leaving academe apparently had little if anything to do with tenure. Of all those interviewed, only three individuals—all Latinas—eventually left or did not find a position after beginning their careers as full-time faculty or administrators in traditional academic institutions. One left to take a more attractive salary in the business sector, another was harassed and left because the traditional university environment was a "bad fit" for her, and the third, who had been teaching part time in a college and could not land a tenure track position, vehemently refused to become an adjunct professor with no chance for tenure and left academia for work in organizations serving the higher education community.

Consensus

One way to eliminate many of the problems faced by new faculty is to institute formal orientation, faculty development, and mentorship programs. At the very least, a faculty mentorship program is valuable, even in the absence of formal orientation and development programs, my respondents said. I asked participants two questions about mentoring: Did you have a mentor on campus? If so, how did she or he help? My interviewees were split evenly: thirteen had no mentor and thirteen had faculty mentors. Of those without mentors, three encountered tenure problems, which they attributed directly to not having a mentor, and the other ten made no mention of tenure difficulties. But few of the women had mentors, and the majority of those who did were also administrators. One creative new faculty member actually negotiated for a mentor as part of his employment contract.

Many respondents believe that without good advice from an experienced mentor, Latino faculty members tend to get sidetracked more than do individuals from many other groups. This was only their collective opinion, not something the data substantiated. However, eight of twenty-six individuals, approximately 31%, mentioned they encountered problems personally or knew others who had problems—they got sidetracked, became frustrated, suffered mistakes in their tenure package, or had difficulty advancing—because they lacked a faculty mentor. One cause for concern is the poor advice they get from other faculty when they don't have a mentor to help them negotiate the tenure process. I asked Jaime (not his real name), a Chicano professor in the Southwest, whether he could find no one to help him through the process. He responded:

> Not really. That's my big complaint. I'm always looking for a mentor. Well, they [other faculty] help you through the process but not really, they talk to you. . . . I have some senior people who will listen to me, but what they keep telling me—and it's what I've been told since graduate school: "Just go and do your research, and just stay away from all these minority issues. Why do you have to carry the torch? Just settle down, teach your courses, let the university run." That's their advice. I think these mentors, if you want to call them that, like me, and they're genuine in their advice. But they can't understand why I'm so committed to Latino issues, and they don't really believe that there are issues about Latinos. They believe that we're playing on a level playing field.

Promotion Problems

Scholarship, publication, promotion, and academic recognition are some key ingredients for academic success and form the basic criteria for gaining tenure at research universities. To achieve tenure remains quite an accomplishment in any department. It is even more difficult to achieve for faculty who are committed to research that is thought to be less mainstream, even marginal, within a demanding and intellectually rigorous discipline (Turner & Myers, Jr., 2000). This is what Latinos and other women and ethnic minority scholars face as they climb the tenure ladder, gain promotions, and seek notice in their fields. If their research interests are geared to ethnicity, diversity, or gender issues, what they accomplish is seen as somehow less worthy (Padilla & Chávez Chávez, 1995). Many faculty in the mainstream of their academic discipline consider it a "no-brainer" for a Chicano or a woman to study and publish books and papers about ethnic culture and women. Never mind that they are doing groundbreaking basic research, or that the academic mainstream crowd considered the topic too mundane or exotic, too commonplace or too obscure to merit attention. Consequently, women and minorities have a difficult time getting strong letters of support for their tenure packages from peers in their discipline. It is still considered less rigorous work, although ethnic and gender research is inherently difficult because it is marginalized in academia. Ethnic scholars and Latina scholars must endure and persevere to gain even local campus recognition, much less the critical national or international notice that has become a prerequisite for tenure and promotion at many research universities.

According to Jaime, the Chicano professor in the Southwest, gaining tenure and promotion are much more difficult for Latinos who engage in ethnic and gender research than many majority professors recognize. The inherent obstacles become even larger when scholars encounter reluctance to publish their work, or they find resistance to promotions within their department. Looking back from his more senior faculty position, Jaime shared the following insights and comments:

> I don't think we're playing on a level playing field. Let me give you this example. I got promoted to full professor last year. Because I am now more senior, I have more opportunities. The [major disciplinary association] calls me, I'm asked to review articles and that kind of stuff. I work with some faculty, and we've had articles sent back from, say, the [disciplinary] Association, manuscripts that haven't even been read, that say things like . . . "This manuscript really is not appropriate for this journal." . . . That's one example. Then my wife did a review of the literature of that [disciplinary] journal for ethnic content [over the last] twenty years, and [that organization] writes back and says it's not appropriate for that particular journal. The methodology we know is sound because we had [a recognized scholar] consulting with us on that article. . . . I've had articles rejected because there's not a great deal of interest by the readership on assessment of minority students. I'm talking about an assessment journal. I see that as problematic in that the journals are not accepting the stuff, so how do you get the [appropriate] numbers [of articles published] to be tenured?

Faculty Culture and Systems

Daniel Seymour attributes the paradoxical nature of tenure to a process he calls "sort and shoot" (1995, pp. 113–115). He views the tenure system as a standardization process that maintains the quality of faculty and staff by sorting out the "bad apples"—a quality-by-inspection mentality. Threshold tenure reviews are simply inspection systems designed to unearth deficiencies, he says. This process may eliminate people who are culturally different if they don't fit into the academy's definition of quality. For example, if a faculty member tends to publish co-authored articles, the academy that prizes sole authorship may count this as a demerit at tenure time. But a preference for sole author-ship is culturally contrary to those whose ethnic backgrounds value true team-work and collaborative engagement. Thus, cultural differences can directly affect one's ability to attain the goal that the academy counts as the only real measure of success: tenure (Seymour, 1995, pp. 115—117).

Seymour points out that similar traps are embedded in many academic processes. Regional accrediting agencies, for example, use a peer review process to generate institutional rankings based on a series of quality indicators that may be culturally biased. Hiring practices acceptable to the accreditation team are merely systems of improvement-by-elimination, not unlike the "bad apple" strategy in the tenure process. The accreditation system has a limited ability to enhance the quality of the faculty or the institution because the overall level of quality is determined by the internal systems, not by outside systems like accreditation. Thus the hiring process, including procedures that create a pool of candidates for faculty positions, the various criteria used to screen candi-dates, and the voting procedures of the hiring committee, is designed to ensure that the position goes to the candidate with the best chance of gaining tenure—who may not be the best teacher or researcher in the pool (Seymour, 1995).

Solutions and Change

One conclusion from my research is that the central conflict regarding campus diversity and demographic change is between culturally different populations and traditional academic values—those that involve how things are done in academia. Now, the pressures for change—the incentives—are mounting. Vot-ers, state legislatures, and court rulings are dismantling thirty years of affir-mative action and antidiscrimination legislation, while women and ethnic pop-ulations on campus argue that the barriers they have always faced in academia remain unchanged. This is a crucial point in the debate about educational reforms. Despite steady increases by underrepresented populations, especially women, real equity and diversity remain elusive on campus.

One of the latest and most promising entries in the arena of higher edu-cation reform is William G. Tierney's edited collection (1998b) of articles that seek to prescribe how to restructure our universities to become more respon-sive to the changing social, demographic, and political forces in the United States today. Couched in terms of "engagement" and "connectedness to the community," the track for systemic change laid down by Tierney's contribu-tors suggests that universities need to become more responsive to "students as customers" (Chaffee, 1998); create alternatives to faculty tenure systems (Tierney, 1998a); devise new ways to form lasting and effective partnerships with public school systems and community-based organizations (Braskamp & Wergin, 1998); and, ultimately, develop new governance structures and policies that are in sync with both internal and external communities (Benjamin & Carroll, 1998). These new models are designed to stimulate institutional or cultural change—collaboration, inclusiveness, community involvement, an orientation to students (people), comprehensive/systemic thinking, and so on. Equally important is the emphasis on the need to redefine the epistemology of faculty work in the context of academic culture change (Braskamp & Wergin, 1998, p. 83).

Tierney's (1997) examination of higher education suggests that the concept of organizational culture and the process of socialization into higher education are literally up for grabs. These are neither coherent nor shared by everyone involved, and thus socialization has no single format. He argues that

> We ought not think of socialization as a series of social acquisitions that occur in unchanging contexts irrespective of individual and group identity. Individuals do not "acquire" static, sedentary concepts. Socialization is not simply a planned sequence of learning activities where recruits learn one fact and then another. (p. 7).

Tierney also suggests that such a perspective helps create "academic communities that honor differences rather than assimilation" (1997, p. 7).

This idea originates from an earlier study by Tierney and Bensimón, *Promotion and Tenure: Community and Socialization in Academe* (1996), which depicts faculty culture and the dynamics of academic organizational systems and reveals the importance of human "difference," which is too often ignored in academe. Their goal is to create what they call "communities of difference" in academia that recognize organized change and do "not demand the suppression of one's identity in order to become socialized to abstract norms" (p. 16). Tierney and Bensimón go on to suggest that, "rather than assuming that 'new recruits' must learn to deal with their situations, we consider how the organizational culture might be changed. Unified, consensual notions of reality are rejected in favor of communities in which it is understood that different individuals and groups will always have competing concepts of reality" (1996, p. 17).

The Emerging Paradigm of Multiple Cultural Contexts

Tierney's work and others suggest that new approaches are needed for dealing with chronic academic issues such as awarding tenure for Latino faculty.

Changing academic cultures to promote lasting solutions to academic issues is becoming an increasingly important strategy in higher education. This became evident in my research and that strategy led to uncovering a new paradigm on diversity I call multicontextuality (Ibarra, 2001). A growing number of individuals now entering higher education bring with them a mix of individualized characteristics described as their *cultural context.* These learned preferences influence how they interact and associate with others, use living spaces, perceive concepts of time, and include many other factors that were imprinted on them in childhood by family and community and continue to help shape their worldview. In addition, they express a variety of personality, cultural, living, and learning styles generated by two distinct cognitive and contextual conditions associated with majority and minority ethnic cultures in this country. In essence, they are multicontextual, a kind of living and learning style combined with different thinking and perception skills formulated around strategies of cultural adjustment that help them adapt to their current circumstances.

The concept of multicontextuality offers a more comprehensive explanation for academic dissonance than multiculturalism or even institutional racism. I argue that popular beliefs claiming that all academic conflict originates in racial prejudice have masked conflict-oriented models that involve culture or cognition. Interactions not easily explained by racism—such as minorities or women who appear to discriminate against other minorities or women—are by default attributed to institutional racism. This mind-set overlooks or ignores the influence of cultural context and cognition.

What distinguishes these ideas from the current paradigm on diversity is the recognition that the cultures of our colleges and universities are permeated by cultural contexts forged from different ethnic roots. Basically, this heritage is a combination of colonial British liberal arts colleges capped by an imported German research model and infused with nineteenth-century Euro-American immigrant ethos dominated by males. While the ethnic markers disappeared long ago, the cultural contexts in higher education, such as preferences for individual learning over group work or technical teaching styles over informal styles, as well as many gender preferences, have not. They have been incorporated into our academic traditions, and especially our science, math, and engineering disciplines, remaining relatively unchanged and unnoticed by nearly everyone. Therein lies the conflict.

Multicontextual students and faculty, and that includes some majority males as well, reveal preferences for cultural contexts and ways of knowing that are often the antithesis of academic culture. Most minority students and faculty who arrive at our doors can and do adapt. But they do so with the historical disadvantage of chronic underperformance in our educational systems. That academic gap continues to take its toll of women and minorities in academe. Latino experiences in higher education, like those of many other ethnic minorities and women, are described as being dominated by conflicts with academic culture that affected them greatly on almost every scale of academic performance tests, classwork, graduate work, and even faculty work toward gaining tenure.

Although higher education has been trying to diversify for thirty years and to figure why it has such difficulty doing so, today's economic, political, and demographic realities mean it is time to try substantially new solutions from very different perspectives. Reexamining what we do generates new ideas, as well as challenges, for changing the face of higher education. When new constructs must be built, the nature of that process is to think expansively and systemically. The implications of such new ideas could improve upon our academic cultural systems, generating fresh guidelines for teaching, research, and tenure while improving the climate for diversity that continues to be such an illusive goal for institutions of higher learning.

References

Alicea, I. P. (1995). Are Latino faculty second-class citizens? *Hispanic Outlook in Higher Education* 6(9): 8–9.

Arnold, B. (1996, October 9). Ward: Tenure central to the soul of universities. *Wisconsin Week* (University of Wisconsin–Madison), pp. 1–3.

Astin, H. S., Antonio, A. L., Cress, C. M, & Astin, A. W. (1997). *Race and ethnicity in the American professoriate, 1995–1996.* Los Angeles: Higher Education Research Institute, University of California.

Benjamin, R., & Carroll, S. (1998). The implications of the changed environment for governance in higher education. In William G. Tierney (Ed.), *The responsive university: Restructuring for high performance* (pp. 92–119). Baltimore, MD: Johns Hopkins University Press.

Bowen, W. G., & Rudenstine, N. L. (1992). *In pursuit of the Ph.D.* Princeton, NJ: Princeton University Press.

Braskamp, L. A., & Wergin, J. F. (1998). Forming new social partnership. In W. G. Tierney (Ed.), *The responsive university: Restructuring for high performance* (pp. 62–91). Baltimore, MD: Johns Hopkins University Press.

Carter, D. J., & Wilson, R. (1997). *Minorities in higher education. Fifteenth Annual Status Report.* Washington, DC: American Council on Education.

Chaffee, E. E. (1998). Listening to the people we serve. In William G. Tierney (Ed.), *The responsive university: Restructuring for high performance* (pp. 13–37). Baltimore, MD: Johns Hopkins University Press.

Chiat, R. (1997, Feb. 7). Thawing the Cold War over tenure: Why academe needs more employment options. *Chronicle of Higher Education,* pp. B4–5.

Garza, H. (1993). Second-class academics: Chicano/Latino faculty. In J. Gainen & R. Boice (Eds.), *Building a diverse faculty* (pp. 33–42). San Francisco: Jossey-Bass.

Harvey, William B. (2001). *Minorities in higher education. Eighteenth Annual Status Report.* Washington, DC: American Council on Education.

Ibarra, R. A. (1996). *Latino experiences in graduate education: Implications for change.* Enhancing the minority presence in graduate education, No. 7. Washington, DC: Council of Graduate Schools.

Ibarra, R. A. (2001). *Beyond affirmative action: Reframing the context of higher education.* Madison, WI: The University of Wisconsin Press.

Leatherman, C. (1996, October 25). More faculty members question the value of tenure. *Chronicle of Higher Education,* pp. A12–13.

Magrath, C. P. (1997, February 28). Eliminating tenure without destroying academic freedom. *Chronicle of Higher Education,* p. A60.

Meyers, S. L., Jr., & Turner, C. (1995). Midwest higher education commission minority faculty development project. Final Report. Minneapolis: Midwest Higher Education Commission.

Mindiola, T., Jr. (1995). Getting tenure at the U. In R. V. Padilla & R. Chávez Chávez (Eds.), *The leaning ivory tower: Latino professors in American universities* (pp. 29–52). Albany, NY: State University of New York Press.

Moody, J. (1997). *Demystifying the profession: Helping junior faculty succeed.* New Haven, CT: University of New Haven Press.

Padilla, R. V., & Chávez Chávez, R. (Eds.). (1995). *The leaning ivory tower: Latino professors in American universities.* Albany, NY: State University of New York Press.

Perley, J. E. (1997, April 4). Tenure remains vital to academic freedom. *Chronicle of Higher Education,* p. A48.

Roey, S., Skinner, R. R., Fernandez, R., & Barbett, S. (1999). "Fall staff in postsecondary institutions, 1997. National Center for Education Statistics, NCES 2000-164, November, Department of Education, Washington, D.C.

Schneider, A. (1997, June 20). Proportion of minority professors inches up to about 10 Percent. *Chronicle of Higher Education,* pp. A12–13.

Seymour, D. (1995). *Once upon a campus: Lessons for improving quality and productivity in higher education.* Phoenix, AZ: Oryx.

Tierney, W. G., (Ed.). (1990). *Assessing academic climates and cultures.* San Francisco: Jossey-Bass.

Tierney, W. G. (1997). Organizational socialization in higher education. *Journal of Higher Education,* 68(1), 1–16.

Tierney, W. G. (1998a). Tenure is dead: Long live tenure. In W. G. Tierney (Ed.), *The responsive university: Restructuring for high performance* (pp. 38–61). Baltimore, MD: Johns Hopkins University Press.

Tierney, W. G., (Ed.). (1998b). *The responsive university: Restructuring for high performance.* Baltimore, MD: Johns Hopkins University Press.

Tierney, W. G., & Bensimón, E. M. (1996). *Promotion and tenure: Community and socialization in academe.* Albany, NY: State University of New York Press.

Turner, C. S. V., & Myers, S. L., Jr. (2000). *Faculty of color in academe: Bittersweet success.* Boston: Allyn and Bacon.

Patricia Arredondo

Patricia Arredondo, associate professor at Arizona State University (ASU), is renowned for her contributions to the development of multicultural counseling competencies, for her dedication to Latina/Latino issues, and her leadership in promoting organizational change through a focus on diversity. She is current president of the National Latina/o Psychological Association and the ASU Chicano Faculty and Staff Association.

Her major publications include three books: *Successful Diversity Management Initiatives, Key Words in Multicultural Interventions: a Dictionary* (co-edited), and *Counseling Latina/os and la Familia: A Practitioner's Guide* (co-authored). She is co-author or "lead author" on several major multicultural competency documents through Association of Multicultural Counseling and Development (AMCD) and the American Psychological Association (APA). These include *Multicultural Counseling Competencies and Standards: A Call to the Profession, Operationalization of the Multicultural Counseling Competencies,* and *Guidelines for Multicultural Proficiency in Education and Training, Research, and Practice.*

Dr. Arredondo is the recipient of many awards including an honorary degree from the University of San Diego. She is also a Fellow of the American Psychological Association, Division 45, Society for the Psychological Study of Ethnic Minority Issues.

She is a former professor at the University of New Hampshire and Boston University. She has been an adjunct professor for Tufts University, Simmons College, and the University of Massachusetts–Boston. In 1985, she established Empowerment Workshops, Inc., in Boston, an organizational consulting firm focusing on workforce diversity initiatives. She also served on the faculty of Columbia University Business School, Executive Training Programs.

Her graduate degrees in counseling psychology are from Boston College and Boston University respectively. Dr. Arredondo is bilingual in English/Spanish and is of Mexican-American heritage.

13

LATINAS AND THE PROFESSORIATE

AN INTERVIEW WITH PATRICIA ARREDONDO

Patricia Arredondo and Jeanett Castellanos

The purpose of this chapter is to provide a brief overview of the current educational statistics and conditions of female faculty in higher education. More specifically, this chapter will highlight Latina faculty experiences and their representation in higher education. Through an extensive interview with a senior academic, the role of gender and culture in this profession will be evaluated. Moreover, the unique responsibilities and additional barriers encountered in her pursuit of the full professoriate will be assessed.

Women, Racial Ethnic Minorities and Latinas in the Professoriate

Women have experienced differences in higher education in their pursuit of the professoriate. Today, women make up over 33% of full-time instructional faculty; they are mostly employed in 2-year colleges (49%) but are minimally represented in research institutions (less than 30%) (NCES, 1999). In reviewing the experience of women in academia, Nettles, Perna, and Bradburn (2000) identified a salary difference by gender of approximately $10,000 in Fall of

1992. In reviewing more recent data by the National Center for Educational Statistics (1999a), figures support that Latina women earn $1,310 less than their white counterparts and $12,100 less than Latino males. Impacting the salary discrepancy, studies have also indicated that women were less likely to be granted tenure than their male counterparts (42% versus 66%, respectively). Moreover, in reviewing academic ranks, NCES (1999) noted women were found primarily in lecturer and instructor positions (over 50% of such positions), compared to their male counterparts who were most often in full and associate professor ranks (66%–79%). Comparing academic promotion, in 1995 White women earned tenure at a 62% compared to 78% of their White male counterparts (Wilds, 2000).

Ethnic/racial minority scholars also encounter unique challenges in the professoriate. In 1997, racial/ethnic minority individuals comprised 13.7% of all full-time faculty in higher education institutions (American Council on Education [ACE], 2001) compared to 86.3 of their White counterparts (National Center for Educational Statistics, NCES, 2000). An examination of the representation of specific ethnic groups reveals the minimum representation levels. For example, in 1997, African Americans made up 5%, Latinos represented 2.6%, and American Indians merely represented .4% of postsecondary institutions professors (NCES, 2000). Caucasians held the majority of academic positions across all ranks. Moreover, in reviewing tenure status, there was an 11% difference between racial/ethnic minority faculty who received tenure compared to White faculty, 64% and 75%, respectively (ACE, 2001).

Latina women experience the double minority status in higher education. There is an acute underrepresentation of Latinas in the professoriate and academia as a whole. Latinas comprise 2.7% (n = 5,078) of the 1995 full-time faculty in higher education (Wilds, 2000). Upon further examination of Latina faculty by academic rank, it appears that Latinas had a participation rate of .4% (n = 558) in full professor ranks compared to 1.2% (n = 1,912) Latino faculty. Moreover, their representation in associate rank was .7% (n = 884) compared to a 1.4% (n = 1723) representation of their male counterparts. Assistant professor levels introduced a slight rise with a 1.3% (n = 1,668) compared to 1.7% (n = 2068) Latino males, and 1.8% (n = 1,421) and 2% (n = 1,538) Latino males were in lecturer and instructor positions respectively. In postsecondary institutions, it has been documented that Latinas have the lowest tenure success of all groups compared by gender and race (Schneider, 1997).

In addition to the Latina underrepresentation, research findings have identified unique challenges Latina encounter while they pursue an academic career in higher education (Turner & Myers, 2000; Escobedo, 1980; Medina & Luna, 2000; Montero-Sieburth, 1996). Specific barriers include additional responsibilities, cultural incongruity/lack of fit, institutional racism, the lack of mentorship, and a limited social network. These women are overburdened by the questioning of their scholarship (Reyes & Halcón, 1988), the demand to be the cultural expert, "cultural taxation" (Padilla, 1994; Tierney & Bensimon, 1996), and the complexity of gender role and stereotypes.

Context: Interview Process and Interviewee Background

The purpose of the interview was to address specific psychosocial cultural issues Latinas face in academic positions. The questions were developed through a theoretical framework whereby the individual was asked to speak about her general experience, the role of culture, and the role of gender and specific barriers encountered throughout her academic career. Questions addressing university efforts, campus climate, and mentorship were also posed. In concluding the interview, the interviewee was asked to provide general recommendations to increase the retention of Latinas in higher education.

The professor invited for the interview is an Associate Professor of Education. Her doctorate (Ed.D.) is from Boston University in the field of Counselor Education, a program that followed a research-practitioner model approach. She is currently at a Research Type I institution and at a top national Counseling Psychology program. In her tenure as a scholar, Dr. Arredondo has addressed multicultural counseling competencies, Latina/os and counseling, and multicultural organizational development models for the field of psychology. Specific awards and recognitions she has received include an Honorary Doctorate of Humane Letters awarded by the University of San Diego (1998); a Distinguished Professional Service Award from the Association for Counselor Education and Supervision of the American Counseling Association (1997); President of American Psychological Association's Division 45; and Chair, Professional Standards Committee, American Counseling Association.

Specific Questions and Responses

> Interviewer: What role has your culture played in your profession? Please describe your experience as a Latina scholar in higher education at a predominantly White institution.

My culture has been the center of my professional life and I've always been mindful about being Mexican American and my Mexican heritage. Growing up as a Mexican in Ohio, I was always aware of how much my interest in education and my cultural background needed to work together. More than anything, I think, realizing how to be a role model, your worldview, and how to be successful is important.

Growing up, I was very self-conscious about being Mexican American and being different from a lot of kids with whom I attended school because I went to Catholic school, and we were the only Mexican family in that school. I think that my situation made me aware of my culture.

I was always aware of the importance of my culture and language as I went through my education and career planning. As an undergraduate, I ended up majoring in Spanish; I think that was my first way of embracing my culture in terms of my professional identity. And then, through that, I began to learn more about the roots of not only being Mexican but the background of Latino culture and how that could be a part of my teaching. I thought that I wouldn't just be able to speak Spanish, but I also had to understand my culture, the Mexican culture.

As I went on to graduate school, again, I found myself in a situation similar to my undergraduate education. I think I was the only Latina, Mexican American, who was studying for their Master's degree. My situation made me aware of what I was missing in the literature and I wanted to investigate the literature available that discussed Mexican people. And I did, but yet there wasn't a whole lot available. Then, by the time I got to my doctoral program, I was more open about being Mexican American, because I was part of the Bilingual Fellowship Program at Boston University. There again, as a part of the admission process, being bilingual did not mean that one was of a certain ethnic minority background, but being bilingual would give me an education that affected ethnic minority populations. I felt this was an opportunity to meet other Latina/os and people from Asian backgrounds who were a part of the Bilingual Fellowship program. More than anything, I wanted to encounter other Mexicans and Puerto Ricans who were in a doctoral program. I think that we all felt very strongly about our culture, and we wanted to intertwine it with our studies. I was able to do that and I centered most of my studies around immigrants.

My culture has always been in my psyche; it is always present when I do my professional work. My *cultura* has given me a voice. At this stage of my career, I'm probably giving it even the greatest voice as possible. Because of my culture, I have the desire to do it. I am very committed to ethnic minority issues, especially Latino issues. I feel that I am in a position of privilege, because I am an academic and a woman with a higher education. I am able to give a voice to the things that other people cannot. Whenever the opportunity arises to talk about culture or be critical of people who are critical of us for focusing on language and bilingual education, I do not miss the chance to speak up both as a Latina and also as a professional.

> **Interviewer:** What role has gender played in your profession? Please describe your experience as a Latina scholar in higher education at a predominantly White institution.

The gender piece is very salient. I think that women in the academy are still minimized. If you are a Latina, or an ethnic minority woman, there is even another way that the organization works. I saw the difference as a junior professor in that there is an expectation that we would do anything that concerns ethnic minority people. Women tend to take on a lot more service-oriented roles and responsibilities. And, I certainly did that as a junior professor and I would not say to my detriment, but I didn't get tenured at that time. Once I realized that no one was getting tenured, I re-evaluated my evaluation and the focus of my work. Originally, I felt that I was not getting tenured because I was spending too much time as a mentor and servicing others and not writing in the area as much as I could have. Then, as I reframed my analysis of my tenure process, I realized that many of my colleagues who were writing more than I was were still not granted tenure. The tenure process was horrible, but it was also good. If I look at it with the culture piece as a junior faculty, I could recall a lot of Latinas in particular dropping out. However, because there was someone who I could identify with, two Latina professors, it was better. I felt good relating to them and we had a sympathetic working and personal relationship; one hard to find with other women and men in general.

There is also a dynamic between Latino men who are academics and Latina women. I do not always think, and this might be men of my generation or older, that men always regard women with the academic respect that they deserve. Sometimes the old boys' network gets perpetuated among Latinos about respecting a man and we, as women, really have to recognize that and either call them on it or somehow make sure it does not get perpetuated. We are not to buy into that myth.

I also find the same challenge with our White colleagues. Often times, we know that they have not had a lot of contact with Latina/o faculty. I am always aware of how people are trying to assess you. We always have to be interacting with mainstream faculty. My comfort level is fine, but I see them a little bit more cautious and it is their discomfort not mine. Whether it is your colleagues or staff, at times you are not sure if they are being careful around you. All such experiences make me very aware of how culture gets introduced in my professional role and my professional environment.

> **Interviewer:** Have you encountered unique challenges as a woman in higher education? What about as a Latina scholar in academia?

Unique challenges are saying as they are, and hoping that you do not insult someone when you call them on it. One example here at ASU is the limited number of Latino/Mexican focus classes. I know that someone might feel upset or embarrassed that they do not do anything about the Latino situation. The campus does not offer enough exposure of the Latina/o experience to our students. When I say such things, I imagine some people grimace—but on the other hand it is true. If we are talking about cultural competence and we are preparing people for real experiences, we have to be able to do that. Those things, I believe, are not well heard or not necessarily agreed with.

In addition, I recall other experiences as a junior professor helping and facilitating something with graduate students who were Latina/o or other ethnic minority and who were often getting stonewalled by colleagues who just did not get it. I had to persist, which was often hard being a junior professor.

Another challenge is the usage of my native language on campus. Today, I feel more comfortable speaking Spanish or speaking it back and forth with faculty or students at ASU. I remember my first year, however, speaking Spanish with some graduate students. They would answer me in English. I finally asked them what that was all about and they said they did not think it was acceptable. I said to them that unless I see it as a rule around here, it is fine by me but it is up to you. I don't need to buy into something either hidden or a phobia. I like to converse in Spanish. Most of my colleagues call me "Patricia" with the Spanish pronunciation because they know that is what I prefer and they make the effort. I think it is important to model and not be shy about our culture.

Other challenges are the stereotypes people have of Latinas; they are not positive. Before Jennifer Lopez and all the popular stars, there was less discussion on Latinas other than maybe "you don't know any" or general assumptions. One of my main challenges is the way Latinas are conceptualized and how that might get generalized to Latinas in the academy. It is sort of like a big blip and this occurs for both Latinos and non-Latinos. In terms of stereotypes, Latinas are viewed as very passive, and quiet *y nos aguantamos* (we repress ourselves). If you don't see that in a Latina, it could be a little confusing to Latinos and non-Latinos alike (I am particularly speaking of men). Latinas are thought of as a stay-at-home wives. Yet, sometimes, we do not fit the stereotype. Moreover, we are professionals in the workplace, and sometimes Latino and non-Latino men do not know how to deal with us.

Stereotypes further impact Latinas who are lesbians in the workplace, because there is still discomfort regarding gay/lesbians in the workplace. Within the Latino culture homosexuality is not a popular issue—it is not acceptable to be lesbian or gay. Thus, the dynamics for a Latina faculty member who is a lesbian are pretty intense.

Another challenge is the role of being a mother or a parent in academia. If you are a Latina mother, there are stereotypes that come into play, such as not being serious about your career or wanting to spend more time with family.

> **Interviewer:** Attaining tenure at a Research Type I institution is a strenuous challenge. Would you say you encountered unique challenges as a Latina scholar during your tenure process? What are some specific challenges you encountered during your tenure process?

Being a junior professor was one thing, and I certainly wasn't mentored well in terms of getting my work published. But it was not because I was not mentored. I think that since there was no encouragement to do extended research on Latinas, my research emphasis was mainly on immigrants. That was the direction I was moving in. However, I was interested in doing research on Latinas and it was a hard shift to make because I was so engaged with mentoring and service issues at the university that I really couldn't focus on a specific population.

Now here at ASU, I came in tenured. Now, I am an associate professor with tenure and I will go for promotion to full professor next fall. It is important, however, that Research Type I institutions have a very strong emphasis on empirical research; this is also evident in my department. I am hearing that message, but it is not the type of work that I have done. My work is more theoretical. At the same time, I recognize there are needs and opportunities to do some empirical research. Candidly, I can say I know how to play the game and still do the research. In fact, I conduct the research, but I do so that it does not in any way exploit populations that are overresearched or underresearched. Furthermore, I ensure it occurs in a culturally competent manner. Therefore, I know that a couple of the projects I am on right now will yield more culturally competent findings even though someone else may be the principal investigator. I know my perspective is going to help conduct culturally competent research, and it does focus on Latinas and other ethnic minorities.

Secondly, I know that with the Latino population here in the Southwest, there are many opportunities to learn from the people. For example, what makes a difference when you want to get health insurance or with health care? And, gathering large amounts of data through surveys is not the most effective way of learning about a community. Therefore, at the moment, I am working with community-based people seeing if they could become our conduits to accessing the population and I still think that the data we gather will be in interview format so that people (again from whom we want to hear) can have a chance to sit down, even if it means going through a checklist in person, but it will get done. This process will probably be more time sensitive, but within the academy, if you want to gather reliable and valid data from ethnic minority populations and, in particular, Latinos, you really have to change your approaches in order to collect data. Some of it will not be an empirical design, and that is what I am beginning to negotiate. I will go as far as I can because in many ways there are opportunities to find new attitudes through culturally sensitive assessment. Culturally sensitive assessment and bilingual therapy are two projects I am working on. I think that one of the challenges in academia, however, if your work is evaluated by people who are not culturally competent or terribly interested in it, is that they will only review the research design and perhaps not sufficiently examine the substance of your work. Ironically, it may even be groundbreaking but if it doesn't meet their requirements, it is invalid.

It is important to note that although I encounter multiple challenges, I do take opportunities—whether it is within my department or on external committees—to be visible and represented. I have to make sure that people know that I have some sort of input that is valuable and sometimes not thought about. I'm aware but I am not self-conscious, because I am older and I feel like I have adapted to a number of different settings in the academic and business world. I should never be surprised if something comes up. I have negotiated a lot of things in different settings, therefore I keep doing it but you always have to be aware.

> **Interviewer:** The professoriate is quite a demanding profession. As a Latina woman, what role has family played in your career? What have you done to balance the two and how do the two interconnect?

Balance is the hardest thing to achieve because none of us could cut our day 50% this, 50% that. Life is not quite as simple. Again, I think that is not well understood for women professionals in general. Being a parent does not mean you are not a professional.

First, I have been married but I do not have children. Not having children puts me in a different sort of situation whereby there are some things that get read in to, as if there isn't any other obligation I would have to attend to. I believe that the word "suspect" is a little strong but I think that sometimes it is suspect to not have children, especially a person of my generation in my fifties. Being a Latina and having children go hand in hand. Sometimes, people are silly enough to ask why I don't have children. I tell them, "Because it was not in the cards." But that is something that could work for or against you.

The other component with being a professional and *la familia* is how Latina professionals are perceived by their family. Most of us are first-generation college students, let alone Ph.D.s. And, we are not unappreciated by our families, instead, our families are proud of us but they do not know how to deal with it. I remember when I was married, my brothers would ask my husband how was his business, but they would never ask me about my business although I was an entrepreneur at the time. Furthermore, up until recently, they wouldn't even ask how my work was going. I find that very remarkable and I wonder if it's just ignorance or if it's just that we are not expected to be part of the workforce.

I find that not being asked about my career is quite disappointing, but it's not that my family is not educated. Just about everyone in my family has a college degree. So, maybe now since I am back in the academy, some people may have a better way to relate to my profession. Being a professor versus being a consultant somehow may be easier to understand for them but I am not making excuses. With friends, we talked all the time, but with family, sometimes there was a lack of curiosity about my work. I know a couple of friends that ask, "Does your family know what you do and your impact in the field?"

I say, "No, I really don't think so." I don't know how to do this without sending them a resume and that's very odd. My first book came out in 1996 and to be honest, there was nothing remarkable that occurred within the family. Then, when my second book came out on counseling Latinos, I sent it to all of my siblings—there are seven of us and a couple of cousins who I thought would be interested. I was really excited about the book, but there is always a list of people who respond to congratulate you and those who say nothing. You know, I got more nothings than congratulations. This whole thing with family is a tricky thing; you don't want to get upset about it, but on the other hand, it is a gender issue and often times it is difficult to explain. My whole family is very much into culture in different ways.

There was only one person, one relative, who told me he read the book and I thought it was funny that it was him. But it's a strange balance. I really want my nieces and nephews to understand culture in their education and their studies. Thus, I believe writing and role modeling is the best I can do in terms of communicating and passing culture on.

On the one hand, I recognize that everyone has a busy life and I really want that family connection around my work. If my work is not connected to my family, then they will never know me. Hence, it is very important to try to bridge the two. Thus, it matters when you are part of a family and you feel in ways close to the family, it's your *familia*. You want them to care. I care about what they do and so I would like them to be somewhat interested in what I do.

> **Interviewer:** When comparing cultural frameworks, many faculty of color have experienced cultural incongruity as professionals in the academy. Have you experienced this phenomenon? If so, how did you navigate this challenge?

There is incongruity for the Latina pursuing the professoriate and I think it occurs in several ways. One obviously incongruity is when you obtain your doctorate; you know you have done a lot of work on your own. More specifically, the continuous focus on individuality runs against gender phenomenon and relationships, and it runs against *cultura,* which is also relationship-oriented. Thus, I'm finding more now than when I was a junior professor—interdisciplinary issues that are all related to one another. Because culture is not taken seriously and especially if you brought it from outside of the institution, culture is viewed as a part of the outside. Fortunately, with the American Psychological Association (APA) and the American Counseling Association (ACA) promoting multicultural congruity in their guidelines, adding the cultural element in practice is less incongruent, culturally speaking. But, the academy is so bureaucratic; it has a bit of a militaristic dimension to it.

Maintaining a relationship with the academy is not always easy especially if it works against a multicultural framework. Certainly, as a Latina, my greatest comfort at the university is when I am with Latina/os; I find that very notable. It is not that I cannot get along with other people. I just feel the greatest comfort with other Latina/os and I have to say that the Chicano Faculty and Staff Association (CFSA) is a great connection for me. In this association, I find that people really care about one another. They are all professors, junior professors, and staff. "*Hay un personalismo y un buen sentido de familismo* (there is a sense of personal connection and a sense of family) that its just automatic; it breathes. I do not have the same experience when I sit in the college committees with others who are my peers or full professors and I certainly do not feel that sense of *cultura* with them. I know that I am with people who I'm doing business with. When I am with CFSA, I am also doing business but it feels different. Yet, it is a very subjective and very palpable feeling. The incongruity really comes from the notion that my non-Latina/o colleagues are collegial, because they have to be. In general, within the university environment you have to be collegial but the aura of the academy prevails *como la gente se comporta* (how the people behave). You are polite and sometimes you disagree and people are a lot more passionate than expected. On the other hand, there is only so much you can do. I come from a background as a consultant and I know that you have to get to the point or you'll lose money.

Ambience is something I always pay attention to. Being an organizational consultant, I'm more in tune with it. I see how things are decorated. If it feels like any other educational institution or *si hay un ambiente* (if there is any unique ambience) that allows Latina/os or Native Americans to see themselves represented. Here, I see a lot more Native Americans artwork around the university. I don't want to be critical of this for I am really glad to see it but there could be also more Latina/o ambience. Furthermore, there could be more bilingual opportunities whether it's a presentation or in signs or other ways that the university can show we are in Mexican territory. I think that there is some cultural incongruity and people always talk it off.

> **Interviewer:** Our cultural beliefs transcend themselves into our daily practices. With your experience in the professoriate, what cultural attributes do you utilize to navigate the professoriate and its challenges?

I began to think of navigational skills back in high school. Just before learning how to play the game of navigating, I realized that on Tuesdays in order for me to learn, I had to show up at practice. I learned that you can do everything the other kids can do, you must just show up to practice. Look at me, I'm Mexican.

I saw the yearbook editor, the high school newspaper business manager, and the president of the honor society; all such positions demonstrated who was in power. In the beginning, you just look around and see the leading positions. You identify the power positions and you position yourself so you can move into them and then you deliver. I think that has been the main lesson in navigating the world—not holding back, seeing the opportunities, and sometimes creating the opportunities. Additionally, it's never a singular achievement because certainly in high school there were things I was more conscious of doing, because I wanted to show that Mexican people can do this. And there were the Latina/os, they were such a small group and I had only one Puerto Rican friend at the time. They were my people as well. As I moved into higher education as a professor now and then as a consultant, I found that what was really clear to me is that there were areas and issues that were not getting the attention they needed. If I wanted to see something happen, I had to give voice to it. Whether there were human rights issues, counseling, multicultural issues, I have to give it a voice. I've been dealing with multicultural issues before they were popular.

I was also involved in other opportunities as an author and different professional associations that were worth navigating through. In the mainstream associations, as a consultant, my clients were primarily Caucasian. I had very few Latina/o clients and if there were, they were community-based organizations; they were not corporations. When I navigated in the corporate world, people were not looking at me as a Mexican American, they were looking at me as a professional who had something that they needed. That is certainly how I communicated it. I also took the opportunity to let people know who I was or if I saw issues or did not see Latina/os in their work environment. Hence, I think it was really about gaining confidence in my ability to be in those worlds in a very physical way.

We talk about our reluctance to self-promote and I certainly have seen that in myself. I'm not shy during the times when I feel I need to get to know my clients. Assuming leadership roles or roles of power is important for your career and issues you feel strongly about. We can also do that by addressing different issues that are not just good for Latina/os, but they are good for the whole profession where you are trying to affect and impact. Finally, you need to follow through and do it in an inclusive way. To me, it is always key that you find out who some of the other talent brokers are, and you must build alliances. Through social networks is how you get your agenda achieved in relationship to others who are Latina/o and non-Latina/o. I firmly believe this. That is the way I perform when I work within the academy and within professional associations. I build alliances and networks with those who are willing to do the work.

Moreover, if you want it done, and you believe it should be done, you have to do it. I rarely have been left standing alone at anything. I say if it is important to me, it is probably important to someone else, because it is a larger issue than a "me" issue.

The other key element to successful navigation in the academia for Latina/os is to bring out our best. You have to present everything in a first-class way, of course without arrogance. We have succeeded in a lot of ways, and I think we have to demonstrate such progress; this too is how I live my life privately. There is no sense hiding my success when I am in a public domain.

> **Interviewer:** For Latinos *la communidad* (the community) is something very important. The academy prides itself on minimizing the

split between "town and gown." Through your work, I know that you are very connected to the community. How do you connect *nuestra gente* (our people) with *la universidad* (the university)? How do you connect *la communidad* (the community) with your own work? How do the university, your colleagues, and the field receive your efforts?

The town and gown split is very pronounced for me in the service profession. I am particularly interested in addressing this issue because of the lack of engagement between our program and the Latino community agencies. There are community counseling programs and community agencies, but the agencies are not necessarily culturally competent. We are also not preparing our students for the real world. My way of becoming involved with the community includes direct contact. Therefore, I have put forth an effort to make a connect. Luckily, this has been facilitated with the help of my colleague Miguel, who has been here for a long time and knows a lot of people.

There are those who have been here quite a while who know who the contacts are. Felipe has been doing research here for a while. There are different starting points, so you don't have to go seek a partnership solo. Again, your first alignment is with people who have been doing community work and then you see how you can create some new agendas. In fact, that is what I've been doing with my colleagues in some community-based agencies here, which have mushroomed into many quality opportunities for faculty and students to conduct research in the field. Such research is probably larger than the two of us could handle, but if we had more resources (i.e., faculty) this effort could lead to a Latino Research Center. We do have a Multicultural Research Center, but I believe its focus is not on mental health issues. What I have found is that you need a few contacts in the community and they will welcome a partnership. Moreover, the social workers and psychologists who are in the community-based agencies are very well educated, and they want to partner *también* (also). They want to feel involved—receiving the benefits we might bring them, besides providing us with participants and knowledge-building opportunities.

I have always believed in order to establish networks, one must find who is on campus and who does what. If the opportunity arises, follow it. For example, the Chicano Faculty and Staff Association is going to meet with the Latino Caucus at the State House. We've never pursued such an effort before but it is important that as Latina/os we remain aware of social and political issues—local and statewide. People can probably say you did your research, but we have to advocate. In order to advocate, you also need to connect with the people who can be helpful. The issues that you want to present in your research are the training and other services you can offer the community. I think that getting connected with political figures is important. I did that in Boston as the president of the Latino Professional Network, because we really have to develop partnerships.

I also recognize the value of press releases and communications to let people know what you are doing. One of my best examples is when Miguel and I developed this course, Counseling Latina/os, about 2 years ago and I thought this was a course a lot people could take. We sent out an article through the university, a press release, and we got calls from people who were interested in it. In addition, we got a call from people in Yuma, Arizona, and we responded to the community's request. We've done the course in Yuma now for two years in a row. I can't tell you how gratifying that was for me because they were so enthusiastic and the majority of our participants were Mexican people, so they were learning about their culture in a different way.

It's taking something that matters and exporting it. Arizona is such a big state, and there are so many needs when it comes to Latina/os. Therefore, you have to be able to let people know what you are doing and what resources are available.

Now, we want to collaborate more in the Greater Phoenix area with providers. However, we have to do business in a different way as a university; you have to communicate what you are doing and invite the community to collaborate. One cannot make it one day of the week, from one to three in the afternoon, that just does not work with most peoples lives unless they are full-time students. Thus, we have to really be creative; bridging the university agenda and Latina/o agendas is about being creative.

> **Interviewer:** There is a dismal representation of Latina Ph.D.s. Some of these *mujeres* (women) are working in the private sector, others work in local communities, and a number of the Latina Ph.D.s are lecturers but are not full-time faculty. What can the university do to recruit these needed women in its attempt to increase their representation?

If there are Latina Ph.D.'s or Latinas in adjunct roles or lecturer roles, an ethnic-specific national association should take the lead (e.g., the National Latina/o Psychological Association, NLPA). Such organizations should serve as great facilitators to help individuals in their journey in academia.

A developmental opportunity for Latinas who would like to become academics will be beneficial. I'm in Arizona, and you are in California—where there may be more of a critical number of individuals like this—and we make the case to the university. We establish our case where women with Ph.D.'s have instructed, written, and have a research agenda. They just have never had the opportunity to start their career in the academy.

Also, since there is a great need for Latinas in the academy, why do we not create developmental opportunities that would support their entry into a tenure track position? With such an opportunity, we would have to create a mutual relationship that would involve the Latina. We would let her know the process and set up the appropriate resources in terms of support and mentorship that would help her to publish and obtain tenure. Thus, the resources would situate her in a more efficient manner, possibly faster than most of the tenured.

Another recommendation is to offer a creative process in developing professional academic opportunities for Latinas. The link, with a national association in the field like NLPA, can help Latinas identify other Latina/o scholars. When they finally know who is out there, their links can help them with their career pursuit. For example, do they want to do something in addition to clinical work? If the academy is not of interest to them how else can we be a resource so they can maximize their skills, or optimize their education? Maybe we can encourage them to come to the conferences. We can have them present, even if it's their dissertation. Mentoring at a latter point in time should also be considered. Maybe finding a career path in the academy did not happen for some Latinas 10 years ago, but if they are still interested and willing, we could start the process now.

> **Interviewer:** The experience of junior faculty has occasionally been associated with loneliness, intellectual isolation, lack of collegial support, and cultural incongruity. What can be done in higher education to minimize the revolving door effects on Latina junior faculty? How can we retain them?

I think that better mentorship can assist the retention of Latina junior faculty in academia. More specifically, if the junior faculty is assigned 2 senior faculty members to monitor their scholarship process with accountability, they will have a better success rate. The junior person is told that she must work with senior faculty and they are told to work with the junior faculty. The senior faculty must be held accountable and must have performance evaluations for the junior faculty. Such performance evaluations would detail what the junior faculty will be doing the first semester in terms of X, Y, or Z. At the end of the first semester, they would sit down and review it. Then, the senior faculty would ask, "Did you accomplish your goal or where are you in the process of doing this?" I think that establishing a relationship and a scholarship agenda is number one. Secondly, in addition to helping them with their scholarship agenda, the senior faculty must also steer them to the appropriate committees, where they will get the right visibility—and visibility counts a lot. Again, junior faculty should consult with senior faculty to check which committees are most appropriate.

Third, the two senior faculty members do not need to be Latina/os. However, Latinas need to connect with other Latina/os on campus. Sometimes, other Latina/o faculty are not available, but the Latinas should make it a priority to find out whomever is Latina/o on campus.

The fourth recommendation is that Latinas either join or somehow connect with a Latino community and local agencies. It is a shame to go to a place and never connect with the people in the greater community. I think this is another way of feeling more integrated. If you are feeling isolated and there is nowhere else you can go, then one is apt to feel pretty bad. Encouraging the Latinas to reach out to the community is also beneficial for the developmental process.

Professional associations are always a piece of the development plan. Latinas should be encouraged to get involved with one or two faculty mentors in their field. Their involvement with faculty will enable them to connect and network with a committee. Indeed, it is a lot of work, but they get recognized either through presentations or being on a committee, and having such visibility will help them get promoted in the future. In essence, the more people who know of you, the more people who can write about you.

I have posed five main recommendations. They include to assign two senior faculty to work with the Latina; develop a performance evaluation or a developmental plan. The plan should have some goals and a timeline on it and it must address scholarship. The Latina must also have on-campus involvement, committee involvement, and connections with Latina/os on campus; she must also connect with Latinos in the community. Lastly, Latinas need to be involved with professional associations both as a presenter and as a member.

> Interviewer: The "browning of America" is not mirrored in higher education. Yet, the academy is working hard to increase the numbers of the majority to be (Latinos) for the year 2030. Even with the influx of Latinos and the new effort to increase our numbers, what do you foresee to be the challenges that forthcoming Latina faculty will encounter? What is the call to the profession to improve these circumstances?

Acknowledging the paucity of Latinas in higher education, it is imperative that we put many more into the pipeline. The biggest challenge is whether the academy will continue to exist and remain in its form. We are asked to transform ourselves, we are asked to be adaptable and flexible as individuals, as Latinas. However, the academies are still heavily archaic and if they continue such practice, Latinas will be stonewalled from bringing their best efforts to the academy. There will be a lot of smart people out there, and although it will be a challenge, I feel we must create our own institution. Also, you find ways of working outside of the cultural mainstream if you can, but that is not easy to do. I hate to say it, but I think that some of these existing issues we are currently experiencing will continue to be with us, whether it's the dropout rate or the sense of isolation and alienation.

Another challenge is the fact that more Latinas get educated than Latinos. Such challenges are probably going to elicit some crisis in relationships among Latinos and Latinas, both within families and within the academy. Are the Latinas going to feel torn and/or be true to their family? I think this is a challenge to the academy. How will acedemia authenticate our professional roles so that we can also feel respected and valued and not feel selfish at the same time? Therefore, the challenges are in fact present. Although it may seem to be a very Latina world in the future in terms of higher education and more Latina professors, there is nothing bad about such a projection. I'm uncertain of what the implications will be when we have more *mujeres* than male counterparts. I certainly know that psychology has shifted in that direction.

There are some professional schools where there are more women than men. Medical and law schools are certainly changing as well. On one hand, you can say for Latinas that such change is a positive, because there will be many more Latina role models for younger generations. Again, you can see that it would not be by having to chose between education and family. Instead, younger generations can realize that a career in education is a valid profession—and that the university is a place where you can realize your academic ambitions.

One main challenge will be the continuing presence of low-income circumstances. Because the disenfranchisement of people is horrific, for Latina professionals going forward, this means they're also going to have to become advocates. We can't just be academics. The luxury of being an academic, I think, is never going to be there for us. Furthermore, it will be a challenge if the rules do not change in terms of how one gets tenure and promotion. It's a really complicated question, because we know of all the trends and all the suggestions.

There are multiple recommendations to improve higher education's current retention efforts for future Latina faculty. First, higher education is to provide access, recruit more actively, enhance its campus, and work on the multicultural competencies of the institution. Better mentorship is to be provided through graduate education, and research on ethnic populations should not be considered "second-tier investigations." On a social level, literature highlights the role of social networks in the private sector—what they call affinity groups. The affinity groups are designed as support mechanisms for people, such as an affinity group for African American and Latinos. An example of such an effort would be a Chicano Staff and Faculty Association. Such organizations meet to advance the mission of Latina/os in higher education. Such associations develop strategic plans, present the needs to the university president, and take the initiative for the group to demand change. Finally, it is imperative that postsecondary institutions provide more fellowships and grants for junior Latina scholars to conduct research on their communities and in the process, attempt to minimize the added academic and social responsibilities (e.g., cultural taxation).

References

American Council on Education (2001). Students of color continue to make enrollment gains in postsecondary education, but the rate of progress is slowing. (www.acenet.edu/news/press_release/2001)

American Council on Education (2000). Facts in brief: Faculty of color continue to be underrepresented on the nations' college campuses. (www.acenet.edu/hena/facts_in_bnet/2000)

Escobedo, T. H. (1980). Are Hispanic women in higher education the nonexistent minority? *Educational Researcher, 9,* 7–12.

Medina, C., & Luna, G. (2000). Narratives from Latina professors in higher education. *Anthropology and Education Quarterly, 31,* 47–66.

Montero-Sieburth, M. (1996). Beyond affirmative action: An inquiry into the experiences of Latinas in academia. *New England Journal of Public Policy, 11,* 65–97.

Nettles, M. T., Perna, L. W., Bradburn, E. M. (2002). Salary, promotion, and tenure status of minority and women faculty in U.S. colleges and universities. (nces.ed.gov/pubs2000/quarterly)

Padilla, A. (1994). Ethnic minority scholars, research and mentoring: Current and future issues. *Educational Researcher, 2,* 24–27.

Reyes, M., & Halcón, J. (1988). Racism in academia: The old wolf revisited. *Harvard Educational Review, 58,* 299–314.

Schneider, A. (1997). Proportion of minority professors inches up about 10%. *Chronicle of Higher Education, 43,* A12–A13.

Tierney, W. G., & Bensimon, E. M., (1996). *Promotion and tenure: Community and socialization in academe.* Albany, NY: State University of NY Press.

Turner, C. S. T. & Myers, Jr., S. L. (2000). *Faculty of color in academe: Bittersweet success.* Needham Heights, MA: Allyn & Bacon.

U.S. Department of Education, National Center for Educational Statistics (1999). *National study of postsecondary faculty.* (NCES 2002–160)

U.S. Department of Education, National Center for Educational Statistics (1999a). Gender and racial/ethnic differences in salary and other characteristics of postsecondary faculty: Fall 1998. (http://nces.ed.gov/das/epubs/2002170/footnotes_es.asp)

U.S. Department of Education, National Center for Educational Statistics (2000). *Digest of Education Statistics.*

Wilds, D. J. (2000). *Minorities in higher education (1999–2000): Seventeenth annual status report.* American Council on Education, Washington, DC.

Richard R. Verdugo

Richard R. Verdugo is the Senior Research Scientist at the National Education Association. He has a doctorate in sociology from the University of Southern California. Dr. Verdugo's areas of specialization are race and ethnic stratification, the labor market, sociology of education, and methods/statistics. At the NEA his primary areas of responsibility are minority student achievement, language minority students, and school safety. His most recent publications include articles in *Education and Urban Society* and the *Trotter Review* as well as two book chapters on the educational outcomes among African American students. Verdugo has won many awards for his scholarly work and was most recently awarded a Fulbright Fellowship.

14

DISCRIMINATION AND MERIT IN HIGHER EDUCATION

THE HISPANIC PROFESSORIATE

Richard R. Verdugo

An emerging body of research points out many troubling aspects of life in academe for Hispanic faculty. For example, a significant number of Hispanic faculty believe they are the targets of racist beliefs by their non-Hispanic colleagues (Reyes & Halcón, 1988; Uribe & Verdugo 1989). In addition, many Hispanic faculty believe that their non-Hispanic colleagues hold low opinions of their scholarship (Uribe & Verdugo, 1989). For many Hispanic faculty, life in academe is not as bucolic as they might have originally thought.

The status of Hispanic faculty is, however, a function of many competing cross-pressures; two of the more demanding are those related to the role of professor, and their role as a member of the Hispanic community.[1] To be sure, higher education is a racially stratified institution with norms, values, and structures that act as significant barriers for status and prestige (Verdugo, 1995). However, higher education is also an environment in which the dominant ideology suggests that individual merit drives one's status position.

---

[1] Note that Garza (1988, 1999) indicates that many Chicano scholars in the 1960s did not want to be detached academics. Instead, they sought to weave their community activism into their scholarly work. While this is admirable, it may jeopardize their careers in higher education.

Higher education institutions are not homogenous; they are in fact highly differentiated on many dimensions including cost, prestige, demography, and institutional norms about success. It is crucial, then, that faculty make wise decisions about how they will comport themselves within a set of boundaries or institutional norms that are institution-specific. In large elite research institutions, for example, institutional norms suggest that research, publishing, and bringing research grants to the institution will increase the likelihood of one's success (Kuh & Hu, 2001). In less elite or teaching institutions, where the focus is on teaching and on student-teacher relations, faculty should focus on those activities and conceive of a plan as to how they can acquire solid marks in such areas. Both structural and individual factors, then, determine one's status among faculty in higher education.

There thus exist at least two competing hypotheses about the status of the Hispanic professoriate in higher education. On the one hand, one viewpoint argues that to the degree to which Hispanic faculty are able to abide by the norms and expectations of their respective institutions, the greater the likelihood that they will be successful. For Hispanic faculty, the ability to identify, prioritize, and meet four basic criteria in their respective institutions can lead to greater status. It is quite plausible that Hispanic faculty who have been unable to do so, for whatever reasons, have either left academe or have remained only to become disgruntled workers in the higher education labor market. On the other hand, another view is that there are structural factors, such as discrimination, that do in fact impede the careers of Hispanic faculty in higher education. A fundamental question is whether the job status of Hispanic faculty is contingent on their ability to meet the respective criteria of their institutions, or if other factors are at work. These other factors might be the perceived and actual racial climates within which Hispanic faculty must work on a daily basis.

I have two objectives in this paper. First, I raise, describe, and provide some brief analysis of key issues surrounding the status of Hispanic faculty in higher education. Second, I raise a somewhat controversial topic within the discrimination research genre. To wit, in studying discrimination directed at Hispanic faculty, researchers need to balance their analyses by addressing the topic of merit/productivity in higher education. It makes little sense to raise the issue of discrimination unless the topic of merit is also raised. Raising and examining both discrimination and merit is sound analysis.

The Hispanic Professoriate: Key Issues

The extant research on the Hispanic professoriate is still open to many questions and concerns. Nevertheless, there are at least three key issues that research addresses: discrimination, the number of Hispanic faculty, and the use of Hispanic faculty as role models.

Discrimination

While not all Hispanic faculty feel they are discriminated against, the number is of sufficient magnitude to warrant our attention. This small body of research addresses at least two domains in which Hispanic faculty are discriminated: their culture, and their work.

Research by some scholars suggests that many Hispanic faculty believe they are discriminated against because of their appearance and language accents (Astin & Burciaga, 1981; Garza, 1988; Rochin & de la Torre 1986).[2] Indeed, some faculty point to incidents in which other non-Hispanic faculty make racist remarks about their accents and about Hispanic culture in general (Verdugo, 1989).

Academic research is a second area in which some Hispanic professors believe they are discriminated against. Some Hispanic professors believe that their colleagues disregard their academic research as "too soft" or "not quite up to par" (Astin & Burciaga, 1981; Bell, 1986; Garza, 1988, 1989, 1991, 1999; Reyes & Halcón, 1988; Smith & Witt, 1990; Willie, 1988). Another related form of discrimination concerns the perception among non-Hispanics that Hispanic faculty owe their positions to affirmative action rather than to any individual accomplishments of their own as scholars and/or teachers (Aguirre, 2000; Aguirre & Martínez, 1993; Delgado, 1991; Niemann, 1999; Valverde, 1975). For many Hispanic professors, work in higher education can be a demoralizing experience.

As a result of work-related discrimination, Hispanic faculty feel their careers in higher education have not moved along as smoothly as possible. Specifically, time to tenure, if at all, is slower for some Hispanic faculty than for non-Hispanic faculty (Uribe & Verdugo, 1989).

The concentration of Hispanic faculty in certain departments, disciplines, and ranks is cited as another form of discrimination. Research has indicated that Hispanic faculty are concentrated in Chicano Studies and departments with a

---

[2]A related concept to discrimination is racial stratification (see Verdugo, 1986, for a discussion). By racial stratification is meant differentiation based on race. A number of scholars have addressed several aspects of racial stratification in academe. For example, Romero (1977) found that Chicano faculty play only a minor role in curriculum development. Astin and Burciaga (1981) found that Chicano faculty have a difficult time in gaining the respect of their Anglo colleagues, lack support from their institutions, and lack adequate numbers of Chicano colleagues on their campus. Other factors affecting Hispanic faculty include isolation (Aguirre, 1987; Garza, 1988), and exclusion (Arce, 1978; Escobedo, 1980; Garza, 1989; Lopez & Schultz, 1980).

decidedly Latino emphasis (Rochin & de la Torre, 1986). Moreover, research has found that Chicano faculty are overrepresented on committees that address Hispanic or equal educational opportunity issues (Aguirre, 1987), or are concentrated in the assistant professor ranks (Milem & Astin, 1993). Hisauro Garza (1988) is most outspoken on these issues, arguing that they lead to the "Barrioization" of the Hispanic professoriate. The segregation of Hispanic professors is a key factor in a system of structured inequality or racial stratification system (Aguirre, 2000; Verdugo, 1986). Such a system segregates Hispanic faculty from others and tends to stigmatize them negatively. In general, the primary function of discrimination is to preserve privilege for those groups in power. In academe, discrimination serves to preserve privilege for White males (Bell, 1986; Bunzel, 1990; Valverde, 1975).

Another work-related issue in higher education is job satisfaction. Research suggests that a significant proportion of Hispanic faculty are not satisfied with their jobs (Garza, 1988). While discrimination plays a role in driving low levels of job satisfaction, other factors are also at work. Uribe and Verdugo (1989), for instance, found that the following clearly played a role:

• Lack of opportunities

• Institutional policies

• Double standards

• Institutional apathy/insensitivity

• Institutional ignorance of minorities

• Lack of recognition

The Number of Hispanic Faculty

A second issue raised by research about Hispanic faculty concerns their number in higher education (Aguirre, 2000; Arce, 1976; Garza, 1988; Haro, 1989; Milem & Astin, 1993; Olivas 1988).[3] Specifically, the primary concern is the

---

[3]It should be pointed out that there are at least two issues surrounding the number of Hispanic faculty in higher education. First, there is the issue of identifiability. Some Chicano scholars take issue with being lumped under the label "Hispanic" because such a designation assumes that all Hispanic ethnic groups are the same (Reyes & Halcon, 1988; Nieves-Squires, 1992). In fact, Leal and Monjivar (1992) found significant differences in worldviews between Hispanic female faculty from Latin America and those from the United States and Puerto Rico (see also Casanova & Budd, 1989; Simoniella, 1981 for discussion of similar findings). A second issue is the cost associated with misidentification; enumeration limits the social networks of individual Hispanic faculty (Rosenblum & Rosenblum, 1990; Smith & Hixson, 1987).

small number of Hispanic faculty in higher education. There are three issues raised by this body of work related to the small number of Hispanic faculty in higher education.

A small body of research on the number of Hispanics in higher education tends to imply that scholarly perspectives and viewpoints are crucial in any academic discipline. It is assumed that the unique experiences brought to academe by Hispanics influences their views and approaches to research and theoretical issues characterizing a specific discipline (see Aguirre, 2000). Scholars argue that introducing new or different views will move the discipline forward in a positive manner.

Second, research indicates that the tremendous increase in the Hispanic population will trigger increases in the number of Hispanic students enrolled in institutions of higher education. In this light, some scholars have argued that there needs to be greater presence of Hispanic faculty in higher education in order to set aside the notion that higher education is a purely Anglo institution (Olivas, 1988).

Third, some scholars are concerned about the validity of reported numbers of Hispanic faculty in higher education (Aguirre, 2000). There are two subissues characterizing this particular strand of research. First, it is argued that the number of Hispanic faculty is overestimated because some universities use Spanish surnames to identify Hispanic faculty, even though they are aware that many of these are not Hispanic at all.[4] A second topic concerns foreign-born Hispanic faculty. There appears to be the practice in higher education of recruiting/hiring foreign-born Hispanic faculty in lieu of U.S.-born Hispanics. This is an egregious practice for two reasons: it assumes that competent U.S.-born Hispanics who are potential faculty members are rare. Second, it is invalid to include foreign-born Hispanics in aggregate data (they are currently so included) because it does not adequately characterize race-based inequality in higher education. If valid data on U.S. Hispanic faculty is the issue, then non-U.S. Hispanics must not be part of the data.

Hispanic Faculty as Role Models

A final issue raised by research concerns role models. The topic of role models hinges on two topics. The first concerns the retention and recruitment of Hispanic students in higher education. The second focuses on the expected

---

[4]In a personal conversation, Adalberto Aguirre informed me that this is indeed the case in the University of California system.

increase in the number of Hispanic students in higher education. It is presumed that the presence of Hispanic faculty will increase the attachment Hispanic students have to higher education. Hispanic faculty will solidify this bond by empathizing with Hispanic students, proffering views and topics with which Hispanic students can relate, and generally being a sounding board for the concerns of Hispanic students (see Verdugo, 1995 for a review).

At least one researcher, however, has questioned the logic of this reasoning (Verdugo, 1995). Verdugo's argument is based on the lack of status and power characterizing Hispanic faculty in higher education. The lack of both these traits among the Hispanic professoriate negates their being used as positive role models.

The Hispanic Professoriate: Demography, Structure and Merit in Higher Education

The Demography of the Hispanic Professoriate

Population   Table 14.1 provides information on the number of Hispanic faculty in higher education from 1989 to 1999.

Data in Table 14.1 indicate that the number of Hispanic faculty increased between 1989 and 1999. In 1989, there were 10,000 Hispanic faculty in higher education. By 1999 their number had increased to 16,000 or an

Table 14.1   Race and Ethnic Data for Full-Time Higher Education Faculty, 1989–1999 (000s)

	Number				
	1989	1995	1997	1999	% Change, 1989–1999
Total	515	538	553	591	14.76
White	456	469	477	489	7.24
Black	23	27	28	29	26.09
Hispanic	10	13	1	16	60.00
A/PI	24	28	31	34	41.67
AI/AN	1	2	2	3	200.00
	White to Other Ratios				
Black	19.83	17.37	17.04	16.86	
Hispanic	45.60	36.08	31.80	30.56	
A/PI	19.00	16.75	15.39	14.38	
AI/AN	456.00	234.50	238.50	163.00	

increase of 60%. How do these data compare to White, non-Hispanic faculty? In 1989 there were 456,000 White faculty in higher education, and by 1999 the figure had climbed to 489,000, or an increase of 7.24%. Thus, the increase, over the period 1989 to 1999, was greater among Hispanic faculty.

Of course, in sheer numbers, White faculty significantly outnumber Hispanic faculty. Indeed, data in Table 14.1 also presents the ratio of White to Other faculty, including Hispanic faculty, from 1989 to 1999. As can be seen, White faculty far outnumber Hispanic faculty; in 1989 the ratio was 46:1, and by 1999 it had dropped to 31:1. In general, then, the total number of Hispanic faculty in higher education has been quite small; the only group they outnumber are American Indian/Alaska Native faculty.

Population by institution type   Data in Table 14.2 exhibit the distribution of professors by institution type for the fall of 1998. These data indicate that the majority of Hispanic faculty are to be found in two types of institutions: public doctoral universities (34.2%) and in public two-year colleges (25.5%). This kind of concentration is also exhibited among White, non-Hispanic, and American Indian/Alaskan Native professors. In contrast, among Black, non-Hispanic faculty, the majority are concentrated in public doctoral, public comprehensive, and public two-year colleges. Among Asian/Pacific Islander faculty, the majority are concentrated in public doctoral and in public comprehensive settings.

Table 14.2   Percent Distribution of Full-Time Faculty by Type of Institution, Fall 1998

Race/ Ethnicity	Public Doctoral	Private Doctoral	Public Comp.	Private Comp.	Private Liberal	Public 2-year	Other
W, N-H	34.8	10.5	14.4	6.9	8.8	18.3	6.3
B, N-H	23.2	8.2	21.8	6.0	10.7	21.5	8.7
A/PI	46.8	14.2	15.0	4.3	4.2	10.6	4.9
Hisp.	34.8	11.7	16.0	5.5	4.1	25.5	2.4
AI/AN	34.2	5.7	10.9	11.4	12.7	19.9	5.2
Total	34.9	10.6	14.8	6.7	8.5	18.3	6.2

Note 1: Public Doctoral Institutions include research, doctoral, and medical institutions.

Note 2: Other Institutions include private not-for-profit 2-year institutions, public liberal arts colleges, and other specialized institutions.

Source: U.S. Department of Education, National Center for Education Statistics, 1999 National Study of Postsecondary Faculty (NSOPF: 99).

Table 14.3   Percentage Distribution of Full-Time Faculty According to Salary Base and Average Salary, Fall 1998

Race/ Ethnicity	Less than $40,000	$40,000– 59,999	$60,000– 79,999	$80,000 or More	Average Salary Base
W, N-H	27.7	36.6	19.7	16.1	$57,000
B, N-H	28.4	49.3	13.6	8.7	50,360
A/PI	18.1	38.0	22.9	21.0	62,800
Hispanic	28.3	40.3	19.6	11.9	54,370
AI/AN	40.1	34.6	16.1	9.2	48,090
Total	27.2	37.4	19.5	15.8	56,850

Note 1: Dollar figures are rounded to the nearest 10.

Source: U.S. Department of Education, National Center for Education Statistics, 1999 National Study of Postsecondary Faculty (NSOPF: 99).

An important measure of discrimination is salary. Salary data are presented in Table 14.3. According to data for the fall term 1998, the lowest average salaries are to be found among American Indian/Alaskan Native faculty, and then among Black, non-Hispanic faculty.

Hispanic Faculty: Discrimination and Merit

In addition to the existence of discrimination and its adverse effects on the careers of the Hispanic professoriate, there is another proposition. It is also possible that some Hispanic faculty fail to recognize the demands placed on them as scholars and teachers within their own institutional environments. For example, teaching in a university means something completely different than teaching at a four-year college or a two-year community college. The basis for such differentiation are the norms about expected forms of productivity characterizing each of these institutional environments.

There are four criteria that drive such differentiation: research, teaching, committee work, and community service. Each factor is not weighed equally by institution type. For example, several scholars have studied how higher education faculty spend their time. Bowen and Schuster (1986) found that faculty at four-year institutions spend about 58% of their time in course preparation, teaching, and research. In contrast, professors in two-year institutions devote about 90% of their time on activities directly related to serving students: office hours, academic counseling, course preparation, etc.

In terms of academic rank, Hispanic faculty tend to be in the middle of the distribution. A quarter of Hispanic faculty are full professors, 19% associate professors, and 24% assistant professors. Interestingly, though, a majority of

Table 14.4   Percentage Distribution of Full-Time Faculty by Academic Rank, Fall 1998

Race/ Ethnicity	Full Professor	Associate Professor	Assistant Professor	Other
W,N-H	32.2	23.5	21.0	23.3
B, N-H	17.5	25.2	32.8	24.6
A/PI	25.9	25.8	30.9	17.5
Hispanic	25.3	19.1	24.1	31.6
AI/AN	17.8	17.4	23.6	41.1
Total	30.7	23.6	22.3	23.4

Note 1: Other includes instructors, lecturers, other ranks, and those without an academic rank.

Source: U.S. Department of Education, National Center for Education Statistics, 1999 National Study of Postsecondary Faculty (NSOPF: 99).

Table 14.5   Percentage Distribution of Full-Time Faculty by Tenure Status, Fall 1998

Race/ Ethnicity	Tenured	Tenure Track	Not on Tenure Track	No Tenure System
W, N-H	54.3	17.4	17.8	10.5
B, N-H	43.9	26.1	20.6	9.3
A/PI	49.1	29.8	17.1	4.0
Hispanic	48.5	22.1	22.9	6.5
AI/AN	29.4	34.4	24.2	12.0
Total	53.1	18.8	18.1	10.0

Source: U.S. Department of Education, National Center for Education Statistics, 1999 National Study of Postsecondary Faculty (NSOPF: 99).

Hispanic faculty are assistant or other faculty (55%). This last figure is not out of pace with the distributions among faculty of other ethnic/racial groups. For example, 46% of White, non-Hispanic faculty are found in these two categories, 57% among Black, non-Hispanic faculty, and 64% of American Indian/Alaskan Native faculty. See data in Table 14.4.

A sizable proportion of Hispanic faculty are tenured. Indeed, in 1998 nearly 49% of Hispanic faculty were tenured. This figure compares favorably with other faculty. For instance, 54% of White, non-Hispanic faculty, 44% of Black, non-Hispanic faculty, and 49% of Asian/Pacific Islander faculty are tenured. Data may be found in Table 14.5.

Hispanic faculty compare favorably with other faculty in terms of time spent on research and research productivity. Data in Table 14.6, for example,

Table 14.6   Among Full-Time Faculty, Average Percent of Time Spent on Various Activities, Fall 1988

Race/ Ethnicity	Teaching Activities	Research	Administration	Service and Other Activities
W, N-H	56.9	14.8	14.4	14.0
B, N-H	58.7	10.6	12.8	17.9
A/PI	51.1	24.5	9.7	14.7
Hispanic	55.6	16.2	11.2	16.9
AI/AN	64.3	10.0	12.6	13.0
Total	56.6	15.2	13.9	14.3

Note 1: Teaching activities include grading, teaching, advising, preparing courses, supervising students, and working with students.

Note 2: Research includes conducting research, participating in professional meetings, reviewing articles, books, or proposals, seeking funding, and giving performances, exhibitions, or speeches.

Note 3: Administration includes departmental or institution-wide meetings or committee work.

Note 4: Service and other activities include professional service, professional growth, and outside consulting, freelance work, and other non-teaching professional activities.

Source: U.S. Department of Education, National Center for Education Statistics, 1999 National Study of Postsecondary Faculty (NSOPF: 99).

indicate that Hispanic faculty say they spend about 16% of their time on research, 56% on teaching, 11% on administrative tasks, and 17% on other and service tasks. The only group of faculty that spends more time teaching are American Indian/Alaskan Natives (64% of their time on average). In terms of research, only Asian/Pacific Islander faculty spend more time on this activity: nearly 25 percent.

The other research issue concerns the proportion of faculty engaged in research. Data in Table 14.7 suggest that a sizable proportion of Hispanic faculty are directly engaged in research (67%). Only Asian/Pacific Islander faculty are more likely to be engaged in some kind of research (79%).

Finally, I examined the average number of recent publications among higher education faculty. These data may be found in Table 14.8. Generally, it appears that Hispanic faculty compare quite favorably with their peers in terms of scholarly productivity. Indeed, on average Hispanic faculty produced 7.9 scholarly works. Compare this output to the 8.3 among White, non-Hispanic faculty, and the 6.7 and 6.8 respectively among Black, non-Hispanic and American Indian/Alaskan Native faculty. Asian/Pacific Islander faculty have been the most productive, having produced 11.2 scholarly products.

Table 14.7   Percentage of Full-Time Faculty Engaged in Research or Other Scholarly Work, Fall 1988

Race/Ethnicity	Any Research	Of those, Percent Funded Research
W, N-H	66.4	51.8
B, N-H	64.6	48.6
A/PI	79.1	63.3
Hispanic	67.1	54.4
AI/AN	62.8	51.7
Total	67.0	52.5

Note 1: Based on responses to the question, "During the 1998 Fall Term, were you engaged in any professional research, proposal writing, creative writing, or creative works (either funded or non-funded) at this institution?"

Source: U.S. Department of Education, National Center for Education Statistics, 1999 National Study of Postsecondary Faculty (NSOPF: 99).

Table 14.8   Number of Various Types of Recent Scholarly Works, Fall 1998

Race/Ethnicity	Other	Articles	Books	Presentations
W, N-H	8.3	3.8	1.0	10.8
B, N-H	6.7	2.5	1.0	9.6
A/PI	11.2	6.4	1.0	11.4
Hispanic	7.9	3.7	1.2	10.1
AI/AN	6.8	2.4	1.6	12.0
Total	8.4	3.9	1.0	10.8

Note 1: Other includes other types of works not shown separately, such as articles or works in non-refereed journals or non-juried media, book reviews, or book chapters in edited volumes.

Note 2: Books includes textbooks, books, monographs, and research or technical reports.

Source: U.S. Department of Education, National Center for Education Statistics, 1999 National Study of Postsecondary Faculty (NSOPF: 99).

Conclusion

The status of Hispanic faculty is a function of competing cross-pressures; the pressures to function as a professor and as a member of the Hispanic community. To be sure, higher education is a racially stratified institution with norms, values, and structures that can act as significant barriers for the acquisition of status and prestige (Verdugo, 1995). However, individual factors also play a role in the status attainment process. Higher education is not a homogenous environment, and faculty must make decisions about how they will comport themselves within the boundaries set by the particular norms of their institutions. In large elite research institutions, for example, the top priorities are research, publishing, and bringing research grants to the institution. In institutions where the priority is teaching, faculty must focus on this activity and determine how to acquire solid marks in such an area. Thus, both structural and individual factors determine status among faculty in higher education.

There are competing hypotheses about the status attainment process among Hispanic faculty in higher education. One argument stresses that structural barriers, such as discrimination, impedes the achievement of status in higher education. Another argument posits that it is the individual behaviors and choices that determine status in higher education; specifically, faculty must meet institutionally driven criteria in higher education if they are to succeed. The discussion and analysis presented in this chapter sought to examine which of these arguments appears most valid.

Using data from the U.S. Department of Education, I found little evidence corroborating the individual or merit hypothesis concerning the status of Hispanic faculty in higher education. Indeed, when compared to other faculty, Hispanic faculty fare quite favorably on time spent on research, and on scholarly productivity. In contrast, while a significant proportion of Hispanic faculty enjoy positions of status and prestige in higher education, their overall position is not in line with their research and scholarly productivity. In conclusion, while these results are not completely conclusive, they do suggest that for Hispanic faculty merit does not appear to be a significant factor in their higher education careers; Hispanic faculty members appear to have pursued activities and accomplishments that should have gained them greater rewards in higher education. If merit is not a significant predictor of status in one's higher education career, then perhaps structural explanations deserve our undivided attention.

References

Aguirre, A. (1987). An interpretive analysis of Chicano faculty in academe. *Social Science Journal, 24,* 71–81.

Aguirre, A. (2000). *Women and minority faculty in the academic workplace: Recruitment, retention, and academic culture.* Washington, DC: ERIC Digests.

Aguirre, A., & Martinez, R. O. (1993). *Chicanos in higher education: Issues and dilemmas for the 21st century.* ASHE-ERIC Higher Education Report No. 3. Washington, DC: George Washington University.

Arce, C. (1976). Chicanos in higher education. *Integrated Education, 14,* 14–18.

Arce, C. (1978). Chicano participation in academe: A case of academic colonialism. *Grito del Sol: A Chicano Quarterly, 3,* 75–104.

Astin, H., & Burciaga, C. (1981). *Chicanos in higher education: Progress and attainment.* Washington, DC: U.S. Department of Education, ED 226–690.

Bell, D., (1986). Strangers in academic paradise: Law teachers of color in still White schools. *University of San Francisco Law Review, 20,* 385–95.

Bowen, H. E., & Schuster, J. H. (1986). *American professors: A national resource imperiled.* New York: Oxford University Press.

Bunzel, J. (1990). Minority faculty hiring problems and prospects. *American Scholar, 59,* 39–52.

Casanova, U., & Budd, A. (1989). *Oral histories of Latino academics: Work in progress.* Washington, DC: U.S. Department of Education, ED 310-716.

Delgado, R. (1991). Affirmative action as a majoritarian device: Or, do you really want to be a role model? *Michigan Law Review, 89:* 1221–31.

Escobedo, T. (1980). Are Hispanic women in higher education the nonexistent minority? *Educational Researcher, 9,* 7–12.

Garza, H. (1988). The "barrioization" of Hispanic faculty. *Educational Record, 68,* 122–124.

Garza, H. (1989). *Second class academics: Chicano/Latino faculty in U.S. Universities.* Fresno: California State University at Fresno, Department of Chicano and Latin American Studies.

Garza, H. (1991). *Academic power, discourse, and legitimacy: Minority scholars in U.S. universities.* Unpublished manuscript, Department of Chicano and Latin American Studies, Fresno, California State University.

Garza, H. (1999). *Objectivity, scholarship, and advocacy: The Chicano/Latino scholar in America.* Occasional Paper No. 58, Julian Samora Research Institute, Michigan State University, East Lansing, Michigan.

Haro, R. (1989). Hispanics and California public universities: Challenges and opportunities. *LA RED/The Net: The Hispanic Journal of Education, Commentary, and Reviews, 2,* 7–11.

Kuh, G. D., & Hu, S. (2001). *Learning productivity at research universities. Journal of Higher Education, 72:* 1–28.

Leal, A., & Monjivar, C. (1992). Xenophobia or xenophilia: Hispanic women in higher education. In L. Welch (Ed.), *Perspectives on minority women in higher education.* New York: Praeger.

Lopez, A., & Schultz, R. (1980). Role conflict of Chicano administrators in community colleges. *Community College Review, 7,* 50–55.

Milem, J., & Astin, H. (1993). The changing composition of the faculty: What does it really mean for diversity? *Change, 25,* 21–27.

Niemann, Y. (1999). The making of a token: A case study of stereotype threat, stigma, racism, and tokenism in academia. *Frontiers, 20:* 111–26.

Nieves-Squires, S. (1992). Hispanic women in the U.S. academic context. In L. Welch (Ed.), *Perspectives on minority women in higher education*. New York: Praeger.

Olivas, M. (1988). Latino faculty at the border. *Change, 20*, 6–9.

Reyes, M., & Halcon, J. J. (1988). Racism in academia: The old wolf revisited. *Harvard Educational Review, 58*: 299–314.

Rochin, R. & de la Torre, A. (1986). *Chicano studies and affirmative action in higher education: Complementarities and prevailing issues*. Chicano Studies Program, University of California at Davis. Mimeo.

Romero, D. (1977). *The impact and use of minority faculty within a university*. Paper presented at an annual meeting of the American Psychological Association, San Francisco, CA.

Rosenblum, G., Rosenblum, B. (1990). Segmented labor markets in institutions of higher education. *Sociology of Education, 63*, 151–164.

Simoniella, K. (1981). On investigating the attitudes toward achievement and success in eight professional U.S. Mexican women. *Aztlan, 12*, 121–137.

Smith, C., & Hixson, V. (1987). The work of university professors: Evidence of segmented labor markets inside the academy. *Current Research on Occupations and Professions, 4*, 159–180.

Smith, E., & Witt, S. (1990). Black faculty and affirmative action at predominantly white institutions. *Western Journal of Black Studies, 14*: 9–16.

Uribe, O., & Verdugo, R. R. (1989). *A research note on the status and working conditions of Hispanic faculty*. Paper presented at the annual American Education Research Association meetings. Boston, MA.

Valverde, L. (1975). Prohibitive trends in Chicano faculty employment. In H. J. Casso & G. D. Roman (Eds.), *Chicanos in higher education* (pp. 106–114). Albuquerque: University of New Mexico Press.

Verdugo, R. V. (1986). Racial stratification and the education of Hispanics. In M. Olivas (Ed.), *Latino college students* (pp. 325–346). New York: Teachers College Press.

Verdugo, R. R. (1989). *The Employment and tenure status of Hispanic higher education faculty*. Washington, DC: National Education Association.

Verdugo, R. R. (1995). Racial stratification and the use of Hispanic faculty as role models: Theory, policy, and practice. *Journal of Higher Education, 66*, 669–685.

Edward A. Delgado-Romero

Edward A. Delgado-Romero is a graduate of the University of Notre Dame in counseling psychology. He is the treasurer of NLPA. Ed is an assistant professor at Indiana University–Bloomington in the Department of Counseling and Educational Psychology. Prior to IU, Ed spent five years at the University of Florida Counseling Center where he became the assistant director. Ed is the outgoing chair of the Section on Ethnic and Racial Diversity of Division 17 (Counseling Psychology) of APA and the by-laws chair for the Association of Multicultural Counseling and Development of ACA. His research interests include Latina/o psychology, issues impacting Latina/o faculty, and narrative psychology.

Lisa Y. Flores

Lisa Y. Flores, Ph.D. from the University of Missouri, is an assistant professor in counseling psychology in the Department of Educational, School, and Counseling Psychology at the University of Missouri–Columbia. She co-directs the Center for Multicultural Training, Research, and Consultation in the Department. Her professional interests include multicultural counseling, multicultural training, and vocational psychology. Her research area focuses on the educational and career development of Mexican Americans.

Alberta M. Gloria

Alberta M. Gloria received her doctorate in counseling psychology from Arizona State University and is currently an associate professor at the University of Wisconsin–Madison. Her primary research interests include psychosociocultural factors for Chicano/Latino and other racial/ethnic students in higher education and issues of cultural congruency for these students within the academic and cultural environment. Other areas of research interest include academic support and cultural congruity for racial and ethnic minorities and professional development issues for counselors in training. Her work has appeared in journals such as *Cultural Diversity and Ethnic Minority Psychology, Hispanic Journal of Behavioral Sciences,* and *The Counseling Psychologist*. She currently is a senior editor for the *Journal of Multicultural Counseling and Development*. An active member of APA, she has served as the secretary and membership chair for the Section for Ethnic and Racial Diversity for Division 17 of APA and is currently the chair-elect for this section. She was awarded the Women of Color Psychologies Award from Division 35 in 1999 and the Emerging Professional Award from Division 45 of APA in 2002.

I5

DEVELOPMENTAL CAREER CHALLENGES FOR LATINA/O FACULTY IN HIGHER EDUCATION

Edward A. Delgado-Romero,
Lisa Y. Flores, Alberta M. Gloria,
Patricia Arredondo,
and Jeanett Castellanos

Education is a powerful vehicle to social and economic advancement for many racial and ethnic minority groups in the United States. Historically, access and representation of racial and ethnic minorities within the educational system has been limited and unfortunately continues to have difficulties (see Chapter 4). More recently, access to higher education has steadily increased for all minority groups over the past few decades, however, the proportion of Latinos and Latinas who graduate with undergraduate and graduate degrees remains relatively low (Wilds, 2000). Consequently, there are few Latinos and Latinas who enter academia as faculty or administrators, particularly in prestigious, predominantly White doctoral degree-granting institutions (Allen et al., 2002).

To accurately understand the process of Latino and Latina faculty in academia, an overview is merited. Next, a specific examination of different professional rankings (e.g., lecturer, assistant, associate, and full) will highlight the developmental processes that are inherent to each rank. This review will reveal the environmental barriers, ethonocultural (Comas-Díaz, 1997) conflicts (e.g., racism, discrimination, and stereotype threat [Niemann, 1999]), and lack of personal and institutional support encountered by Latino and Latina faculty. Unfortunately, these challenges often influence scholars to avoid academia as a career and prematurely terminate their faculty careers.

Throughout this chapter we will refer to superordinate value orientations (Altaribba & Bauer, 1998) in the Latino culture that are common to Latina/o professionals (Comas-Díaz, 1997), including higher education faculty. These include *personalismo* (a preference for close personal relationships), *respeto* (respect for elders and authority, which is maintained by all family members), *familismo* (an emphasis on the family including the extended family and friends), *simpatía* (need for behaviors that promote pleasant and non-conflicting social relationships) and the cultural value of allocentrism (high levels of conformity, mutual empathy, willingness to sacrifice for the welfare of the group, and high levels of personal interdependence) (Marín & Marín, 1991).

Status of Latina/o Faculty

Latino and Latina full-time faculty (16,498) currently represent 2.9% of all U.S. faculty (Harvey, 2002). This represents a 44% increase from 1991 to 1999 and is the largest increase among all racial/ethnic minority groups. Of special note are the needs of Latina faculty (see Chapter 13, Arredondo, 2002), as their numbers have increased 70% in that period.

Represented in various academic areas and disciplines (see Tables 15.1 and 15.2), Latino and Latina faculty are concentrated in humanities, social sciences, education, and engineering (although primarily in part-time positions). It is speculated that the representation of Latino and Latina faculty in certain academic areas is due to personal choice (opportunity to address social justice issues in the humanities) and institutional racism (see Villalpando & Delgado Bernal, 2002). In addition to faculty positions, Latinos and Latinas have dismal representation as administrators (3%) and as college presidents (4%).

Despite progress, there are several inaccuracies that misrepresent the national data of Latino and Latina faculty. First, the data are aggregated, obscuring the differential rates of academic representation among the various Latino and Latina ethnic groups. Second, the information about Latino and Latina faculty are not differentiated by institutional type (e.g., community college, 4-year teaching university, 4-year doctoral-granting university). For example, the number of Latina/o presidents decreases from 4% to 2.5% if the 44 Latina/o presidents at Puerto Rican universities are not included. Third,

Table 15.1   Percentage of Full-time, Part-Time, and Total Hispanic/Latina/o Faculty and Staff in Degree-granting Institutions, by Field, Fall 1998

	Full-time	Part-time	Total
All fields	3.3	3.7	3.5
Agriculture and home economics	1.4	3.9	1.9
Business	1.6	1.4	1.5
Education	3.3	3.5	3.3
Engineering	3.9	11.2	5.9
Fine Arts	1.1	3.1	2.2
Health	3.3	1.9	2.7
Humanities	6.5	5.8	6.2
Natural sciences	2.9	2.4	2.7
Social sciences	3.0	4.8	3.7
Other	2.6	4.1	3.3

Source: U.S. Department of Education, National Center for Education Statistics, National Study of Postsecondary Faculty (NSOPF), 1993 and 1999 (July, 2001: Table 232).

some faculty are inaccurately identified as Latino and Latina based on their surname, rather than by their own ethnic background (e.g., someone married to a Latino). Finally, many institutions continue to count Latino and Latina faculty as part of their representation long after their departure (e.g., leaving faculty information on department Web pages and in print brochures).

Saturated at the bottom levels of the academic prestige hierarchy (Allen et al., 2002), Latino and Latina faculty predominantly enter into entry-level and non-tenure positions (e.g., lecturer, adjunct faculty) and are concentrated at Hispanic Serving Institutions (HSIs) and 2-year colleges. A review of the Latino and Latina faculty data reveals a pyramid structure, in which there are more Latino and Latina instructors, lecturers, and non-tenure line faculty (6,187) than there are tenure-track assistant (4,237), associate (3,161) or full (2,913) professors. In contrast, the pyramid of professorial rank is inverted for White faculty, who have the most representation as full professors (142,852) than any other faculty rank.

Research regarding Latina/o faculty careers generally falls into two categories: empirical studies and narratives. Empirical studies often focus on faculty of color (e.g., Fouad & Carter, 1992) in the aggregate, and unfortunately most of the research fails to address issues specific to Latina/o faculty. For example, counseling psychology research that addresses scholarly research productivity (Kahn, 2001; Mallinckrodt & Gelso, 2002; Tinsley, Tinsley, Boone, & Shim-Li,

Table 15.2 Percentage of Full-Time, Part-Time, and Total Hispanic/Latina/o Faculty and Staff in Degree-Granting Institutions, by Program Area, Fall 1998

	Full-Time	Part-Time	Total
Communications	3.1	2.0	2.5
Teacher education	1.4	3.7	2.5
Other education	4.3	3.3	3.9
First-professional health sciences	3.6	2.7	3.4
Nursing	3.7	1.7	3.0
Other health sciences	2.6	1.4	2.0
English and literature	4.4	3.1	3.7
Foreign languages	17.6	20.4	18.8
History	4.7	3.9	4.3
Philosophy	2.0	1.6	1.8
Law	1.3	5.1	3.5
Biological sciences	1.9	.9	1.7
Physical sciences	2.5	1.5	2.2
Mathematics	4.8	3.7	4.3
Computer sciences	3.1	2.2	2.6
Economics	1.4	1.3	1.4
Political science	4.3	2.4	3.7
Psychology	3.1	2.6	2.9
Sociology	2.0	5.4	3.4
Other social sciences	3.7	10.5	6.7
Occupationally specific programs	2.8	3.5	3.2
All other programs	2.7	4.5	3.5

Source: U.S. Department of Education, National Center for Education Statistics, National Study of Postsecondary Faculty (NSOPF), 1993 and 1999. (July 2001: Table 235).

1993) either does not report demographics (treating findings as universal) or uses samples that are predominantly White (with less than 3% Latina/o subjects on average). Further, salient issues in faculty development (e.g., mentorship, cultural congruity), have not been thoroughly investigated (Hollingsworth & Fassinger, 2002; Smith, Smith, & Markham, 2000). Although some studies focus on issues relevant to Latinos and Latinas (Atkinson, Neville, & Casas, 1991; Pope-Davis, Stone, & Nielson, 1997), the results are discussed broadly, having minimal relevance to Latina/o students and faculty. More recently, scholars have conducted studies that separate different racial and ethnic groups in their data analyses (i.e., Villalpando & Delgado Bernal, 2002).

Personal narratives generally give voice to unaddressed barriers in academia, providing validation and psychic relief to Latina/o faculty about important interpersonal and sociopolitical dynamics (see Niemann, 1999; Olivas, 1996; Padilla & Chávez, 1995; Reyes & Halcón 1996). Proponents of Critical Race Theory (Delgado, 1989; Villalpando & Delgado Bernal, 2002) point out that the viewpoints of marginalized groups are rarely heard, and by sharing what they term as "counterstories," there are both personal and professional benefits. First, narratives can provide a source of connection among Latina/os who are isolated in the academy both socially and psychologically, and second, these writings provide a challenge to the dominant discourse. The sharing of narratives allows for a sense of connection and strength for those Latina/o faculty who feel isolation, alienation, and are without norm group for comparison. Comas-Díaz (2000, 2002) calls attention to the value of testimony as a type of narrative that focuses on a first-person account of the past, allowing the narrator to transform painful experiences and identity, thereby leading to ethnopolitical understanding, healing of pain, political activism, and hope for the future.

Purpose

This chapter is guided both by the available empirical research and the need to share our narratives. The authors of this chapter represent many dimensions of diversity in terms of gender, Latino national origin (e.g., Mexican, Cuban, and Colombian), and academic status (tenured/non-tenured/non-tenure line; instructor, assistant, and associate professor). Despite our diversity, we share navigational experiences within the university system at doctoral-granting predominantly White academic institutions (Delgado-Romero, Flores, Gloria, & Arredondo, 2002). In this chapter we will examine the developmental career challenges that Latina/o faculty encounter at various levels in the higher education system using a combination of available research and our personal narratives (we have chosen to present our experiences without individually identifying ourselves since some of us are still in vulnerable positions). We conclude by suggesting directions for future research and interventions that will enhance Latina/o faculty recruitment and retention in higher education.

Part-Time Faculty: Full-Time Work

Currently, Latina/o faculty represent 3.7% of all individuals classified as Instructors, Lecturers and "other" faculty (Harvey, 2002). Referring to Tables 15.1 and 15.2, Latina/os comprise a disproportionate number of the part-time faculty in Foreign Languages (20.4%), Engineering (11.2%), and other social sciences

(10.5%). Whether hiring of Latina/os in temporary positions to deal with budgetary issues, faculty shortages, or fulfill diversity quotas, Latina/os are typically found in academic positions that are poorly paid, have no benefits (medical insurance, retirement plans, permanent office space), and lack opportunities for advancement. Universities may often choose to deal with budgetary problems and faculty shortages by hiring temporary positions such as lecturers, visiting professors, instructors, and adjunct professors.

Lecturer positions typically do not offer the benefits that tenure line faculty enjoy, such as academic freedom, opportunities for advancement, and social support. Moreover, these positions often carry heavy teaching and service expectations. The following section highlights the challenges of a Latina lecturer. These challenges include: organizational and social barriers, cultural responsibilities, and *navegando* (navigational means) the system, and *la política* (politics).

Lecturer positions hold limited prestige in the academic hierarchy (Allen et al., 2002) without the protection of long-term contracts, and they are overscrutinized. In particular, the importance of teaching evaluations, student opinions, maintaining high class enrollments, and teaching efficiency and productivity become paramount. This is particularly challenging for Latina/o lecturers who are assigned race-based or culture-specific (e.g., Latina/o issues) classes that cover topics such as White privilege, racism, ethnic identity, and cultural competency. Students are often uncomfortable with the challenging content of ethnic identity and race consciousness and can target their discomfort at the lecturer (who they accurately perceive as having limited power in the system). Programs often offer classes that deal with race-based or cultural content as curriculum fillers, which further marginalizes part-time faculty, and impacts the difficulty of teaching emotion-laden courses. All of these experiences may reflect the lack of value the institution bestows upon these courses, or one's field of study and academic/professional interests.

Lecturers have numerous teaching responsibilities as a result of an ever-expanding student enrollment, and the working conditions for non-tenure line faculty continue to deteriorate. In particular, most lecturers are hired on an "as needed" basis (by quarter, semester, or yearly basis), requiring them to continuously reapply for their own positions. This furthers the perception of lecturers as "disposable," and is also often dehumanizing and emotionally draining to the individual.

The long-term rewards for lecturers are rare—for example, some Research I Institutions require lecturers to teach for 6 years before becoming eligible for a 3-year contract. Additionally, the salaries for lecturers are often substandard relative to the services provided. To complement the dismal salaries, many lecturers are considered "freeway flyers." That is, they lecture at various institutions in order to piece together a sustainable income. These factors prohibit lecturers from developing courses and rule out the development of a research agenda. Latina/os who take a part-time job, hoping for entry into a permanent position soon find that without a research agenda, many permanent positions for which they apply are then denied to them. Thus, the cycle of exploitation perpetuates itself.

In addition, part-time faculty are faced with marginalization, isolation, and "free-floater" status, without professional networks to provide support and normalization. Lecturers experience an academic hierarchy (Allen et al., 2002) that dichotomizes faculty and academic staff (i.e., lecturers, adjunct faculty). A sense of dispensability resounds for lecturers given their limited social network and collegial ties with other academic scholars. As a result, lecturers are often considered second-tier faculty as they are not part of the long-term mission of the department or institution. Ironically, higher education is dependent on part-time faculty to teach students, yet at the same time it devalues and exploits part-time faculty.

> At my institution Latina/o tenure-track faculty have welcomed me and they seem to value my contributions. Despite their efforts, I am well aware that I am not fully involved in the organizational structure and decision-making processes. Many White faculty, while cordial, are careful to distinguish themselves from lecturers by encouraging students to "seek out tenure-track faculty for mentorship as oppose to lecturers, who are temporary and who will probably not be here next year."
>
> In addition to being excluded (systemically and personally) I have been unable to foster professional relationships, in-depth academic dialogues with colleagues, and collaborative research opportunities due to the overwhelming demands of my position. This is further impacted by an institutional culture that permits limited Latina/o faculty representation in the academy. Although I have been able to foster relationships with other Latina/o faculty, it has been a challenge to coordinate schedules, have lunch, or dialogue about our research interests given my heavy teaching and advising loads. Although there are three Latino male senior faculty down the hall, it is few times in the academic year that time permits us to discuss our experiences or mutual academic interests.

Adding to the social isolation experience of Latina/o lecturers, they also experience discrimination, disrespect, and a pronounced interrogation of their credibility.

As a lecturer, I have been mistaken for a member of the cleaning crew, a student, an administrative assistant, or a visiting community member. Because many people hold stereotypes of Latinas as uneducated, menial workers who are only good for childbearing, I constantly combat cultural stigmas and stereotypes of Latinas in the workplace. When I inform other faculty of my educational training and my teaching load (i.e., four classes a quarter), many are shocked. They interrogate me about which university I earned my degree and inquire about my teaching history.

The lack of respect is pervasive, and students quickly pick up on this disrespect as many students do not see the need to address me properly (i.e., as "Dr."), continuously challenge my teaching or advising, or even curse in front of me (as if I were a peer). In particular, students feel entitled to abruptly open my door without knocking or shout outside my door when I do not open it, yelling "Open the door, I know you are in there." Some students treat me like I am their maid, I am here to serve them and they feel entitled to my help.

As a Latina lecturer who has over 4 years of teaching experience in academia, I can clearly identify the additional cultural responsibilities that I have in comparison to my fellow White lecturers. For example, I regularly (7 times in a quarter, over 21 times in a year) present to Latina/o undergraduates about graduate school opportunities. In addition, I mentor over 30 students throughout the academic year and have chaired a total of six undergraduate honors theses per year in ethnic issues and minorities in higher education. Moreover, I attend luncheons sponsored by MEChA and other student groups to promote faculty interaction, student retention, and improve campus climate representing *mi gente* (my people) and promote knowledge about Latinos in higher education.

Other additional community responsibilities include being invited to deliver bilingual presentations to Latina/o students' parents. I also attend end-of-year recruitment efforts with parents of color, demonstrating that the school is student-centered and that there are people who look and think like their children. Finally, in that there are only two tenure-track Latinas in my area of study, I am frequently asked to serve on panels with senior Latina/o faculty. Thus, my service activities are considerable and my institution relies on me (but does not reward or recognize me) for these important activities.

Overall, being a Latina lecturer consumes emotional and psychological energy given the constant organizational, social, and cultural responsibilities coupled with a lack of respect and active exploitation. Yet, it is at least *un pie* (one foot) in the institution. I have considered transferring to a teaching institution, but I realize the importance of placing Latina/o undergraduates into the Research I graduate pipeline.

Further, the access to research resources allows me to pursue my emerging research agenda.

The three main social networks that have sustained me as a lecturer include my family, my academic mentors (who are faculty), and *La Causa*. My family (parents, grandparents, nieces and nephews) motivates me to make an impact on Latino undergraduates' lives, their educational aspirations, and the graduate school and professional pipeline. My mentors provide guidance, direction about research, insight into academic politics, and advise me in how to sustain myself in my current position. Their own professional successes, research agendas, and drive further ignite my passion for academia. Because of the struggles regarding social injustice and limited academic access for Latinos, the motivated students of color who daily enter my office with academic dreams, and the wave of brown students (i.e., Latinos) that I know is forthcoming, keeps me holding on.

However, in my position as a lecturer I am at the first, the last, and the only step that this position offers. Therefore I am going to seek a tenure-track appointment. Because I have been able to establish a research agenda (on my own time) I am still marketable, but many Latina/o lecturers end up burned out, feeling used and leave academia.

Beginning Career Issues

We intentionally position this discussion of beginning career issues after the section on part-time faculty to underscore the fact that the entry-level position in academia is the assistant professor, not part-time faculty. Decisions about a career in the academy typically begins in graduate school as Latina/o graduate students become familiar with the requirements of academic life. In most professions, this involves teaching and establishing a program of research. During graduate school the advisor or dissertation chair is extremely influential and can ensure that the graduate student obtains the right type of experiences (i.e., presenting at conferences, research, networking) to prepare them for a faculty position. This type of support and mentoring is even more important for Latina/o graduate students because they may lack role models from their own families or communities who have gone through such experiences. Advisors or other faculty can also steer Latina/o graduate students away from academic careers and toward clinical or applied careers by providing a "null environment" (Betz, 1989), by the types of reinforcement they offer (Pope-Davis, Stone, & Nielson, 1997), or by controlling access to salient professional networks within the academic hierarchy (Allen et al., 2002).

Career Considerations

After a decision has been made to apply for an academic position, it is important to determine which institutions and departments might provide the best fit for the Latina/o candidate. An essential part of that fit is cultural self-understanding and the potential receptivity of an institution to one's culture. Latina/o job applicants should consider how ethnically focused they are going to be in all aspects of professional life, and how much of their culture they will bring into the workplace. A candidate might not always be aware that they are making these decisions or of the long-standing impact that these decisions can have.

> When searching for a position I had to make a decision of how Latino-focused I wanted to be personally and professionally and find an environment, both at work and in the community, that would fit my needs. I decided that I was going to use both of my Spanish surnames and insist that people not shorten my name or mispronounce it. A few search chairs seemed put off when I corrected their pronunciation of my name, but I felt it was worth the effort, especially if I ended up working with them for many years.

However, not every Latina/o can fully decide how Latina/o they want to be, especially in the eyes (and ears) of others. For example, those Latina/o with strong Spanish accents or those who phenotypically (skin and eye color, hair color and texture) represent what Latina/os are expected to look like, may find that they are strongly identified as Latina/o by others. Conversely, light-skinned Latina/os without accents may struggle to be seen as legitimate (Delgado-Romero, under review), and dark-skinned Latina/os may face additional challenges when identified as Black or African American by others (Comas-Díaz, 1994). The general issue of the relationship of stereotypical expectations, both internal and external, to the decreased sense of competence and self-defeating behavior that may result for Latina/o faculty is something the Latino/a candidate should be aware of.

> Other things I had to consider in my job search included the type of Latina/o community in the town or within driving distance from the town, the availability of Latino food, music, and cultural events, and the support for Spanish/English bilingual education in the local school system. Of course I also had to consider my geographical proximity to my family, especially *mi Mama*. Of all the variables in my job search I feared her reaction the most if I were to move too far away from her and take her *nieto* (grandson) away from her.

Although some of these considerations sound trivial, I knew I had to change my mentality from "I can put up with anything for a few years," which is how I ended up in a snowy area of the Midwest for graduate school. I had to think relatively long-term. One site told me that despite the previous faculty person leaving due to community intolerance of Latinos and a severe racial divide in the town, that I should still consider applying. They actually thought that I would be able to survive and thrive without a supportive context outside of the department!

Latina/o faculty applicants may want to consider the number of faculty and administrators of color (as well as Latina/o faculty and administrators) at an institution. As the only Latina/o faculty, one runs the risk of experiencing tokenism and further exacerbating the negative association that some senior faculty equate with affirmative action or "special" hires (Niemann, 1999). It is also important to inquire about the tenure history of recent Latina/o hires. Part of the early career decision-making process requires candidates to inquire about the tenure history of recent Latina/o hires. Situations to avoid are ones where the "revolving door" of Latina/o and other faculty of color occurs. In these institutions, faculty of color are brought in to enhance diversity in the department and work on diversity issues, but they typically do not achieve tenure.

An important source of support and advocacy in a university can be Ethnic Studies or Latino/Chicano Studies programs. However, affiliating with a Chicano, Latino, or Ethnic Studies program can be a complicated decision. Although these programs can provide resources and like-minded colleagues, conversely they may also serve to increase a sense of alienation from home program faculty (Atkinson, Brown, Casas, & Zane, 1996). Furthermore, program faculty may resent the influence of outsiders on their own junior faculty and question the loyalty of the Latina/o seeking support elsewhere. One Latina faculty member cited an example when, in response to a competing offer for a postdoctoral position in an Ethnic Studies program, a senior faculty member asked her "What are you, a scholar or a Mexican American?" (Niemann, 1999, p. 116). On the other hand, faculty in Ethnic Studies programs may be some of the few people on campus that are aware of the issues facing junior Latina/o faculty.

Latina/o applicants need to inquire about the departmental and institutional expectations related to research, teaching, and service for the positions for which they apply.

One search chair put it to me like this, "We count six things for tenure: research, research, research, research, teaching, and service."

My research interests were in Latino issues, so I had to assess whether or not senior faculty would support this. My work is in Latina/o psychology and "Brown on Brown" research can carry with it a stigma of being unprofessional, subjective, and a form of service, so it was important to me that Latina/o research was valued and publications in minority-focused journals would not be looked at as inferior research. Some programs only count "mainstream" research as being tenure worthy.

With regard to teaching, often Latina/o faculty are expected to teach courses with ethnic and cultural content. This expectation is a double-edged sword because although these courses can be professionally and personally rewarding, Latina/o faculty might be subject to marginalization both by students (lowered teaching evaluations or accusations of a lack of objectivity) and by other faculty, especially when ethnic courses are only taught by junior faculty of color.

It is also important for a candidate to get a sense of what kind of service is expected and how service is defined. For example, one university may define conference presentations as service while another defines it as research. This issue is critical since Latina/o faculty can be inundated with service requests, especially related to ethnic minority issues. It is important to know that senior faculty are aware of this potential problem and will help protect junior colleague's time.

The Interview

Once a Latina/o candidate makes the finalist pool for a position he or she is faced with new challenges. The job interview in the academy manifests the ultimate professional value of individualism. Candidates are often closely scrutinized and judged on their ability to be an independent scholar. A lack of awareness of this individualistic emphasis may leave a Latina/o candidate unprepared for this experience. The interviewing process, including traveling without family and dealing with powerful strangers, who may skip over *platica* (small talk) to get to business, may result in uncomfortable feelings for Latina/o candidates accustomed to the Latino cultural norm of *personalismo*.

My job search was successful, but interviewing was very stressful. One department sat and listened to my job talk in total silence and did not ask many questions or give any feedback on the talk whatsoever. In my hotel room I fell apart, certain that the job talk was a failure and that I was a fraud. I later found out that the department gave minimal feedback to candidates in order to be "fair and objective." In another interview I was told to sit in an empty conference room for an hour upon my arrival because the faculty were too busy to greet me until my scheduled meeting time. Talk about impersonal!

Interviews can also become complicated if the Latina/o candidate is subject to subtle or overt prejudice or racism by faculty members who are ambivalent about affirmative action or hiring racial/ethnic minority candidates. The issue of hiring faculty of color can often be a highly political situation, even if the applicant is not an affirmative action or "special" hire. Many people (both within and outside of academia) endorse a view of faculty hiring, reward, and promotion in higher education based on "neutral, objective, and meritocratic" criterion (Villalpando & Delgado Bernal, 2002, p. 244). However, this is often not the case for Latina/o applicants as they soon discover the complex and political nature of faculty hiring.

> Although the department had brought me in for an interview and assured me they were looking to diversify their faculty, I soon became aware that they had no intention of hiring me. Naively, I had believed them. However, once I got to campus it became apparent that the only reason that I was brought in for an interview was to appease the Dean about diversity hiring. After relentless criticism, a sabotaged job talk and second-guessing by White senior faculty, it became clear to me that the faculty used me to support their contention that there were no qualified Latina/o applicants available. Furthermore, I was not the only Latino treated this way. I never stood a chance of getting the job, and I felt stupid, incompetent, and dehumanized in the process. I felt even worse when I found out that a White person was hired for the position. Luckily not every department behaved this way, and I had some very positive interview experiences as well that led to job offers.

When the Latina/o candidate is successful in the interview process, he or she must then negotiate the terms of the academic appointment. The terms of the initial appointment are critical because all subsequent merit raises are built from this base. Negotiations are handled with powerful senior faculty and administrators that, for Latina/os accustomed to the cultural norm of *respeto*, can be quite a challenge.

> My mother taught me never to argue with authority and to show elders *respeto*—communication was one way: they spoke and I listened. So it came as a shock to have to negotiate for salary and benefits with the Dean. I was not very good at it but I had friends who helped me a great deal. I was lucky that I had a Dean who made a fair offer to

start with, because I have heard horror stories of low-ball negotiating tactics from other faculty of color. However in the long run I realized that this was just the first time I had to justify how much I was worth, and I had to get used to it. So even though it felt totally alien, I had to learn to stand up for myself.

Assistant Professors: The Early Professional Years

Research demands and teaching are often cited as two of the most challenging tasks for new professionals in academia (Taylor & Martin, 1987). Although each new faculty member will experience a range of demands that are specific to his or her institution and program, previous scholars have identified general professional issues encountered by beginning faculty, including: (1) concerns about competency, (2) fears of being tenured, and (3) socialization to the job (Fouad & Carter, 1992; Mintz 1992). Feelings of anxiety and incompetence may be especially heightened for Latina/o faculty because of the lack of role models in academia. Moreover, new Latina/o faculty members may face additional challenges when they start their academic careers. Discrimination, feelings of isolation and tokenism, and expectations to provide ethnic minority service are unique issues in the experience of people from underrepresented racial, ethnic, or gender groups in academia (Fouad & Carter, 1992; APA, 2000; Mintz, 1992).

In addition to tackling the universal issues faced by new assistant professors—which in and of themselves can feel like a considerable load, Latina/os often face supplemental stressors in comparison to their White counterparts. These stressors stem from the subtle and not so subtle acts of racism and prejudice, including and establishing authority with students and colleagues. Although such microaggressions may not occur on a daily basis, they have a cumulative effect, wearing down the recipient over time. Interpersonal disrespect and other institutional behaviors toward Latina/o academics undermine the new professional's competencies and power, and may add unnecessary stress and doubt, or a need to prove oneself during a time when the new professional may already be feeling vulnerable.

> I have experienced several instances of bias in the academy, ranging from being accused of getting the position due to affirmative action (message: you did not earn your position), to being mistaken as a student (message: you do not look like someone who fits our image of a faculty member), to hearing disparaging remarks of faculty or students who are pregnant (message: if you get pregnant, want to have a family, or have a family and make them a priority in your life, you are not committed to your job).

At times I felt approached or challenged by some students in ways that I was sure they would never interact with other faculty, such as questioning the legitimacy of a class I was teaching, addressing me by my first name, or arriving late to class even after being told that it was distracting and disruptive and telling the student that the tardiness must stop.

Stigmas Facing the New Professional

Latina/o faculty still deal with the stigma of affirmative action, "target-of opportunity" (Atkinson et. al. 1996) or "special hires" regardless of the actual circumstance of their hire. Affirmative action programs are often blamed because of a perception that they give Latina/o faculty preferential treatment. Yet, paradoxically, affirmative action programs are often criticized for failure to make a difference (Atkinson et al., 1996). Thus institutional ambivalence about affirmative action, and the broader question of diversifying faculty, can often leave Latina/o faculty in another defensive posture.

> While transitioning into my job as an assistant professor, I was introduced to an acquaintance of a colleague who, within 15 seconds of being introduced, asked me whether I was hired because the department needed a "female" or an "ethnic minority." This person had no idea what my academic record was, and yet within seconds reduced me to being a hire based solely on my group affiliation!

Latina/o assistant professors also face challenges that their White colleagues do not in the areas of research, teaching, and service, and are evaluated for their performance in each area based on White, Eurocentric values and standards. As mentioned earlier, Latina/o faculty may be expected to teach race-based courses, yet their teaching evaluations for these courses are weighed similarly to other classes despite the fact that such courses typically produce lower ratings. In addition, research quality and productivity may be evaluated on the impact rating of a journal or citation counts of an article, both of which are heavily influenced by the number of researchers doing similar work. These standards do not take into account that there are fewer academics doing culture-based research and that research in culture- or race-based journals are less likely to be cited by "mainstream" researchers.

Ethnic Minority-Specific Service Demands

Finally, Latina/o faculty may be pressured to provide service around ethnic minority issues, conduct diversity training, and recruit and advise ethnic minority students (in addition to the White students). However, excessive service may consume valuable time that can be devoted to research and writing activities, and may ultimately result in tenure denial (Suinn & Witt, 1982). Moreover, the people who are often requesting the services of Latina/o faculty are those who will be voting on their tenure and promotion (e.g., department chair, vice-provosts for academic affairs).

> By the end of my second year, I was a member of two university work-group committees, two university search committees, two departmental search committees, organized a recruitment weekend for racial/ethnic undergraduate students for the department, and chair of the department's diversity committee. The diversity committee was comprised of two full professors and one associate professor, one of whom consistently attended meetings. In addition, I was providing guest lectures on Latino issues in undergraduate and graduate courses, conducting training for psychology interns at the counseling center, and presenting during the annual Latino Awareness Week on campus.
>
> It's not just an issue of learning to "just say no." The implication behind this advice is that as a Latina I do not have the sufficient personal and professional boundaries to manage multiple demands. The key is helping other faculty to understand the unique demands on Latina/o junior faculty, accurately understanding the political consequences of saying no, and getting support from senior faculty for doing so. I have to keep a long-term perspective on what it means to help.

Tenure and Associate Professors

Without a doubt the most significant and essential shift from Assistant to Associate Professor is receiving tenure. Once tenure is granted, it serves as the gateway to academic longevity, status, and professional advancement within academia. Ultimately, promotion and tenure ensure permanent employment and academic freedom. Because of its importance within academia, a substantial amount of literature has been generated about the tenure process, and about the tenure grievances and difficulties of Latina/o faculty in particular (see Chapters 11 and 12). The research indicates that the overall tenure rate for all faculty is 73%, while White faculty (75%) have higher tenure rates than Latina/o faculty (64%). Further, Latino men are more likely to be tenured (68%) than are Latinas (59%) (Harvey, 2002).

Challenges to Credibility

Academic credibility is one of the most salient issues confronting Latina/o faculty, particularly relative to White faculty who generally do not experience the same scrutiny. One credibility issue that is often raised during the tenure process is whether a Latina/o faculty member is developing and presenting a programmatic research agenda or a political/personal agenda. More specifically, the faculty member is often questioned whether he/she is working out personal issues through his/her research agenda.

> Part of my research examines how cultural values inherent to the university system impact campus climate and the potential inclusion of Latina/o students. This work was perceived as a political agenda rather than research about a people who are often discriminated against within higher education and who typically have fewer college degrees than other racial and ethnic groups. (See Chapter 4.)

Another credibility concern is whether Latina/os have "what it takes to get published." Research conducted by Latina/o faculty is often not well received by colleagues, journal reviewers, or journal editors and is not published in "mainstream" or top-tier journals because its focus on Latina/o research is often deemed as out of the mainstream—and therefore inferior—research. Tenure reviewers give little attention (at either the departmental or divisional levels) as to whether the research is considered relevant to "seminal" journals.

> Unfortunately, I found that the top-tier journals in my area of research were considered "specialty journals" and were scrutinized as "less than scholarly outlets" for my research.
>
> A similar credibility question is that of intellectual capability. Although I was never directly asked how smart I was, the question took the covert form of a directive that I not publish with other colleagues. In other words, I was asked whether I was doing my own research, particularly if I published with more senior colleagues (with the assumption that the more senior scholars were doing all of the work). I am still often and "innocently" asked by both academic colleagues and students if I analyze my own statistics for my research. This is another thinly disguised approach to assess my intellectual capabilities. Perhaps the most denigrating experience was being told that I should not publish with students because it was assumed that students were doing my work for me.

At the heart of the credibility issue is whether Latina/o faculty are qualified for the faculty positions and tenured posts to which they are hired. Because of the disparate hiring practices that have occurred throughout history, the importance of Equal Employment Opportunity (EEO) processes are integral to balance past inequities (Niemann & Dovidio, 1999). At the same

time, discrimination is perpetuated as faculty colleagues of all races and eth-
nicities question the qualifications of recently hired Latina/o faculty.

> For example, the issue of whether I was hired for my qualifications or
> to meet a diversity quota was something that I had not seriously con-
> sidered until I was faced with blatantly differential treatment by col-
> leagues and students. For example, I often wonder whether students
> would challenge my lecture material or my choice of course require-
> ments if I were White? If I were male? If I were a White male?

The Tenure Process

Credibility issues are prominent for the Latina/o professional entering academia; however, these issues continue to be raised during the tenure process.
While these issues may be expected among White colleagues, the constant
challenges to credibility are most unsettling when they come from the Latina/o
community.

> In attempting to meet the required research, teaching, and service
> expectations to earn tenure, I found myself having less and less time to
> spend in the community. Even though I always made some time for the
> Chicano/a and Latina/o students on campus, many questioned
> whether I was a *vendida* (cultural sell-out). Why was it that I missed
> so many Chicana/o student events? Why didn't I make it to the
> MEChA social? Why wasn't I volunteering my weekend at the local
> Latino community center? The task of balancing my time to publish
> research manuscripts, teach Multicultural Counseling (an extremely
> difficult and emotionally taxing class) and other courses, fulfill a
> diversity role on multiple campus committees, advise numerous under-
> graduate and graduate students from various departments, and take
> care of a family (in which I perform the majority of household respon-
> sibilities) was/is a physical and psychological challenge that left little
> time for me to give back to my community. Ultimately, what use would
> I be to the Chicana/o and Latina/o students if I did not earn tenure and
> was required to leave the campus at which they needed my support?
>   When both the academic and student communities questioned my
> credibility, it unfortunately became easy for me to question myself as
> well. Although I had a Latino colleague with whom to address these
> credibility questions, the gender expectations that he had of me as a
> Latina were all the more difficult. As a result, I looked to others for
> mentoring, but with few Latina tenured faculty, I found that I was
> making up my role as a tenured Latina faculty member as I went.
> Although I was searching for ongoing mentorship, it was evident from

the system that as a Chicana I was expected to be a "good little minority" by following the systems' rules.

For example, I was expected to be quiet about the differential handling of tenure cases for a White male colleague and myself. I wasn't supposed to ask questions or became angry about post-tenure inequities. Instead, my need to understand the workings of the system was met with defensiveness. When I was "put up for tenure review" I was told that my outside reviewers should not be Latina/o or faculty of color, because it would be assumed that I would somehow personally know all of them. When my White colleague's reviewers were all White, I questioned why he could have all White individuals and why he did not need to have any people of color review his materials. My questions were met with defensiveness and academic rhetoric. Although not overtly confirmed, I felt that others perceived my questioning of the tenure system as my being ungrateful.

In navigating the questions of credibility (from the internal and external forces) I found that my survival in academia required changes in my attitudes about the system and the educational elite. First and foremost, I remember who I am, particularly as the current tenure system attempts to strip and devalue any approach or values that are contrary to it. In staying rooted to my personal and cultural values, I remind myself to not take myself so seriously. More specifically, I remind myself of the internal energies (i.e., *ganas*) and familial responsibilities that support my seeking a career as a faculty member. At times I had to fight the system expectations to stay grounded to what I believed was best for me and my family.

In maintaining my family (and my sanity), I shifted my perspective of who and where my family is. Applying the flexibility to reconfigure, common to many Latina/o cultures, I created an academic family with other faculty colleagues (many of whom are Latina/o) at my home institution and abroad. Further, conferences are reframed as reunions where I spend time with those who give me cultural energy and support, thereby challenging the political norms of "having dinner with the right people" or "being seen with the names in the field." Ultimately, in letting go of the expectations and unmet needs of the academy, I find true joy and passion in being a tenured Chicana faculty member.

Tenure and Beyond

Advancing through academic ranks may or may not increase one's sense of belonging or acceptance. Some Latina/os might argue, from their personal experiences, that tenure does not necessarily mean increased respect from colleagues or reduced performance stress. However, with tenure status comes power, privilege, seniority, and recognition. Latina/o academics report that they take advantage of the opportunities that come to one with tenure. This may mean the freedom to promote a Latino-centered research agenda or one that is needed in a particular context, teaching advanced seminars and specialty courses, and influencing organizational changes that are inclusive and fair for faculty and students of color.

Latina/o senior faculty might assume the role of training director, program leader or coordinator, department chair and other administrative positions. At the college and university levels, individuals may become members and chairpersons of personnel committees, institutional review boards (IRBs), dean/presidential advisory councils, advisors to Latina/o student group, mentors to undergraduate and graduate students, and leaders of ethnic-focused professional associations. At some institutions, Chicana/o or Latina/o Faculty and Staff Associations give academics the opportunity to lead among their peers while also influencing university-wide policy changes that benefit Latinos and the university community in general.

Latina/o faculty account for 1.4% of full professors, which is the second lowest number (after Native Americans, who account for only 0.2%) of full professors in racial/ethnic groups (there are 2.5% African American and 4.4% Asian American). This statistic pales in comparison to Whites, who account for 91.5% of full professors (Harvey, 2002). The historic pipeline issue, as well as the lack of attention to the retention of Latina/os and other people of color in the faculty ranks can explain this inequity. Yet, it is important to tout other indicators of success in addition to tenure and full professor status. There are Latina/os who have received Fulbright and other prestigious fellowships to advance their research interests. A few have endowed chairs, a statement of their accomplishment as scholars. Others have been recognized through honorary degrees, or other important awards and recognition in other institutions, from professional associations (such as the American Psychological Association in our profession), and from community-based groups. The latter, in many respects, speaks volumes about the credibility and contributions of those academics to social justice and empowerment agendas for *la comunidad* (the community).

Indeed, power, privilege, and status mean responsibility to *la gente* (the people) and leaving a legacy for those who will follow us. Getting beyond tenure in some institutions may signal that it is time for the Latina/o academic to give back, to engage in behaviors that benefit other Latina/os at the university as well as in local communities. It may also mean that some may step in to visible leadership roles thereby demonstrating that Latina/os can also be leaders. In short, achieving tenure and beyond is a personal and collective milestone for *la gente;* it is one that must be celebrated, nurtured, and respected. The narratives in this chapter underscore this value of connection to one's primary cultural *familia*. Even though our career development challenges may not be appreciated by those who are near and dear, there is always a conveyance of *respeto* for our positions in the academy.

Critical Analysis from Developmental and Contextual Perspectives

Sigmund Freud (1856–1939) is credited with the often-used quote: "The tasks of adulthood are to love and to work." Julia de Burgos, a Puerto Rican poet and social justice advocate, wrote about creating *mi ruta* (my route), because she "could not be what men wanted her to be" (1953). These sentiments provide context for the challenges of many Latina/o academics—attempting to respond to multiple messages about who they should be, now that they are educated, and have their own personal strivings and ambitions.

The narratives of the other authors may be reminiscent to other faculty of color of moments of excitement and apprehension, of triumphs and disappointments, and of indignities versus respect. The *ruta* (route) each person has taken to reach the revered faculty appointment, promotion, and tenure is similar and different because each one of us has a different life story. However, there appears to be a developmental process with critical decision points that each individual has faced. It is these experiences that inform the processes for life in the academy for those seeking it and for those who are on the hiring and evaluation end. In our estimation, these are interactional and acculturation processes, involving Latina/os and non-Latina/os. All have a role to play in understanding the career development blueprint (see Figure 15.1).

The Latina/o Career Development Blueprint

It is fair to say that any family's values about education, its usefulness and meaning, are influenced by a number of factors. Economics, family history, family experiences in educational contexts, and of course, abilities, are a few of the variables that may account for who pursues higher education, particularly graduate studies, and who decides to enter the academy. The Latina/o Career Development Blueprint indicates that values clarification occurs throughout one's career development process as one weighs the benefits and liabilities personally and professionally of life in the academy.

The narratives in this chapter underscore some of the personal conflicts that occur intra- and interpersonally. There is considerable psychic energy

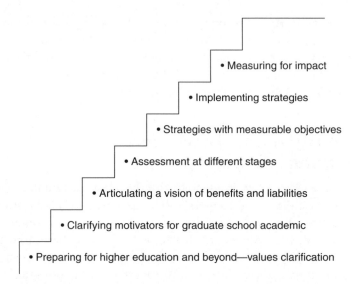

• Measuring for impact

• Implementing strategies

• Strategies with measurable objectives

• Assessment at different stages

• Articulating a vision of benefits and liabilities

• Clarifying motivators for graduate school academic

• Preparing for higher education and beyond—values clarification

FIGURE 15.1   The Latina/o career development blueprint.

expended in an individual's attention to "goodness of fit" and sense-of-belonging dynamics. If a Latina is the only person of color, it may be difficult or impossible to share this psychological unrest with others, including family. For junior faculty, measuring up is an extremely pressured expectation. The "publish or perish" mantra is one that weighs heavily and constantly.

Metaphorically, this speaks of the borderlands or "wild zone" language introduced by Latina feminist writers (Anzaldúa, 1987; Candelaria, 1993) and anthropologists (Ardener, 1975). These metaphors speak of individuals having to walk a tightrope, of at times feeling like an imposter because of a lack of validation from any source, and having to exercise enormous adaptation skills in different contexts. As Latina/o academics, there is an ongoing need to be bicultural and culturally and contextually responsive. While we have the experience of operating in the dominant Euro-American society, many of our colleagues have not worked with Latina/o colleagues. Again, this means that quite often the Latina/o must manage the relationship, excuse "inadvertent" microaggressions (e.g., ethnic jokes), explain oneself, and adapt to dysfunctional situations. The narratives underscore the process of hypersensitivity because of mistrust and other uncertainties in the academic setting. Yes, institutional and interpersonal racism is and may be a daily experience for many Latina/os, but it is one that we have to manage (Arredondo, 1999).

Stifling emotions in the midst of interpersonal and professional racist acts is a debilitating experience. Perceptions about Latina/os as emotional and emotive people are ones that Latina/o academics must keep in our conscious awareness. On the one hand, all faculty have frustrations and moments of anger but in the experiences of many of us, it is best to suppress these emotions. If there is not a climate of safety in one's department or institution, one takes a tremendous risk in demonstrating aggravation, annoyance, or anger— even if this appears to be the norm.

Empowerment Perspectives

Courage, tenacity, belief in personal values and one's self, and focus are attributes that contribute to being stalwart, self-directed, and ultimately successful in the academy. Along the way, cultural identity is challenged, but as Erikson's psychohistorical construct indicates (1975), the search for self, meaning, and identity are tasks for those who are outsiders or see themselves in contexts of cultural incongruity. Latina/os in academic positions are creating their own personal histories as well as preparing a roadmap for others. We have to draw from our *Mestizo* (indigenous) roots that are about survival in the midst of oppression, of collectivism to advance the common good of Latina/os who will follow us, and of the belief in multiculturalism and multiple realities (Ramirez, 1998). Finally, we have to congratulate ourselves, one another, and our *familias,* for giving us *las ganas* (motivation) to be pioneers, role models, and leaders in the privileged world of academics.

Recommendations/Future Directions

Latina/o success needs to be celebrated and studied. There are stories to be shared that provide valuable learning to hiring institutions as well as to Latina/os evaluating a career in the academy. Qualitative methodology lends itself to understanding and examining the counterstories (personal narratives) of Latina/o faculty. Through a narrative approach, barriers and enablers in the academic environment can be better understood. A second area of inquiry lies in exploring the strengths and resilience that flow from a positive conceptualization of Latina/o culture or *Mestizo* psychology. In the face of overwhelming amounts of data that document the lack of success of Latina/o faculty and the leaking pipeline to academia, there must emerge new notions of hope, of common purpose and of empowerment.

Understanding the factors that enhance or reduce Latina/o faculty success becomes a matter of cultural competence for academic institutions. Borrowing from the Multicultural Competencies of the Association of Multicultural Counseling and Development (Arredondo et al., 1996), and the adaptation of these competencies from Latino-centered perspectives (Santiago-Rivera, Arredondo, & Gallardo-Cooper, 2002), it is recommended that institutional agents, including deans, program directors, and senior faculty evaluate their values, knowledge, and skills with respect to engagement with Latina/o faculty. We encourage that Latina/os be seen as an investment in the future of the department and the profession of psychology. Far too often, our presence in the academy is seen as a liability or as a compromise of standards in the hiring process. From a values orientation, retention of Latina/o faculty should be seen as the necessary infusion of intelligence, passion, and energy that this institution needs to survive in the twenty-first century.

With respect to the knowledge aspect of cultural competence, institutional agents must understand Latina/o faculty in terms of the multiple cultural contexts that influence us. As has been discussed in this chapter, career development planning and decisions are typically collectivistic, taking *la familia* and *la comunidad,* both on and off campus into consideration.

Cultural competency in terms of skills means actions and behaviors. We recommend that academic deans and other hiring agents engage in dialogues with senior Latina/o faculty to learn more about how they can nurture and retain us. There are several professional associations with a Latina/o-specific focus. These include the National Latina/o Psychological Association and Hispanics in Higher Education, among others. Again, institutional agents responsible for hiring and tenure processes must reach out to us for counsel. Simultaneously, our Latina/o professional associations must also monitor the tenure and promotion process. The American Council of Education is a valuable source in this process, but beyond this, we too must exercise our self-efficacy skills on our own behalf and for our Latina/o *hermanos y hermanas* (brothers and sisters).

Closing Thoughts

"To survive the borderlands you must live *sin fronteras* (without borders), be a crossroads"(Anzaldúa, 1987, p. 195). The experiences of Latina/o faculty are more than an academic issue. This chapter has punctuated the intersections of roles and identities, challenges that accompany these, and the importance of courage and values to pursue one's career. As we do so, we bring *orgullo* (pride) to our communities and to ourselves.

References

Allen, W. R., Epps, E. G., Guillory, E. A., Suh, S. A., Bonous-Hammarth, M., & Stassen, M. L. A. (2002). Outsiders within: Race, gender and faculty status in U.S. higher education. In W. A. Smith, P. G. Altbach, & K. Lomotey (Eds.), *The racial crisis in American higher education: Continuing challenges for the twenty-first century* (rev. ed.), (pp. 189–220). Albany, NY: State University of New York Press.

Altaribba, J., & Bauer, L. M. (1998). Counseling the Hispanic client: Cuban Americans, Mexican Americans, and Puerto Ricans. *Journal of Counseling and Development, 76,* 389–396.

American Psychological Association Task Force on Women in Academe [APA]. (2000). *Women in academe: Two steps forward, one step back.* Washington, DC: Author.

Anzaldúa, G. (1987). *Borderlands/la frontera.* San Francisco: Spinsters/Aunt Lute Book.

Ardener, E. (1975). Belief and the problem of women. In S. Ardener (Ed.), *Perceiving women* (p. 275). London: Malaby Press.

Arredondo, P. (1999). Multicultural counseling competencies as tools to address oppression and racism. *Journal of Counseling and Development, 77,* 102–108.

Arredondo, P. A. (2002). Mujeres Latinas—santas y marquesas. *Cultural Diversity and Ethnic Minority Psychology, 8,* 308–319.

Arredondo, P., Toporek, R., Brown, S. P., Jones, J., Locke, D. C., Sanchez, J., & Stadler, H. (1996). Operationalization of the multicultural counseling competencies. *Journal of Multicultural Counseling and Development, 24,* 42–78.

Atkinson, D. R., Brown, M. T., Casas, J. M. & Zane, N. W. S. (1996). Achieving ethnic parity in counseling psychology. *The Counseling Psychologist, 24,* 230–258.

Atkinson, D. R., Neville, H., & Casas, A. C. (1991). The mentorship of ethnic minorities in professional psychology. *Professional Psychology: Research and Practice, 22,* 336–338.

Betz, N. E. (1989). Implications of the null environment hypothesis for women's career development and for counseling psychology. *The Counseling Psychologist, 17,* 136–144.

Brinson, J., & Kottler, J. (1993). Cross-cultural mentoring in counselor education: A strategy for retaining minority faculty. *Counselor Education and Supervision, 32,* 241–253.

Candelaria, C. (1993) *Arroyos to the heart.* Santa Monica, CA: Lalo Press: Santa Monica College.

Comas-Díaz, L. (1994). LatiNegra: Mental health issues of African Latinas. *Journal of Feminist Family Therapy, 5,* 35–74.

Comas-Díaz, L. (1997). Mental health needs of Latinos with professional status. In J. G. García & M. C. Zea (Eds.), *Psychological interventions and research with Latino populations* (pp. 142–165). Boston, MA: Allyn and Bacon.

Comas-Díaz, L. (2000). An ethnopolitical approach to working with people of color. *American Psychologist, 55,* 1319–1325.

Comas-Díaz, L. (2002). *Liberación Latina: Psychology's role in transformation.* Keynote address presented at the 2002 Latino Psychology Conference, Providence, Rhode Island.

DeBurgos, J. (1953). Y yo misma fui mi ruta. In *Río Piedras: Editorial Huracán*. Poesía. Encuadernación rústica.

Delgado, R. (1989). Storytelling for oppositionists and others: A plea for narrative. *Michigan Law Review, 87,* 2411–2441.

Delgado-Romero, E. A., Flores, L., Gloria, A., & Arredondo, P. (2002). *Developmental career challenges for Latino and Latina psychology faculty.* Symposium presented at the Latino Psychology 2002 Conference, Providence, Rhode Island.

Delgado-Romero, E. A. (under review). *No parece: The privilege and prejudice inherent in being a light skinned Latino without an accent.*

Erikson, E. H. (1975). *Life history and the historical moment.* New York: W. W. Norton.

Fouyad, N., & Carter, R. (1992). Gender and racial issues for new counseling psychologists in academia. *The Counseling Psychologist, 20,* 123–140.

Harvey, W. B. (2002). *Nineteenth Annual Status Report on Minorities in Higher Education.* Washington, DC: American Council on Education.

Hollingsworth, M. A., & Fassinger, R. E. (2002). The role of faculty mentors in the research training of counseling psychology doctoral students. *Journal of Counseling Psychology, 49,* 324–330.

Kahn, J. H. (2001). Predicting the scholarly activity of counseling psychology students: A refinement and extension. *Journal of Counseling Psychology, 48,* 344–354.

Mallinckrodt, B., & Gelso, C. J. (2002). Impact of research training environment and Holland personality type: A 15-year follow up of research productivity. *Journal of Counseling Psychology, 49,* 60–70.

Marín, G., & Marín, B. V. (1991). *Research with Hispanic populations.* Newbury Park, CA: Sage.

Mazon, M. R. & Ross, H. (1990). Minorities in the higher education pipeline: A critical view. *The Western Journal of Black Studies, 14,* 159–165.

Mintz, J. B. (1992). Assistant professor: Paranoid or self-preserving? *The Counseling Psychologist, 20,* 39–46.

Niemann, Y. F. (1999). The making of a token: A case study of stereotype threat, stigma, racism, and tokenism in academe. *Frontiers: A Journal of Women Studies, 20,* 11–34.

Niemann, Y. F., & Dovidio, J. F. (1999). Tenure, race/ethnicity and attitudes toward affirmative action: A matter of self-interest? *Sociological Perspectives, 41,* 783–796.

Olivas, M. A. (1996). Latino faculty at the border: Increasing numbers key to more Hispanic access. In C. S. V. Turner, M. Garcia, A. Nora, & L. I. Rendón (Eds.), *Racial and ethnic diversity in higher education* (pp. 376–380). Needham Heights, MA: Simon & Schuster.

Padilla, R. V., & Chávez, R. C. (Eds.). (1995). *The leaning ivory tower: Latino professors in American universities.* Albany, NY: State University of New York Press.

Pope-Davis, D. B., Stone, G. L., & Nielson, D. (1997). Factors influencing the stated career goals of minority graduate students in counseling psychology programs. *The Counseling Psychologist, 25,* 683–698.

Ramírez, M. (1998). *Multicultural/multiracial psychology: Mestizo perspectives in personality and mental health.* Northvale, NJ: Jason Aronson.

Reyes, M. D., & Halcón, J. J. (1996). Racism in academia: The old wolf revisited. In C. S. V. Turner, M. Garcia, A. Nora, & L. I. Rendón (Eds.), *Racial and ethnic diversity in higher education* (pp. 337–348). Needham Heights, MA: Simon & Schuster.

Santiago-Rivera, A. L., Arredondo, P., & Gallardo-Cooper, M. (2002). *Counseling Latinos and la Familia: A practical Guide.* Thousand Oaks, CA: Sage Publications.

Smith, J. W., Smith, W. J., & Markham, S. E. (2000). Diversity issues in mentoring academic faculty. *Journal of Career Development, 26,* 251–262.

Suinn, R. M., & Witt, J. C. (1982). Survey on ethnic minority faculty recruitment and retention. *American Psychologist, 42,* 37–45.

Taylor, S. E., & Martin, J. (1987). The present-minded professor: Controlling ones career. In M. P. Zanna & J. M. Darley (Eds.), *The compleat academic: A practical guide for the beginning social scientist.* Mahwah, NJ: Lawrence Erlbaum Associates.

Tinsley, D. J., Tinsley, H. E. A., Boone, S., & Shim-Li, C. (1993). Prediction of scientist-practitioner behavior using personality scores obtained during graduate school. *Journal of Counseling Psychology, 40,* 511–517.

Villalpando, O., & Delgado Bernal, D. (2002). A critical race theory analysis of barriers that impede the success of faculty of color. In W. A. Smith, P. G. Altbach, & K. Lomotey (Eds.), *The racial crisis in American higher education: Continuing challenges for the twenty-first century* (rev. ed.) (pp. 243–270). Albany, NY: State University of New York Press.

Wilds, D. J. (2000). *Minorities in higher education: Nineteen annual status report.* Washington, DC: American Council on Education.

16

AN INFRASTRUCTURE THAT FACILITATES THE RETENTION OF LATINA/OS IN HIGHER EDUCATION

Jeanett Castellanos and Lee Jones

As noted in the previous chapters in this book, given the demographic profile of Latinos in the United States, an increase in Latina/o college participation is expected (U.S. Census, 2000). Moreover, the number of Latinos will represent a large proportion of the student body in higher education. However, extensive research has highlighted the lack of fluid access, the experience of marginalization and isolation of Latina/os in the academy, and the hostile environment toward diversity and multiculturalism that still permeates academia. Consequently, educational institutions need to better serve this population by providing a culturally inclusive campus climate (with proper services, programs, and opportunities) that will foster a positive university environment and quality experience.

This chapter will address the need to provide a better infrastructure to accommodate Latina/os in higher education. First, a section on the importance of change to address the issue of retention and Latina/os in higher education is presented. In this section, specific strategies needed for a successful retention process are identified. Second, general university-wide recommendations are presented. Following, specific directions in addressing the retention of the students, faculty, and administration in higher education are presented.

Change: The Need and Process

Arvizu (1994) contends that the failure to envision and prepare for the future of a diversified higher education population will adversely impact Latinos and prove costly to society as a whole. The attention on this social change is even more important considering that Latinos will constitute an increasingly larger percentage of Americans. Consequently, there is a social responsibility for America to educate and train its people with the goal of creating well-qualified leaders (Weaver, 1994). A failure to understand the characteristics contributing to persistence among Latinos presents long-term cost (Ramirez-Lango, 1995). Thus, the future advancement of the Latino population and their subsequent contribution to society makes the focus on their academic persistence of paramount importance. An important step in alleviating this problem is to address the multiple variables identified throughout this book that contribute to the academic persistence of Latina/os in higher education.

To improve the current conditions of Latina/os in higher education, it is necessary that higher education pursue a process of planning, organizing, leading, decision making, and initiating new ideas (Hersey & Blanchard, 1993) to achieve the retention of Latina/os in academia. A culturally invested university will guide decisions, shape the view of the organization, and increase awareness of the Latina/o issues in the academy. An innovative institution with the commitment to retain Latina/o college students will (1) enable the representation of Latina/o colleges students to grow, (2) identify Latina/o needs, (3) evaluate its current services and attempt to address it current shortcomings, and (4) provide proper programmatic intervention (academic and social) for the prevention of attrition.

Change is a challenge that requires tremendous effort and consistency. This shift of paradigm will establish benefits for the university, community, and society in general. However, change must be organization-wide and *everyone* needs to gain an understanding of the Latina/o experience in higher education. To accomplish change, it will require senior leadership commitment, faculty support, time, and training (Horine & Hailey, 1995). Furthermore, cross-functional teams should be implemented, and isolated day-to-day operations should not be the target. Instead, there should be long-term goals, projects, and quarterly assessments of progress and improvement with Latina/o retention. The issue cannot be fixed with a short-term solution. Instead, a long-term intuitional commitment to Latina/o students, faculty, and staff is required.

Recommendations for Latina/os' Retention in Higher Education

In order to improve Latina/o student, faculty, and staff retention in higher education, postsecondary institutions must do more. Not only does retention require the design of elaborate models that include mentorship, financial incentives, and other support services, but also top leadership and tenured faculty must become and remain involved beyond current and past levels. Following, four recommendation sections will be provided to increase the representation and improve the experiences of Latina/o students, faculty, and administrators in higher education institutions.

University-Wide Efforts

- Leaders must know how to identify relevant research and data to implement change in processes as well as in organizational culture (Kinnick and Ricks, 1993). More specifically, it is imperative that each institution keep a track record of their Latino student, faculty, and administrator retention rates. Offices of Multicultural Services must stay abreast on reoccurring issues and patterns of attrition throughout U.S. colleges and universities.

- Assessment must be used in administration to continuously improve quality and initiate change (Gray, 1997). Individual focus groups should be offered quarterly to allow Latina/o students, faculty, and staff to express their concerns and needs. Surveys should also complement this assessment to attain both qualitative and quantitative data on the issues surrounding Latino retention on campus. Outside consultants should be hired for this process to enable the university to receive a nonbiased assessment of the progress or lack of progress in relation to campus climate, student, faculty, and staff satisfaction.

- Tenured faculty must be encouraged to participate in retention efforts, which include establishing formal and informal relationships with students and junior faculty. The call for faculty involvement is not exclusive to Latina/o faculty. Hence, this call is also for non-Latino tenured faculty who are established; they can assist this underrepresented group (both students and colleagues) in their retention efforts. This recommendation reinforces the ideology that the retention of Latina/os at the university is a community responsibility and not an individual problem solely resting on the shoulders of the marginalized group.

- "Zero" tolerance policies for racism should be established on college campuses (Madison, 1993) to address discriminatory practices. Students, faculty, and administrators should have a process where they are able to report and address such incidents to alleviate circumstances through mediation. Individuals who partake in racist and discriminatory behaviors should be sanctioned via promotion evaluations and student conduct regulations.

- Faculty and staff should be continuously trained on multiculturalism and related professional topics. Diversity dialogues should be offered through each college and school for faculty and staff. All faculty should be required to attend yearly sessions and they should be asked to implement their educational gains in syllabus and curriculum. Students should also be offered the opportunity to have dialogues about ethnic identity, privilege, stereotypes, campus climate, and racial consciousness.

Latina/o Students Retention Efforts

- Students should be viewed as customers in both the classroom and student service areas. It is imperative that the university stop viewing ethnic racial minority students as affirmative action students. Although some students may enter academia through special admittances processes, they are well qualified and must meet university requisites for admissions.

- Encourage Latina/o student involvement in campus activities and their use of campus facilities and services. However, it is critical to provide services that match their values and needs for retention (e.g., Latina/o sorority and fraternities).

- View the institution as an entire system by which everyone has a role in the education of students. Latina/o students are not to be considered solely responsible for their own retention. As the university provides solutions for the recruitment and retention of their student population as a whole, Latina/o students should be in the center of this discussion within administration and academic departments.

- Help bridge the gap between the Latino community and the university community for the student. Provide bilingual parent sessions that identify university expectations of the student, ways to cover the costs, financial aid seminars, etc.

- Make the curriculum relevant for the student to appreciate the classes and their content (see Chapter 4). An example of such effort can include internship opportunities for students to learn the social problems in the local community.

Faculty

- Latina/o and other diverse faculty should be hired.

- Develop a Latina/o faculty series where different Latina/o scholars come to campus to share their work with other Latina/o faculty, staff and students. This will allow Latina/o faculty to share their work and build research partnerships with other Latino scholars (see Chapter 4).

- Develop a mentorship program where senior faculty are responsible for guiding junior faculty and their scholarly efforts (see Chapter 13). Senior faculty should be held accountable for their mentees' progress and this evaluation should be considered part of their own promotion package.

- Provide grants and funding to do research in the local community addressing Latino-specific issues.

- Offer fellowship opportunities for junior faculty in order to decrease their teaching responsibilities and increase their time to conduct research.

- Establish a Latina/o support group/network for Latino faculty and staff on campus (as has been done at Arizona State University, for example). The group can come together monthly to address issues on campus encountered by the group as a whole and individual instances unique to individual members of the group. This group can serve as the voice for the Latina/os on campus and could identify specific goals for the academic year (see Chapter 13).

Administrators

- Latina/o and other diverse staff should be hired. There should not be one Latina/o per unit, meeting the status quo or serving as a token. Instead, universities should provide a comfortable environment with an abundance of diversity and multiculturalism.

- Opportunities for advancement and promotion should be available for entry-level management. More specifically, managers should elucidate the proper socialization process for Latina/o administration aspiring to move up to top administration. Furthermore, grants for conferences and professional development should be offered to promote professional growth and the opportunity for upward mobility in the system.

- Mentorship programs should also be established in the administrative units. Latina/o administrators could benefit from direction provided by senior administrators. Particular issues to address include career development needs, goals, and personal aspirations. Recommendations for specific leadership style, means to achieve promotion, and proper protocol to attain employment opportunities can also prove very beneficial.

- Establish a proactive support network to discuss and address main issues encountered as a Latina/o administrator. (See above.)

Our suggestions will improve the retention of Latina/o students, faculty, and administrators in higher education and the recommendations can also serve to address the issues of other diverse groups and their retention on university campuses.

Summary

The representation of Latina/o students, faculty, and administrators has increased in predominantly White institutions. Over the years, despite their growing numbers, Latina/o students have left predominantly White institutions without bachelor degrees in disproportionate numbers and faculty and administrators find themselves marginalized and leaving academia for other employment opportunities. Research indicates that a large part of the reason for these departures (including student, faculty, and staff) is because of the poor institutional climates and instances of racism. As discussed in previous chapters, top administrative positions and tenured faculty play a large role in the perpetuation of these environments. In addition, retention models have not maximized their potential. Management that focuses on quality, continuous improvement and assessment, and teamwork will assist the issue of retention among Latina/o students, faculty, and administrators in higher education. If leadership were successful in implementing these recommendations, which demonstrate a strong commitment to diversity, institutions would improve the retention for Latina/o students, faculty, and administrators tremendously.

Conclusion

Latina/os continue to be an underrepresented group in higher education. There is a disequilibrium between the number of ethnic students, faculty, and staff and their White counterparts in postsecondary institutions. Scholars and leaders need a wake-up call to become more active in the policy progress by creating new standards and assessment that are more useful to the current population. University administrators must realize the Browning of Higher Education calls for a pluralistic perspective. Furthermore, institutions must increase the support system for ethnic students in higher education and provide appropriate services and resources for its new growing clientele.

Change will not occur overnight. However, the awareness that homogeneity has limited the scope and practice of higher education is the first step to the journey toward institutional change. The system must take responsibility; it must develop sensitive and skilled cultural teachers, counselors, and administrators. Academia needs to evaluate its practice, values, and mission while keeping in mind the effect of the Browning of America of the times. In essence, multicultural initiatives will provide strength and the ability to conceptualize and account for the effects of culture. Moreover, a multicultural programmatic perspective will generate a more culturally sensitive paradigm and as a result, be of great benefit to higher education, all ethnic/racial minorities, and the Latina/o community.

References

Arvizu, S. F. (1994). Latinos in higher education: Underreduction vs. empowerment. In T. Weaver. (Ed.), *Handbook of Hispanic cultures in the United States: Anthropology* (pp. 282–307). Houston, TX: Arte Público Press.

Gray, P. J. (1997). Viewing assessment as an innovation: Leadership and the change process. *New Directions for Higher Education, 25*(4), 5–15.

Hersey, P., & Blanchard, K. H. (1993). *Management of organization behavior* (6th ed.). Englewood Cliffs, NJ: Prentice-Hall.

Horine, J., & Hailey, W. (1995). Challenges to successful quality management implementation in higher education institutions. *Innovative Higher Education, 20*(1), 7–17.

Kinnick, M. K., Ricks, M. F. (1993). Student retention: Moving from numbers to action. *Research in Higher Education, 34*(1), 55–69.

Madison, E. (1993). Managing diversity: Strategies for change. *CUPA Journal, 44*(4), 23–27.

Ramirez-Lango, D. (1995). Mexican American female enrollment in graduate programs: A study of the characteristics that may predict success. *Hispanic Journal of Behavioral Sciences. 17*, 33–48.

U.S. Census Bureau, U.S. Department of Commerce (2000). *Overview of race and Hispanic origin.* Washington, DC: U.S. Government Publications.

Weaver, T. (1994). The culture of Latinos in the United States. In T. Weaver (Ed.), *Handbook of Hispanic cultures in the United States: Anthropology* (pp. 15–38). Houston, TX: Arte Público Press.